A Clinical Introduction to Lacanian Psychoanalysis

A CLINICAL INTRODUCTION TO LACANIAN PSYCHOANALYSIS

Theory and Technique

BRUCE FINK

Harvard University Press
Cambridge, Massachusetts
London, England

Library of Congress Cataloging-in-Publication Data

Fink, Bruce, 1956–
A clinical introduction to Lacanian psychoanalysis: theory and technique / Bruce Fink.
p.   cm.
Includes bibliographical references and index.
ISBN 0-674-13535-0 (cloth)
ISBN 0-674-13536-9 (pbk.)
1. Lacan, Jacques, 1901–. 2. Psychoanalysis. I. Title.
BF109.L28F54   1997
150.19′5′092—dc21
96-52127

To Héloïse

ACKNOWLEDGMENTS

Jacques-Alain Miller—the general editor of Lacan's seminars and head of the Ecole de la Cause Freudienne, who is widely recognized as the foremost interpreter of Lacan's work in the world today—taught me the lion's share of what I know about Lacanian psychoanalysis. I am greatly indebted to his ongoing "Orientation lacanienne," the weekly seminar he gives as chairman of the Department of Psychoanalysis at the University of Paris VIII, Saint-Denis, which I attended from 1983 to 1989. He provided many of the keys that have allowed me to read Lacan, and—as was true of my previous book, *The Lacanian Subject* (above all, Chapters 2–5 and 10 and the appendixes)—I rely considerably on his published and unpublished lectures here. Chapters 6, 9, and 10 are in part based, respectively, on his essays "An Introduction to Lacan's Clinical Perspectives," "On Perversion," and "Commentary on Lacan's Text," and a number of the figures I use in Chapters 8, 9, and 10 are derived from figures that he discusses extensively. Indeed, references to his work occur throughout, since it forms the backdrop for the view of Lacan's work I present.

Colette Soler, one of the most experienced Lacanian psychoanalysts affiliated with the Ecole de la Cause Freudienne, has been especially influential in my understanding of Lacan's clinical work, and her work is quoted extensively here as well. Her essay "Hysteria and Obsession" was extremely useful to me in Chapter 8. Still, neither Jacques-Alain Miller nor Colette Soler would necessarily endorse the views expressed in this book—they would no doubt take issue with various interpretations proffered here.

Héloïse Fink made many useful comments that helped improve the readability of this book, and provided moral support throughout the writing process.

CONTENTS

PREFACE

The goal of my teaching has always been, and remains, to train analysts.

—Lacan, Seminar XI, 209

Despite the great complexity of Lacan's writings, many of his clinical notions and innovations can be clearly and simply formulated. Yet few if any books on Lacan available today talk about how one goes about doing Lacanian psychoanalysis, what it really involves, and what thus distinguishes it from other forms of therapy, whether psychoanalytically oriented or not.

This book sets out to rectify that situation. It is designed for clinicians (psychoanalysts, psychologists, psychiatrists, psychotherapists, counselors, social workers, and so on) and for people in—or interested in going into—therapy. It grew out of my work training new therapists at Duquesne University, and supervising clinicians already in practice—some for quite a number of years. Few of them had much prior knowledge of Lacan's work, yet we were able to find common ground in our clinical experience, dealing with the kinds of problems faced by a wide range of practitioners: getting our patients involved in the therapy, dealing with their anxiety and demands, handling transference love, setting aside our own feelings for (or against) the patient, keeping our own prejudices out of the therapeutic setting, working with the patient's aggression, sarcasm, and criticism, and so on.

In my experience, clinicians of many different persuasions find Lacan's work quite accessible when it is used to elucidate concrete clinical situations and individual case histories. Thus, I have done my best here to discuss everyday aspects of a practitioner's experience, and to use as many examples as possible to illustrate my points.

I assume no prior knowledge of Lacan's work, and I provide suggested reading to supplement my discussion in a separate section at the end of the book, including books and articles by Freud, Lacan, and Lacan's students. Unlike much of my previous work on Lacan, this book does not include meticulous interpretation of complex Lacanian concepts or painstaking deciphering of formulations from his extremely dense writings. I assume that the reader is confronted with the myriad practical problems presented by therapeutic work with patients, and is not yet sure Lacan's approach interests him or her enough to devote hours and hours, or more likely months and years, to working through the finer points of Lacanian theory.

My approach here can thus be viewed in at least two different ways. (1) It constitutes an unjustifiably bowdlerized popularization of Lacan's work, involving gross generalizing and reductionism—I am bound to be accused of this by some. (2) It attempts to provide a sorely lacking meeting place for theory and practice, of the type that exists in many Parisian hospitals and outpatient clinics run by Lacanians. In such clinical settings, new therapists and therapists-in-training engage in daily work with Lacanians—not on the nicer points of Hegelian dialectics, modal logic, topology, Heideggerian theories of being and truth, or literary tropes, but on concrete cases where diagnosis, medication, hospitalization, and involvement of the patient in therapy are vital issues. It is in the context of case presentations, discussion of what needs to be done for a particular patient, or interpretation of a dream, fantasy, or daydream that clinicians in France often first encounter concepts such as the analyst's desire, the symbolic, object *a*, jouissance, and so on. They do not automatically grasp them even then, but at least there is in France a context in which basic Lacanian concepts are used in everyday clinical settings to formulate what is going on for particular patients at particular times and to make recommendations to the therapists seeing them.

Not everyone is born an analyst, and the French man or woman in the street understands nothing of Lacan's grammar, much less of his multilayered, polyvalent pronouncements. No one in France comes to understand Lacan by reading his main written work, the *Ecrits*; as Lacan himself says, "they were not meant to be read" (Seminar XX, 29). French therapists learn about Lacan in academic and clinical contexts, where they are taught by one or more of the thousands of practitioners who worked directly with Lacan and his associates, attended lectures, went to case presentations at the hospitals, spent years on the couch, and so on. They learned about Lacan's work first hand—as a practice.

In America, Lacanian psychoanalysis has thus far been viewed as little more than a set of texts—a dead, academic discourse. For Lacan's discourse to come alive here, his *clinical approach* will have to be introduced through analysis, supervision, and clinical work—in other words, through subjective experience. Books are just a beginning. If, by reaching clinicians at the level of their everyday experience, I am able to motivate them to take a longer look at Lacan's often impenetrable opus, and to take more seriously his view of analytic experience, I shall have accomplished my purpose here. This book by no means purports to be a total expression of Lacan's view of clinical practice. It is, rather, an introduction and an invitation to read.

This book should be suitable for analysts-in-training, practitioners of all ilks, and advanced undergraduate and graduate seminars in psychology and other related areas. It provides a broad overview of Lacan's approach to therapy, while at the same time introducing many of his basic concepts: imaginary, symbolic, real; need, demand, love, desire, fantasy, jouissance; subject, object, Other; signifier and signified; the three forms of negation (foreclosure, disavowal, and repression) and the clinical structures determined by them; the analyst's desire, punctuation, and the variable-length session; and so on. Four detailed case discussions are included in the later chapters, illustrating the Lacanian approach to practice laid out here, as well as the different psychoanalytic diagnostic categories. In the earlier chapters, too, I include a certain amount of case material (though it is more fragmentary in nature), much of which I have borrowed from my supervisees; I often find it easier to extract specific interventions and illustrations from their work than from my own, as I am always inclined, when it comes to my own cases, to engage in more extensive discussion than the context allows. The two case studies provided in Chapter 8 are from my own practice and provide quite a lot of background material.

The Lacan I am presenting is not the "early Lacan"—that is, the clinician of the 1950s—but rather the later Lacan of the middle to late 1960s and the 1970s. My understanding of his work derives from seven years of professional training in Paris at the institute that Lacan founded just before his death (the Ecole de la Cause Freudienne), from my personal analysis and supervision with Lacan's students, from graduate study at the University of Paris VIII, Saint-Denis, and from years of ongoing private practice, supervision, study, and translation.

It should be noted that I have taken the liberty of changing the translation of many of the passages I quote from Lacan's work. I am currently in the process of preparing a new complete edition of Lacan's major written work, *Ecrits* (Paris: Seuil, 1966), and it is quite clear to me that the existing translation, *Ecrits: A Selection* (New York: Norton, 1977), is not only misleading but often totally misguided. In every case I have aimed at faithfully rendering the meaning(s) of Lacan's French, but also at expressing it in good idiomatic American English so that it has the same kind of power and impact on the American ear as it has on the French. This, it seems to me, is an aspect of translation that is sorely missing in most translations of Lacan's work to date.

A Clinical Introduction to Lacanian Psychoanalysis

I

DESIRE AND PSYCHOANALYTIC TECHNIQUE

1

DESIRE IN ANALYSIS

"How many psychologists does it take to change a light bulb?"

"Only one, but the light bulb has to really want to change!"

So went the joke in the 1970s and 1980s. The joke was not as uninformed as it might at first seem, since many psychologists do in fact believe that all the therapy in the world would be of no value if the patient did not *genuinely want to change*. If Woody Allen stayed in therapy for twenty years, it was no doubt because "deep down" he did not really want to change. And if psychotherapy met with so little success, it was because most people's will to change was simply not strong enough, not fervent enough. The onus was thus placed on the patient.

Lacan's approach is radically different. Of course the patient does not *really* want to change! If symptoms have developed, if the patient engages in symptomatic behavior, it is because a great deal of energy has become tied up in those symptoms. The patient has a great deal invested in keeping things the way they are, for he or she obtains what Freud referred to as a "substitute satisfaction" from symptoms, and cannot be easily induced to give it up (SE XVI, 365–371). Although the patient may initially claim to want to be relieved of his or her symptoms, he or she is ultimately committed to not rocking the boat.

This is, quite simply, an essential feature of symptoms: they provide satisfaction of one kind or another, even though it may not be obvious to outside observers or even to the individual saddled with the symptom (SE XVI, 365–366). At some level, the individual enjoys his or her symptoms.[1] Indeed, generally speaking, this is the only way the individual knows how to obtain enjoyment. Now why would anyone genuinely strive to give up his or her only satisfaction in life?

From a Freudian/Lacanian perspective, it is clear that the therapist cannot rely on some sort of "will to get better" on the patient's part—some kind of "genuine desire to change." There is no such thing.[2] Indeed, patients often go into therapy because they no longer have any will to live, or to do anything at all, or because they sense that their libido is stifled and withering; in short, their desire is dying. How then could it possibly serve as the mainspring of change?

If there is a desire in therapy that serves as its motor force, it is the analyst's, not the patient's. Many therapists and therapists-in-training with whom I have worked feel that it is inappropriate for therapists to express any *desire* at all to their patients. They do not even call patients who miss scheduled sessions,[3] or who stop coming to therapy altogether. "It is the patient's right to stop," they claim, and if a patient does not want to come, "who am *I* to tell him or her what to do?" Indeed, many therapists simply feel hurt and rejected when patients fail to show up or stop coming altogether, and are inclined to say to themselves, "Good riddance!" Or they feel inadequate, believing that they have done something wrong.

What such therapists fail to realize is that the patient's desire to continue therapy *must,* at certain times, wane or disappear altogether—otherwise the patient's essential conflicts tied up in his or her symptoms are not being affected. It is true that the patient has the legal right to stop coming, and it is true that the therapist may have done something stupid that led the patient to leave therapy; but *in the majority of cases the patient is looking for an excuse to leave,* and virtually any excuse will often do. Patients tend to skip sessions or even break off therapy when they sense that they are being asked to give up something or make a sacrifice they are not prepared to make.

It is the analyst's desire, not their own flagging desire, that allows them to continue. Even very subtle expressions of the analyst's desire may suffice to keep certain patients in therapy when they have no will of their own to continue. The analyst's "I'll see you tomorrow" may be enough to bring certain patients back even though they believe they have nothing more to say and feel stuck. Though they feel absurd for coming, and think they must be boring the analyst, the latter's request that they return, and that they continue to return, may sustain them and allow them to wade through the quagmire of libidinal stasis and associative stagnation.

The majority of patients require far stronger expressions of the analyst's desire in order to overcome their tendency to withdraw and avoid sacrifice. The analyst must often tell them that he or she *wants* them to continue, *wants* them to come on such-and-such a day, *wants* them to come more often—twice a week, not once, or five times a week, not four.

An example of the importance of the analyst's desire was given to me by a French friend who had been in analysis with someone for a couple of years and wanted to continue. Her analyst told her that she, the analyst, could do nothing further for her, indicating to the patient that she wished the patient would stop coming. This not only distressed the patient deeply, but also discouraged her from ever going back into analysis. She was left with the impression that nothing could be done for her. It may well have been true that her analyst could no longer be of any help to her, but the analyst's approach should have been radically different. The very fact that the patient wished to continue meant that she had more to say, had not finished her analytic work; and thus her analyst should have expressed a desire for the patient to *continue* her analysis, but to continue it with Dr. So-and-So, an extremely knowledgeable and experienced analyst.

In working with neurotics, the therapist must *always* express a desire for patients to continue, even if he or she feels that these patients have completed their work. Such patients will break off when their own desire to move on has become strong enough and determined enough. (If this never happens, of course, it means that the therapy is making the patient ever more dependent on the therapist instead of more independent—a point to be discussed in later chapters.)[4]

This obviously implies that the analyst is an actor or actress who plays a part which does not necessarily convey his or her "true feelings." The analyst is not "authentic," not communicating his or her deepest beliefs and reactions to the patient as one human being to another. The analyst may find a patient unpleasant and annoying, but what use is it to let the patient know this? The patient may very well react to an expression of the analyst's antipathy by leaving analysis altogether, or by trying to make him- or herself pleasant and interesting to the analyst, censoring certain thoughts and feelings which he or she thinks might annoy the analyst, instead of getting down to true analytic work. Counterproductive reactions to say the least! The analyst must maintain a position of desire—desire for the patient to talk, dream, fantasize, associate, and interpret—regardless of any dislike he or she may have for the patient. The analyst is called upon to maintain this same position, this same strictly analytically oriented desire, in the opposite case as well—that is, when he or she is drawn to or turned on by the patient.[5]

Virtually every movie that portrays a psychiatrist, psychoanalyst, or psychologist, from Robert Altman's *Beyond Therapy* to Phil Joanou's *Final Analysis* (with Kim Basinger and Richard Gere), focuses on the therapist's desire insofar as it transgresses the limits of the therapeutic relationship. The contemporary therapist is almost always portrayed as being lonely and vulnerable, becoming enamored of a patient, and succumbing to the temptation of abusing his or her power over the patient by sleeping with him or her. This perception of the therapist in mass-media productions parallels contemporary therapists' own fascination with one aspect of countertransference: the feelings of the therapist that are elicited in his or her relations with the patient.

Lacan does not deny the existence of countertransferential feelings: everyone who has ever seen patients in a therapy setting has felt drawn to or angered by, sympathetic toward or frustrated by patients at one time or another. Lacan's originality lies in the fact that he requires analysts to put these feelings aside when interpreting or otherwise intervening in therapy. Such feelings may be of value to analysts in understanding themselves in their own analysis, and in gauging where the patient is attempting to situate the analyst in his or her libidinal economy, but they should not be displayed or revealed to the patient.

Lacan's expression "the analyst's desire"[6] refers not to the analyst's countertransferential feelings but rather to a kind of "purified desire"[7] that is specific to the analyst—to the analyst not as a human being with feelings but as a function, a role, a part to be played and one that *can* be played by many extremely different individuals. "The analyst's desire" is a desire that focuses on analysis and only on analysis. Many therapists tell me that they have plans for their patients, that secretly (or not so secretly) they hope one patient will become this, another that, that one will split up with her husband and another will settle down and have children; these wishes have absolutely nothing to do with "the analyst's desire" as Lacan formulates it. "The analyst's desire" is not for the patient to get better, to succeed in life, to be happy, to understand him- or herself, to go back to school, to achieve what he or she says he or she wants, or to say something in particular—to say, for example, that the pig in the dream represents her father or that she had something to do with the disaster that occurred in her family when she was eleven. It is an enigmatic desire that does not tell the patient what the analyst wants him or her to say or do.[8] Neurotics are only too eager to figure out what other people want from them so they can fulfill or thwart those other people's desires.

"The analyst's desire" is a kind of pure desiring that does not alight on any particular object, that does not show the analysand (the person engaged in analyzing him- or herself) what the analyst wants from him or her—though the analysand almost inevitably tries to read a specific desire into even the slightest intervention or interpretation. One of my analysands was convinced that I believed she was a homosexual because I encouraged her to talk about a couple of homosexual encounters she mentioned a number of times in passing without ever going into them in any detail. Several "huh's" on my part were enough for her to conclude that I wanted her to realize she was a homosexual; she protested against my supposed desire by never discussing those encounters at all. "The analyst's desire" is a desire that walks a fine line, emphasizing every manifestation of the unconscious (even when it interrupts something the analyst is personally interested in hearing about, even when it does not seem to fit in with what the analyst had managed to understand thus far), and thus indicating to the patient the kind of work expected of him or her in the therapy, without suggesting that the analyst has a certain agenda and is attempting to lead the patient to say or do something in particular.

I will have a great deal more to say about the analyst's desire in the chapters to come, but it should already be clear that it is an unflagging desire for the patient to come to therapy, to put his or her experience, thoughts, fantasies, and dreams into words, and to associate to them. It is not a "personal" desire, and it is not the kind of desire that anyone who wants to can maintain without first going through a long period of analysis him- or herself. It is, nevertheless, what Lacan considers the motor force of analysis.

Knowledge and Desire

If the perception of reality entails unpleasure, that perception—that is, the truth—must be sacrificed.

—Freud, SE XXIII, 237

Just as patients do not come to therapy with a "genuine desire to change," they do not come with a "genuine desire for self-knowledge." Although at the outset many patients express a desire to know what went wrong, what they are doing that keeps backfiring, why their relationships always fall apart, and so on, there is—Lacan suggests—a more deeply rooted wish *not to know* any of those things. Once patients are on the verge of realizing exactly what it is they have done or are doing to sabotage their lives, they very often resist going any further and flee therapy. When they begin to glimpse their deeper motives and find them hard to stomach, they often drop out. Avoidance is one of the most basic neurotic tendencies.

Freud occasionally talked about a drive to know *(Wissentrieb),*[9] but Lacan restricts such a drive to children's curiosity about sex ("Where do babies come from?"). In therapy, Lacan says, the analysand's basic position is one of a refusal of knowledge, a will not to know (a *ne rien vouloir savoir).*[10] The analysand wants to know nothing about his or her neurotic mechanisms, nothing about the why and wherefore of his or her symptoms. Lacan even goes so far as to classify ignorance as a passion greater than love or hate: a passion not to know.[11]

It is only the analyst's desire that allows the analysand to overcome this "wanting to know nothing," sustaining the analysand through the painful process of formulating some kind of new knowledge. If the analysand resists knowing, and the analyst fails to bring his or her desire to bear, new knowledge cannot be formulated. Lacan goes so far as to say that the only resistance in analysis is the analyst's resistance,[12] for the patient's resistance to knowing can be surmounted *if* the analyst is willing to intervene. If the analyst balks, missing the chance to bring his or her desire into play, the crucial resistance in the therapy is his or her own, not the patient's. For the patient's resistance is taken as a given: from the outset it is assumed that the patient does not to want to change, know, or give up anything. There is nothing to be done about the patient's structural resistance. But there is, as we shall see, something that can be done about the analyst's.

Satisfaction Crisis

What the subject finds is not what motivated his attempt at refinding.

—Lacan, Seminar XI, 199/219

If people do not really want to change or know, why does anyone ever actually go into therapy? What are they hoping to achieve by doing so?

In the majority of cases, people go into therapy at moments of crisis, at times when their usual modus operandi is breaking down. If, as Freud says, symptoms provide substitute satisfactions, these substitutes do not always work· forever. They may come into conflict with society at large, with the tolerance of an individual's loved ones, with an employer's temper, or with the individual's own expectations. Or they may intensify: an individual's agoraphobia may progressively worsen, restricting his or her movements ever more completely, rendering life unbearable. People tend to seek therapy when the satisfaction provided by their symptoms is no longer as great, when it is threatened by others, when it is rapidly waning or being outweighed by other factors.[13]

"Satisfaction" is, however, perhaps too "clean" or "clean-cut" a term to describe the kind of pleasure symptoms provide. We all know people who are ever complaining of their lack of satisfaction in life, but who never seek therapy. This is because they obtain a certain satisfaction from their very dissatisfaction, and from complaining: from blaming others for their lack of satisfaction. So, too, certain people derive a great deal of pleasure from torturing themselves, from subjecting themselves to painful experiences, and so on. The French have a fine word for this kind of pleasure in pain, or satisfaction in dissatisfaction: *jouissance*. It qualifies the kind of "kick" someone may get out of punishment, self-punishment, doing something that is so pleasurable it hurts (sexual climax, for example), or doing something that is so painful it becomes pleasurable. Most people deny getting pleasure or satisfaction from their symptoms, but the outside observer can usually see that they enjoy their symptoms, that they "get off" on their symptoms in a way that is too round-about, "dirty," or "filthy" to be described as pleasurable or satisfying.[14] The term "jouissance" nicely captures the notion of getting off by any means necessary, however clean or dirty.[15]

The moment at which someone seeks therapy can thus be understood as one in which a breakdown occurs in that person's favorite or habitual way of obtaining jouissance. It is a "jouissance crisis." The jouissance-providing symptom is not working anymore or has been jeopardized.

The people who seek out a therapist who are *not* experiencing some sort of jouissance crisis are generally sent by family, friends, or employers. Their spouses may be in a jouissance crisis, but they are not. And generally speaking, they are primarily interested in thwarting their spouses' desire and are not open to the effect of the analyst's desire.

Those who do come in the middle of a jouissance crisis are hoping that the therapist will fix it, patch things up, make the symptom work the way it used to. They are not asking to be relieved of the symptom but rather of its recent ineffectiveness, its recent inadequacy. Their demand is that the therapist restore their satisfaction to its earlier level.[16]

Instead, what the therapist offers at the outset is a different substitute satisfaction: the strange sort of satisfaction that comes from the transference relationship and from deciphering the unconscious. This is *not* what patients are asking for—they are not demanding a replacement. Rather, they want a patch kit with which to repair the old one.

This is essentially why therapy cannot be characterized as a contract, and why the widespread use of the term "client" to qualify patients seems to me misguided. To be a "client" suggests that one is a consumer, and that one knows exactly what one is asking for and what one will receive—something which is certainly *not* true of any kind of real therapy situation. The notion of "contract" suggests that the parties enter into an agreement as equals, the contract spelling out each party's obligations to provide something. But in therapy the therapist sidesteps the patient's demands, frustrates them, and ultimately tries to direct the patient to something he or she never asked for. Some contract! While "client" may be preferable in certain respects to "patient," which tends to pathologize or stigmatize the person in therapy, Lacan proposes a different term: "analysand." The *-and* ending of "analysand" is a gerund form (like *-ing* at the end of a word), which implies that it is the person in therapy who does the work of analyzing, not the analyst.

The analysand who comes to therapy at a time of crisis may be willing to compromise, may be willing to accept the substitute satisfaction of deciphering the unconscious in exchange for the flagging satisfaction of the symptom. The analysand may ask for promises: "What can I hope for? What can I expect from therapy?" Although the therapist can promise neither happiness nor cure, he or she can, if need be, hold out for the analysand the promise of a new approach to things, a new way of dealing with people, a new way of operating in the world. Some analysts refuse to respond in any way to such requests by analysands, but in asking the analysand to make a sacrifice—to give up the jouissance of the symptom—the blow may be temporarily softened by offering something else in exchange: something vague, something that will no doubt fall short of their expectations, but something that may make the first step possible.

Thus, it may not be necessary for the light bulb to really *want* to change: it may be enough for the light bulb to be burned out or flickering. When coupled with the freefall of jouissance provided by the symptom, the analyst's desire may be intriguing enough to get people involved in the analytic process and, when brought to bear regularly, keep them there.[17]

2

ENGAGING THE PATIENT IN THE THERAPEUTIC PROCESS

The "Preliminary Meetings": Analytic Pedagogy

Few people who seek out a therapist have any real idea at the outset what the therapeutic process involves. Depending on their background, their preconceptions about what goes on in therapy may run the gamut from complaining about life to confessing sins, from receiving advice to learning new "tricks" useful in dealing with problems, from having disturbing thoughts removed to having so-called repressed memories restored. Generally speaking, people tend to think that, once in therapy, you talk about what went on since you last spoke to your therapist—in other words, that you recount your day or week, your feelings and thoughts about this person and that, and so on. Such notions are easily gleaned from the media, and indeed there are therapists who encourage their patients to engage in some or all of the above.

None of this is, however, of interest in psychoanalysis, and the question that arises is how to take patients from their everyday notions about what to do in therapy to the point of doing genuine analytic work. The early part of analysis involves a kind of explicit and not-so-explicit pedagogy.

At the outset, many patients view their relationship with the analyst as being like any other relationship. If they find an interesting article in the newspaper and want to show it to someone, they bring it to the analyst just as they might send it to a parent or show it to a friend. If they read a good book, see a good movie, or whatever, they recommend it to the analyst or even "lend" it to him or her by leaving it on his or her desk. To their mind, such acts are of no significance, reflecting "normal friendly interest."

From the outset, however, the analyst has to make it clear that everything in their relationship is significant, and that their relationship is unlike any other. The analyst is not a friend who will exchange stories or secrets, lend books or tapes. There is no point trying to amuse him or her with entertaining stories or jokes, since the analyst will not be amused. And though the patient believes certain parts of his or her story to be the most significant, the analyst always seems to be paying attention to something else.

The early part of analysis is thus devoted to establishing that *there is no reciprocity between analyst and analysand* ("you tell me your stories and I'll tell you mine"),[1] as there usually is, at least to some degree, between friends; and that the analyst is not interested in hearing most of what the analysand is prepared to talk about. The analyst requests that the analysand say whatever comes to mind, without censoring any of his or her thoughts, no matter how senseless, unimportant, out of context, distasteful, or insulting they may seem; and that the analysand pay attention to things he or she probably paid little attention to before: dreams, fantasies, daydreams, fleeting thoughts, slips of the tongue, bungled actions, and the like.

This is a fairly tall order for most people, especially for those who have never been in analysis before. But one of my patients who had supposedly been in analysis for several years before coming to see me told me that his previous analyst had never even asked him to try to remember his dreams and recount them during his sessions, much less to engage in the specifically psychoanalytic technique of associating to each element of a dream or fantasy. Doing analysis requires a learning process, and the analyst must not abstain from repeatedly encouraging the analysand to pay attention to all manifestations of the unconscious. This is what I would call the pedagogical aspect of the early stages of analysis.

The "Preliminary Meetings": Clinical Aspects

Lacan's term for the early stages of analysis, "preliminary meetings," could also be translated as "preliminary interviews" [*entretiens préliminaires*], indicating that the analyst plays an active role in them. They serve a specific purpose for the analyst, who must fairly quickly situate the patient with respect to diagnostic criteria. Many therapists consider diagnosis to be nothing more than pigeonholing, which is ultimately of no use to the therapy process and is required only for the usually nefarious purposes of health insurance companies. True, the latter sometimes base therapy allowances on diagnosis, and thus those who are obliged to work with such companies have to learn how to walk a fine line, providing the latter with a diagnosis that will not forever stigmatize the patient but that will allow treatment to continue, while perhaps reserving their real diagnostic judgment for themselves or a small group of colleagues.

Nevertheless, an analyst cannot treat psychotics in the same way as neurotics, and a general diagnosis, subject to possible revision and careful substantiation later, is important to the analyst's proper positioning in the analytic relationship with the patient. I have supervised many therapists who will refrain for several months from asking any questions about the patient's parents or the patient's sexuality, if the patient does not bring up these topics spontaneously. But if a therapist does not quickly obtain a fairly global view of the patient's history, family life, and sexual life—in cases in which perversion or psychosis cannot be almost immediately ruled out—he or she may inadvertently commit grave errors (such as triggering a psychotic break).

Thus, the preliminary interviews, in which the analyst may ask very specific questions in order to clarify certain points crucial to making a preliminary diagnosis, allow the analyst to form an overall view of the patient's life and clinical structure. This does not mean that the analyst directs the preliminary sessions, telling the patient what to talk about; as Freud says, in these sessions "one lets the patient do nearly all the talking and explains nothing more than what is absolutely necessary to get him to go on with what he is saying" (SE XII, 124). Nevertheless, when a doubt persists in the analyst's mind regarding diagnosis, which could be such as to preclude treatment of this patient by the analyst (if, for example, the latter is unfamiliar with the treatment of psychosis, as outlined here in Chapter 7, or is uncomfortable with the position he or she is likely to be put in when engaged in the treatment of perversion, as discussed in Chapter 9), pointed questions are in order.

Second, the preliminary interviews seek to transform what may be a vague sense of uneasiness in the patient's life (depression, anxiety, unhappiness, and so on) into an isolable symptom.[2] For example, the patient may initially be convinced that his or her problems are really physical in nature, but be willing to follow his or her physician's advice to go into therapy while medical treatment begins to take effect. The preliminary meetings provide a context in which the patient can begin to view some of his or her problems as perhaps psychosomatic, and thus as accessible to the talking cure.

Many patients come to therapy with a very specific demand to be relieved of one or more specific symptoms. Every therapist, except for behaviorists working on the surgical model of psychotherapy (where a symptom is considered to be an isolated behavior that can be removed like a swollen appendix), realizes that one cannot remove a patient's symptom, as isolated as it may at first seem, without probing into many aspects of a person's life. A "simple" facial tic is a complex psychosomatic phenomenon, and may be but the one visible, public manifestation of a "larger problem." Yet this tic does not become a psychoanalytic symptom, strictly speaking, until the patient has exchanged (perhaps more or less reluctantly) the single-minded demand for the tic to go away for the satisfaction of deciphering the unconscious—that is, until the patient is willing to put the whole of his or her life in question, not just one little corner of his or her face.

This may take quite a bit of time: it may well take a year of daily face-to-face meetings before the patient can truly be said to be engaging in the analytic process. What we are hoping for, in the words of Jacques-Alain Miller, is that "an 'autonomous' demand . . . will emerge from the relationship itself"[3]—in other words, that the demand that the symptom be excised like a tumor will give way to a demand for analysis, and that the relationship with the analyst in and of itself will transform the analysand's will to know nothing into a will to pursue his or her analysis.

During this period of time, which varies in length, the analysand generally feels the need to be supported or propped up to some extent: people are not used to talking without there being a face attached to the person they are addressing, and they feel a need for eye contact. In their mind, the analyst is, to begin with, a person like any other, and it is only gradually that the "person" of the analyst gives way before the analyst as an actor, a function, a placeholder, a blank screen, or a mirror.[4] This transition takes time, and thus one cannot immediately put patients on the couch,[5] as a number of psychiatrists and analysts have a tendency to do. The preliminary meetings must take place face to face, and even people who have already been in analysis should not immediately be put on the couch.

The "Preliminary Meetings": The Analyst's Interventions

As long as the patient views the analyst as another human being like him- or herself, interpretations made by the analyst generally carry little weight. They may be accepted or rejected, but they have little or no impact on the patient's libidinal economy. Interpretations that are rejected by the patient (whether they are on target or not) are, when offered in sufficient number, likely to lead a patient to change analysts or leave therapy altogether.[6] Interpretation has virtually no beneficial effect until the analysand has formulated a true demand for analysis, and the analyst begins to operate as a pure function.

Punctuation

This does not mean that the analyst need say nothing at all during the preliminary meetings; rather, it means that his or her interventions should consist of "punctuations"[7] of the patient's speech, the analyst proffering a meaningful

"Huh!" or simply repeating one or more of the patient's words or garbled sounds. Just as the meaning of a written text can often be changed by changing the punctuation (commas, dashes, periods), the patient's own punctuation of his or her speech—emphasizing ("underlining") certain words, glossing rapidly over mistakes or slurs, repeating what he or she thinks is important—can be modified, the analyst suggesting through his or her own punctuation that another reading is possible, but without saying what it is or even that it is clear and coherent. By emphasizing ambiguities, double entendres, and slips, the analyst does not so much convey that he or she knows what the patient "really meant" as hint that other meanings, perhaps revealing meanings, are possible. The analyst's punctuation does not so much point to or nail down one particular meaning as suggest a level of meanings the patient has not been attentive to: unintended meanings, unconscious meanings.

The punctuation of manifestations of the unconscious (repeating a patient's slip of the tongue, for example) may annoy certain patients at first, for such manifestations are what we learn to correct quickly in everyday conversation, attributing little if any meaning to them. When carried out systematically, however, punctuation suggests to patients that they are not masters in their own homes.[8] The result tends to be the arousal of curiosity about the unconscious, at times a passionate interest in it. Many patients reach a stage at which they point out and analyze their own slips and slurs, even ones they were about to make but avoided because they caught themselves in time.

The analyst's interest in such slips, double entendres, and garbled speech arouses the patient's interest in them; and though the analyst, by punctuating, has not provided a specific meaning, the patient begins to try to attribute meaning to them. Avoiding "full-blown" interpretation, the analyst can nevertheless get the patient engaged in—even hooked on—the process of deciphering the unconscious.

Scansion

No medical instrument or procedure is guaranteed against abuse; if a knife does not cut, it cannot be used for healing either.

—Freud, SE XVII, 462–463

Another way in which the analyst can intervene in the early stages is by interrupting the session at what he or she deems a particularly important point: the patient may be vigorously denying something, may be asserting something he or she has discovered, may be recounting a telling part of a dream, or may have just made a slip. By stopping the session at this point, the analyst nonverbally accentuates it, making it clear to the patient that he or she believes it is significant and not to be taken lightly.

The analyst is anything but a neutral listener. He or she makes it very clear that certain points—points that virtually always have to do with the revelation of unconscious desire and previously unavowed enjoyment—are crucial. He or she directs the patient's attention to them, more or less directly recommending that the patient mull them over, associate to them, and take them seriously. Patients do *not* spontaneously home in on the subjects that are most important, psychoanalytically speaking; they spontaneously avoid them, for the most part. Even if they recognize that sexuality should be dwelt upon, for example, they nevertheless tend to avoid associating to the elements in dreams and fantasies that are the most sexually charged.

"Free association" is a fine thing (riddled though it is with paradoxes at a deeper level), but it is often quite a task to get the patient to free associate to the most important material. *The analyst must not be afraid to stress the material he or she considers important.* Not necessarily to the exclusion of all else, of course, since the analyst cannot possibly know what lies behind each element; but by stressing the unconscious, the analyst manifests "the analyst's desire" to hear about *this.*

Yes, this! Not how the patient spent his or her Saturday night going from club to club, or the patient's theories about Dostoevsky's poetics,[9] or what have you—all of which is the blah, blah, blah of everyday discourse that people talk about with friends, family, and colleagues, believe they are supposed to re-count in therapy, or wind up talking about in therapy because they do not know what else to say or are afraid of what they might have to say. The interruption or "scansion"[10] of the session is a tool with which the analyst can prevent patients from filling up their sessions with empty chatter. Once they have said what is important, there is no need to continue the session; and indeed if the analyst does not "scand" or end the session there, patients are likely to supply filler till the end of the psychoanalytic "hour" and forget the important things they said earlier on. Scanding the session upon a particularly striking formulation by the analysand is a way of keeping attention focused on the essential.

Analysis does not require one to recount one's whole life in every detail, one's whole week in four-part harmony, or one's every fleeting thought and impres-sion. Such an approach automatically turns therapy into an infinite process that a lifetime could never encompass.[11] Many therapists are, however, reluctant to interrupt their patients, to change the subjects they spontaneously embark upon, or to manifest in any way that they are bored or exasperated. Exasperation, in any case, often indicates that the analyst has missed his or her chance to change the subject, ask a question, or probe more deeply into something, and now cannot find an "elegant" way back to it; that is, it reflects the analyst's frustration at having missed his or her own opportunity to intervene.

If the analyst is to engage the patient in true analytic work, he or she cannot be afraid of making it clear to the patient that storytelling, blow-by-blow accounts of the past week, and other such superficial talk are not the stuff of analysis (though, of course, they can at times be put to analytic use). The therapist would do better to *change the subject* than to obstinately attempt to find something of psychological significance in the excruciating details of the patient's everyday life.[12]

In and of itself, the systematic elimination of superficial talk—of the blah, blah, blah of everyday discourse[13]—and the accentuation of important points is enough to justify the introduction of what Lacan called the "variable-length session." But when Lacan began varying the length of the sessions he conducted with his patients, many in the psychological and psychoanalytic establishment were scandalized, and pejoratively referred to the practice as the "short session," thereby veiling the important element: the *variability* of the length of the session. There are many reasons for varying the length of sessions, some of which I will discuss in later chapters; here I would simply like to mention a few more of the simple reasons for doing so.

Manifestations of the unconscious are often accompanied by *surprise:* surprise at a slip of the tongue—as when the analysand says precisely the opposite of what he or she meant to say by adding the word "not," or by inverting "you" and "me" or "he" and "she" in a sentence—or surprise at something the analysand did. An example of the latter was given to me by a therapist I supervise. One of her patients had consciously hated his stepmother for many long years but, running into this stepmother on the street shortly after his father's death, was astonished to find himself treating her with great fondness and kindness. He had been unaware that for years he had transferred anger toward his father onto his stepmother, and his unexpected reaction was a window through which he could glimpse feelings and thoughts of which he had previously been unaware.

When the analyst suddenly ends a session, he or she may accentuate surprise the analysand has just been expressing, or introduce the element of surprise through scansion, leaving the analysand wondering what it was the analyst heard that he or she had not heard, wondering what unconscious thought had been manifesting itself. This element of surprise is important in ensuring that analysis does not become *routine*, such that, for example, the analysand goes in every day, recounts his or her dreams and fantasies for forty-five or fifty minutes, and goes home, nothing being shaken up, nothing bothering or preoccupying him or her all day and night. Lacanian analysis seeks to keep the analysand off guard and off balance, so that any manifestation of the unconscious can have its full impact.

When fixed-length sessions are the norm, the analysand becomes accustomed to having a set amount of time to talk, and considers how to fill up that time, how best to make use of it. Analysands are very often aware, for example, that the dream they had the night before about their analyst is what is most important to their analysis, yet they try to fit in plenty of other things they *want* to talk about before they get to the dream (*if* they get to the dream). They thus attempt to minimize the importance of the dream in their own eyes, minimize the time that can be devoted to associating to it, or maximize the amount of time the analyst gives them. Analysands' use of the time allotted to them in the session is part and parcel of their larger neurotic strategy (involving avoidance, neutralization of other people, and so on), and setting session length in advance merely encourages their neurosis.

The variable-length session throws analysands off guard, to some extent, and can be used in such a way as to encourage the analysand to get right to the good stuff. In and of itself, the variable-length session is not a panacea: certain analysands continue to plan their sessions, deliberately talking about things of less importance first because, for narcissistic reasons, they want the analyst to know about them (for example, "I did really well on my exams," "I read your chapter yesterday on feminine sexuality," and so on), and saving the best for last; other analysands, especially obsessives, plan their sessions to the extent that they know exactly what they want to talk about beforehand, and make of their session a well-rehearsed performance in which slips are not possible and there is no time or place for free association.

An eminent writer on Lacanian matters openly admits to having pursued just such a strategy in his analysis every day for years; he assiduously wrote down his dreams, and memorized a large stock of them for his sessions so that if his analyst kept him longer than usual, he would still never run out of well rehearsed lines.[14] He was quite aware of the obsessive way in which he had handled his anxiety about being in analysis, ensuring that nothing therapeutic could occur during the sessions, and referred to what he had done as "sabotaging" his analysis. And he had been in analysis with a Lacanian who practiced the variable-length session!

Thus, the latter is clearly not a cure-all, but can be useful in dealing with such obsessive strategies. Consider, for example, the following case.

A friend of mine was in analysis with a Lacanian and, for more than a week at one point in his analysis, his analyst sent him on his way after sessions lasting no more than a few seconds. At the time, my friend and I were shocked, and considered the treatment altogether unfair, inappropriate, and brutal. I am not aware of the analyst's precise reasons for the harsh treatment, but it seems quite likely to me in hindsight that this friend—an obsessive accustomed to overintellectualizing, with a somewhat grandiose sense of his own self-worth—was no doubt proffering well-constructed discourses on highfalutin subjects during his analytic sessions, and the analyst had decided it was high time he realized that there is no room for that in analysis and learned to get to the point without beating around the academic bush.

In most schools of psychology and psychoanalysis, such behavior on the analyst's part would be considered a serious breach of professional ethics—abusive, unconscionable, and downright nasty. After all, people would argue, the analysand did not seek out an analyst to be treated in that way! But analysis is not a contract, and the analysand may well be hoping for something that he or she nevertheless unconsciously strives to stave off. The eminent writer I mentioned above was still hoping to achieve something in his analysis, despite his unconscious and at times not so unconscious self-defeating strategy. The very fact that he continued to go to analysis every day for such a long period of time meant that he was, at some level, looking for something else, hoping against hope, perhaps, that the analyst would wean him from his long-standing self-sabotaging tendencies.

This friend who received several extremely short sessions in a row was, in a sense, *asking for it*. Not openly, necessarily; not even verbally, perhaps. But he may very well have known, at some level, what he was doing; he simply could not help it. He went to that particular analyst (one of the most experienced Lacanians) asking to be trained as a psychoanalyst, and then conducted himself as if he were in a classroom with a professor, discoursing upon theoretical matters of the utmost interest to him. Since my friend was by no means ignorant of Freud's work, he knew very well that that is not the stuff of analysis; nevertheless, he could not break himself of his intellectualizing habits, and tried (somewhat successfully at first, it seems) to engage the analyst at the level of psychoanalytic theory. His challenge to the analyst was, in some sense: "Make me stop! Prove to me that you won't get caught up in my game!"[15] In this sense my friend *was* asking for it. He kept going back to see the analyst, despite the seemingly harsh treatment, and the remedy fortunately was not stronger than the patient. It was, admittedly, strong medicine, but his analysis took a very positive direction thereafter, whereas with an analyst who was not willing to intervene in such a forthright manner, his analysis might have bogged down indefinitely in academic speculation.

Nothing Can Be Taken at Face Value

Just because people ask you for something doesn't mean that's what they really want you to give them.

—Lacan, Seminar XIII, March 23, 1966

Desire is the central point or crux of the entire economy we deal with in analysis. If we fail to take it into account, we are necessarily led to adopt as our only guide what is symbolized by the term "reality," a reality existing in a social context.

—Lacan, Seminar VI, July 1, 1959

The examples I have just provided point to the fact that what analysands blatantly or latently demand must not be taken at face value. Explicitly, they may be asking to become analysts—that is, to undergo thorough analysis—while their behavior suggests that they do not really want to rock their own psychical boat. They may obstinately discuss certain issues, all the while secretly hoping the analyst will interrupt them. Their demands are often quite contradictory, and if the analyst gives in to one demand—say, to change the number of sessions per week from three to two—it is as if he or she were taking the demand at face value, instead of seeing through the obvious demand to its deeper motives. Perhaps the patient is asking to go to two sessions a week only because his or her spouse does not want to spend the money, and the patient is actually hoping the analyst will say no; or perhaps the patient is going through a rough period and feels a need for the analyst to express his or her *desire* for the patient to continue to come three times a week. While at one level the patient is demanding fewer sessions, at another he or she wants the analyst to say no.[16]

Nothing in analysis can be taken at face value. This may be a shocking position to some, but, as we have just seen in the case of the patient's demands, demands are rarely as simple as they may at first seem. Indeed, nothing the patient says or does can be assumed to concern "reality pure and simple." A patient says, for example, "I can't come to my Tuesday appointment because I have to take my child to the doctor." But why did the patient schedule an appointment for her child at that particular time when she knew she had an appointment with her analyst? Couldn't she have found some other time? How important was it to her to find another time? Did she even ask for a different time, or did she accept the first appointment suggested to her? Perhaps she says that the child was very sick and she had to take the first possible opening. This *could* be true, but it could also be true that it was the first possible opening that was convenient for her, because she had to schedule it around, say, a haircut and a PTA meeting.

What is important here is not "reality"—the "real events" that impinge upon the patient's continuation of therapy—but psychical reality: the way the patient weighs in her own mind the importance of her sessions, compared with that of other aspects of her life, other things she wants to do. When a patient says, "I had to miss my appointment because of such and such," the therapist must always be somewhat skeptical about the validity of the reason given. "I had to miss my appointment because I was in a car accident" sounds like a perfectly valid excuse, but perhaps the accident was the day before her appointment, the patient was not in any way injured, and her car still worked just fine. Perhaps the accident was extremely minor and the patient could have made it to her appointment a mere ten minutes late.

The pretext given can never be immediately assumed to be the whole story. The complex comparisons in the patient's mind of which is more important, her session with the therapist or her other responsibilities and/or pleasures, reflects what is going on in her therapy and the place it has in her life, and ma constitute a message to the therapist: "I put everything above you!" *There ai no inherently "reasonable" excuses.* The patient is supposed to structure her day or week around the therapy, and not vice versa; there are emergencies which occasionally make it *impossible* to make an appointment. But they are very rare indeed. Freud and numerous other analysts mention that analysands who are inclined to miss appointments, claiming that they are physically ill, curiously stop falling ill and missing so many appointments when they are charged for sessions they miss (SE XII, 127).

The analyst must not be tractable when it comes to possible manifestations of the patient's resistance; he or she must not give in.[17] The patient's sessions are, to the analyst's mind, the most important thing in the patient's life; the patient's analysis is the number one priority. If the analyst is to negotiate, he or she has to make it clear that the session must be rescheduled, earlier or later than originally planned, but that it will not be sacrificed. And if the patient makes a habit of rescheduling, the analyst must make it clear that he or she does not give sessions on demand. A colleague of mine who was prone to sleeping late and missing and rescheduling his 10:00 A.M. sessions was given only one alternative by his analyst: he could have an appointment at 7:30 A.M. Needless to say, he stopped sleeping through his 10:00 A.M. appointments![18]

Nothing can be taken at face value in analysis because everything between analyst and analysand potentially has psychological significance. But there is another reason nothing can be taken at face value.

22

Meaning Is Never Obvious

The very foundation of interhuman discourse is misunderstanding.

—Lacan, Seminar III, 184

Apart from the fact that every assertion may constitute a denial, meaning is never obvious. The patient may use a vague colloquial expression like "I'm just not feeling up to snuff, you know what I mean?" but the analyst cannot possibly know what the patient means. Meaning is extremely individual, in certain ways, and everyone uses words and expressions in highly particular senses.[19] The analyst cannot agree to understand *à mi-mot*, as the French say, implying that the patient has merely intimated, implied, or "half-said" what he or she means. In ordinary speech with friends or family, we are often glad that other people understand what we mean without our having to go into detail, or that a simple word or reference to a shared event brings to mind for them myriad feelings and meanings. In a word, we feel at home with them because "they speak our language."

In analysis, however, the analyst and analysand do not "speak the same language," even though they may both be native English speakers. Their idioms may be very similar if they are from similar socioeconomic back-grounds and from the same part of the country, but they never ultimately "speak the same language."

When people use an expression as banal as "low self-esteem," in some cases it could mean that they have been told they have low self-esteem but do not really see themselves this way, whereas in others it could mean that they hear voices telling them they will never amount to anything—meanings which are worlds apart. The analyst must draw out the particular meanings from such seemingly transparent statements, despite patients' occasional annoyance at not receiving the kind of immediate "I know what you mean" reaction they usually get in conversation with others.

Meaning is never transparent, and the analyst must act uncomprehending to the point of pretending to be hard of hearing, if need be, to get the patient to spell out what he or she means when he or she says "Sex is distasteful," "Women are scary," or "I'm afraid of spiders." As Michel Sylvester, a prominent Lacanian analyst, once put it, the analyst must not be afraid of seeming dense, thick, brutish, and dumb to get patients to provide more detail:[20] "I mean oral sex is okay, but intercourse repulses me"; "Kissing and petting don't scare me, but I could never understand why other guys are so anxious to get into a girl's pants"; "It's the spiders with black hairy legs that give me shivers down my spine." The analyst who assumes he or she knows what a patient means when he says "Sex is distasteful" may be surprised to find out later that the patient (felt he) was referring to sex between his parents.

Meaning Is Always Ambiguous

Words, since they are the nodal points of numerous ideas, may be regarded as predestined to ambiguity.

—Freud, SE V, 340

A male homosexual whose case I was supervising said to his therapist that he felt his father was "a hundred percent behind" him. With very little stretch of the imagination, we can hear that in at least two different ways: he felt that his father truly supported him in what he did,[21] or he felt his father behind him in a more spatial sense—standing behind him, lying behind him, or looking over his shoulder. *Speech is, by its very nature, ambiguous.* Words have more than one meaning, expressions we use can often be taken in a number of different ways, and prepositions allow of many metaphorical meanings. Indeed, it is an interesting exercise to try to come up with a statement which is in no way, shape, or form ambiguous—which cannot, when taken out of context or accentuated differently, have more than one meaning.[22]

Thus, what is important is not the simple fact that what a patient says is ambiguous, for all speech is ambiguous. What is important is his or her choice of words. Why didn't the patient say that his father supports him in his decisions a hundred percent, instead of saying that his father is "behind" him a hundred percent? The patient has at his disposal numerous ways of expressing the same idea,[23] and thus it seems likely that his choice of an expression involving "behind" is significant. Perhaps some other thought has led him to choose that expression over the others available to him.

That indeed was the case for this homosexual, for he later repeated the same expression almost word for word, but conveniently left out the "me" at the end: "My father was a hundred percent behind." This formulation amounted to a bona fide Freudian slip, allowing of the following translations: "My father was a complete ass," "My father was only interested in ass," "My father was only interested in anal sex," and so on. The patient, not surprisingly, denied having meant anything other than that his father was supportive of his decisions, but *psychoanalysis is concerned not so much with what he meant but with what he actually said.*

"What I meant"—a phrase patients often repeat—refers to what the patient was consciously thinking (or would like to think he or she was thinking) at the moment, thereby denying that some other thought could have been taking shape in his or her mind at the same time, perhaps at some other level. Many patients vigorously deny the existence of such other thoughts for a long time in therapy, and there is little point insisting to them that the fact that they said something other than what they meant to say must mean something. In time, once they have learned to associate to dreams, slips, and so on, they may begin to accept the notion that several thoughts may occur to them almost simultaneously, though perhaps at different levels. In short, they come to accept the existence of the unconscious, the existence of a level of thought activity that they do not usually pay attention to.[24]

This does not mean that the analyst relentlessly emphasizes every single ambiguity in a new analysand's speech—which is, in any case, patently impossible—or stresses every slip of the analysand's tongue. The punctuation of ambiguities and slips must be introduced slowly and gradually with most analysands, and the analyst must select those ambiguities that seem to have some particular meaning to the analysand. It may, for example, be more worthwhile to punctuate a metaphor like "to shove something down someone's throat" when used by an anorexic or bulimic analysand than it would be when used by an obsessive. Such punctuations, like all other interventions, must be timed sensitively in terms of what a particular analysand is prepared to hear, and should have some bearing on the context in which they appear. Garbled speech—where the context may be very unclear—is certainly worth stressing, nevertheless, for its elucidation may lead to new and particularly unexpected material.

In psychoanalysis it is thus what the analysand actually says, not what he means, that is important. For "what he means" refers to *what he consciously thinks he means, what he intends to say at the level of consciousness, what he intends to convey.* And what he *intends* to convey is something that is consonant with his view of himself, with the kind of person he believes himself to be (or would like to believe himself to be, or is at least willing to believe himself to be). "What he means" thus refers to a level of intentionality that he views as his own; it refers to an intentionality that fits in with his self-image.

This is why Lacan said that "meaning is imaginary" (Seminar III, 65). He did not imply thereby that meaning does not exist, or that it is simply something we dream up in our imagination. He implied that it is tied up with our self-*image*, with the image we have of who and what we are. In a word, meaning is related to the "ego" or "self" (two words I use synonymously in this book), to what we view as part and parcel of ourselves; hence, meaning excludes that which does not fit in with our own self-image.

What Lacan referred to as his "return to Freud"[25] in the 1950s involved a return to the importance of the unconscious, as opposed to the emphasis upon the ego so prevalent in "ego psychology" at that time and still so prevalent today in many schools of psychology and psychoanalysis. Insofar as the ego is essentially that which we view as part of ourselves, that which we refer to when we say "me," that which fits in with our self-image, the ego excludes all that we consider foreign, all thoughts and desires that slip out in parapraxes (slips of the tongue, bungled actions, and so on) for which we deny responsibility. By privileging what patients actually say over what they mean, by stressing the ambiguities and slips that appear in their speech, Lacan, like Freud, gave priority to the unconscious over the ego.

Lacan is well known for having paid a great deal of attention to the letter. The expression "the letter of the law" implies emphasizing the way the law actually reads, as opposed to its overriding meaning or spirit. "To obey the letter of the law" may mean that one follows to a T what is written in the text of the law, without concerning oneself with the spirit in which the law was penned. Lacan paid great attention to the letter of his analysands' discourse: to what they actually said, as opposed to what they consciously meant or intended to say. By never assuming that he understood what they meant, by never giving the impression that he spoke their language, by attending to the ambiguities in their speech and to that which was expressing itself between the lines, as it were, he made room for new meanings to emerge, and for his analysands to realize that, in fact, they had little idea what they were saying, why they were saying it, or even *who* was speaking when they opened their mouths.

It is when patients begin to throw such things into question—when the what, why, and who of their utterances become problematic to them—*that they are genuinely engaged in analysis.* It is at this point that they are engaged in something which goes beyond the simple demand to be relieved of one or more specific symptoms. Everything becomes questionable; what was most certain is no longer at all certain, and they are now open to listening to the unconscious, to hearing the other voice that speaks through them, and to attempting to decipher it.

The space thus opened up is one in which analysands no longer know what they are saying or even what they are pursuing, but place their faith in the ability of the unconscious—in the formations (dreams, fantasies, daydreams, forgettings, and slips) it produces in the course of analysis—to guide them. It is a space of desire, insofar as "desire is a question," as Lacan says,[26] a wondering. Once patients begin to wonder about the why and wherefore of their words, thoughts, and fantasies, begin to formulate questions about them, their desire is engaged in the analysis.[27]

Demand is, of its very nature, repetitive. The patient's insistent, repetitive demand for an instantaneous cure gives way to something that moves, that is intrigued with each new manifestation of the unconscious (or "unconscious formation"),[28] that attaches itself to each new slip and explores it; in a word, the patient's demand gives way to desire, desire which is always in motion, looking for new objects, alighting here and there but never sitting still. In a sense, the patient has exchanged demand for desire—not completely, of course, since patients make further demands on their analysts throughout their analyses, demands for interpretation, recognition, approval, and so on. But the patient has been willing to let go of certain demands, and a demand always involves a kind of fixation on something (which is why one repeatedly asks for the same thing, that thing one feels one cannot do without). Thus, the patient has given up a certain fixation for desire, for the pleasure stemming from the metonymy of desire, the term "metonymy" here implying simply that desire moves from one object to the next, that in and of itself desire involves a constant slippage or movement. Desire is an end in itself: it seeks only more desire, not fixation on a specific object.[29]

Lacan's term for this shift—this exchange of demand for desire, this giving up of fixation for movement—is "dialectization." The patient, when this shift occurs, enters the dialectical process of analysis—"dialectical" in the sense that the patient becomes free to say, "Well yes, I want that; on second thought, I don't really; come to think of it, what I really want is . . ."[30] The patient no longer feels he or she has to be consistent; he or she can assert a wish during one session, contradict it during the second, reassert it with slight changes during the third, and so on. There is method in the seeming madness, but the logic of the movements of desire is not propositional logic or the logic of everyday common sense (whereby you cannot both want something and not want it at the same time).

Lacan's use of the term "dialectic" here (the "dialectic of desire")[31] does not mean that desire follows the widely taught version of Hegel's dialectic—affirmation, negation, synthesis; it means that *desire is set in motion, set free of the fixation inherent in demand*. This is a momentous step, and it signals the analysand's true entry into analysis. I do not mean to imply that the patient's desire is set in motion once and for all, and never gets stuck or bogged down at any point thereafter. Rather, a first exchange occurs: the patient agrees to accept the pleasure of desire in exchange for his or her initial demands.

With certain patients, however, the analyst is never able to elicit a question of any kind; the patient does not wonder about any of the things she did or said in the past, and does not problematize anything she says or does in her present relationship with the analyst. Though the patient continues to come to talk with the analyst, she never sees anything else in what she says than what she meant. The unconscious is never accepted, the imaginary (meaning) predominating. This may imply one of two things. The patient may be psychotic, a possibility I'll return to in Chapter 7; or the analyst may not have created a space in which desire can come to the fore, and thus needs to reconsider his or her own position in the therapy. The latter is likely to involve an oppressive demand that the patient talk, talking being associated for certain patients with performing, and simply giving other people what they want to hear as opposed to speaking "one's own" thoughts and desires.

3

THE ANALYTIC RELATIONSHIP

Knowledge and Suggestion

The role in which the analyst is cast by his or her analysands at the beginning of treatment depends a great deal on what they have heard and read about analysis, which in turn depends on their socioeconomic background, their education, and their cultural milieu. Generally speaking, however, people's view of doctors and healers in modern-day society, above all in consumer societies like the United States, is not what it once was. The respect for the doctor or healer which seems to have prevailed in certain eras in certain parts of the world has given way to an increasing lack of respect, attested to in the medical field by the often heard demand for "a second opinion."

As early as 1901, Freud mentioned a medical colleague of his who told him that the Turks in Bosnia and Herzegovina were "accustomed to show great confidence in their doctor and great resignation to fate. If [their doctor] has to inform them that nothing can be done for a sick person, their reply is: 'Sir, what is there to be said? If he could be saved, I know you would have saved him'" (SE VI, 3). Freud was no doubt struck by the contrast between the respect for doctors among the Turks and the treatment he received from his own patients in turn-of-the-century Vienna.

In America today, people tend to be somewhat skeptical of what their physicians tell them, and extremely skeptical of the therapeutic powers of psychotherapists.[1] Study after study in the popular press has thrown into question the usefulness of psychotherapy; therapists of different schools sling mud at one another to win partisans; health insurance companies often consider any therapy with the prefix "psycho" in it to be worthless; and the media depict nothing but therapists who take advantage of their patients and who are more deranged than their patients in the first place. In short, *psychotherapy has been largely discredited in the United States, and is frequently no more than a last resort.* It is often only after someone has been to general practitioners, gastroenterologists, chiropractors, psychiatrists, and acupuncturists—all to no avail—that a psychotherapist is finally contacted.

To the American mind, the psychotherapist is often assumed to be someone who could not hack medical school, who flunked college math or science, and whose experience of human nature may be no more profound than that of radio talk-show hosts. Americans have no more faith in psychology or psychoanalysis than they do in astrology and palmistry (indeed, they may have less). People very often come to therapy absolutely unconvinced that the therapist can help them, and openly skeptical of the kind of knowledge the therapist professes to wield.

How then are we to understand Lacan's well-known claim that the motor force of analysis is "the subject supposed to know,"[2] usually presumed to imply that the analysand attributes vast knowledge of human suffering to the analyst, assuming, right from the outset, that the latter has the knowledge necessary to make a difference? Clearly this calls for some explanation. Is it simply that what works in France does not work in America?

In our day, respect for the analyst's knowledge is greater in some countries, cities, and circles than in others. In Paris, for example, psychoanalysis is a daily topic of discussion in the media, is introduced in high school philosophy classes, and is generally held in fairly high esteem. The French do not seem to believe, as do Americans, that biology is at the root of everything and that medicine will someday be able to eliminate all mental anguish and suffering. Indeed, in Paris the individual psychoanalyst benefits from the fact that the population at large has a generally positive view of the field of psychoanalysis.

Such a view can be found on a smaller scale in New York and Los Angeles, for example, above all in artistic and intellectual circles. In those microcosms, people (whether they are in analysis or not) tend to assume that analysts have knowledge about human problems such as anxiety, fear, stress, and guilt. And if, in the course of their lifetime, they are led to consult an analyst, they tend to immediately view that analyst as someone who knows more than they do about their symptoms and neurosis. In other words, such people automatically consider the analyst "a subject supposed to know."

What is the effect of this cultural difference? It simply means that certain people (Parisians, for example) are *more open to the effect of analysis* right from the outset. When people attribute knowledge and thus power to a doctor, it means that they are open to any and all *suggestions* he or she might make. If we think back to Mesmer and Charcot, it is clear that their patients were extremely *suggestible* due to their reputations as miracle healers. If Charcot hypnotized a patient who apparently had been unable to walk for years and made the suggestion to her that she could now walk, the patient was very often *ready and willing to believe him.* Freud, on the other hand, complained that when he practiced hypnosis, he was rarely able to hypnotize people the way clinicians could in the well-known clinics where "miracle cures" were every-day events, for the patients who came to him did not have the same faith in his powers. In the early years of his practice, there was no "aura" of healing around him. His patients thus were not very suggestible.

This changed as Freud's reputation grew, but since the effects of suggestion are generally short-lived, requiring the therapist to repeat the same sugges-tions over and over at regular intervals, Freud gradually moved away from relying on suggestion alone. If his patients presumed he had a vast store of knowledge and were thus more open to the effect of the treatment, so much the better; if not, he could do without that presumption. In other words, a patient *may* be quite suggestible and open to the analyst's influence at the outset, and may even feel somewhat relieved of anxiety that has been mount-ing over time just by making an appointment with an analyst (in some cases merely by *thinking* he or she could make such an appointment), but this improvement is due to what is known as the "placebo effect."[3] In other words, it is an effect not of psychoanalytic treatment, strictly speaking, but merely of the patient's preconceived notions.

In certain cases, the fact that the patient puts the analyst in the position of "the subject supposed to know" can actually be detrimental to his or her analytic work. Indeed, a patient who comes to the analyst in a highly suggestible state, sure that the analyst is the one with all the knowledge, is far less likely to realize that it is the patient who must engage in the serious analytic work of association. Such a patient may be more inclined to briefly state his or her consciously formulated problem and await the analyst's indubitably brilliant solution.

The analyst may have all the diplomas in the world, and a reputation second to none, but if he or she is unable to go beyond suggestion with the patient and engage the patient in the analytic process, the treatment will amount to nothing more than the administering of placebos.

The Subject Supposed to Know

If psychoanalysis does not rely on the analysand's *belief* in the knowledge and power of the analyst—if it is not, therefore, a form of faith healing—what is the role of knowledge in the establishment of the analytic relationship?

The subject supposed to know something of importance in psychoanalysis is the analysand's unconscious.[4] If there is an authority to be respected in the analytic setting, it is the manifestations of the unconscious in the analysand's slips, mistakes, expressions of surprise, and so on.

The "final authority" in the analytic setting thus resides in the analysand's unconscious, not in the analyst as some sort of master of knowledge who immediately grasps what the analysand is saying and the meaning of his or her symptoms. The analyst, by systematically emphasizing the unconscious, and by initially confining his or her interventions to punctuation and scansion, does not present him- or herself as someone who has already seen it all a hundred times and thus immediately understands.[5] Yet the *analysand*, who is perhaps paying attention to manifestations of the unconscious for the first time, *tends to view the analyst as the representative or agent of every such manifestation.* The analysand does not take such manifestations upon him- or herself, but instead refuses responsibility for them. Responsibility is thrust upon the analyst, and the analyst must agree to occupy the place of those manifestations, those unknown quantities. It might therefore be said that it is not the *analysand's* unconscious that is the ultimate authority, but rather the unconscious as manifested *via* the analysand; for such manifestations are disowned by the analysand as foreign or other, as not his or hers.

Thus it is that, in a roundabout way, the analyst becomes associated with the analysand's unconscious, with its incomprehensible manifestations, with the unknown, or x, that appears in the analysand's speech. *The subject supposed to know—that is, the unconscious "within" the analysand—is rejected by the analysand and projected onto the analyst.* The analyst must agree to occupy the space of or stand in (or sit in) for the unconscious—to make the unconscious present through his or her presence.

The "Person" of the Analyst

The analyst may encourage this or discourage it. Clearly, insofar as the analyst is unwilling to keep his or her own personality out of the analytic relationship (that is, *resists* being a placeholder for or representative of the analysand's unconscious), he or she reinforces the assumption made by most new analysands that the analyst is a person more or less like themselves.

In the course of the preliminary meetings, the analyst must allow a shift to occur in the analysand's mind: the analyst must shift from being an other person to being an other ~~person~~ ("person" under erasure [*sous rature*]). In other words, the "person" of the analyst must disappear if he or she is to stand in for the unconscious. He or she must become a more abstract other, the other that seems to speak inadvertently, in the slips and cracks in the analysand's discourse. In a word, he or she must stand in for what Lacan calls the Other with a capital "O": that which the analysand considers to be radically foreign, strange, "not me."

This is not the analyst's final position, as we shall see below, but it already makes clear why analysts must keep their personal feelings and character traits out of the therapy, revealing as little as possible about themselves, their habits, likes, and dislikes. Every individualizing feature of the analyst gets in the way of the analysand's projections. The less concrete and distinct the analyst seems to the analysand, the easier it is to use him or her as a blank screen.[6]

When the analyst is viewed by the analysand as just another person like anyone else—that is, as similar to the analysand—the analysand is likely to compare him- or herself to the analyst, seeing him- or herself in the analyst, imitating the analyst, and ultimately competing with the analyst. The relationship that arises in this situation is characterized by Lacan as predominantly imaginary. By qualifying it as "imaginary," Lacan does not mean that the relationship does not exist; he means that it is dominated by the analysand's self-image and the image he or she forms of the analyst. The analyst is loved insofar as the analysand's image of him or her resembles the analysand's self-image, and hated insofar as it is different. As the analysand measures him- or her*self* against his or her image of the analyst, the foremost question is, "Am I better or worse, superior or inferior?" *Imaginary relations are dominated by rivalry*, the kind of rivalry most of us are familiar with from sibling rivalry.

It is at the level of imaginary relations that analysts who are concerned with acting the part of the master of knowledge are challenged, if not unseated, by their analysands, such analysts mistaking their authority as representatives of the unconscious with the authority associated with keeping the upper hand.[7] In other words, the ultimate authority in the analytic situation lies, to their minds, in the "person" of the analyst, and they thus set out to prove to their analysands that they know more than their analysands, and attempt to establish their power on that basis.

The imaginary is the level at which Lacan situates what most analysts refer to as "countertransference." It is the level at which the analyst gets caught up in the same game of comparing him- or herself to his or her analysands, sizing up their discourse in terms of his own: "Are they ahead of me or behind me in their comprehension of what is going on here?" "Are they submissive to my wishes?" "Do I have any control over the situation?" "How come this person makes me feel so lousy about myself?" As I mentioned in Chapter 1, Lacan's perspective is not that countertransferential feelings do not exist, but rather that they are situated at the imaginary level and must thus be set aside by the analyst. They must not be revealed to the analysand, since this would situate the analyst and analysand at the same level, as imaginary others for each other, both of whom are capable of having similar feelings, hang-ups, and insecurities.[8] It prevents the analysand from casting the analyst in some Other role.

Often it is not easy for analysands to give up the notion that the analyst is not going to act with them like everyone else with whom they interact. When the analyst consistently maintains his or her position, however, a good many imaginary phenomena tend to subside. One patient manifested his grudging acceptance of this unusual sort of relationship when he said to a therapist I supervise: "So I guess this means you're not going to be my *woman*." Up until then he had been propositioning her, asking her to coffee, lunch, and dinner, acting as if she were just any other woman he might meet somewhere and strike up a relationship with. Here he seemed to have finally accepted the fact that she was an Other like no other.

Symbolic Relations

At an early stage in Lacan's work, the goal in analysis was to eliminate the interference in symbolic relations generated by the imaginary—in other words, to get imaginary conflicts out of the way so as to confront the analysand with his or her problems with the Other.

What are symbolic relations? One simple way of viewing them is as one's relation to the Law, to the law laid down by one's parents, one's teachers, one's religion, one's country. Symbolic relations can also be thought of as the way people deal with *ideals* that have been inculcated in them by their parents, schools, media, language, and society at large, embodied in grades, diplomas, status symbols, and so on. Are they inhibited in their pursuit of the objects and achievements that have been recommended to them? Do they pursue them compulsively? Do they avoid pursuing them altogether, by dropping out? Do they pursue them only indirectly, in the hopes of attaining them *without really trying*, without really putting themselves on the line?[9] Do they furtively break the law in the secret hope of being caught? Do they think about getting married and having children (widely advocated as the ideal way of life), yet feel anxious about this course and indefinitely put it off? Do they embark on a career and aim at social and financial success only in such a way as to ensure failure? In short, what is the stance they adopt with respect to the ideal objects designated by the parental Other, the educational Other, the social Other?

Symbolic relations include all the conflicts associated with what is commonly referred to in psychoanalysis as "castration anxiety." Analysands, for example, often cannot directly pursue things they claim to want because that would involve giving in to what (they think) their parents want them to do. To attain a particular goal would thus, to their minds, be tantamount to satisfying their parents' wishes. "Anything but that!" "God forbid!" "I would never give them such pleasure." They would sooner live their whole lives in opposition to the demands made and the ideals fostered by the parental Other than let anything they do serve that Other.[10] Thus, all of their behavior is, in some sense, a protest: it secretly or not so secretly defies the Other's wishes. Consciously, of course, they may believe there are all sorts of reasons for their behavior that have nothing to do with their parents or with rebellion against social ideals. Nevertheless, they have made themselves into living symbols of protest.

In his work from the early 1950s, Lacan suggests that one of the aims of analysis is to clarify and modify the analysand's symbolic relations—that is, the analysand's stance with respect to the Other (the parental Other, the Law, social ideals, and so on). With two simple categories, the imaginary and the symbolic, he provides a model (Figure 3.1) of the analytic situation which suggests that symbolic relations involve the unconscious (hence the word "subject" in the upper left-hand corner) and the Other, whereas imaginary relations involve the analysand's own ego or self-image and the ego of other people like him- or herself ("ego'" in the upper right-hand corner).[11] Analysis aims at progressively dissipating the analysand's imaginary relations[12] with his or her friends, colleagues, brothers, and sisters (relations which tend to preoccupy analysands in the early stages of analysis) through the work of association—known as "working through" or, as Lacan often puts it, "the work of transference"[13]—in order to bring into focus the analysand's symbolic relations. Indeed, very often the key to the analysand's imaginary relations lies in the symbolic. A man's intense rivalry with a brother, for example, may well stem from the way the parents (the parental Other) gave that brother special treatment, or considered him smarter or better looking; his homosexual attachment to another man his own age may well be related to their

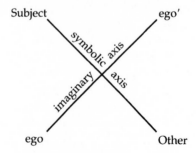

Figure 3.1. Simplified L Schema

similar positions with respect to a symbolic Other—an older teacher or supervisor, for example.

Thus, the goal of analysis, as Lacan conceptualized it in the early 1950s, is to pierce through the imaginary dimension which veils the symbolic and confront the analysand's relations to the Other head on. The imaginary and the symbolic are at cross-purposes in this conceptualization.[14] To emphasize the symbolic is to diminish the importance of the imaginary. If, however, the analyst allows him- or herself to be cast in the role of someone like the analysand (an imaginary other as opposed to the symbolic Other), it is the analyst's ego that becomes situated at one end of the imaginary axis in juxtaposition to the analysand's ego, and analysis bogs down in rivalrous power struggles and identifications. By falling into the trap of imaginary identifications, the analyst loses sight of the symbolic dimension—"the only dimension that cures," as Lacan says.

The Analyst as Judge

Who is the analyst? He who interprets by taking advantage of transference? He who analyzes transference as resistance? Or he who imposes his idea of reality?[15]

—Lacan, *Ecrits*, 592/232

Carefully avoiding the pitfall of situating him- or herself as an imaginary other in relation to the analysand, the analyst must be aware that further pitfalls await. For the analysand has, as we all have, come to expect certain things of parental and authority figures: approval, disapproval, recognition, punishment—in a word, *judgment*.

Not only does the analysand expect judgment; he or she may well demand it! The analyst who successfully skirts the trap of being viewed like the analysand (and of comparing him- or herself to the analysand) may well become viewed as a kind of priest to whom one confesses one's sins, and then awaits the exaction of penitence and atonement. The analyst here may be projected into a God-like position: that of the all-knowing Other fit to deliberate on all questions of normality and abnormality, right and wrong, good and bad.

Apart from the fact that the analyst is by no means fit to deliberate on such issues, providing such judgments is detrimental to therapy. Telling analysands that certain thoughts or fantasies are bad, for example, or that certain impulses or desires are abnormal, is likely to make them stop talking about them in therapy, despite their persistence outside the therapy context. Telling analysands that other thoughts or fantasies are fine and normal can have the same effect, for it impedes analysands from bringing out all the reasons they themselves don't consider such things fine and normal. It may at first be relieving and gratifying to the analysand to hear an authority deem normal what the analysand had considered problematic, but this salutary effect of suggestion ultimately stops the analysand from delving into his or her own qualms and reservations. And since speech is the only lever in therapy, as soon as an analysand stops talking about something, the analyst cannot hope to bring about any change whatsoever in that area. If analysands stop talking about certain aspects of their experience because the analyst has inhibited them with positive or negative judgments, the analysis can do nothing for them; indeed, the withholding of thoughts regarding one aspect of life is likely to make all of the therapist's efforts regarding other aspects fruitless as well.

More problematic still is that the analysands of even the most vigilant analyst often interpret a sigh, a cough, or even silence as a sign of disapproval or censure. Analysands are so used to being judged by the parental, academic, or juridical Other that they supply the judgment in their own minds even when it is not forthcoming from the analyst, even when the analyst has in no way, shape, or form passed judgment. Judgment has become so thoroughly internalized that it is pronounced without any action being required on the analyst's part.

In other words, the analyst not only has to be careful not to suggest disapproval, but has to vigilantly preempt or undo the analysand's tendency to attribute disapproving attitudes to the analyst. Whenever the analysand expresses his or her sense that the analyst disapproved of something, the analyst has to make it matter for interpretation: the analyst neither accepts nor refuses the projection, but finds it a fruitful field for association, elaboration, and interpretation. The analyst obviously suggests thereby that it is the analysand who has projected such an attitude onto the analyst (assuming that the analyst did not, consciously or unconsciously, convey such an attitude), and incites the analysand to wonder why he or she has projected *that particular attitude.* By not directly denying having had such an attitude and focusing instead on interpretation, the analyst tries not to thwart future projections by the analysand—for this would dissipate the transference which is so essential to the working through of conflictual relations. Instead, the analyst allows transferential projections to continue, *interpreting not the fact of transference* ("You're projecting that attitude onto me") *but its content*—that which is transferred or projected—seeking to link it anew with its source or point of origin.[16]

By the very nature of his or her work, the analyst is often associated, in the analysand's eyes, with Establishment values: hard work, academic success, seriousness, capitalism, and so on. The fact that the analyst dresses in a particular way, lives in a certain part of town, decorates his or her home or office in a certain style, and subscribes to specific magazines found in the waiting room often leads the analysand to view the analyst as the representative of certain values—values the analysand may utterly reject, unsuccessfully try to embrace, or successfully pursue, though feeling alienated in that very pursuit. Such values are obviously attached to the "person of the analyst"—that is, to the analyst as an individual—but the analysand is likely to attribute these values to the analyst even in his or her role as analyst. The analyst must thus vigilantly highlight such attributions as interpretable—as more telling of the analysand than of the analyst.

The same is true of positive judgments the analysand attributes to the analyst. The analyst is not there to approve of the analysand's behavior, but analysands very often seek to win the analyst's approval by second-guessing his or her values and attempting to realize them, second-guessing his or her desire and attempting to fulfill it, becoming what they believe the analyst wants them to become. This is but another neurotic strategy which, instead of leading to the subject's separation from the Other, brings on ever greater dependence. It generally repeats prior relations to the parental Other in which the subject has tried to satisfy the parents and then secretly disobey or disappoint them, or satisfy them at his or her own expense.

When the analyst knowingly or unknowingly provides the analysand with a sign of approval, the effect is often one of pure suggestion: the analysand comes to believe that he or she is doing the right thing or getting better, attempts to build upon the approved behavior, yet remains dependent upon the Other's opinion. Should the analysand then spend his or her vacation with people who do not endorse the analyst's view, the analysand, still slavishly influenced by other people's views, ends up throwing everything back into question. The question in such a case becomes, "Whose influence is stronger, the analyst's or the friends'?"—which is ultimately the wrong question. The effects of suggestion last only as long as the relationship with the analyst lasts, assuming the analyst has the most influence over the analysand's life.

A therapist I supervise was somewhat astonished by what seemed to be a miraculous improvement in one of her patients, to whom she had indicated that therapy was not about the therapist befriending the patient and supporting her as a friend might, but rather about making the patient able to support herself, so to speak. By the next session, the patient's insistent demands for support had already ceased, and within four sessions the patient reported a newfound sense of independence and happiness. Despite the immediate therapeutic value for the patient of such a solution, it seemed quite clear that the improvement was due primarily to suggestion, and that the patient had as yet made no enduring progress.[17] She had glimpsed one facet of what the therapist wanted from her, and had set out to provide it, thereby subordinating her own desire to the therapist's.

The Analyst as Cause

Abdicating the role of imaginary other, the analyst is very often cast in the role of Judge by the analysand, yet the analyst must abdicate this position as well.[18] Highly discriminating in terms of what he or she emphasizes during analytic sessions, encouraging the analysand to talk about certain things and not about others, he or she must nevertheless abstain from passing judgment on the analysand's actions in the "outside world" or on the analysand's fantasies and thoughts. Neither imaginary other nor symbolic Other, what role is left for the analyst?

As I mentioned earlier, many new analysands tend to refuse responsibility for their slips and slurs, thrusting responsibility for them onto the analyst. As one patient said to her therapist, "You're the one who always sees dark and dirty things in everything I say!" At the outset, analysands often see no more in a slip than a simple problem regarding the control of the tongue muscles[19] or a slight inattention. The analyst is the one who attributes some Other meaning to it.

As time goes on, however, analysands themselves begin to attribute meaning to such slips, and the analyst, rather than standing in for the unconscious, for that strange Other discourse, is viewed by the analysand as its cause: "I had a dream last night because I knew I was coming to see you this morning." In such a statement, very often heard in analysis, the analyst is cast in the role of the cause of the analysand's dream: "I wouldn't have had such a dream were it not for you." "The dream was for you." "You were in my dream last night." Unconscious formations, such as dreams, fantasies, and slips, are produced for the analyst, to be recounted to the analyst, to tell the analyst something. The analyst, in that sense, is behind them, is the reason for their production, is, in a word, their cause.

When the analyst is viewed as an other like the analysand, the analyst can be considered an imaginary object or other for the analysand. (Lacan writes this as *a'*, "a" being the first letter of *autre*, the French word for "other." Lacan puts it in italics to indicate that it is imaginary. In contrast to *a'*, the subject's own ego is denoted by *a*.) When the analyst is viewed as a judge or parent, the analyst can be considered a sort of symbolic object or Other for the analysand (which is denoted by A, for *Autre*, "Other"). When the analyst is viewed as the cause of the analysand's unconscious formations, the analyst can be considered a "real" object for the analysand (which is denoted by the expression "object *a*").

Once the analyst has maneuvered in such a way that he or she is placed in the position of cause by the analysand (cause of the analysand's dreams and of the wishes they fulfill—in short, cause of the analysand's desire), certain manifestations of the analysand's transference love or "positive transference," typically associated with the early stages of analysis, may well subside, giving way to something far less "positive" in coloration.[20] The analysand may begin to express his or her sense that the analyst is "under my skin," like an irritant. Analysands who seemed to be comfortable or at ease during their sessions at the outset (by no means the majority, however) may well display or express discomfort, tension, and even signs that they are rebelling against the new configuration, the new role the analyst is taking on in their lives and fantasies. The analyst is becoming *too* important, is showing up in their daydreams, in their masturbation fantasies, in their relationships with their significant other, and so on.

Such a predicament is generally not what people expect when they go into analysis, and indeed non-Lacanian analyses often never go this far. Certain analysands are inclined to break off their treatment when they sense that the analyst is taking on an "intrusive" role in their lives, and many analysts are loath to invite, shoulder, and deal with such feelings (sometimes referred to as the "negative therapeutic reaction"). Indeed, the very theory of therapy such analysts embrace considers such an intrusive role to be unproductive. Lacan, on the contrary, considers it the *Archimedean point of analysis*—that is, the very point at which the analyst can apply the lever that can move the symptom. The analyst in the position of *cause* of desire for the analysand is, according to Lacan, the *motor force of analysis;* in other words, it is the position the analyst must occupy in order for transference to lead to something other than identification with the analyst as the endpoint of an analysis (identification with the analyst being considered the goal of analysis by certain psychoanalysts).

"Negative transference" is by no means the essential sign indicating that the analysand has come to situate the analyst as cause of desire; it is but one possible manifestation of the latter. Nevertheless, the attempt by therapists of many ilks to avoid or immediately neutralize any emergence of negative transference—which, after all, is but the flipside of transference love (love and hate being intimately related through the essential ambivalence of all affect)[21]—means that aggression and anger are turned into feelings which are inappropriate for the patient to project onto the therapist. Patients thereby learn not to express them in therapy; or, if they do express them, the therapist quickly seizes the opportunity to point out that the patient is projecting—that the anger and aggression are *not really directed at the therapist*—thereby defusing the intensity of the feeling and the possible therapeutic uses of the projection. Anger and aggression are thus never worked out with the therapist, but rather examined "rationally."

Consider, by way of contrast, Freud's characterization of analysis as a struggle or battle between analyst and analysand:

> The patient regards the products of the awakening of his unconscious impulses as contemporaneous and real; he seeks to put his passions into action without taking any account of the real situation. [The ensuing] struggle between the doctor and the patient . . . is played out almost exclusively in the phenomena of transference. It is on that field that the victory must be won—the victory whose expression is the permanent cure of the neurosis. It cannot be disputed that controlling the phenomena of transference presents the psychoanalyst with the greatest difficulties. But it should not be forgotten that it is precisely they that do us the inestimable service of making the patient's hidden and forgotten erotic impulses immediate and manifest. For when all is said and done, it is impossible to destroy anyone *in absentia* or *in effigie*. (SE XII, 108)

In other words, it is only by making psychical conflicts—such as aggression against one's parents or hatred of a family member—*present* in the relationship with the analyst that the patient can work them through. To work them through means not that they are intellectually viewed and "processed," but rather that the internal libidinal conflict which is holding a symptomatic relationship to someone in place must be allowed to repeat itself in the relationship with the analyst and play itself out. If verbalization (putting things into words) is the only technique allowed the analysand, a true separation from the analyst and from analysis never occurs.[22] Projection must be allowed to go so far as to bring out all the essential aspects of a conflict-ridden relationship, all the relevant recollections and dynamics, and the full strength of the positive/negative affect. It should be recalled that one of the earliest lessons of Freud and Breuer's *Studies on Hysteria* was that verbalizing traumatic events without reliving the accompanying affect left symptoms intact.[23]

Transference, viewed as *the transfer of affect* (evoked in the past by people and events) *into the here and now of the analytic setting*, means that the analysand must be able to project onto the analyst a whole series of emotions felt in relation to significant figures from his or her past and present. If the analyst is concerned with "being himself" or "being herself," or with being the "good father" or "good mother," he or she is likely to try to immediately distance him- or herself from the role in which the analysand is casting him or her by saying something like, "I am *not* your father" or "You are projecting." The message conveyed by such a statement is, "Don't confuse me with him" or "It is not appropriate to project." But the analyst would do better to neither encourage nor discourage the case of mistaken identity that arises through the transfer of feelings, and to let the projection of different personas occur as it will—unless, of course, it goes so far as to jeopardize the very continuation of the therapy.

Rather than interpreting the *fact* of transference, rather than pointing out to the analysand that he or she is projecting or transferring something onto the analyst, the analyst should direct attention to the *content* (the ideational and affective content) of the projection, attempting to get the analysand to put *it* into words. Not to dissipate it or prohibit it, not to make the analysand feel guilty about it, but to speak it. Here the analyst works—often more by asking questions than by interpreting—to reestablish the connections between the content (thought and feeling) and the persons, situations, and relationships that initially gave rise to it.[24] I provide a concrete example of this approach in the case of obsession I present in Chapter 8.

This discussion of the analyst as cause (cause of the analysand's slips, dreams, and fantasies, cause of the analysand's love and hate—in a word, cause of the analysand's desire) has led me to get rather far ahead of myself; I'll return to the topic in Chapter 5, after introducing a number of other concepts. The concept of the cause of desire plays an essential role, for example, in what Lacan calls the "fundamental fantasy," the fantasy that stages the satisfaction implied in the analysand's principal symptom. As will become apparent in the discussion of fantasy, it is only when the analyst stands in for the cause in the analysand's fantasy that this fantasy can be modified.

4

INTERPRETATION: OPENING UP THE SPACE OF DESIRE

Desire is the very essence of man.

—Spinoza, *Ethics*

Our technique involves handling desire, interfering with it, and even rectifying it.

—Lacan, Seminar X, May 22, 1963

Demand versus Desire

As we saw in Chapter 2, the analysand's demands can never be taken at face value. While ostensibly demanding two sessions a week instead of three, the analysand may merely be going through the motions imposed upon her by her husband (concerned as he is about saving money and ensuring that she not change too much), rather than expressing any real desire of her own. She may be knowingly or unknowingly hoping that the analyst will vehemently disagree or even refuse to continue to see her if the original frequency is not maintained. Even if she is making the demand on her own account, she may still, in some sense, be hoping that the analyst will refuse.[1]

If the analyst easily yields to the analysand's request for fewer sessions, he or she indicates to the analysand that, to the analyst's mind, the request was something very simple—the expression of a "real need" or a "straight-forward demand"—rather than something potentially far more complex, a statement in which competing thoughts and wishes played a part.[2] Indeed, the analyst has the ability to interpret any statement made by the analysand as the expression of a "simple" demand or as the expression of a desire or nexus of desires.

Just as an audience can make a lecturer's statement into a joke by laughing at it, or a joke into a boring statement by remaining deadpan—and just as a mother can turn every cry by her infant into a demand for food by feeding her baby every time it cries—so too, the analyst, as listener, can read what the analysand says either as a demand or as an expression of desire. The listener or public has the power to determine what someone has said. There is obviously a distinction between what a speaker "means" or "means to say" and what the public hears. Meaning is determined by the public or, as Lacan says, in the locus (or place) of the Other. Despite your conscious intention to communicate something very specific, the meaning of your words is always determined by other people, by the Other.

The politician's nightmare is the way the press or the opposing party "twists" his or her words, making them say something he or she did not mean. Yet this is the nature of "communication": we speak to express something to other people, but *they* determine—often to our dismay—what it is we meant, and sometimes base serious decisions on *their* interpretation of what we said. The listener's power is considerable.[3]

So too, the analyst's power as listener is considerable, and by constantly "hearing" the analysand's statements as something other than "simple" demands, the analyst can open up a space in which desire is glimpsed beneath or behind demand.[4] Indeed, as I mentioned in Chapter 2, an extremely important goal of analysis is to go beyond the constancy and fixation of demand to the variability and mobility of desire: to "dialectize" the analysand's desire. One of the means at the analyst's disposal is to listen for potential desires behind every statement, every request, and everything the analysand intends as a demand "pure and simple."

Having been an analysand myself for many years, I know how infuriating this method can be at times, yet it is the key to getting analysands to probe their own motives more profoundly.[5] As an analysand, one may have the impression that one's analyst is constitutionally unable to call a spade a spade, or to accept that there are *real* circumstances (such as work, money, and matters of health) that sometimes impinge on treatment. But *the analyst must remain intractable in any matter which smacks of resistance,* and indeed most analysands would probably agree that, in hindsight, other motives were often behind what they themselves initially believed to be "simple demands" (to miss sessions, come less frequently, and the like).

Thus, the familiar strategy of "frustrating the patient's demands" is adopted not so much to "maintain the limits of the analytic situation" as to bring desire to the fore. To interpret a patient's stated request as a simple demand and accede to it is to squelch whatever desire may have been lurking, or even seeking expression, behind it. To yield to a patient's every demand may even, in the end, make him or her anxious; for when there is no lack—when everything demanded is surrendered—desire is stymied. Nothing is left to be desired.

Interpretation: Bringing Forth
the Lack in Desire

Desire disappears under pleasure's sway.

—Lacan, *Ecrits*, 773–774

What a man actually lacks he aims at.

—Aristotle, *Nicomachean Ethics*, 1159b14

Desire springs from lack. If one were given everything one asked for, would one want anything anymore? A spoiled child, who is always given whatever it requests, typically complains of boredom. In the words of the old song Marilyn Monroe used to sing, "After you get what you want, you don't want it." Satisfaction buries desire.[6]

So does a certain type of interpretation. In Chapter 2, I discussed the kinds of interventions at the analyst's disposal during the preliminary meetings (including punctuation and scansion), suggesting that interpretation has little or no useful effect in most cases until the next stage has been reached. But even then, *not all interpretations are alike.*

In my experience, the most common form of interpretation in contemporary psychotherapy and psychoanalysis can be characterized as follows: the therapist tells the patient, in no uncertain terms, what the therapist believes the meaning of the thought, dream, fantasy, or symptom to be. Certain therapists wait until the patient is very close to arriving at the same interpretation, ensuring thereby that the patient understands the interpretation more or less immediately. Nevertheless, the therapist (as listener or Other) generally provides a very specific meaning, communicating to the patient that *this* is the true meaning.

Interpretation, understood in that way, is familiar to certain parents who calm their child when he has had nightmares by interpreting his nightmares for him. Such parents attempt to supply a simple, reassuring interpretation, designed to soothe the child's nerves and give the child something tangible to connect it to: a TV show seen earlier in the day, a fairy tale character, or something of the sort. Parents who make such interpretations may or may not be aware that, by tying down one possible association to the dream, they are blocking the way to others (for example, the fact that the frightful fairy tale character has become associated in the child's mind with the child's father). But their overriding concern is a very practical one: to calm the child.[7]

Interpretation as Oracular Speech

An interpretation whose effects one understands is not a psychoanalytic interpretation.

—Lacan, *Cahiers pour l'Analyse* 3 (1966): 13

It should be clear from the example I have given that this kind of interpretation is rather limited in scope, serving only immediate ends (say, allowing one's child to fall back asleep quickly). According to Lacan, interpretation in the analytic situation should generally serve a very different purpose. *Rather than tying down one particular meaning, it should seek to suggest numerous meanings.* To tie down one meaning brings on what I would refer to as an "adjustment" in the analysand's ego: the analysand learns that the analyst sees him or her, or understands his or her dream, in a particular way, and tries to fit this in with his or her self-image. The analysand adjusts his or her conscious ideas about who and what he or she is in accordance with the analyst's.[8]

The analyst here plays the role of the Other, the listener who determines the meaning of what the analysand says. The analyst does not accord the role of the Other to the analysand's unconscious, but rather usurps it. To adopt a Lacanian position, on the other hand, the analyst has to both play the role of the Other who hears something other than a simple demand in the analysand's request, and abdicate that role when it comes to interpretation. Giving the analysand clear, predigested meanings institutes a kind of dependency that is given up only with great difficulty: the analysand learns that he or she need but demand interpretation to receive it, the analyst being identified as the one who knows (the full vase) whereas the analysand (the empty vase) knows nothing but what the analyst communicates.[9] Nothing creates a more child-parent, student-teacher relationship between analysand and analyst than this. Nothing fosters greater dependency than this, infantilizing the analysand right from the outset and making analysis into a structurally endless parenting or educative process. Nothing feeds the analysand's demands faster than this, leading to a vicious cycle of demand (by the analysand) and response (by the analyst), action and reaction, wherein the analysand ultimately leads the analyst around by the nose. A typical sign that an analysis has come to such a pass is when the analyst devotes a great deal of time outside the sessions to trying to interpret the case in order to have something to offer to the analysand at the next session. Rather than spoon-feeding meaning to the analysand, regardless of how brilliant and insightful that meaning may be, the analyst must arouse the analysand's curiosity and kick-start his or her associative processes. The analyst must interpret in such a way that the analysand has to work hard to attempt to fathom the meaning of the analyst's interpretations.

This is done by providing interpretations that are enigmatic and polyvalent. The analysand tries to figure them out, at the conscious level inevitably, but also at the unconscious level. Such interpretations *resonate:* they put the unconscious to work. Conscious thought processes, abhorring ambiguity and multiple meanings, committed as they are to the belief that there must always be *one true meaning,* are soon frustrated and cease. The unconscious, however, is set in motion, and the enigmatic words spoken by the analyst find their way into the dreams and fantasies produced thereafter. "Rational thinking" gives way to the associative processes of unconscious desire.

A wide array of psychoanalysts accept Freud's notion that an interpretation is not so much true or false, correct or incorrect, as it is productive or unproductive.[10] But the productivity of interest is at the level of unconscious formations, not ego discourse (the latter being witnessed in such statements as, "I was thinking about what you said yesterday, and I agree in certain respects, but . . ."). What concerns us is what the analysand's unconscious finds in the interpretation—that is, what is seen or projected by the analysand's unconscious when it is granted the role of Other (here, the Other who knows).

Hence Lacan's description of genuine analytic interpretation as "oracular speech."[11] Much like the Delphic oracle, the analyst says something sufficiently polyvalent that it resonates even though it is not understood, arouses curiosity and a desire to know why the analyst said what he or she said, and invites new projections.

Let me illustrate Lacan's point with an altogether nonoracular interpretation, made by someone I once supervised. It functions almost exclusively at the level of meaning, the level at which the therapist simply provides the meaning of the analysand's speech. The patient was a young woman who enjoyed smoking marijuana in a circle with "a group of guys." The therapist told his patient that she was "using marijuana as an escape." Apart from the fact that nothing in her discourse had yet suggested such an interpretation (the latter reflecting the therapist's prejudices more than the patient's circumstances), the therapist's statement neglected the oral level of the drug experience and the possible sexual and social connotations of the group of guys. It not only stressed a conventional, stereotypical meaning, as opposed to an individual one, but also closed down the meaning-making process, rather than opening it up. True, the word "escape" can imply many things, but "using marijuana as an escape" does not. It seals a particular meaning, which can, of course, be accepted or rejected, giving rise to a long *conscious* thought process (it may be grudgingly or eventually accepted, or immediately rejected only to be later accepted), but does not inspire much at the unconscious level. Thus, it is not terribly productive, and may even be counterproductive; for the clearer the meaning attributed by the therapist, the easier it is for the patient to identify the therapist with a particular view, opinion, or theory and rebel against it at a conscious level. The therapist comes to stand for a specific perspective (social, economic, political, psychoanalytic), and regardless of whether the patient is for it or against it, it impedes the progress of the therapy.

The point is not that the analyst must never say anything directly so as not to let him- or herself be pinned down or held responsible for a particular psychoanalytic interpretation. But when an analyst knows relatively little about an analysand, he or she should avoid unambiguous formulations; the more direct a formulation is in the early stages of treatment, the more likely the analyst is to be barking up the wrong tree and for that to be plain to the analysand. When a formulation is more ambiguous, the analyst is able to see how the analysand takes it up—that is, what the analysand reads into it.

The timing of interpretation is thus quite important: interpretation should be avoided altogether during the preliminary meetings or interviews, and kept more polyvalent than univalent for much of the analysis. Relatively direct, relatively unambiguous interpretation—when it has its place at all—is reserved for the construction phase of analysis, as we shall see in the context of a case study in Chapter 8.

The interpretation mentioned above came too early in the treatment and articulated something of which the patient could not have failed to be aware, since the dominant discourse in our society today views drugs as an escape. Interpretation should, instead, seek to surprise, to derail the analysand's usual trains of thought. If it emphasizes sexual elements that the patient seems loath to discuss (for example, oral pleasures, involvement with a group of guys), it must nevertheless not become so predictable that the analysand always knows in advance what the analyst will highlight. Most analysands eventually catch on to sexual motifs repeatedly stressed by the analyst, and begin to stress such themes themselves without any outside help. But *there is always something that they do not catch on to.*

Interpretation Hits the Real

One's of Lacan's most noteworthy remarks about interpretation is that it hits the real,[12] and one of the things he means by this is that it hits what the analysand has been circling around and around without being able to formulate. The analyst at times has the sense that the analysand comes back to something again and again, approaching it from numerous angles, without ever feeling satisfied with what he or she has been able to say about it. The Lacanian real, as manifested in the patient's discourse, is that which makes the analysand come back to the same subject, event, or notion over and over, revolve around it endlessly, and feel unable to move on. The patient dwells on it and feels stuck, something essential remaining unformulated.

In such a case, the analyst, if he or she has a fair sense of what it is the analysand is circling around and around, might offer an interpretation which attempts to speak it: "Your mother turned you against your father"—an example of an interpretation I made with an analysand (whose analysis is described at some length in Chapter 8) who had become increasingly angry with her mother after years of pitying her as the victim of her husband's rage. The analysand's long-repressed love for her father had recently come into view, and anger with her mother had been the central topic of numerous recent sessions; the two themes had never been connected, however, and while the analysand related her anger toward her mother to many specific events, she did not feel satisfied with her own explanations. The interpretation restored a missing link in the chain of the analysand's thoughts and feelings, and it could be said to have "hit the real" in the sense that it verbalized (or symbolized) something that had never before been put into words. This something served as the *cause* of her anger, and the anger could not be worked through without its symbolization. Which is not to say that the anger suddenly disappeared— by no means. But it became focused on the mother's attempt to achieve something with her daughter which involved the father (that is, to get her daughter to side with her against her husband, thus turning the daughter away from her own father) and no longer monopolized all of the analysand's sessions.

It could, of course, be said that I simply gave her the meaning of her anger, and that she then set about trying to prove me right, adjusting her ego to my view of it. A good deal of case material would have to be presented to refute that claim, and I shall supply it in Chapter 8. Let us simply note here that the very wording of the interpretation ("Your mother turned you against your father"), like virtually all wording, was ambiguous: it could be taken in the physical sense of being turned in such a way (in bed, say) as to be up against your father. And while this may not be the first meaning that comes to the reader's mind, it certainly came to my analysand's mind in the time between sessions, and led to a number of interesting associations to events in her life (some of which she had already told me about). The point is that, while aiming quite directly at something that the analysand had been circling around, there was still something oracular about even this interpretation: it deliberately played on two levels simultaneously (figurative and literal, affective and physical).

Interpretation as oracular speech thus does not mean that an interpretation cannot be understood *at all* by the analysand; rather, it means that an interpretation plays off ambiguities in its very formulation. The analyst deliberately seeks provocative, evocative ways of expressing him- or herself, preferring, for example, formulations that include words containing sounds that are part and parcel of words or names that have been important in the analysand's discourse.

Certain analysands are inclined to become impatient when presented with oracular speech, but the analyst only defeats his or her own purpose by giving in to requests for explanation. Rather than provoking the analysand to ponder the why and wherefore of the analyst's intervention, explanations feed the analysand's demand, leading only to more demand.

The real, as I have presented it thus far, is what has not yet been put into words or formulated. It can be thought of, in a certain sense, as the connection or link between two thoughts that has succumbed to repression and must be restored.[13] It can also be thought of as what Freud calls trauma—traumatic events (usually sexual or involving people who have been libidinally invested by the subject) that have never been talked through, put into words, or verbalized. This real, according to Lacan, has to be symbolized through analysis: it has to be spoken, put into signifiers ("signifierized"). As Jacques-Alain Miller has put it, analysis involves the progressive "draining away" of the real into the symbolic.[14] Aiming at the real, interpretation helps the analysand put into words that which has led his or her desire to become fixated or stuck.

5

THE DIALECTIC OF DESIRE

Subjectification [is] the essential moment of any and every institution of the dialectic of desire.

—Lacan, Seminar VIII, 251

People come to analysis in a variety of states. Some people claim that they no longer want anything and can barely drag themselves out of bed anymore; others are so worked up about something they want that they can no longer concentrate or sleep at night. Whatever their specific state, it is problematic from the standpoints of desire and jouissance.

In many cases, the analyst can understand the new analysand's predicament as one of libidinal stasis: *his or her desire is fixated or stuck.* Consider, for example, a male analysand who repeatedly gets "hung up" on women who refuse his advances, manifest disinterest in him, or dump him. He meets a woman at a party, is vaguely attracted to her, and asks her out a couple of times. He remains somewhat indifferent toward her until the day she says she does not want to see him anymore. Suddenly he comes alive: he desires her passionately, and pursues her doggedly. She becomes the focus of all his attention, all his love, all his desire. She is *it,* his one and only. And the more she refuses him and remains disinterested, the more his desire blossoms.

Prior to the refusal, his desire is half asleep, barely in play. Refusal by a woman is not so much the ardently sought object *of* his desire as what *arouses* his desire, bringing it to life. It is the *cause* of his desire. Though his desire is slumbering at the outset, he becomes intrigued, indeed captivated, by the refusal. What demonstrates that *she* (the real, live, flesh-and-blood woman) is not what captivates him is the fact that the moment she succumbs to his never-ending endeavors to win her back, "she's history"—he has no further use for her. As long as she agrees to refuse him (perhaps letting him get closer only to push him away the next moment), she enflames him, setting his love ablaze. As soon as she shows him that she is really letting him in, his desire fades: its cause disappears and it can make no further use of the object at hand.

We might be tempted to think that it is his desire that makes him go out and find a woman, as if his desire were a given, some sort of constant force in his life. The fact is, however, that he merely happens upon women, gets involved with them without much conviction, and becomes impassioned only when one of them turns him down or tries to repel him.

As long as he associates the cause (refusal by a woman) with an object (a specific woman), it seems to the outside observer that his desire is incited by the object—that it is correlated with a specific object, that it reaches out to a specific object. But as soon as that association is broken, as soon as it becomes impossible for him to imbue the object at hand with the trait or characteristic that turns him on—refusal—we see that what is crucial is not the object, the specific woman he gets involved with, but the trait or characteristic that arouses his desire.

Desire thus is not so much *drawn toward* an object (Desire → Object) as *elicited by* a certain characteristic that can sometimes be read into a particular love object: desire is pushed not pulled (Cause → Desire). For a while, the object is seen as "containing" the cause, as "having" the trait or feature that incites this analysand's desire. At a certain point, however, the cause is abruptly subtracted from the object and the object promptly abandoned.[1]

Desire Has No Object

Although I've been talking about one specific case, Lacan's argument is far more general. *Human desire, strictly speaking, has no object.* Indeed, it doesn't quite know what to do with objects. When you get what you want, you cannot *want* it anymore because you already have it. Desire disappears when it attains its ostensible object. In the case of the analysand discussed above, when a woman gives in to his repeated entreaties and supplications (perhaps flattered that someone could want her so badly), his desire evaporates. Satisfaction, as I mentioned in Chapter 4, kills desire. Getting what one wants is not the best strategy for keeping one's desire alive.

Indeed, hysteria and obsession can be understood as different strategies for keeping one's desire alive. The obsessive desires something that is unattainable, the realization of his or her desire thus being structurally impossible. The hysteric, on the other hand, works to keep a certain desire unsatisfied; Freud refers to this as a wish for an unsatisfied wish, and Lacan refers to it as a desire for an unsatisfied desire.[2] In both hysteria and obsession, obstacles are placed in the way of any possible realization of desire (except, of course, in dreams, fantasies, or daydreams—the wish fulfillment *they* stage does not lead to the fading of desire).

Desire thus does not seek satisfaction; rather, it pursues its own continuation and furtherance—it merely seeks to go on desiring.[3] It might be objected that this is the case only in neurosis, because neurotics cannot pursue their own desire, due to inhibitions, fears, anxiety, guilt, and revulsion. But Lacan's claim is that even after a "successful analysis," desire essentially seeks its own continuation; due, however, to a reconfiguration of the subject in relation to the cause of his or her desire, desire no longer hinders the subject's pursuit of satisfaction (as we shall see further on).[4]

Lacan's term for the cause of desire is "object a."[5] One may wonder why, if desire has no object as such but rather a cause, Lacan continues to use the term "object" at all. It seems to have to do, in part, with the evolution of his own thought over time (in the early 1950s he was influenced by Karl Abraham's notion of the partial object and by D. W. Winnicott's notion of the transitional object), and also with an attempt to preempt discussion of what more commonly, in psychoanalytic theory, goes by the name "object." For, according to Lacan, the object as studied in certain forms of Kleinian psychoanalysis and object relations theory is of only secondary importance: it misses the cause. The only object involved in desire is that "object" (if we can still refer to it as an object) which *causes* desire.[6]

Fixation on the Cause

Object *a* can take on many different guises. It may be a certain kind of look someone gives you, the timber of someone's voice, the whiteness, feel, or smell of someone's skin, the color of someone's eyes, the attitude someone manifests when he or she speaks—the list goes on and on. Whatever an individual's characteristic cause may be, it is highly specific and nothing is easily put in its place. Desire is fixated on this cause, and this cause alone.

When someone comes to analysis because a relationship is going badly and yet he or she is clinging to it with all his or her might, it is generally the case that the partner has been imbued with the analysand's characteristic cause—is seen to have or contain the cause—and desire thus cannot be found elsewhere. To give up this partner is to give up desire altogether. If he or she is forced to do so (if, say, the partner cuts him or her off altogether), the analysand's desire may well enter the quagmire of libidinal limbo, a nether world which is desireless and in which the analysand drifts aimlessly.

It is the analysand's fixation on this cause that leads to a crisis of desire or in desire.[7] The analyst attempts to get the analysand's desire into motion, to shake up the fixation when the analysand can think about nothing else, and to dissipate the stasis that sets in when the analysand's desire has seemingly ebbed to the point of no return. The analyst attempts to arouse the analysand's curiosity about every manifestation of the unconscious, to bring the analysand to wonder about the why and wherefore of his or her life decisions, choices, relationships, career. Desire is a question, as I remarked in Chapter 2; and by getting the analysand to throw things into question, the analyst makes the analysand want to know something, find out something, figure out what the unconscious is saying, what the analyst sees in his or her slips, dreams, and fantasies, what the analyst means when he or she punctuates, scands, and interprets, and so on. The analyst, by attributing meaning to all these things, becomes the cause of the analysand's wonderings, ponderings, ruminations, dreams, and speculations—in short, the cause of the analysand's desire.[8]

No longer quite so fixated on that which served the analysand as cause at the outset of analysis, the analysand begins to take analysis and, by extension, the analyst as cause.[9] A new fixation is thereby established, but it is one that, as Freud tells us, is "at every point accessible to our intervention." The original fixation has become a transference fixation, and the pre-existing neurosis has become a "transference neurosis" (SE XII, 154).

The Other's Desire as Cause

Once the analyst has successfully maneuvered into the place of the analysand's cause—being neither an imaginary other for the analysand (someone like him or her), nor a symbolic Other (judge or idol), but the real cause of the analysand's desire—the true work begins: the "work of transference" or working through. The analyst endeavors to shake up the analysand's fixation on the cause.

Before the process involved here can be described, however, we must first understand more about the cause and how it comes into being. In other words, we must first examine the nature and development of human desire. My discussion here will be somewhat schematic, since I have written on this subject at great length elsewhere.[10]

During infancy, our primary caretakers are immensely important to us, our lives being intimately tied to theirs. We make demands on them; they, in turn, demand that we behave in certain ways and not others, and that we learn many things: to speak their language (using words, expressions, and grammar not of our own making) and to regulate our needs for nourishment, warmth, excretion, and so on in accordance with their schedules. They are our primary source of attention and affection, and we often attempt to win their approval and love by conforming to their wishes. The better we satisfy their demands, the more approval we are likely to obtain. The more completely we satisfy their wishes, the more love we are likely to win from them.

Yet they do not always tell us what they want. Often they confine themselves to telling us what they do *not* want, punishing us after the fact for a faux pas. To garner favor and to avoid such punishment and disapproval, we seek to decipher their likes, dislikes, and wishes: "What is it they want?" "What do they want from me?"

Even when they do tell us what they want—"You're going to be a lawyer when you grow up, and that's final!"—the message may not be as transparent as it seems. Apart from the fact that we may opt to accede to such wants or revolt against them in protest, we may sense that, while our parents are saying this (perhaps even demanding this), they would actually prefer something else: that we be something they had always wanted to be but were unable to be—or that we *not* be what they had always wanted to be but were unable to be, since they would feel threatened by this, preferring to see us as failures or "ordinary people" like themselves.

In our attempt to decipher their wants, we are confronted with the fact that people do not always mean what they say, want what they say they want, or desire what they demand. Human language allows people to say one thing and mean another. One parent may be merely mouthing what the other parent ardently wants, and we sense this, wondering what it is that the parent "really wants."

Our parents' desire becomes the mainspring of our own: we want to know what they want in order to best satisfy or thwart them in their purposes, discover where we fit into their schemes and plans, and find a niche for ourselves in their desire. We want to be desired by them; as Lacan says, "Man's desire is to be desired by the Other" (here the parental Other).[11]

It is their desire, often quite opaque or enigmatic, that arouses our own: our own curiosity, our own determination to find out certain things, investigate the world, read and interpret gestures, actions, tones of voice, and conversations intended to be out of earshot or beyond our ken. Their desire is what makes us tick, makes us do things in the world; it brings our desire to life.

In the attempt to discern their desire—which I will henceforth refer to as the Other's desire (the desire of the parental Other)[12]—we discover that certain objects are coveted by the Other and learn to want them ourselves, modeling our desire on the Other's desire. Not only do we want the Other's desire to be directed onto us (we want to be the object, indeed the most important object, of the Other's desire); we also come to desire like the Other—we take the Other's desires as our own.[13]

When a mother, in the presence of her young daughter, expresses admiration for a certain actor because of his cocksureness and no-nonsense approach to women (the hero in Shakespeare's *The Taming of the Shrew*, to take a concrete example), her daughter is likely to incorporate those attributes into her own image of Prince Charming. Such attributes, discovered years later in the course of the analysis of the daughter's fantasies, are likely to give rise to a sense of indignation and alienation on the daughter's part: "How could I have adopted *her* fantasies?" "How disgusting! Even my fantasies aren't really my own."

While the assimilation of the Other's desires is an inevitable aspect of the formation of desire, it is experienced later as an intrusion or violation: the Other did this to me, put this in me, made me be this way, made me want this and not that. Even my desire is not my own.

The Other's desire causes ours. What we sometimes consider to be most personal and intimate turns out to come from elsewhere, from some outside source. And not just any source: our parents, of all people!

Separating from the Other's Desire

Freud says that the most important task during adolescence is to detach ourselves from our parents, a task neurotics fail to accomplish.[14] Translated into Lacanian terms, this means that neurotics remain stuck on the Other's desire. Their parents' desire continues to function as the cause of their own; their parents' desires continue to operate in them as if they were their own; what they want remains utterly dependent upon what their parents wanted. Even when neurotics devote all of their time and energy to doing precisely the opposite of what their parents wanted, their lives are still constituted entirely in opposition to the Other's desire, and thus remain dependent upon it: without it their lives have no focus, no *raison d'être*. The most important task for the neurotic is thus to separate from the Other, from the Other's desire.

Yet this is not always the first task at the beginning of an analysis, for many people come to analysis claiming to have little if any idea what they really want. They express uncertainty about their own wants, about the legitimacy of what they want, and even about wanting in general. With such analysands, the early part of analysis involves a decanting process in which what they want begins to come into focus, and a discovery process in which buried, forgotten, or unknown wants come to the fore.

Slowly, however, it dawns on them that what they want is closely linked to what significant others in their life want or once wanted. They come to realize that they are "alienated," that their desires are not their own, as they had thought; even their most secret desires often turn out to have been someone else's before becoming their own, or seem fabricated to satisfy or support someone else at the outset.

The aim of separating the subject from the Other's desire may not seem to be the order of the day in other cases either—when, for example, the analysand complains essentially of being inhibited or shy: "I know what I want but am unable to pursue it. Every time I try, I feel guilty; I feel I'm betraying someone, or that something terrible will happen." In such cases, we are inclined to think that neurotics simply have knots in their desire, that they want something but are inhibited from pursuing it by a conflicting desire or force (for instance, a prohibition stemming from their parents that they are unwilling to transgress). Indeed, as Freud says, all symptoms arise from at least two conflicting desires, forces, or impulses: love and hate, lust and inhibition, and so on (SE XVI, 349, 358–359). Analysis, in such cases, would simply seem to involve untying the knots in the analysand's desire.

But the neurotic's subjection, submission, or subjugation to the Other is far greater than is suggested by such a metaphor ("untying the knots in desire"). The neurotic's desire is not his or her "own" in the first place, for it has never been subjectified. *Subjectification is the goal of analysis:* subjectification of the cause—that is, of the Other's desire as cause.

The Fundamental Fantasy

Lacan refers to the analysand's fixation on the cause as the "fundamental fantasy": the fundamental relationship between the subject (not the ego) and his or her elective cause, the subject as positioned with respect to the cause. Lacan's notation or formula for that is ($\mathS \lozenge a$), where S with the bar through it stands for the subject as split into conscious and unconscious, a stands for the cause of desire, and the diamond stands for the relationship between the two.[15]

What does fantasy stage but the way the subject imagines him- or herself in relation to the cause, to the Other's desire as cause? If, at the most profound level, a woman's desire comes into being because a man looks at her in a particularly impertinent way, her fantasy depicts her being looked at in that way; it brings together in one and the same scene the look and herself (being provocative, perhaps, or passively inert).[16] Even in the case, discussed by Freud, of a conscious or preconscious fantasy in which the subject seems to be absent—namely, "A child is being beaten"—we can reconstruct the unconscious fantasy at work, "I am being beaten by my father" (SE XVII, 179–186), which involves a relation between the subject and the Other's presumed desire (to punish).

People obviously have many different fantasies, some of which are conscious or preconscious (we can become aware of them if we pay attention to them), others of which are unconscious, our only mode of access to them often being via the royal road of dreams. Lacan suggests that there is one single fantasy—an unconscious fantasy for most of us—that is absolutely fundamental. This notion is related to Freud's theory of a "primal scene," a scene that plays a fundamental role in the constitution of the analysand's sexuality and life in general. The way one reacted to the scene (real or imagined) as a child colors the whole of one's existence, determining one's relations to one's parents and lovers, one's sexual preferences, and one's capacity for sexual satisfaction. (Such a scene is discussed under "A Case of Hysteria" in Chapter 8.)

As the analyst assumes the role of cause of the analysand's desire, the analysand transposes his or her fantasies onto analysis. The relationship with the analyst takes on the characteristics and tenor of the analysand's fundamental fantasy: the latter is projected into the here and now, and the analysand expects the analyst's desire to coincide with the Other's desire as he or she has always construed it. In other words, the analysand falls into his or her habitual way of seeing and relating to the world of (parental) others, presupposing that the Other's desire is the same as it has always been in his or her experience. The analysand begins to play out his or her usual stance or position in relation to the Other's desire, attempting to satisfy or thwart it, be its object or undermine it, as the case may be.

The analyst is considered to want from him or her the same thing the parents wanted, whether that was blood, solace, pity, or whatever. The analysand's notion of what the Other wants is projected and reprojected, but the analyst continually shatters it or shakes it up by not being where the analysand expects him or her to be. Embodying the Other's desire as cause, standing in for it in the analytic setting, the analyst does not conform to the analysand's expectations in his or her behavior, responses, or interventions. The analysand was expecting the analyst to highlight a specific word or point, or to end the session on a particular note or statement—because in his or her view that is what of interest or concern to the analyst—but the analyst does not. Just when the analysand believes that the analyst wants to hear about each and every dream ("The dream is, after all, the royal road to the unconscious"), the analyst changes tack. Discussion of all those things the analyst spent so many sessions encouraging (dreams, fantasies, daydreams, slips, sex, mom, dad, family) may become rote, automatic, and unproductive, serving as a defense mobilized to deal with the Other's desire: "If I give the Other what he or she is demanding, maybe I'll be able to hold onto my desire and the little pleasure I still manage to derive from it." The analyst has to be vigilant regarding the routinization of analysis and the way in which fantasy—the analysand's defense against the Other's desire—affects the work that goes on there.

The analysand is continually recreating his or her fantasized situation in relation to the Other's desire, confident that his or her discourse is of great interest to the analyst or anxious about its being unsatisfactory, neglecting altogether the analyst's presence in the room or listening intently for any sign of life from behind the couch. By countering the analysand's assumptions about what the analyst wants, by manifesting interest in something other than what the analysand is expecting, the Other's desire is thrown into question: it is not what the analysand has been assuming it to be. Indeed, *perhaps it never was* what the analysand has always assumed it to be. Perhaps it is a creation or a construction on the analysand's part. Perhaps it represents a solution the analysand provided to the enigma of his or her parents' desire.

By way of example, let us consider Freud's work with the "Rat Man," described in detail in Freud's well-known "Notes upon a Case of Obsessional Neurosis" (SE X, 155–249). My comments here will obviously be very schematic, given the amount of material Freud provides in the case study, but one point which seems amply clear is that all of the Rat Man's problems are intimately related to his father. The desire to take revenge on his father is central to many of the symptoms he describes, which run the gamut from his childhood belief that a certain girl whose affections he wished to attract would take notice of him and pity him *were his father to die*, to the "horrifying" thought that a certain form of torture he had heard about (whereby rats bore into a victim's anus) *was being inflicted on his father*. It is no exaggeration to conclude that the Rat Man's father was the *cause* of the Rat Man's anger, resentment, and desire for revenge.

In the course of his work with Freud, the Rat Man unwittingly began to vent rage upon Freud, "heaping the grossest and filthiest abuse" upon him and his family; while doing so, he would get up from the sofa so that he could distance himself from where Freud was sitting. The Rat Man himself eventually concluded that he was afraid Freud would hit him, as his father often had; his father, having had a "passionate temper," sometimes had not known where to stop in his violence (209). Freud had been put in the place of the Rat Man's father and had come to play the part of the cause of the Rat Man's recriminations, angry outbursts, and desire for violent revenge. At the same time, the Rat Man fully expected Freud to react to such expressions of rage as his father had, by beating him.

We see here a crucial fantasy, if not the fundamental fantasy itself: the Rat Man engaging in provocative behavior in the expectation of receiving rough treatment from his father. The father is assumed to want to beat his son—indeed, perhaps, to enjoy beating his son—insofar as he seems to have been prone to getting carried away in the "heat of the moment," not knowing when to stop. Freud's office becomes the site of an enactment of the subject's relation to the object: the Rat Man's provocative eliciting of the father's desire to beat his son (this being perhaps one of the only ways the Rat Man could get any attention from his father). The fantasy is thus reenacted in the therapy situation, Freud playing the role of the father as cause of the Rat Man's desire.

Freud obviously does not react to this staging of the Rat Man's fantasy as the Rat Man expects him to. Freud assumes that the filthy remarks his analysand makes are addressed at his role, not at Freud as an individual with his own particularities, dignity, and history. He is thus able to respond not by throwing the analysand out and demanding respect for his "person," or by physically hitting the analysand, but by interpreting. In this way, Freud indicates that it is not always the Other's desire to beat the Rat Man, opening up the possibility for the Rat Man to call into question his view of the Other's desire: "perhaps it was not so much that my father desired it as that I pushed him to it . . ." Such wondering is not mentioned by Freud, but was rendered possible by Freud's intervention: it became possible for the Rat Man to question his own role in interpreting his father's words and deeds. Perhaps his interpretation was, in fact, self-serving in some respect; perhaps it was pleasing or convenient for him to see things in that light.[17] I shall return to this notion of one's subjective involvement in the fundamental fantasy in the next section, and to the case of the Rat Man further on in this chapter.

Here I would simply like to reiterate the idea that the analysand's interpretation or construction of the Other's desire can be thrown into question only insofar as the analyst does not react as the analysand expects and does not show his or her cards—does not allow the analysand to read his or her desire. Instead, the analyst must maintain a position of enigmatic desire.

Just as the analyst must not be predictable in terms of how long he keeps the analysand in session, his or her interventions and interpretations must not become predictable. Analysands occasionally make the remark, "I knew you were going to end the session on that point" or "I knew you were going to say that"—a sign that the analyst's style of practice has become too evident and that the element of surprise is fading. The analyst's interest, curiosity, and desire must be hard for the analysand to read, hard to pin down, and thus the analyst must not be where the analysand is expecting him or her to be. Otherwise, the fundamental fantasy can never be thrown into question, shaken up, and reconfigured.

The Reconfiguration of the Fundamental Fantasy

Analytic therapy does not make it its first task to remove the symptoms.

—Freud, SE XVI, 436

The analyst asks neither that the subject get better nor that he become normal; the analyst requires nothing, imposes nothing. He is there so that the subject may gain access to the truth of his desire, his own desire, and not so that he may respond to the Other's demand.

—Anny Cordié, *Les cancres n'existent pas* (Paris: Seuil, 1993), 299

All speech is demand.[18]
Every demand [is] a request for love.

—Lacan, *Ecrits*, 813/311

I have been simplifying Lacan's views thus far in my presentation of the fundamental fantasy, and a number of other points must now be raised. I have been speaking, for example, as if the neurotic's desire were fully constituted prior to analysis. This is not entirely obvious, however, since according to Lacan the neurotic is to a great extent stuck at a level shy of desire: at the level of demand.[19]

Lacan formulates this by saying that, at the commencement of an analysis, the neurotic's fundamental fantasy involves the subject's stance with respect to the Other's demand, rather than with respect to the Other's desire.[20] The subject much prefers to deal with the Other's demand that he or she do things, become this or that, than to deal with the Other's desirousness, pure and simple (we shall see a clinical example of this under "A Case of Obsession" in Chapter 8). The neurotic even prefers to believe that the Other wants something truly horrible—that the Other is demanding something of him or her that is very onerous and unpleasant[21]—to remaining uncertain as to what the Other wants.

The encounter with the Other's desire is anxiety producing. To illustrate this point, Lacan borrows an example from animal behavior—that of the female praying mantis, which bites off the head of her male partner during copulation—and asks us to imagine the following hypothetical situation (admittedly not easy to put to the test experimentally). You are wearing a mask that makes you look like either a female or a male praying mantis, but you do not know which; a female praying mantis approaches, making you extremely anxious. The anxiety you feel may well be worse in the case in which you do *not* know whether you are disguised as a male or a female, than in the case in which you know you are disguised as a male. (Indeed, in the latter case what you experience is simply *fear* of a specific fate that is soon to befall you.) Hence, you may prefer to *assume* or *conclude* that your death is nigh because you are dressed as a male, even if you are not sure this is true. If we take the female praying mantis here as the Other (the real, not the symbolic Other),[22] you may prefer to assume the Other is out to get you—to assume that you know what it is you are for the Other, what object you are in the Other's desire—than to remain anxiously uncertain. Lacan refers to the latter form of anxiety as angst *(angoisse)*, which is far more upsetting and unsettling than awaiting certain death (leading to what Freud calls "realistic anxiety"—in other words, fear).[23]

Rather than anxiously waiting to find out what you are, you may well prefer to jump to conclusions (precipitate answers) about what the Other wants of you, with you, from you, and so on. The unknown nature of the Other's desire is unbearable here; you prefer to assign it an attribute, any attribute, rather than let it remain an enigma. You prefer to tie it down, give it a name, and put an end to its angst-inducing uncertainty. Once it is named, once you conclude that *this* is what the Other wants of you—to stay out of the way, for instance— the angst abates, and you can set about trying to make yourself scarce.

This jumping to conclusions transforms the Other's desire—which, strictly speaking, has no object—into something with a very specific object. In other words, it *transforms the Other's desire into a demand* ("Stay out of my way!"), a demand addressed to the subject who does the naming. Whereas desire has no object, demand does.

The interpretation by the subject of the Other's desire takes an inherently nameless wanting, longing, or desiring, and makes it a concrete desire, a specific want—in short, a demand for something quite precise. Such a demand can be negotiated or dealt with by the child: it causes less angst and gives the child direction. Indeed, the child believes that by conforming to the demand— to stay out of the way—it will garner love and approval; it is only insofar as he or she stays out of the way that the parent will love and approve of him or her. If, on the other hand, the child believes that the parent pays attention to the child only when he or she is in the way, he or she may adopt the strategy of being in the way as much as possible in order to be paid attention to, even if this attention comes only in the form of punishment.

In the clinical setting, one hears neurotics make all kinds of claims about what their parents wanted from them, and their interpretations of their parents' wants are often strikingly at odds with the interpretations forged by their twin brother, sister, or other siblings. Different interpretations are made by different siblings, and often even by children who seem to be treated virtually identically. This highlights the fact that parents' wants are never "known" in some absolute sense; *they can only be interpreted*. Neurotics try to identify the reasons for which their parents view them as lovable and worthy of attention, and to take on those reasons as their own. In a word, they come to see themselves as they believe their parents see them, value what they believe their parents value, and attempt to be what they believe their parents want them to be. They identify with their parents' ideals, and judge themselves in accordance with those ideals.

In Freudian terms, the neurotic's concern to discern his or her parents' demands is related to the formation of the ego-ideal *(Ichideal)*, the ideals one sets for oneself and against which one measures one's own (usually inadequate) performance. Freud equates the ego-ideal with the superego, and talks about it as "an individual's first and most important identification, his identification with the [parents]" (SE XIX, 31).[24]

Not surprisingly, neurotics seek to identify with the analyst as they did with their parents: they attempt to read between the lines of the analyst's desire and discern demands, values, and ideals. If they can discern what it is the analyst values or wants of them, they believe they can render themselves lovable and curry favor with the analyst by conforming to them (or revolting against them, hoping in this case to garner attention in a different form). They thus attempt to adopt his or her ego-ideal as their own and become like the analyst. While the formation of the ego-ideal may be inevitable in the course of the child's psychical development (we shall see in Chapter 7 how Lacan explains it in terms of his 1960s revision of the mirror stage), *the repeated attempt by neurotics to adopt the Other's ego-ideal is at the very crux of their neurosis:* they are stuck on the Other's demand. In analysis, they want to know what the analyst wants of them; indeed, they may well demand that the analyst tell them what he or she wants them to do—anything but have to ask themselves what *they* want![25]

In certain approaches to psychoanalysis, the analysand is encouraged to *identify with* the analyst's "strong ego" in order to prop up his or her own "weak ego." In other words, the neurotic is never weaned from the vicious cycle of the demand structure. The analyst does not confront the analysand with the enigma of the Other's desire, bringing into being thereby the analysand's own desire; instead, the analysand learns to see him- or herself through the analyst's eyes and to adopt his or her values and ideals. As long as the analyst, his or her analytic institute, or psychoanalysis itself continues to be situated in the position of Other by the analysand, a certain stability may be witnessed (though the analysand may, in neurotic fashion, repeatedly seek approval and recognition from the analyst, institute, or analytic journals and associations); but as soon as some new representative of the Other comes along—if, say, the analysand has not so thoroughly identified with the analyst that he or she is still able to pursue a different profession, with a boss to impress, other successful professionals to emulate, and so on—the same problem is likely to ensue: the neurotic attempts to discern what this new Other wants of him or her and to conform to it (or revolt against it, but for the same reasons).

An important thrust of Lacan's development of the notion of the analyst's desire is to show how and why the goal of analysis must *not* be identification with one's analyst, identification with the "healthy part" of the analyst's ego, or identification with any other part of the analyst. Such a goal leads either to permanent transference with the analyst, instead of what Freud calls the "liquidation of the transference" or what Lacan refers to as the "falling away of the subject supposed to know"—the situation in which the analysand no longer assumes that the analyst has any knowledge that can be of use or value to him or her—or simply to the return of the problem in another context (the neurotic search for approval and recognition from the next Other to come along).

Outside analysis, neurotics demand that their parents tell them what to do, that their teachers, bosses, spouses, and anyone else who comes to incarnate the Other for them, tell them what to do. Neurotics stave off the anxiety associated with the Other's desire by encouraging, cajoling, or (if all else fails) forcing the Other to make demands—and the more specific the demands, the better. We can see this, for example, in the case of an analysand who had basically been taking care of himself prior to getting into a relationship, but who suddenly adopted a stance of childlike helplessness with his new lover, trying to impress upon her that he had to be told what to do; he manipulated her to the point that she finally did take control and make highly specific demands on him—lists of chores he had to complete, and so on.

In the perhaps better-known case of the "henpecked" husband, it is often because the man is unable or unwilling to deal with his wife's enigmatic desire—characterized as "fickle," "fleeting," "inconsistent," and "incomprehensible" (these are the more polite adjectives employed)[26]—that he demands she tell him exactly what she wants (for her birthday, in bed, and so on) and then refers to her as bossy. She is upset that he never seems capable of "reading her desire," of realizing that she wants something from him that reflects how *he* sees her, what *he* wants from her, what *his* desire is regarding her.[27] He laments that he is unable to express any desire of his own in the relationship (this being reserved for his fantasy life, in which she plays no part), but has in fact orchestrated the modus operandi himself, albeit in spite of himself.

Unable to deal with the enigma of the Other's desire, neurotics demand that the Other make specific demands on them; demand leads to more demand, in a kind of vicious cycle. What the neurotic wishes not to recognize is that desire is not so much something you have as something you do not have. It springs from lack, and no one can say what he or she really wants, desire having no unique object.[28] A demand is a specific want, not a vaguer, more diffuse want*ing*. It is something you seem to "have," like a need, a biological need to eat. It is the Other's wanting—or as Lacan says, "the lack in the Other," the incompleteness of the Other—that the neurotic cannot abide. A specific want is like a possession; the Other seems not to be poorer for it, but richer. Wanting, however, is different: it suggests a lack, inability, or inadequacy of some sort.[29] The neurotic flees it like the plague.

When the analyst refuses to allow his or her desire to be pinned down, discerned, or named by the analysand, the confrontation with the Other's wanting is no longer forestalled, but actualized, brought into the present. The confrontation is best represented by the abrupt end of the analytic session, wherein the analysand is brought face to face with the analyst whose enig-matic desire has just brought the session to an unexpected close, scanding the analysand's last words.

Here the analysand is brought face to face with the analyst's desirousness, the manifestation of a desire that is not easily discerned or predicted, for otherwise it could be read as a demand, yet another demand that the ana-lysand can choose to grant or refuse, give in to partially or negotiate. The analyst must walk a fine line, for while she must direct the treatment, eliciting unconscious material in the form of dreams, fantasies, and daydreams, the analysand must never be able to conclude for very long, "Aha! That's what she wants me to talk about!" Anytime the analysand latches onto one of the analyst's demands (to talk, say, more about dreams), reconstituting him- or herself in relation to that demand, satisfying it or deliberately frustrating it, the analyst must shift ground to ensure that her desire remains an unknown.[30] This breaks the vicious cycle of demand, whereby the analysand demands to be freed of his or her symptoms, to be fed interpretations, to be cured, and—in order for this to happen—to be told what to do, to receive orders from the analyst which, when executed, make the analysand lovable to the analyst (all demands are, according to Lacan, ultimately demands for love: I demand that you tell me what I have to do in order to win your love). Breaking the cycle forces a reckoning with the Other's desire that is so traumatic to the neurotic, and that is at the crux of his or her fixation.

There are thus, in some sense, two stages to the work of transference here: (1) the analyst must side-step the analysand's demands in order to encourage the analysand's desire to come to the fore, suffocating though it is in the stranglehold of the Other's desire, implying a shift from $\text{\$} \lozenge \text{D}$ to $\text{\$} \lozenge a$; and (2) the analyst must bring about a revamping of the analysand's interpretation of the Other's desire and a shift in his or her subjective position, which is based on this interpretation. The first stage might be referred to as *dialectization* (of desire) and the second as *reconfiguration* (or traversing, of the fundamental fantasy). As we shall see in Chapter 10, they constitute crucial logical moments of "subjectification," whereby the analysand moves from being the subject who demands (as well as being subject to the Other's demand) to being the subject who desires (as well as being subject to the Other's desire), and then to being the subject who enjoys (who is no longer subject to the Other).

A Freudian analogy may be useful here. In *Beyond the Pleasure Principle*, Freud puts forward various theories to explain why shell-shocked soldiers relive the same scene again and again in their dreams (nightmares), suggesting that the psyche revives a trauma in order to attempt to experience it differently. Repetition of a traumatic scene is viewed in the early part of the book less as a pure expression of the death drive than as an effort by the mind to "live" the event differently this time. One hypothesis Freud advances here is that we attempt to insert anxiety into a situation—anxiety as a form of preparedness or readiness—where there was none at the outset; that is, we retroactively attempt to change the way we experienced the event by taking a certain distance from it, a distance that anxiety provides.

This theory (like that of "binding," elaborated in the same work) seems to have be abandoned by Freud by the end of his book, but it is very much in keeping with his deferred-action model of symptom formation: a first event can retroactively become traumatic (and lead to the formation of a symptom) due to the effect of a second, later event.[31] Perhaps the psyche spontaneously attempts the contrary: to *retroactively* undo the nefarious effects of a traumatic event.

In any case, Freud's abandoned 1920 theory can serve us as an analogy for what Lacan proposes here. *By continually reactualizing the analysand's encounter with the Other's desire that left fixation in its wake, the analyst hopes to introduce a certain distance retroactively.* It can be an anxiety-provoking process at times, to be sure, but an effective one, according to a great many accounts.[32] Indeed, it is the only approach considered effective by many analysts in going beyond what Freud termed the "bedrock" of castration.[33]

Castration and the Fundamental Fantasy

What the neurotic does not want, and what he strenuously refuses to do right up until the end of his analysis, is to sacrifice his castration to the Other's jouissance, allowing it to serve the Other.

—Lacan, *Ecrits*, 826/323

Lacan's notion of the fundamental fantasy encompasses two complex facets of Freud's theory: his early stress on the "sexual overload" at the origin of neurosis (see Chapter 8 below),[34] but also his later stress on a loss of sexual pleasure. In the course of a child's "education," its parents impose many sacrifices: immediate gratification of the need to eat and excrete is withheld or punished, and autoerotic behavior is progressively discouraged (thumb sucking, at first tolerated, is eventually discouraged or even punished; touching one's genitals in public, while perhaps allowed the infant, is forbidden the schoolchild; and so on). It is this loss of gratification—whether autoerotic or alloerotic (involving another person such as the mother)—that Lacan refers to as "castration."

This loss is *imposed* in a sense, but the child also *adopts* a position with respect to the parents' demands regarding that loss, for certain children continue to suck their thumbs and/or touch their genitals in private, in defiance of their parents' demands; in other words, they refuse to give up this satisfaction completely. Others do give it up altogether, for a variety of reasons. They may do so, as Freud tells us, because of very blatant castration threats uttered by their parents (a number of my analysands have convinced me that such threats still occur in our day and age, especially in lower- and lower-middle-class milieus)—in the case of little boys, out of fear of losing forever the pleasurable sensations derived from their genitals (they give up autoerotic pleasure for fear of losing all genital pleasure)—or because they fear losing their parents' love and esteem.

This loss of satisfaction or jouissance—which Lacan refers to as "castration"—is *accepted* to some extent by neurotics. They may not seem to have had much of a choice in the matter, but their acceptance of it constitutes a *solution* to a problem presented by their parents, teachers, and other representatives of the social order: "If I give up this satisfaction, I get to keep something else." Nevertheless, the jouissance thus sacrificed is not so easily parted with at every level: the subject constitutes him- or herself as a stance adopted with respect to that loss of jouissance. Object *a* can be understood as the object (now lost) which provided that jouissance, as a kind of rem(a)inder of that lost jouissance.[35]

The pleasure given up seems all the more valuable now that it is lost (it seems we didn't know we had it so good). And, as we saw in Chapter 1, the process of prohibition transforms the "simple" gratification or pleasure derived from autoerotic acts (for example) into jouissance, *stricto sensu*. For the pleasure, when prohibited by the parents, takes on a further meaning, a meaning that involves the parents and the parents' desire. "Naive," "simple" bodily pleasure is transformed into jouissance—something far more erotic, dirty, bad, and evil, something *really* exciting—thanks to prohibition. Prohibition eroticizes. The stronger the prohibition, the more erotically charged the specific act prohibited becomes.

The fundamental fantasy stages the relationship between the subject and the lost object that provided this now prohibited satisfaction.[36] Desire, as expressed in and propped up by the fundamental fantasy, is determined and conditioned by the satisfaction that has been prohibited and renounced. We see here why prohibition is so central to desire: it conditions desire, fixating it on that which is prohibited. As Lacan says in "Kant with Sade," "Law and repressed desire are one and the same" (*Ecrits*, 782). We also see the intimate relationship between desire and castration qua loss of satisfaction: I desire precisely what I sacrificed.

Let us once again use Freud's case of the Rat Man as an example here. It comes out, in the course of his analysis, that the Rat Man was severely beaten by his father at a very early age because he had been involved in some kind of sexual play (biting) with a nurse who worked for the family, though the exact nature of the event was never really determined (SE X, 205–208). The Rat Man seems to have concluded from this punishment that his father intended to make him give up *all* sexual contact with *all* females, not just this or that kind of contact with the nurse or mother. This is attested to by the fact that, from this day forward, he perceives his father to be "an interferer with [his] sexual enjoyment" (205). He is unable to spontaneously express his affection for women in the household, as he did prior to the beating; his father shows up in all of his thoughts regarding women as an obstacle to his relations with them (163, 178–179); masturbatory activity seems to cease thereafter, until the time of his father's death when the Rat Man is twenty-one; and several years later, when he first has sexual relations with a woman, he thinks, "This is glorious! One might murder one's father for this!" (201).

A major symptom that the Rat Man discusses—indeed, it is part of the larger set of symptoms that drives him to seek therapy—involves his inability to make up his mind regarding women he is interested in. His mother and father believe he should "marry well" and have selected, as his future wife, a second cousin whose family is well connected in the business world. Seemingly uninterested in the second cousin, the Rat Man devotes his attention for some time to a "lady" whom his father disapproves of and who refuses all of his proposals. One day, out on maneuvers with the army, the Rat Man finds himself faced with the choice of returning to Vienna, where his "lady" lives, or of going to a town (known in the case study as Z—) where there are two women who he believes are favorably disposed toward him (the innkeeper's daughter and the woman at the post office who paid the COD charges for his glasses).

The Rat Man's indecision here is many layered, but one important factor at work is his father's (perceived) desire for him to marry "the right kind of girl" and the Rat Man's twofold wish to please his father and thumb his nose at him. During his lifetime, the father disapproved of the lady in Vienna; hence one of the attractions of going to Vienna to see her. And the Rat Man believes that the two women in Z—, since they are of a lower social class than he is, are likely sexual conquests that will enable him to fly in the face of his father's perceived prohibition of all sexual satisfaction.[37]

Thus, the Rat Man unwittingly constructs for himself a situation that in some sense conforms precisely to his father's (perceived) Law, the prohibition of his son's sexual satisfaction with women; for the Rat Man is completely unable to choose between Vienna and Z— and can take no concrete action, deriving instead a "substitute satisfaction" from torturing himself—a kind of mental masturbation. His desire revolves around what his father has, to his mind, *prohibited*.

The second cousin chosen for him plays no part in this symptom, though the Rat Man does fall ill so as not to complete his education, which is the precondition the girl's father has set for the marriage (198–199). This behavior evinces his refusal to give in to his father's demands—that is, his refusal to give his father pleasure. Indeed, many of his obsessive thoughts involve punishing his father or making him die.

Though the Rat Man has given up a good portion of his directly sexual pleasure in life, he keeps trying to find a little here and there. He cannot bring himself to rebel openly against his dead father's wishes by marrying someone with whom he could secure himself such pleasures,[38] but he engages in clandestine relations with a nurse at a sanitarium where he is supposedly undergoing hydrotherapy, and occasionally with servant girls and waitresses. He still fantasizes about winning his father's esteem (for example, studying late at night, he sometimes opens the front door, imagining that his father's ghost has come to see him and finds him hard at work) but simultaneously tries to affirm his own sexuality (in the same fantasy in which his father sees him studying, the Rat Man stands in front of the mirror and looks at his erect penis; 204). All of these activities and fantasies (though far more complicated and multilayered than I have suggested here) indicate that the Rat Man keeps regretting the sacrifice of sexual pleasure he has made: he has in no sense made his peace with his own castration.

In "Analysis Terminable and Interminable," Freud suggests that analysis, when carried out as far as it can go with neurotics, butts up against the "rock of castration," the bedrock beyond which analytic exploration is often unable to penetrate. Analysis can bring us to the point of discovering castration—the sacrifice of satisfaction made at our parents' behest—but often can go no further.[39]

To rephrase in Lacanian terms: the analysand has handed over a certain jouissance to the parental Other, but never seems to stop regretting it. He or she remains stuck on that loss, and refuses (in his or her psychic economy) to allow the Other to enjoy what the subject has given up, to take advantage of the jouissance sacrificed. "Yes, I gave it up, but God forbid I should ever do anything you ask of me from now on!" The neurotic may follow his or her parents' demands to a T (marry, have children, follow the exact career choice they "forced" upon him or her), but never let the parents know that: "I did what you asked, but I'll never give you the satisfaction of knowing!" Resentment is never relinquished. "My parents took something precious from me, but I fixed them good: I made them suffer for it, held it against them for decades, and never let them live it down."

Every neurosis entails such a resentful stance toward the Other's satisfaction. The neurotic has made the sacrifice (unlike the psychotic, as we shall see in Chapter 7), but attempts to rip off compensatory satisfactions under the Other's nose. Masturbating, stealing, cheating, speeding, breaking the law, and getting away with it—these are among the illicit satisfactions the neurotic is able to find which, in his or her psychic economy, represent a taking back from the Other of the jouissance lost, or a recompense, retribution, or indemnification by the Other to the subject for the loss incurred. Neurotics' claims against the Other (for example, "My parents didn't give me enough love, recognition, and approval") know no bounds. They gave up jouissance in the hope of receiving the Other's esteem and got less than they bargained for.[40] In Freudian terms, women never stop resenting their mothers for having deprived them of a penis; the love and esteem provided by way of compensation for that imaginary loss are considered inadequate. Men never overcome their castration anxiety in the face of what they perceive to be major life decisions, and feel that regardless of what they do, they will never be able to satisfy their fathers—their fathers' expectations, requirements, criteria, and ideals. The approval their fathers provided is considered to have always been conditional upon achievement, and a man can never rest, regardless of how much he achieves.

According to Freud and many other analysts, psychoanalysis is only rarely able to take the analysand beyond that stance. The neurotic's protest against castration, against the sacrifice made, is generally insurmountable, unsurpassable.

Lacan, however, would beg to differ. His answer to what has been construed as the monolithic "bedrock of castration" is the traversing of fantasy made possible by the confrontation with the analyst's desire. The analyst's interventions, including the scansion of the session, can lead to a new configuration of the analysand's fundamental fantasy, and thus to a new relation (stance or position adopted with respect) to the Other—the Other's desire and the Other's jouissance. The initial fixation of the analysand's desire is shaken up, and the analysand's desire no longer serves as a substitute for or hindrance to the pursuit of satisfaction.[41]

It should be noted that the fundamental fantasy is not so much something that exists per se prior to analysis, as something constructed and reconstructed in the course of analysis. In a certain sense, it is distilled out of the whole network of fantasies that come to light in the course of analysis. It can be seen, after one's analysis has gone far enough, that *this* is the position or stance the subject adopted with respect to the cause that has been responsible for so many of the subject's choices and actions.

By the time such a position or stance has been discerned in analysis, it has, no doubt, already changed to some degree. The same is true of what Freud calls the "primal scene." It is not so much a real scene witnessed by the child at a particular moment in time, as a construction by the child—perhaps based on numerous scenes observed, overheard, and/or imagined—that is reconstructed and yet simultaneously transformed in the course of analysis.[42]

Separation from the Analyst

The ultimate struggle in analysis—that of getting the analysand to assume responsibility for his or her castration instead of demanding compensation for it from the Other—is played out between the analysand and the analyst, who stands in for the Other (and for the lost object at the same time). The analysand must be brought to the point where he or she no longer blames the analyst (as object or Other) for his or her troubles, and no longer seeks compensation or retribution. At the same time, the analysand must, faced with the analyst's constant desire for him or her to continue the analysis, reach a point at which the analyst's wishes have no hold on him or her.

If this is indeed the conjunction of forces operative at the end of analysis—and Freud and Lacan certainly seem to indicate that it is—then we should not be surprised to see analysis end with a kind of struggle or battle in which the analysand's attitude toward castration, toward the jouissance sacrificed, changes, and the lost object is finally given up. It is given up not so much in resignation as in what Lacan refers to as a "precipitation," a sudden reversal of things: a reconfiguration of the fundamental fantasy. The process is more likely to be messy, unwieldy, and hot to handle than to be cool, calm, and collected. As Freud says, "When all is said and done, it is impossible to destroy anyone *in absentia* or *in effigie*," and the object is no exception. The separation occurs in the present, and the stakes are very real.

I am always a bit puzzled when I hear talk of analysands ending their analysis in a peaceful and friendly manner, and then hear of them befriending their analysts afterward—as if the choice of their former analyst as a friend were an indifferent choice, as if there were not enough other people in the world to befriend. Friendship is not, in and of itself, out of the question, assuming one has surpassed the stage of blaming the Other for one's problems or one's fate.[43] But it suggests that a certain demand toward the Other—a demand for recognition and approval, in short, for love—may well remain unresolved. Peaceful "termination" hardly seems consonant with *the reversal of position regarding the onerous renunciation that is required to go beyond castration.*

II

DIAGNOSIS AND
THE POSITIONING OF
THE ANALYST

6

A LACANIAN APPROACH
TO DIAGNOSIS

The Lacanian approach to diagnosis is bound to seem strange to those schooled in the DSM-III or DSM-IV; it is in some ways far simpler, yet in other ways more discriminating, than what passes for diagnosis in much of the contemporary psychological and psychiatric world. Lacanian diagnostic criteria are based primarily on Freud's work—a certain *reading* of and *extension* of notions found in Freud's work—and on work done by a handful of French and German psychiatrists (most notably Emil Kraepelin and Georges Gatian de Clérambault). Rather than tending to multiply ever further the number of diagnostic categories, such that every new clinically observable symptom or set of symptoms is taken to constitute a separate "disorder," Lacan's diagnostic schema is remarkably simple, including only three main categories: neurosis, psychosis, and perversion. And unlike the categories developed in the DSM-IV, which provide little concrete direction for the psychotherapist regarding how to proceed with different categories of patients, Lacanian diagnoses find immediate application in guiding the practitioner's aims and in indicating the position the therapist must adopt in the transference.

At the most basic level, Lacanian theory demonstrates that certain aims and techniques used with neurotics are inapplicable with psychotics. And not only are such techniques inapplicable—they may even prove dangerous, triggering a psychotic break.[1] Diagnosis, from a Lacanian standpoint, is not merely a matter of performing perfunctory paperwork required by institutions and insurance companies; it is crucial in determining the therapist's general approach to treating an individual patient, in correctly situating him- or herself in the transference, and in making specific kinds of interventions.

This should not be taken to imply that Lacanians are always able to make a precise diagnosis immediately. As many clinicians are aware, it can sometimes take quite a long time before one manages to discern the most basic mechanisms in a person's psychical economy. Nevertheless, a preliminary situating of the patient as most likely neurotic or psychotic is quite important, and the clinician's very *inability* to situate a patient at this level must incline him or her to tread lightly during the preliminary meetings.

Lacan attempts to systematize Freud's work on diagnostic categories, extending certain of Freud's terminological distinctions. Freud himself separates neurosis from perversion by theorizing that whereas repression *(Verdrängung)* is characteristic of neurosis,[2] the primary mechanism characteristic of perversion is disavowal *(Verleugnung)*.[3] Lacan points out that Freud employs another term—*Verwerfung*—to talk about a still more radical mechanism (though not in theoretical detail). This term is found in a number of contexts in Freud's work,[4] and Lacan suggests (especially through a close reading of Freud's 1925 paper "Negation")[5] that we understand it as the primary mechanism characteristic of psychosis; he translates it first as "rejection" and later as "foreclosure."[6] I will discuss this term at some length in Chapter 7. Suffice it to say here that Freud uses it to describe not simply a rejection of something from or by the ego (repression might be talked about in some such way), or the refusal to admit something that was nevertheless seen and stored in memory (disavowal might be talked about in this way), but an ejection from oneself—not simply from the ego—of some part of "reality."

Thus, the three main diagnostic categories adopted by Lacan are *structural* categories based on three fundamentally different mechanisms, or what we might call three fundamentally different forms of negation *(Verneinung)*:

Category	Mechanism
Neurosis	Repression
Perversion	Disavowal
Psychosis	Foreclosure

Regardless of whether one accepts these mechanisms as fundamentally different and as defining three radically different categories, it should be clear that *Lacan's project here is essentially Freudian in inspiration,* and in direct continuity with Freud's efforts to discern the most basic differences among psychical structures. (In Chapter 8, we shall consider Freud's attempt to distinguish between obsession and hysteria—an attempt that is perhaps more familiar to the reader.)

It will, I hope, be immediately clear that the possibility of distinguishing among patients on the basis of such a fundamental mechanism—the way in which they negate something—would constitute a diagnostic contribution of major proportions. It would allow the practitioner to go beyond weighing the relative importance of certain clinical characteristics, comparing them with lists of features in manuals such as the DSM-IV, and to focus instead on a *defining* mechanism—that is, a single determinant characteristic. For, as Freud was wont to say, repression is the *cause* of neurosis. In other words, repression is not simply associated with neurosis; it is constitutive of neurosis. One becomes neurotic due to repression. Similarly, Lacan puts forward a causal argument: foreclosure is the cause of psychosis. It is not simply associated with psychosis; it is constitutive of psychosis.

An important consequence of this structural approach is that there are three and only three principal structures. (There are, of course, various subcategories. For example, the subcategories of neurosis are hysteria, obsession, and phobia—these are the three neuroses.) People referred to in common parlance as "normal" do not have some special structure of their own; they are generally neurotic, clinically speaking—that is, their basic mechanism is repression. As Freud himself said, "If you take up a theoretical point of view and disregard the matter of quantity, you may quite well say that we are *all* ill—that is, neurotic—since the preconditions for the formation of symptoms [that is, repression] can also be observed in normal people."[7] Obviously, it is conceivable that other forms of negation could be found, leading to four or more principal structures; but on the basis of current research and theory, these three seem to cover the entire field of psychological phenomena. Thus, *"borderline" does not constitute a genuine diagnostic category in Lacanian psychoanalysis, as no specific mechanism corresponds to it.*

This does not mean that Lacanians never hesitate in making a diagnosis; for example, they may note certain psychotic traits in patients, though they are not convinced of the existence of a true psychotic structure. They may, in other words, wonder whether the patient is neurotic or indeed psychotic; but they view this ambiguity as resulting from their own inability to make a convincing diagnosis. The patient is not on the border between two clinical structures; it is the clinician who is hesitating at the border in his or her diagnostic ponderings.[8]

The defining mechanisms of the three major clinical structures will be discussed in detail in subsequent chapters. Here I shall merely point out that, however sophisticated our theoretical understanding of these structures may be, determining which mechanism is at work in the case of an individual patient is still a matter which requires a great deal of clinical experience and expertise. Foreclosure, like repression, is not something that the clinician can "see" directly; it is not perceptually available. It has to be inferred from the clinical material with which analysts are presented and which they are able to elicit. Lacan was a highly experienced clinician by the time he gave Seminar III, *The Psychoses* (he was fifty-four and had been working with psychotics for at least twenty-five years), but in this seminar he attests to how difficult it can be—even in a case in which psychosis seems more than likely—to elicit the "signature" of psychosis,[9] the feature which makes it absolutely clear that the patient is psychotic.

Fine *theoretical* distinctions between neurosis, psychosis, and perversion do not eliminate clinical difficulties, but it seems to me that Lacan also details the essential clinical features associated with, say, foreclosure which allow the analyst to diagnose psychosis with a great deal of confidence. Some of these essential clinical features may be immediately manifested by a particular patient, whereas others may require a good deal of questioning and probing on the clinician's part. The more familiar the analyst becomes with them, however, the easier they are to discern.

7

PSYCHOSIS

Foreclosure and the Paternal Function

Foreclosure involves the radical rejection of a particular element from the symbolic order (that is, from language), and not just any element: it involves the element that in some sense grounds or anchors the symbolic order as a whole. When this element is foreclosed, the entire symbolic order is affected; as has been noted in a great deal of the literature on schizophrenia, for example, language operates very differently in psychosis from the way it does in neurosis. According to Lacan, the element that is foreclosed in psychosis intimately concerns the father. He refers to it as the "Name-of-the-Father" (as we shall see, the French, *Nom-du-Père*, is far more instructive). For my present purposes, I will refer to the "father function" or "paternal function," since they cover more or less the same ground. The latter term can occasionally be found in Freud's work, but it is Lacan who rigorously formulates it.[1]

The absence of the paternal function is the single most important criterion to consider in diagnosing an individual as psychotic, yet it is by no means immediately visible in the majority of cases. The paternal function is not the function played by the individual's father, regardless of his particular style and personality, the role he plays in the family circle, and so on. A flesh-and-blood father does not immediately and automatically fulfill the paternal function, nor does the absence of a real, live father in any way automatically ensure the nonexistence of the paternal function. This function may be fulfilled despite the early death or disappearance of the father due to war or divorce; it may be fulfilled by another man who becomes a "father figure"; and it may be fulfilled in other ways as well.

A complete understanding of the paternal function requires knowledge of a good deal of Lacan's work on language and metaphor. For our purposes here, let it suffice to say that the father who embodies the paternal function in a nuclear family generally comes between mother and child, stopping the child from being drawn altogether to or into the mother and stopping the mother from engulfing her child. Lacan does not claim that *all* mothers have a tendency to smother or devour their children (though some do); rather, he says that children "perceive" their mOther's desire as dangerous or threatening. This "perception" reflects in some cases the child's wish for the mother to take her child as her be-all and end-all (which would ultimately annihilate the child as a being separate from its mother), and in other cases a reaction to a genuine tendency on the mother's part to obtain a kind of satisfaction with her child that she has not been able to obtain elsewhere.

In either case, the result is the same: the father keeps the child at a certain distance from its mother, thwarting the child's attempt to become one or remain forever one with the mother, or forbidding the mother from achieving certain satisfactions with her child, or both. Stated differently, the father protects the child from *le désir de la mère* (which means both the child's desire for the mother and the mother's desire)—that is, from a potential danger. The father protects the child from the mother as desire (as desiring or as desired), setting himself up as the one who prohibits, forbids, thwarts, and protects—in a word, as the one who lays down the law at home, telling both mother and child what is allowed and what is not.

The father I have been describing thus far is a stereotypical figure seen less and less frequently in our times (at least according to sociologists): the "head of the household" who is the authority at home, the master in his own castle who has no need to justify his orders. Even if he generally does provide reasons for his commands, he can always put an end to any controversy by saying, "Because *I* said so."

We are familiar with this rhetorical strategy, since it is adopted in a great many contexts. In a leftist study of political economy, a particular line of reasoning may be merely suggested, not proven, and then followed by the fateful words, "As Marx says in volume 3 of *Capital* . . ." This is known as the "argument from authority," and is as prevalent in psychoanalysis as it is in politics, philosophy, and virtually every other field. In my own writing, I do not appeal to "Freud" and "Lacan" as living, breathing individuals; I appeal to their names. Their names lend the weight of authority (only, of course, to those who accept them as authorities).

In the same way, when a father says, "You'll do it because *I* said so," there is often an implicit "I am the father here, and the father is always to be obeyed." In modern Western society, many contest the principle that "the father is always to be obeyed," but it seems to have been widely accepted for centuries and is still commonly appealed to. The point is that in many families the father is granted a position of authority not so much because he is a "true master"—a truly authoritative, brilliant, or inspiring figure who commands total respect—but simply because he is the father and is expected to take on the functions associated (in many people's minds) with "father."

The paternal function is a *symbolic function*, and can be just as effective when the father is temporarily absent as when he is present. Mothers appeal to the father as judge and castigator when they say to their children, "You'll be punished for that when your father gets home!" But they appeal to the father as a more abstract function when they ask a child to consider what its father would do or say if he found out that the child had done such and such. They appeal, in such cases, to the father as a name, as a word or signifier associated with certain ideas. Consider the case of a woman whose husband has died; she can keep him alive in her children's minds by asking them, "What would your father have thought about that?" or by saying, "Your father wouldn't have liked that one bit." It is above all in such cases that we see the functioning of *the father as a part of speech—that is, as an element in the mother's discourse.* The paternal function here is served by the noun "father" insofar as the mother refers to it as *an authority beyond herself,* an ideal beyond her own wishes (though in certain cases she may be appealing to it simply to prop up or lend credence to her own wishes).

What has thus far been rendered in English translations of Lacan's work as the "Name-of-the-Father" is much more striking in French: *Nom-du-Père. Nom* means both "name" and "noun," and with this expression Lacan is referring to the father's name (for example, John Doe), to the name insofar as it plays the role of father (for example, in the case of a child whose father died before it was born, the father's name as pronounced by the mother, as it is given a place in the mother's discourse, can serve a paternal function), and to the noun "father" as it appears in the mother's discourse (for example, "Your father would have been very proud of you").[2] Lacan is also playing off the fact that, in French, *nom* is pronounced exactly like *non,* meaning "no," evoking the father's "No!"—that is, the father's prohibition.

Now a mother can undercut her husband's position by constantly telling her child "We won't tell your father about that, will we?" or "Your father doesn't know what he is talking about!", and by disobeying all of his orders as soon as he turns his back. Thus the paternal function may never become operative in cases where a child's father is clearly present, yet it may be instated in cases where a child's father is absent from birth. The presence or absence of a father in someone's clinical picture provides no immediate indication.[3] I shall more fully explain the paternal function and the purposes it serves after a discussion of the consequences of its failure.

Consequences of the Failure of the Paternal Function

What happens if a certain lack has occurred in the formative function of the father?

—Lacan, Seminar III, 230

In Lacanian psychoanalysis, the paternal function is considered to be all or nothing: either a father (as noun, name, or "No!") *has* been able to take on the symbolic function in question or he has not. There are no in-betweens.[4]

Similarly, either the paternal function is operative by a certain age or it never will be. Lacanian psychoanalysis, though it purports to help the psychotic, cannot change the psychotic's structure: once a psychotic, always a psychotic. There is, of course, some question about the maximum age at which the paternal function can be instated—that is, the age beyond which one's psychical structure cannot be further modified. It seems likely that appropriately oriented analytic work with young children can, up to a certain point, bring about the establishment of the paternal function.

In the case of adults, however, no amount of analytic or other work can, according to Lacan, change a psychotic structure. Such work can make certain psychotic traits recede from a patient's clinical picture, ward off further psychotic episodes, and allow the patient to carry on life in the world; but there is no such thing as a "cure" for psychosis in the sense of a radical change in psychical structure (for example, transforming the psychotic into a neurotic).

This structural approach to psychosis also means that a patient who has a "psychotic break" at age thirty has always had a psychotic structure—it was simply "untriggered." The patient could, in theory, have been diagnosed as psychotic by a clinician long before an obvious break occurred—that is, long before the appearance of obvious psychotic phenomena.

The clinically observable consequences of the failure of the paternal function are many and varied, and the clinician needs to be on the lookout for them in establishing a diagnosis. I will begin with the best-known psychotic phenomenon, hallucination, and then take up less well-known phenomena that can be helpful in diagnosing untriggered psychosis—that is, cases in which no psychotic break has yet occurred.

Hallucination

Hallucination, *in its widest sense,* is not a consequence of the failure of the paternal function. Freud tells us that hallucination is the infant's first path to satisfaction: when hungry, for example, the child first hallucinates an earlier experience of satisfaction, rather than engaging in motor activity, such as crying, to attract a parent's attention so that nourishment will be provided. Hallucination is a typical form of primary-process "thinking," and plays a role in daydreaming, fantasizing, and dreaming. Thus, it is present in all of the structural categories: neurosis, perversion, and psychosis.

Taken in its widest sense, therefore, hallucination is *not* a criterion of psychosis: its presence does not constitute definitive proof that the patient is psychotic, nor does its absence constitute definitive proof that the patient is not. In the words of Jacques-Alain Miller, since "hallucination [may be found] in both hysteria and psychosis, [it] is not, in and of itself, proof of structure . . . If you find an element like hallucination, you still have to ask very precise questions to distinguish between the different structural categories."[5]

Lacan nevertheless provides us with the wherewithal to understand hallucination in a narrower sense as well. And given the contemporary tendency in the United States to immediately classify people who report anything vaguely resembling a hallucination as psychotic (or at least borderline), and to prescribe drugs to them or commit them, I think that it is important to insist that *not all hallucinations are alike.* It seems to me justifiable to distinguish psychotic hallucinations—what I'll call bona fide hallucinations—from the run-of-the-mill voices and visions that so many nonpsychotics report.[6]

A patient in therapy with someone I supervise once said he had had the impression that he'd seen his ex-wife standing in a hallway. The therapist could have added the clinical trait "hallucinations" to his list, and indeed his other supervisors did just that. Yet the patient never used the term "hallucination," and even if he had, it would probably have been because a previous consulting psychiatrist had used the term in his presence.

If we probe the subjective nature of the experience, a number of distinctive features stand out. For example, the patient had been surprised by this image or vision, and had said to himself that *his ex-wife could not have gotten into the house without his noticing,* thus calling into question the reality not of his experience (the image or vision) but of the image's content. He had glanced over at two people sitting next to him, and when he had looked back toward the hallway his ex-wife was gone. He never once believed that the person had *really* been there; he believed that he had seen something—that is, he believed in the vision—but did not believe *it.*[7] He did not believe that what was presented was real, or had any claim to be taken as real. Superficially speaking, we could say that he was able to distinguish between fantasy (psychical reality) and reality (the Western notion of social/physical reality he has assimilated in the course of his lifetime).

When the discussion is cast in terms of fantasy and reality, however, we cannot clearly distinguish between neurosis and psychosis, for many neurotics are unable, at certain moments, to tell fantasy from (our socially constructed notion of) reality. The most obvious example would be that of the hysteric (consider Freud and Breuer's *Studies on Hysteria*) whose fantasies have become so lifelike as to have rewritten the subject's historical account of his or her past. Neurotics and psychotics may both manifest difficulty distinguishing psychical reality from socially constructed reality. Indeed, important questions could be raised about the very validity of this distinction. For example: Whose notion of socially constructed reality is to prevail—the patient's or the analyst's? Is there a clear watershed between the psychical and the social?[8]

I will leave these epistemological questions for another occasion, emphasizing instead Lacan's suggestion that "reality" is not all that helpful a concept by which to distinguish fantasies from hallucinations or neurosis from psychosis. A far more useful concept is "certainty."[9]

Certainty is characteristic of psychosis, whereas doubt is not. The psychotic is convinced not necessarily of the "reality" of what he or she sees or hears, but of the fact that it means something, and that this meaning involves him or her. While the psychotic may agree that what he or she heard or saw was not audible or visible to others (Seminar III, 87)—in other words, that it was not part of a socially shared reality—this may make it all the more special to him or her: he or she has been *chosen* among all others to hear or see it, or it concerns only him or her. "The president of the United States is trying to contact *me* personally through brain waves." "God has *chosen* me as his messenger." The subject is certain with regard to the message (the content of what was heard or seen) and the identity of the addressee: him- or herself. The psychotic manifests that what was "true" or "real" to him or her in the experience were the implications of the message for his or her life: "They are trying to get me," "They want my brain." There is no room for error or misinterpretation: the meaning of the experience is self-evident.

In contrast, what dominates the clinical picture in the case of neurosis is doubt. *Doubt is the very hallmark of neurosis.*[10] The neurotic is unsure: maybe the person was there, maybe not; maybe the voices are coming from some outside source, maybe they are not; maybe what they say has some meaning, maybe not; the meaning seems to have something to do with the person, but perhaps he or she is misinterpreting it. The neurotic wants to know: "Am I crazy to be seeing (hearing) such things? Is it normal? How should I be viewing such experiences?" The neurotic has a certain distance from them; as gripping and anxiety-producing as they may be when they occur, it is never entirely clear what they signify, what they mean in the larger scheme of things. "God spoke to me, but does that mean that I am to be his messenger? What does he want of me?"

The psychotic knows. For example: "God wants me to be his wife."[11] "The Devil wants to have his way with me." "The Martians want to take my brain to study it; then they can control all my thoughts."

In the case of the man who had the impression he'd seen his ex-wife in a hallway, his "vision" was not what I call a bona fide hallucination but rather something on the order of a waking fantasy or daydream. His desire to see her was so strong that she "appeared" before him. What seemed to be a persecutory note in his alleged hallucination (in his vision she said, "I'm gonna get you!") seemed indicative of his own wish to take revenge on her, transformed into a fear that *she* would harm *him*—the typical neurotic mechanism of a fear disguising a wish.[12] If she were to try to hurt him, he would feel justified in hitting back (and perhaps pummeling her, as he had done to someone else when provoked in the past).

Thus, I believe we are justified in referring to this patient's experience as a fantasy or daydream rather than a hallucination. Indeed, when Freud tells us that hysterics sometimes hallucinate, what he seems to mean is that their thoughts and wishes become so powerful (so hypercathected—that is, so highly investe with energy or libido) that hysterics "see" or "hear" them as if they were bein enacted or fulfilled in the present. They fantasize so intensely that the event seems palpable or real. Yet some doubt remains in their minds about the fantasized events. Indeed, they find it hard to say what is real and what is not.

Obsessives, too, sometimes hallucinate,[13] and their "hallucinations" are generally auditory in nature. Their auditory experience can usually be understood in terms of the voice of the punishing superego. When someone claims to hear voices saying, "You'll never amount to anything," "It's your fault—you ruin everything," "You don't deserve any better," "You'll be punished for that," and so on, we need not jump to conclusions with a diagnosis of paranoia. The punitive superego is a well-known and documented phenomenon, and patients often recognize the voice as the father's and the phrases as typical of the things the father used to say (or was believed to have thought).

It would be difficult in the course of any one book to exhaust the panoply of voices that are heard by neurotics and that can hardly be considered pathological. What certain patients and nonpatients describe, for example, as a kind of running commentary that accompanies them in their daily lives— "Now she's going into the restaurant, and now she's smiling at the person behind the counter . . ."—can be understood on the basis of Lacan's work on the mirror stage:[14] insofar as the ego is essentially the self *seen* by "oneself" (as in a mirror reflection)—that is, viewed as if by another person, or seen from the outside by someone else—a running commentary may well be provided in a form of *self*-consciousness, or consciousness of one's self doing things in the world.[15] A philosopher may observe his or her thought processes as if they were those of another person; and one can observe oneself interacting with others as if that self were someone else. The "mystery of self-consciousness"— thought by some to be a gift of evolution, dependent on the numerous interconnections in the human brain, soon to be duplicated in computer chips—is explained by the nature of the ego (which is identical to the "self" in my terminology)[16] as an external view or image of the subject which is internalized or interjected. The ego is thus an object,[17] and consciousness may adopt it as an object to be observed like any other object.[18]

Neurotics may well see and hear all kinds of things—they may have visions and hear voices, have tactile sensations and smell odors—but they do not have bona fide hallucinations. They may fantasize, hear superego and other endopsychic voices, and so on. But a bona fide hallucination requires a sense of subjective certainty on the patient's part, an attribution of external agency, and is related to the return from the outside of something that has been foreclosed.[19]

One conclusion of this discussion is that when a patient reports having hallucinations, the clinician should never take the report at face value and should spend time exploring the nature of the experience. In cases in which the clinician cannot find convincing evidence one way or another—in other words, cannot determine whether or not it is a bona fide hallucination—*other* diagnostic criteria, such as those described below, should be given the most weight.

Language Disturbances

Before making a diagnosis of psychosis, we must make sure that [language] disturbances exist.

—Lacan, Seminar III, 106

Whereas the neurotic inhabits language, the psychotic is inhabited or possessed by language.

—Lacan, Seminar III, 284

We are all born into a language that is not of our own making. If we are to express ourselves to those around us, we are obliged to learn their language— our parents' language, which we can refer to here as the Other's discourse— and in the process this language shapes us: it shapes our thoughts, demands, and desires. We have the sense, at times, that we cannot find the words to say what we mean, and that the words available to us miss the point, saying too much or too little. Yet without those words, the very realm of meaning would not exist for us at all. Lacan refers to this as our *alienation* in language.[20]

The problem we face is how to come to be in language, how to find a place for ourselves in it and make it our own to the greatest extent possible. We may seek out and adopt a vocabulary that is rejected, scorned, or repressed by the powers that be: the rebellious son may adopt a slang dominated by four-letter words, the anarchist a jargon free of the language of power, the feminist a nonpatriarchal lexicon. We may feel more ourselves when we speak in a subcultural dialect, or with an assumed accent. More radically still, we may reject our mother tongue almost completely, if we associate it with our parents and a discourse (educational, religious, political, and so on) we abhor, feeling at home only in a foreign tongue.[21]

The neurotic succeeds, to a greater or lesser extent, in coming to be in language, in inhabiting some subset of language (no one can ever inhabit the whole of a language as developed and variegated as most natural languages are). Alienation is never completely overcome, but at least some part of language is eventually "subjectified," made one's own. While language speaks *through* us more than most of us would care to admit, while at times we seem to be little more than transmitters or relays of the discourse around us,[22] and while we sometimes initially refuse to recognize what comes out of our own mouths (slips, slurred speech, and so on), we nevertheless generally have the sense that we live in language and are not simply lived by it.

The psychotic, on the other hand, "is subjugated by the phenomenon of discourse as a whole" (Seminar III, 235). Whereas we are all inhabited by language as a kind of foreign body,[23] the psychotic has the sense of being possessed by a language that speaks as if it were coming not from inside but from outside. Thoughts that come to mind are considered to be placed there by some outside force or entity. Although the Rat Man refuses responsibility for certain thoughts that come to him, he never attributes them to an agency outside himself, loosely speaking.

Lacan's thesis is that *the psychotic's relation to language as a whole is different from the neurotic's.* In order to understand this, we must examine more closely the imaginary and symbolic orders, as Lacan defines them, and consider their different roles in neurosis and psychosis.

The Symbolic's Failure to Overwrite the Imaginary

The best-known aspect of Lacan's work to date in the English-speaking world is the "mirror stage,"[24] a concept Lacan developed in 1936. Briefly stated, the mirror stage corresponds to the time in a child's life when it is still extremely uncoordinated and is merely a bundle of perceptions and sensations lacking in unity. According to Lacan, it is the child's mirror image that first presents the child with an image of its own unity and coherence which goes beyond anything that it has yet achieved developmentally. The mirror image is jubilantly invested with libido by the child and internalized, becoming the nucleus, core, matrix, or mold of the child's ego. Successive "self-images" reflected back to the child by parents, teachers, and others crystallize around it. Lacan views the mirror stage as providing a structuring image—one that brings order to the prior chaos of perceptions and sensations. It leads to the development of a sense of self, anticipating a kind of unity or self-identity that has yet to be realized. And it is what allows a child to finally be able to say "I."

More important than this early description of the mirror stage, however, is Lacan's 1960 *reformulation* of the mirror stage, currently available only in French.[25] Here Lacan suggests that the mirror image is internalized and invested with libido because of an approving gesture made by the parent who is holding the child before the mirror (or watching the child look at itself in the mirror). In other words, *the mirror image takes on such importance as a result of the parent's recognition, acknowledgment, or approval*—expressed in a nodding gesture that has already taken on symbolic meaning, or in such expressions as "Yes, baby, that's you!" often uttered by ecstatic, admiring, or simply bemused parents. This is what makes it different from the power of certain images in the animal kingdom. A female pigeon, for example, must see an image of another pigeon (or of a decoy, or even a mirror image of itself) for its gonads to mature (*Ecrits*, 95/3), but the image alone suffices for a developmentally significant process to occur. In human beings, the mirror image may, as in chimpanzees, be of some interest at a certain age, but it does not become formative of the ego, of a sense of self, unless it is *ratified* by a person of importance to the child.[26]

Lacan associates this ratification with what Freud calls the ego-ideal (*Ichideal*): a child internalizes its parents' ideals (goals that are symbolically expressed), and judges itself in accordance with those ideals. Indeed, a child brings its parents' (perceived) view of the child into itself, and comes to see itself as its parents do. Its actions become seen as its parents see them, judged as worthy of esteem or scorn as its parents would (the child believes) judge them.

A whole new order is instated in this way: a reorganization (or first organization) takes place in the early chaos of perceptions and sensations, feelings and impressions. The imaginary register—that of visual images, auditory, olfactory, and other sense perceptions of all kinds, and fantasy—is restructured, rewritten, or "overwritten" by the symbolic, by the words and phrases the parents use to express their view of their child.[27] The new symbolic or linguistic order supersedes the former imaginary order, which is why Lacan talks about the dominance and determinant nature of language in human existence. This is at the crux of his critique of certain forms of object relations theory,[28] which he sees as focusing on an imaginary order or set of relations that is, in fact, superseded by the symbolic and that is inaccessible to psycho-analysis, whose sole medium is speech.

The overwriting of the imaginary by the symbolic (the "normal" or "ordi-nary neurotic" path) leads to the suppression or at least the subordination of imaginary relations characterized by rivalry and aggressivity (as discussed in Chapter 3) to symbolic relations dominated by concerns with ideals, authority figures, the law, performance, achievement, guilt, and so on. This overwriting is related to Freud's notion of the castration complex, which, in the case of boys, brings about an ordering or hierarchization of the drives under the dominance (or "tyranny," to use Freud's term)[29] of the genital zone. The boy's blithely polymorphous sexuality becomes organized, owing to the father's function in bringing about repression of the boy's Oedipal attachment to his mother. The father—who in Freud's work is par excellence the symbolic father, the demanding, prohibiting father—brings about a socialization of the boy's sexuality: he requires the boy to subordinate his sexuality to culturally accepted (that is to say, symbolic) norms.

This occurs, Freud tells us, even in the case of perverts: their polymorphous sexuality gives way to a hierarchization of the drives, but under the domi-nance of a zone other than the genital zone—oral, anal, scopic, and so on. Similarly, in accordance with Lacanian criteria, the pervert's imaginary has undergone symbolic rewriting of some kind—not the same rewriting as in neurosis, but a rewriting nevertheless, evinced by the ordering or structuring of the imaginary (see Chapter 9).

In psychosis this rewriting does not occur. We can, at the theoretical level, say that this is due to the unsuccessful establishment of the ego-ideal, the nonfunc-tioning of the paternal metaphor, the noninitiation of the castration complex, and a variety of other things. The point here is that the imaginary continues to predominate in psychosis, and that the symbolic, to the extent to which it is assimilated, is "imaginarized": it is assimilated *not* as a radically different order which restructures the first, but simply by imitation of other people.

Insofar as the ego-ideal serves to anchor one's sense of self, to tie it to the approval or recognition of a parental Other, its absence leaves one with a precarious sense of self, a self-image that is liable to deflate or evaporate at certain critical moments. Rachel Corday, a psychotic who has made an ex-tremely instructive videotape entitled *Losing the Thread* (Insight Media, 1993), which details her first-hand experience of psychosis, repeats numerous times that she "loses her self" during psychotic breaks, likening her self to a balloon that is rising out of sight in the sky and that she is unable to recapture. She tells us that she can then no longer relate to other things, as there is no *I* to do the relating, no longer any recognizable center of intentionality. "Everything in reality disintegrates, including my own body," she says, detailing how difficult it becomes to move from one point to another without the "CEO in her office," that homunculus known as the ego which gives us the sense that our bodies are organized wholes that move harmoniously, as a unit. The nerves, muscles, and tendons in her body still have all the same connections that allowed her to execute complicated movements before, but the sense of self that allowed her body to function as a whole dissipates.[30]

Corday tells us that she is prone to telling herself, "Get hold of yourself!"— just like many other patients (for example, Gérard Primeau, interviewed by Lacan in "A Lacanian Psychosis")[31] who use the very same words to describe their sense that their self is slipping away. The disintegration of the ego is not always so complete in psychosis, and we perhaps more often witness a confusion between self and other, a difficulty in determining who is speaking. As Corday says, "I don't know where my own voice is coming from." The "boundaries" of the ego are not simply flexible, as they are sometimes described in neurosis, but virtually nonexistent, leading to a dangerous sense that another person or force is trying to usurp one's place.[32] Without the help of language that names and delimits—when its structure is assimilated and not simply imitated[33]—imaginary relations predominate, as we shall see a bit further on.

The Inability to Create New Metaphors

While Schreber is certainly a writer, he is no poet. He does not introduce us to a new dimension of experience.

—Lacan, Seminar III, 91

The fact that the essential structure of language is not assimilated by psychotics is attested to by the fact that they are unable to *create* metaphors the way neurotics can. They obviously *use* metaphors, since metaphors are part and parcel of every natural language; they are quite capable of employing the metaphors used by those around them, those found in their reading, and so on. They are incapable, however, of forging new metaphors.

It would appear, then, that the very structure of language—noun, verb, and object—is not assimilated in the same way, for example. For this structure allows us to replace a noun, such as "womb," with another noun, such as "theater," or with a phrase such as "theater of menstrual activity," to create a metaphor (a specific kind of metaphor known as a "substitutional metaphor").[34] The psychotic's discourse is curiously devoid of original metaphors, specifically poetic devices through which most people are able to create new meanings. Thanks to imitation, a psychotic can learn to speak the way other people speak (Seminar III, 285), but the essential structure of language is not integrated in the same way.

The metaphorical use of language is not available to psychotics, according to Lacan, due to the failure of *the essential metaphor: the paternal metaphor*. Lacan refers to the paternal function as having the structure of a (substitutional) metaphor, where the term on top replaces or cancels out the one below it:

$$\frac{\text{Father's name}}{\text{Mother as desire}}$$

Or more simply:

$$\frac{\text{Father}}{\text{Mother}}$$

The father—as name, noun, or No!—cancels out the mother (as desiring or desired), neutralizes her, replaces her; loosely speaking, the father puts himself as name or prohibition in her stead. Stated thusly, the paternal metaphor has considerable affinity with the castration complex, as Freud describes it: a child is forced to give up a certain jouissance, a certain relationship with the mother, due to a demand made or a threat issued by the father. In a word, this corresponds to what Freud calls "primal repression," or what we might term the "first repression."[35]

Let us assume that the child has been accepted into the world of its mother or primary caretaker. This is often a big assumption, for as we see in certain extreme cases of childhood autism, some children are granted no place whatsoever in their mother's world, not having been wanted at the outset; only their most minimal biological needs are attended to (often not even by their parents, but by indifferent, paid caretakers) and their attempts at talking and engaging with others are met with shouts and slaps.[36] Figure 7.1 represents the situation in which a child *is* given some space within its mother's world.

In a nuclear family in Western cultures, it is typically the father who gets in the way of the child's otherwise exclusive relationship with its mother.[37] The

Figure 7.1

father is often experienced by the child as hampering or cutting off access to its mother at various times of day and night and, indeed, as imposing limitations on the kind of satisfactions the child can achieve with the mother, claiming, for example, "You're too old for that now—only babies need their mommies."

Father

Figure 7.2

Here, in a very straightforward way, the father serves a separating function: he acts as a bar or barrier between mother and child, refusing to allow the child to be no more than *an extension of the mother* (see Figure 7.2). The wish to maintain as close a mother-child link as possible may be the wish of the child, the mother, or both (though, strictly speaking, it becomes a "wish" only once it is obstructed); in any case, the father serves here as that which separates the child from the (typically) primary source of its satisfactions. He thus functions. as the one who prohibits jouissance.

The Father's No!
Mother as Source of Jouissance

Prohibition, as we have seen, creates desire: it is only when something is refused me that I first see what I want, what I lack, what I cannot have. The father's prohibition constitutes a desire for certain pleasures with my mother (contact with her body, her caresses, the warmth of her embrace, the sound of her voice, her loving looks, and so on), but this desire must go underground: it is unacceptable to this father person, and must be put out of mind. The first repression, thus, for both male and female children, involves the forgetting of one's desire to achieve certain satisfactions with one's mother. This repression is often stronger in boys than in girls, since the father typically makes greater efforts to separate his son (as rival) from the mother; often he allows his daughter to maintain a far closer relationship with the mother for a far longer period of time. Nevertheless, limits are drawn to the kinds of satisfactions the child is allowed to achieve with the mother (or the mother with the child), and repression occurs; this is often evidenced when the child begins to find the mother's caresses and embraces to be repugnant, disgusting, unseemly, and so on, all of which are telltale signs of repression. I schematize repression by putting that which is repressed under the bar:

$$\frac{\text{The Father's No!}}{\text{Mother as Jouissance}}$$

The paternal metaphor involves yet another moment, which we shall have occasion to talk about in later chapters.[38] What I would like to stress here is the sense in which this first moment already ties word to meaning (meaning being the "stuff" of our socially/linguistically constituted reality—that is, of the reality we share because we talk about it). As we saw in Part I of this book, meaning is determined after the fact, and the child's relationship with its mother is given meaning by the father's prohibition; that meaning is, we might say, the "first meaning," and it establishes a solid connection between a sternly enunciated interdiction and an indeterminate longing for closeness (which is transformed into desire for the mother as a result of the prohibition). The first meaning, the fundamental meaning brought into being by the paternal metaphor, is that my longing for my mother is wrong. Whatever else I may come to think of it later—believing, for example, that I should not have given in to my father's prohibition because he never offered me anything in return, never provided me with substitute satisfactions—that first meaning, once established, is unshakable and cannot be uprooted.

Everything else may be open to interpretation, up for grabs. And certainly there is room for misunderstanding even when the father prohibits something about the mother-child relationship: "Is it the way she's holding me, the way I'm holding her, or the noise we're making?" A child is not obliged to immediately conclude that it is certain kinds of touching and caressing that the father is objecting to. Assuming, however, that the father has been assiduous (or simply lucky) enough to drive home to the child what is prohibited, a link is established between language and meaning (reality as socially constituted), between signifier and signified, that will never break.

This is what Lacan refers to as the "button tie" (point de capiton, sometimes also translated as "anchoring point" or "quilting point"). A button tie, in the upholsterer's vocabulary, is a type of stitch used to secure a button to fabric and stuffing in a couch or chair, whereby the button and fabric are held together not in reference to a wooden or steel frame but simply in reference to one another. There is no true anchoring here, strictly speaking, since an anchor suggests an unmovable terra firma to which something is attached. Rather, the result of the paternal metaphor is to tie a specific meaning to particular words (Figure 7.3) without regard to an absolute referent (that is, without appealing to a mythical absolute reality beyond the reality created, or hewn from the real, by language). The paternal metaphor creates a foundational, unshakable meaning.[39]

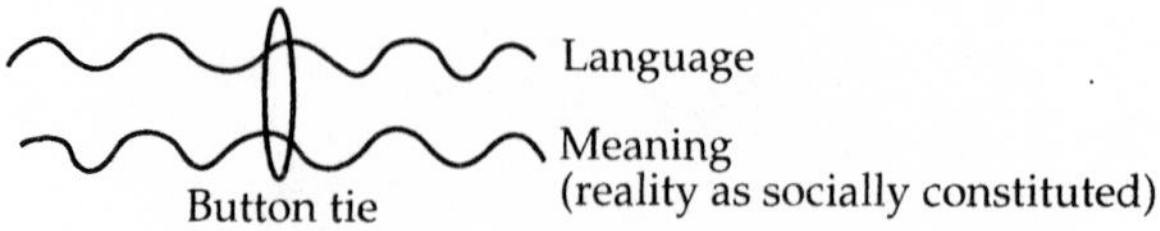

Language

Meaning
(reality as socially constituted)

Button tie

Figure 7.3

When everything else can be thrown into question later, even the why and wherefore of this foundational meaning, it is precisely because that original button tie—a kind of knot—was tied in the first place. It is this one stitch that allows someone to assimilate the *structure* of language. Without it, everything comes undone. As Rachel Corday says, try as she might to gather up some sense of self at one end, it constantly "unravels at the other end." The fabric of her self unravels without that all-important stitch, which is why she so often "loses the thread."[40]

Interrupted Sentences and Neologisms

In psychosis, the paternal metaphor fails to function and the structure of language (allowing for the possibility of metaphorical substitution) is not assimilated. When language operates without that structure, other distur-bances may appear as well. For example, the voices the psychotic hears often speak in interrupted phrases or sentences that break off just before the most important term is uttered, and the patient feels obliged to supply the missing part of the sentence.

It is part and parcel of the structure of speech that a sentence takes on its full meaning only after the last word has been pronounced. For each word or phrase in a sentence paves the way for the words that are to follow it and bears a relation to the words that precede it. In the partial sentence "The most important thing is . . .," the verb is determined as a third-person singular by the subject and leads us to *anticipate*, when we take it in conjunction with the subject, a single thing or activity that is deemed crucial by the speaker (such as ". . . to please yourself"). A sentence can be understood as a *chain*, in the sense that the verb is linked to the subject, the adjectives to the nouns they qualify, and the formulation of the last part of the sentence to the structure of the first: the elements are thus all interrelated. Certain elements prepare the way for others, and none of the elements is completely independent: they are all "chained together" (this is why Lacan uses the expression "signifying chain").

One cannot fully understand the beginning of a sentence in isolation; its meaning or meanings become clear (if they ever become clear) only at the end of the sentence. The anticipatory and retroactive movements involved in the creation of meaning are depicted in Lacan's diagram of the button tie,[41] and are related to the process by which new meaning is created through metaphorization. For our purposes here, it should suffice to say that the interruption of a sentence pronounced by the voice a psychotic hears severs the chain that had been forming, exposing its components as isolated units or things, not links.[42] This suggests a disturbance in the usual process of meaning making, and is related to the sense in which *words are things* for the psychotic.

One patient, whose therapist I supervise, illustrated the psychotic's fundamentally different relation to language when she began speaking of her fear that someone wanted to "strip her of her assets," and then remarked on the curious connection between this phrase and "Strip District" (a market area in Pittsburgh she had just been to), and "New York Strip Steak" (which she had seen on a menu recently). She was intrigued not by the different *meanings* of the word "strip" (for example, its sexual connotations), but simply by the fact that the word had appeared in her life in three different contexts. Her "associations" were not to closely related words (such as, "stripe," "trip," or "tripe") or to different meanings, but simply to the reappearance of the same word qua thing. This patient also saw a sort of "cosmic connection" between David *Letter*man and a certain David who had been interested in Saint Paul's *letters* in the *New Testament.* One of my own patients said the following about the importance to him of words: "They are my crown jewels that no one should piss on." To him, *words are things one can piss on.*

It has often been noted that psychotics show a predilection for neologisms. Unable to create new meanings using the same old words via metaphor, the psychotic is led to forge new terms, and attributes to them a significance that he or she often describes as ineffable or incommunicable. Unlike every other term we employ, which can be defined with known words, such neologisms cannot be explained or defined. The meaning of an ordinary word or expression always refers to other meanings, but the psychotic employs words that do not refer to any other known or explainable meanings. Lacan describes neologisms as one of the "signatures" of psychosis (Seminar III, 43–44).

The Predominance of Imaginary Relations

In the beginning was rivalry . . .

It is in a fundamental rivalry . . . that the constitution of the human world as such takes place.

—Lacan, Seminar III, 51

The elementary Lacanian distinction between imaginary and symbolic can serve as a powerful clinical tool in distinguishing psychosis from neurosis. The neurotic, while likely to bring up a variety of more or less significant conflicts with friends and colleagues—that is, with others like him- or herself—often lets the therapist know right from the first few sessions that his or her main beef is with the symbolic Other. This may be expressed through complaints about parents, authority figures, social expectations, or self-esteem issues, all of which suggest a conflict at the level at which the patient sees him- or herself in terms of the Other's ideals (that is, at the level of his or her ego-ideal or superego)—as inadequate, underachieving, guilty, and so on.

The psychotic, on the other hand, presents things differently: the conflict seems to be with others his or her own age—rivals, competitors, or lovers. They are not all trying to garner approval from the same authority figure; rather, one of them is usurping the psychotic's place.[43]

The familiar phenomenon of *persecution* clearly falls in the category of imaginary relations, and is the predominant feature in paranoia (one of the psychoses). As Lacan says, "It is insofar as [the patient] has not acquired . . . the [symbolic] Other [language with its underlying structure] that he encounters the purely imaginary other. This other negates him, literally kills him" (Seminar III, 236). Nevertheless, Lacan reminds us that just because a patient complains that someone is trying to do him or her harm, we cannot automatically assume that the patient is psychotic: the complaint may be true, or it may be so outrageous as to be obviously false, but often it is not very easy to tell. In this context, Lacan once again reiterates that in order to be sure the patient is suffering from psychosis, "there must be language disturbances" (Seminar III, 106).[44]

The Invasion of Jouissance

In psychosis, just as the imaginary is not overwritten by the symbolic, so the drives are never hierarchized in the body except by imitation. In other words, the hierarchy that may be apparent is not irrevocable: it does not represent as definitive a sacrifice of jouissance as does the hierarchization the neurotic undergoes during socialization, whereby libido is channeled (more or less completely) from the body as a whole to the erogenous zones.

Lacan asserts that the body, in neurosis, is essentially dead. It is written with signifiers; in other words, it has been overwritten or codified by the symbolic.[45] The body as a biological organism is what Lacan calls the "real," and it is progressively socialized or "domesticated" to such an extent that libido retreats from all but a very few zones: the erogenous zones.[46] Only in these zones is the body still alive, in some sense, or real. Here libido (or jouissance) is channeled and contained. This is not the case in psychosis: the hierarchy of drives achieved imaginarily can collapse when the imaginary order that supports it falters. The body, which has been for the most part rid of jouissance, is suddenly inundated with it, invaded by it. It comes back with a vengeance, we might say, for the psychotic may well experience it as an attack, an invasion, or forcible entry.

Thus, when the patient speaks, as does Schreber,[47] of the "voluptuousness" of his body, of the indescribable ecstasy or "electric sensation [he feels] in [his] whole body" (as one of my patients described it), or of the unbearable shooting pains he feels (for which no biological cause can be found), the therapist can feel confident of having uncovered a likely indicator of psychosis. It is not positive proof, since religious mystics (of whom there is not an overwhelming number) sometimes report similar experiences, but it is a good first indication that the symbolic has been unable to rewrite the body, and that whatever organization of libido may have occurred via the imaginary has collapsed.

Lack of Control over the Drives

Neurosis is generally characterized by extensive ego and superego control over the drives. When the neurotic engages in truly physically aggressive acts, he or she usually has to be drunk or in some other sort of altered state (for example, repeatedly angered by someone, pushed to the limit, sleep deprived, or on drugs); only then are the restraints of conscience lifted sufficiently for the neurotic to take direct action. To act directly and effectively is, indeed, one of the hardest things for a neurotic to do.[48]

The absence of the paternal function affects all symbolic functions, and thus it should be no surprise that it affects everything we commonly associate with morality and conscience. This does not mean that a psychotic always acts "immorally"; rather, it means that even slight provocation can lead the psychotic to engage in seriously punishing behavior. The reigning in of the drives that occurs in the course of the neurotic's "education," socialization, Oedipalization, and de-Oedipalization—often manifested in the laborious weighing of alternatives by the neurotic before any kind of lust or aggression can be displayed to others—does not occur in a durable way in psychosis. Thus, the psychotic is more prone to immediate action, and plagued by little if any guilt after putting someone in the hospital, killing someone, raping someone, or carrying out some other criminal act. The psychotic may manifest shame, but not guilt. Guilt necessitates repression: one can feel guilty only if one knows one secretly wanted to inflict harm or enjoyed doing so. In psychosis, nothing is repressed and thus there are no secrets one keeps from oneself.

Feminization

An interesting facet of psychosis *in men* is the feminization that often occurs. Schreber, in the course of his delusions, begins to see himself as the wife of God. In certain other cases of psychosis, we see a tendency toward transsexualism, repeated requests for sex change operations, and homosexual activity.[49] Freud analyzed Schreber's psychosis as indicative of an inadequate defense against homosexuality, but Lacan suggests that Schreber's feminization occurs due to the very nature of psychosis.[50]

Psychosis is by no means a direct result of the physical absence of the father in a family; as I have said, the father is a symbolic function, and this function may be served by other people in or around the family or even by the mother's discourse. Psychosis is, no doubt, more likely to result when the father or father figure is absent from a patient's childhood—and it is always important for the clinician to try to get a sense of the degree of that physical or psychological absence—but it may result when the father or father figure is present as well.

Lacan suggests that certain fathers—often men who are very successful, socially speaking—are characterized by an unrestrained ambition or "unbridled authoritarianism" (Seminar III, 230), and establish a relationship with their sons, in particular, which is not that of the symbolic pact but one of rivalry and antagonism. *The imaginary is war, the symbolic peace.* The symbolic—the law—divides things up, providing a kind of distributive justice: this is yours, that is mine. The father who incarnates the law—*the symbolic father*—says, "Your mother is mine, but you can have any other woman"; "This is my bedroom and my bed, but you can have your own space and a bed for yourself." The symbolic father makes a tacit pact with his son: "This part of the day must be spent on homework, and the rest is yours to do with what you will"; "This is what I will oblige you to do, and what you do apart from that is your business."

In contrast, the unbridled father acts unilaterally toward his son, punishing, for example, without listening to the son's possible reasons for having behaved the way he behaved. There are no limits to his demands—no symbolic criteria that specify and delimit boundaries for both the demander and demandee—and thus they can never be satisfied. The father is perceived as a monster, and Lacan suggests that the only relationship possible is an imaginary relationship[51] characterized by rivalrous, erotically charged tension. No triangulated Oedipal relation can form, and the child assumes a feminine position in relation to the domineering, monstrous father—the imaginary father.[52]

This feminine position may be covered over for a long period of time, as the male psychotic identifies with his brothers and friends, imitating them in his attempt to act like a man. When a psychotic break occurs,[53] the patient's imaginary identifications or "imaginary crutches" (Seminar III, 231) collapse, and his essentially feminine position reemerges or forces itself upon him. In other cases, the male psychotic may claim to have felt he was a woman since his earliest childhood.[54] Such male psychotics are the most likely patients to request sex change operations.

Feminization in psychosis thus seems to be indicative not of a total absence of a real father in the child's family, but of the (at least occasional) presence of a father who established only an imaginary relationship with his son, not a symbolic one. Interestingly enough, the psychotic may also describe himself as in a feminine or passive relation to language itself, passively submitting to it, invaded by it, or possessed by it.[55]

In Lacan's later work, it becomes clear that feminization occurs for more structural reasons as well, and need not necessarily be restricted to male psychotics who had only imaginary relationships with their fathers. I cannot present here all of the concepts Lacan develops in Seminars XVIII through XXI regarding masculine and feminine structure, for it would take us too far afield and I have done so elsewhere.[56] Very briefly stated, Lacan suggests that masculine structure is related to a kind of "totalization" brought on by the symbolic father (who imposes limits on the male child), whereas feminine structure is related to a kind of nontotalization (*pas tout*) or impossibility of totalization; when the paternal function is missing from a boy's life, totalization does not occur and the boy takes on a certain element of feminine structure.[57] However, the "Other jouissance" characteristic of feminine structure often becomes, for the psychotic, a very long-lasting if not constant experience (characterized as invasive), whereas for the neurotic with feminine structure, this particular form of jouissance is more likely to be occasional and fleeting.

The Lack of a Question

We are sure that neurotics have asked themselves a question. With psychotics, this is not so clear.

—Lacan, Seminar III, 227

At the end of Chapter 2, I mentioned that the therapist is not always able to discern anything like a question that the analysand asks him- or herself. Even after months of regular sessions, certain analysands never wonder aloud about anything, never mention that they wonder or once wondered about why they did what they did at a certain point in time, what their dreams mean, or why they seem to react in a particular way to things. Nothing in their own lives raises a question in their mind, nothing seems incomprehensible, no motives are called into question. There is no food for thought.

Desire is a question, according to Lacan, and what such a situation suggests is either that the analyst has been unable to create a space in which desire can show itself or come into being, or that it does not exist as we know it in neurosis. Desire—human desire, not the kind of desire we anthropomorphically attribute to animals or inanimate objects (for example, "The squirrel wants to find the acorns it buried in the fall," "The sun is trying to come out")—forms in language and exists only in language. And it is subject to a dialectic or movement typical of language:

> One forgets that the dialectical changeability of actions, desires, and values is characteristic of human behavior and that it makes them liable to change, not only from one moment to the next, but constantly, and even that it makes them shift to strictly opposite values . . . The ever-present possibility of bringing desire, attachment, or even the most enduring meaning of human activity back into question . . . is such a common experience that it's stupefying to see this dimension forgotten. (Seminar III, 32)

We are accustomed, in work with neurotics, to witnessing an evolution in the neurotic's desires, fantasies, values, and beliefs in the course of therapy. Of course, we are sometimes disheartened by the inertia we encounter in certain areas of the neurotic's life, but perhaps more common is the neurotic who expresses surprise at the ease with which he or she has been able to shed identities and ideas that had seemed so central to his or her "personality" such a short time before. The fiercest defender of machismo soon recognizes homosexual tendencies in himself, the staunchest advocate of family ties soon breaks with his or her parents, and so on. Ego identifications collapse, new ones form, and desire is allowed to pursue its own course ever more completely.

The psychotic, on the other hand, is characterized by inertia, by the lack of movement or dialectic in his or her thoughts and interests. The obsessive, too, complains of having the same thoughts over and over, but generally in the course of therapy at least some of his or her ideas change rapidly, while those more closely linked to the symptom change slowly if at all. The psychotic, however, reiterates again and again the same phrases; repetition replaces explanation. The "dialectic of desire" has no place. There is no properly human desire at all in psychosis. Where the structure of language is missing, desire too is missing. Where repression is missing—where transparency has not given way to the opacity regarding my own thoughts and feelings that results from repression—there too questioning and wondering are missing: I cannot call into question my past, my motives, or even my thoughts and dreams. They simply are.

The Treatment of Psychosis: Analysis of a Case

The most particular cases are those whose value is the most universal.

—Lacan, Seminar VI, February 11, 1959

Lacan does not merely provide us with a radically new way of understanding psychosis; he also helps lay the groundwork for its treatment. As I mentioned above, this does not mean that Lacan believed he could alleviate or cure psychosis—in other words, instate the paternal function in a patient in whom it had not been instated. He does not hold out for us the hope of naming the mother's desire or desire for the mother, and thus constituting it as prohibited and requiring repression, twenty years after the fact, say.

The symbolic order, missing a crucial element (the Name-of-the-Father, cannot be structurally repaired, to the best of our knowledge; it can, however, be propped up or "supplemented" (to use Lacan's term) by another order. In his early work, it is the imaginary that is relied upon to cover over the hole in the symbolic. Indeed, according to Lacan, it is the imaginary—in this case, the mimicking of others engaged in by the psychotic—that often allows the psychotic to make it to age twenty or thirty without suffering a psychotic break or "episode." The goal, superficially stated, is to return the imaginary to the stable state that characterized it prior to the psychotic break.[58]

I cannot provide here a thoroughgoing discussion of Lacan's approach to the treatment of psychosis, since this would require the introduction of too many new concepts. Instead, I will provide a brief case history of a psychotic who was treated by two different psychotherapists; the case illustrates a number of Lacan's claims about psychosis and the possibilities for its treatment.

Unlike Freud's study of Schreber, the case is quite contemporary, dating back only to the late 1960s and early 1970s. Although it is not one of my own cases, I have decided to introduce it here because it exemplifies a number of points highlighted in this chapter, is readily available in English (though probably not well known), and is a mere eleven pages long. It is entitled "Bronzehelmet, or the Itinerary of the Psychotherapy of a Psychotic," and was written (in French) by Jean-Claude Schaetzel.[59] The case study does not contain a wealth of biographical information, but instead concentrates on what occurs in the course of the patient's treatment.

Schaetzel refers to his French patient as Roger Bronzehelmet—a pseudonym, but the patient's last name does literally mean "bronze helmet" in the Slavic language from which it derives. As we shall see, Roger's last name—that is, the name handed down to him by his father—is of considerable importance in his history. Regarding Roger's family, Schaetzel tells us that Roger's father allows himself to be completely dominated by his wife's mother, to the extent that Roger believes his maternal grandmother to be the "father" of the family. When the mother-in-law dies (Roger is four at the time), the father becomes an alcoholic and allows his wife to dominate him as her mother had before her. The father devotes all his attention to Roger's sister, who is seven years Roger's senior; Roger's mother devotes all of her attention to Roger. Born in 1943, Roger has no known psychiatric history or documented difficulties during his childhood or teenage years. It is only as a college student in the mid-1960s that Roger begins to show signs of obvious disturbance.

As a child, Roger plays "sexual games" with his sister, the nature of which is unclear, and it is when he is about to have his first sexual encounter as an adult that he becomes profoundly disoriented. A woman in Roger's apartment building, whose blind husband has recently died in an accident, invites him to visit her, and her intentions seem overtly sexual. As the time of their rendezvous approaches, he anxiously flees the apartment building and goes in search of his professor at the university, "to tell him of his state of utter confusion" (185). An assistant there, perceiving his difficulty, directs him to a social worker, who in turn directs him to a psychotherapist for treatment.

Of particular relevance here are certain things Roger says and does in the course of his therapy that are related to his father and his father's name. "There is no name for a father like mine," he tells his therapist.[60] He refers to his father as a "poacher," an unscrupulous "crook" who wanted his son to play the part of the "lookout to prevent them from being found out by the law" (187)—a far cry from the father who lays down laws that both he and his child must obey! An event that occurs during the therapy is indicative of Roger's lifelong lack of recognition and attention from his father: wishing to start anew, to build a relationship with his father from the ground up, Roger asks his father to put the past behind them, saying that "to live, a father needs a son, just like a son needs a father." His father's reply says it all: "I'd sooner grow fond of a dog."[61]

Roger's attempt to establish a relationship with his father does not, at first sight, differ much from the neurotic's all-too-common attempt to renew ties with a father who did not, the neurotic feels, provide sufficient praise, recognition, or love. But Roger's quest is more all-encompassing, more vital: rebuffed by his father, Roger becomes convinced that the "unscrupulous" man who lives with his mother must not be his real father. He visits the county recorder's office to look up his birth certificate and his parents' marriage license, in order to see with his own eyes the name of the man who signed them—that is, in order to be sure of the name of his true father. But despite what he sees, he remains unsure that he is the son of the man whose name appears there in black and white, or that the name he sees is in fact the same as that of the scoundrel who lives with his mother; in other words, he remains unsure that he is that man's son. He feels a vital need to establish a paternal genealogy for himself, to find an identity and a place for himself as someone's son. The neurotic may wish his or her father had been different, hate or despise the father, wish he or she had had someone else (indeed, anyone else) for a father, but generally does not throw into question in this way who his or her father is.[62]

Here we see, in a very concrete case, that the father, as we generally understand it in our society, is a symbolic function, not a biological (real, physical, genetic) function. The father is someone who plays a specific role in his child's life, not simply someone whose name appears on a piece of paper, no matter how official it may be. Some male obviously provided Roger's mother with the sperm necessary for her to conceive Roger, but the latter nevertheless feels himself to be no man's son, to have no father.

Needing an identity, Roger goes on to create for himself "a secret name that finally allows him to live" (188). He senses that he can be born from himself and his therapist, and combines the letters of his first name with those of his therapist's last name (the combination turns out to be a simple anagram of the therapist's name). Roger writes this name down on a piece of paper which he considers to be his true birth certificate (in French, *acte de naissance* also evokes the act of birth, the fact of being born), sticks it in a hole in the foundation of his family home, and plugs up the hole. The joy he feels that day is ineffable. Only a name can give birth to the subject, can give a child a place in which to come to be in the symbolic world of family trees and genealogies. Roger has no place; the name he bears, Bronzehelmet, cannot really be his name, to his mind, since his so-called father prefers even a dog to him.

Roger mechanically goes to his sessions with his first therapist for two years, bringing the therapist mountains of writings: he meticulously writes down his dreams, types them up, memorizes them, and recites them by heart in his sessions. (This sort of prolific "literary" production is an extremely common feature in psychosis.) The therapist holds on to the writings and allows Roger to recite his dreams in therapy for a long time, but one day, after Roger recites a dream in which he is in a gilded cage "strewn with roses, watched by the therapist" (186), the therapist suggests that this may be an image of his life at present: perhaps he sees the world as if from within a gilded cage where everything is rosy and he is admired by his doctor.

Without taking up the question of the well-foundedness or groundlessness of this interpretation, we need first to note its effect: *it leads to a psychotic break.* The therapist, by providing a kind of interpretation, suggests to Roger that his dreams have meaning of which he is unaware; up until this time, Roger views his dreams as no more than pretty images and stories that he finds very pleasing. With this intervention, the therapist attempts to situate himself not in the place of the witness, the willing repository of the patient's dreams, writings, and thoughts, but in that of the Other: the place or locus in which meaning is determined.

In work with neurotics, a therapist must, as we saw in earlier chapters, situate him- or herself as the Other who hears something in what the neurotic says that is not what the neurotic consciously intended. For it is in this way that meaning becomes problematized and that the analysand begins to realize that he or she does not always know what he or she is saying. In the case of the neurotic, *this place or locus already exists,* and the therapist simply maneuvers in such a way as to occupy it, if he or she is not situated there from the outset by the neurotic. In the case of the psychotic, however, this locus does not exist. Roger's therapist can thus be understood as trying, with this intervention, to take on *a symbolic role for which there is no precedent.* The therapist tries to go beyond the imaginary axis, on which everything had until then been situated in Roger's case, and to bring something into "symbolic opposition" (*Ecrits,* 577/217) with the imaginary. In a word, he tries to triangulate, or introduce an "outside" into a dyadic relationship.[63]

In terms of the L Schema introduced in Chapter 3, Roger and his therapist have been situated at either end of the imaginary axis (Figure 7.4), the only axis involved in their relationship. But the therapist, no doubt unwittingly, tries to occupy a position in symbolic opposition to a subject (along the symbolic axis in Figure 7.5) *in a case in which there is no subject to be found.* That

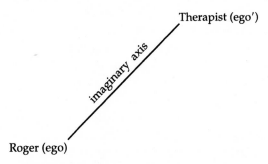

Figure 7.4 L Schema (imaginary axis alone)

is, he tries to situate himself in a symbolic relationship to Roger when those places, subject and Other, do not exist for Roger.[64] Instead of a subject who can respond to the Other, what appears is a giant hole or vacuum. In the absence of a subject of meaning—a subject rooted in a first meaning established by the paternal metaphor—Roger begins to attribute a menacing meaning to all kinds of things that, prior to the therapist's interpretation, had no such meaning. A hammer inadvertently left in the therapist's waiting room is suddenly understood by Roger to imply that the therapist thinks Roger has "a screw loose."[65] A question on the cover of a journal in the therapist's waiting room, "Are students crazy?" (announcing an article on discontent among college students), leads Roger to believe that that question is aimed directly at him, and that it is intended specifically for him. In other words, interpretations begin to present themselves to Roger of which he is absolutely convinced; in a word, he begins to have delusions.

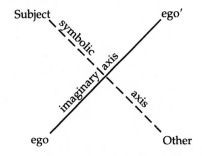

Figure 7.5. L Schema (imaginary and symbolic axes)

It should be kept in mind here that while Roger has seemingly been trying to erect this therapist into a father figure by christening himself with an anagram of the therapist's name, he nevertheless tells Schaetzel (his second therapist) that his first therapist was "like a mother to me." Once he even tried to leave a photograph of his mother in the therapist's office, so that the therapist would keep it and perhaps take the hint that he should attempt to be like her. Roger strives to create for himself a new genealogy, one that provides a space or place for him in the world, a role in a specific lineage, but he does not adopt his therapist as a symbolic father; rather, he takes him as a kind of supportive maternal figure. The therapist's presence remains reassuring to Roger until the therapist attempts to become somewhat more like a symbolic father, attempts to "situate himself in a tertiary position in a relationship based on the imaginary couple a-a' [ego to alter-ego]" (Ecrits, 577/217). Lacan refers to such a father as Un-père, "A-father," or perhaps better, "One-father."[66] This role involves not just any older man, but a man who attempts to intervene in a dyadic (usually mother-child) relationship and establish a genuinely symbolic relation with the psychotic.

It is the encounter with the One-father, with the Father as a pure symbolic function[67] (and this often takes the form of an encounter with a particular person, male or female, who plays or tries to play a symbolic role), that leads to the triggering of psychosis—that is, to a psychotic break. Lacan makes this into a very general thesis, inviting us to try to verify it by seeking dramatic encounters with such a One-father at the origin of *every* psychotic break— whether it is found, in the case of "a woman who has just given birth, in her husband's face, [in that of] a penitent confessing his sins in the person of his confessor, [or in that of] a girl in love in her encounter with 'the young man's father'" (Ecrits, 578/217). The encounter with the Father as a pure symbolic function may also occur without the intermediary of another person, as, for example, when a man learns that he is about to become a father, or is called upon to play the role of a social/political/juridical father figure (Seminar III, 344–345; Lacan has Schreber in mind in the latter case).

One of the immediate consequences of this encounter in Roger's case is that Roger sets out in search of a new name, a new secret name by which to bring himself into being. The first secret name he concocted, based on his therapist's name, was not solid enough to allow Roger to answer "Present!" when cast into the position of the subject of the symbolic order—that is, the subject of the signifier—by the therapist's interpretation. When he was interpellated, called upon to come into being as a subject of language, as a subject capable of taking responsibility for the hidden meanings in his own dreams, the secret name caved in. Logically enough, Roger's search for a new name then leads him to try to discover the name of his therapist's analyst, the spiritual or symbolic father of his own therapist, but he is unsuccessful in this endeavor. He next tries to speak with the most prominent professor at his university—"the biggest name," as he puts it[68]—but it is suggested to him that he continue therapy, this time with a therapist of his own choice.

Roger chooses his new therapist, Jean-Claude Schaetzel, for largely unknown reasons, though it seems quite likely that the therapist's last name sounds a good deal like a nickname Roger used for his sister who was so adored by his father. Prior to the first session, Schaetzel is lucky enough to attend a case presentation on Roger by Roger's first therapist, and is thus well aware that Roger is psychotic, is prone to delusions, and attaches tremendous importance to his oneiric-literary production. Schaetzel never refuses to accept Roger's written work and always allows Roger to recite dreams during his sessions, but gives precedence in his interventions to "casual remarks" Roger makes before and after sitting down and to seemingly spontaneous comments Roger makes about his dreams that are not included in the written version he hands his therapist. Obviously feeling more at ease speaking to Schaetzel, Roger reveals the following: "Words frighten me. I've always wanted to write, but couldn't manage to put a word on a thing . . . It was as though the words slipped off things . . . So I thought that by studying the dictionary from A to Z and writing down the words I didn't know, I would possess them all and could say whatever I wanted" (190–191). Of course, Roger never manages to "possess" them all—that is, stop them from "sliding off of things"—for there is no anchoring point for him that could ever tie word to thing, or, more precisely, signifier to signified. In the absence of the fundamental button tie that links the father's name or "No!" with the mother's desire, words and meanings, signifiers and signifieds, are condemned to drift aimlessly. Roger nevertheless feels a bit safer when he writes things down, as writing seems to fix or freeze meaning to some extent (things are thus "set in type," if not in stone); speech, he feels, is dangerous because meanings become slippery, and he feels he can never grab hold of them or tie them down.

Schaetzel is very patient with Roger, and by devoting attention to Roger's more spontaneous comments and by repeating in later sessions what Roger said offhandedly in earlier sessions, Schaetzel allows Roger to view him as "someone he can talk to" (191). Roger almost completely stops reciting dreams by heart, sensing that, unlike his first therapist, Schaetzel will not try to explode the meaning of his speech (which is already tenuous in his own mind), to evoke or insinuate meanings that Roger does not intend.

Schaetzel makes an important intervention in this vein when Roger recounts a dream whose principal figure is the "203 man."[69] The number "two hundred and three" *(deux cent trois)*, is pronounced in French exactly like "two without three" *(deux sans trois)*. Aware of the problem Roger's former therapist had provoked by attempting to introduce a tertiary position, a three, into the dyadic relationship between Roger and himself (a two), Schaetzel intervenes by saying, "There is two without three," implying thereby that two without three is permitted and that the therapist is not going to attempt to play the role of the One-father with Roger, being content to have a dyadic, mother-child type relationship with him. After a moment of silence, Roger says, "It's like with my mother . . . I was always with her as if I didn't have a father" (193).

Indeed, Roger has no more than a real (biological) or imaginary father, not a symbolic father—that is, a father who lays down the law by saying, "Your mother is off limits, I found her first. Go find your own woman." There were two without three throughout Roger's childhood, and now it is too late: to try to introduce an outside (a three) at Roger's age would lead only to delusions and suicidal depression. The father's name, like the father's prohibition, was never accepted by Roger or never imposed upon him in the first place, and the Other as locus never came into being. Primal repression never occurred, and we thus see in Roger's case what Lacan refers to as the foreclosure of the father's name or "No!" While "foreclosure" suggests an active attempt to refuse or reject something, we see here, as we so often see, a simple absence of paternal prohibition leading to no inscription or instating of the father as symbolic Other. Roger seems not to vigorously *refuse* to grant his father a symbolic role; rather, he is never given the opportunity to either accept it or reject it. Indeed, he tries in vain to replace his father's name with some other—with the therapist's name (in the form of an anagram), or a "big-name" professor's name—but nothing "sticks," so to speak: nothing can do the job for which there has been no precedent. He appeals to or calls upon the Name-of-the-Father, but to no avail: there is nothing there to respond. The therapist cannot hope to triangulate now; he must focus all his efforts on the imaginary register that is there and operative, to make it as sturdy and solid as possible.

What exactly does this mean in Roger's case? Roger tells Schaetzel that he wants to "understand what has happened" to him (193). And this is precisely what the therapist can hope to achieve with a psychotic: help the patient *construct an understanding,* edify a world of meaning that allows the individual to live and find a place for him- or herself. Meaning is imaginary, as we saw in Chapter 2, and it is the level at which the psychotic can be successfully engaged in therapy. With neurotics, the therapist must work hard to stop them from understanding too quickly, because they see what they want to see, understanding what it is pleasing to them to understand. Since the ego recrystallizes or reconstitutes itself around every new meaning, every new under-

standing, the therapist tries to disrupt the neurotic's all too quick and convenient meaning-making activity, hoping to affect what is unconscious, not the
ego. But with the psychotic, the therapist must encourage such meaning-making activity because the ego is all one can work with: the therapist must build
up a sense of self in the psychotic that defines who the psychotic is and what
his or her place is in the world.

In Roger's case, we see that while Roger suffers from delusions after his first
therapist proposes an interpretation, his delusional activity never foments a
new cosmology or world-view—one like Schreber's, for example. Delusional
activity, when it is allowed to run its course rather than being silenced by a
therapist's intervention, eventually leads—and this process may well take
years—to the construction of what Lacan calls a "delusional metaphor" (*Ecrits*,
577/217), a new starting point on the basis of which the psychotic establishes
the meaning of the world and everything in it.[70] In Roger's case, this new
starting point might be a delusional genealogy explaining that Roger is actually, say, the son of God (if not the wife of God), explaining how his mother's
and father's family trees were destined to come together, and so on. Lacan
refers to such a new world view as a delusional metaphor because, in certain
respects, it stands in for the paternal metaphor, allowing words and meanings
to be bound together in a relatively stable, enduring way. Schreber, for example, spends years fomenting a new, highly idiosyncratic cosmology, but the
end result is a stable world of meanings—meanings not shared by many, but
meanings all the same—in which a space, a bearable role, is reserved for
Schreber. Schreber at last manages to find a place for himself in a world of his
own making. Lacan refers to this as the "terminal" point of Schreber's "psychotic process" (*Ecrits*, 571/212).

As we shall see in Chapter 9, the paternal metaphor serves as an explanatory
principle, explaining the Other's desire from which we are born (for, *as subjects*,
we are born of our parents' desire, not of their bodies), explaining why we are
here, why we were wanted, to what extent we were wanted, and so on. In the
absence of such an explanatory principle, the psychotic attempts—via the delusional process—to elaborate an explanatory principle of his or her own.

In contrast, Roger's delusional activity is halted, for the most part, by his
therapist's interventions. Schaetzel sets out to help Roger construct meanings
that can sustain him in life without recreating the entire universe à la Schreber.
Schaetzel does not tell us what the constructed system of meanings looks like
in Roger's case, for his case study reports on only two years of work; nevertheless, it does give us a good idea of the type of work Schaetzel envisions
carrying out with Roger over the years to come. A discussion of Lacan's
approach to the treatment of psychosis beyond this point would, in any case,

require the introduction of much more theoretical material; in particular, it would require me to indicate and justify the precise nature of the interventions Lacan advocates as means of curtailing hallucinatory activity and helping the psychotic construct a new meaning system. I will present such material in the sequel to this book.

Much more could obviously be said about Roger. I have not, for example, said anything about why his problems seem to begin when the possibility of sex with a woman presents itself (a woman whose blind husband has recently died). Is this predicament related to his early sexual play with his sister—that is, with the girl who was his only means of access to his father while growing up? Nor have I addressed the question of feminization in his case. It seems to me, however, that Schaetzel does not provide enough background for us to do anything more than speculate about such questions. The case primarily illustrates what is meant by the foreclosure of the Name-of-the-Father, and helps us understand the radical difference in the therapist's role when the treatment involves psychotics instead of neurotics.

From Father to Worse

Sociologists and historians have, for some time now, been announcing the decline of the father function in Western society. This announcement must, it seems to me, be taken with a grain of salt; after all, the ancient comedies of Terence and Plautus depict the father in ways quite reminiscent of what we see all around us. Nevertheless, changes in family structure (such as the rising percentage of single-parent families today), and changes in ideology and discourse regarding sexual roles, suggest that the importance of men in families and of their symbolic roles as fathers is being ever more widely contested.

More and more single women are deliberately having children, ostensibly rejecting the importance of triangulation (for example, the introduction of a third term in the mother-child dyad, an outside, a symbolic Other; or the institution of the paternal metaphor); and more and more lesbian couples are raising children, seemingly eschewing or downplaying the importance of the father. Combined with the de facto increase in the divorce rate and the consequent increase in the number of children being raised solely by their mothers, and with the growing antiauthoritarian attitude toward children among men (no doubt at least in part encouraged by certain modern-day feminist discourses), the paternal function seems to be in danger of extinction in certain social milieus.

Lacan does not claim that the paternal or father function—the instatement of a father figure in a role of authority beyond the mother—is the nec plus ultra of family structure. His discourse is not that of "family values," pitting Dan Quayle against Murphy Brown. Lacan does not assert that the father should be propped up in our society. Rather, he issues a warning: to reject the father's role, to undermine the father's current symbolic function, will lead to no good; its consequences are likely to be worse than those of the father function itself, increasing the incidence of psychosis. This is one of the things Lacan had in mind when, in 1971, he entitled Seminar XIX ". . . ou pire" (". . . or Worse"), one of the possible elided words being *père* ("father"). If we view the father as the lesser of two evils, to reject the father is to opt for the worse.

Lacan's challenge to discourses that encourage the elimination of the paternal function would run something like this: "Can something like the paternal metaphor—providing the fundamental link between signifier and signified, between language and meaning—be instated without the father as symbolic function? If so, how? If not, is there some other way to introduce an outside— that is, to triangulate the mother-child relationship and stave off psychosis? How can this be done without relying on the symbolic order and its ability to intercede in the imaginary, the world of rivalry and war? Doesn't one sex have to play the part of symbolic representative?"

Unless some other way of achieving the same effect is found—Lacan's work would seem to suggest—the practices that stem from such discourses run the risk of increasing the incidence of psychosis.[71]

8

NEUROSIS

Fantasy provides the pleasure peculiar to desire.

—Lacan, *Ecrits*, 773

Many features of neurosis have already been described in this book. Indeed, the approach to analysis outlined in the first five chapters applies, above all, to neurotics; as I mentioned in Chapter 7, a different approach is required in the case of psychotics and (as we shall see in Chapter 9) the approach required in the case of perverts is also different in certain respects.

Neurosis can, of course, be characterized in many ways. In contradistinction to psychosis, it implies the instating of the paternal function, the assimilation of the essential structure of language, the primacy of doubt over certainty, considerable inhibition of the drives as opposed to their uninhibited enactment,[1] the tendency to find more pleasure in fantasy than in direct sexual contact, the mechanism of repression as opposed to foreclosure, the return of the repressed from within, as it were, in the form of Freudian slips, bungled actions, and symptoms—the list goes on and on. Unlike perversion, neurosis involves the predominance of the genital zone over the other erogenous zones, a certain degree of uncertainty about what it is that turns one on, considerable difficulty pursuing it even when one does know, the refusal to be the cause of the Other's jouissance, and so on.

Repression

The first thing to say about the unconscious . . . is what Freud says about it: it consists of thoughts.

—Lacan, *Scilicet* 1 (1968): 35

What is essential in repression . . . is not that affect is suppressed, but that it is displaced and misrecognizable.

—Lacan, Seminar XVII, 168

The fundamental mechanism that defines neurosis is repression. Repression is responsible for the fact that, whereas the psychotic may reveal all of his or her "dirty laundry" with no apparent difficulty, airing all of the scabrous feelings and deeds anyone else would be ashamed to divulge, the neurotic keeps such things hidden from view, from others and from him- or herself. Lacan expresses the psychotic's situation by saying that his or her unconscious is exposed for all the world to see (à ciel ouvert).[2] Indeed, in a certain sense *there is no unconscious in psychosis*, since the unconscious is the result of repression.[3]

Repression—however its motor force is described (whether as the putting out of mind by the ego or superego of thoughts or wishes that do not fit in with one's view of oneself or with one's moral principles; or the attraction to the "nucleus" of primally repressed material of elements linked to it; or both)—leads, according to Freud, to a separate inscription or recording of a perception or of a thought that once passed or flashed through one's mind. Thus, it does not imply the utter and complete obliteration of that perception or thought, as we might understand foreclosure. As Freud tells us in his essay "Negation," repression cannot occur unless the reality in question (the perception of a scene, for example) has already been accepted or affirmed at some level by the psyche.[4] In psychosis, the reality in question is never affirmed or admitted—it is foreclosed, refused, rejected. In neurosis, the reality is affirmed in some very basic sense, but pushed out of consciousness.

Just as Freud likens the manifest content and the latent content of dreams to two different languages (SE IV, 277), Lacan suggests that the unconscious is a language (Seminar III, 20), a kind of foreign language that we are not immediately able to read. Following Freud's most rigorous formulations in his paper "Repression" (which are repeated many times elsewhere), Lacan sustains that *what is repressed is neither perception nor affect, but the thoughts pertaining to perceptions,[5] the thoughts to which affect is attached.* In other words, the unconscious consists of thoughts, and thoughts cannot but be expressed or formulated in words—that is, with signifiers. Affect and thought are generally connected or linked at the outset; but when repression occurs, affect and thought are generally detached from each other, and the thought may be put out of consciousness.

This is why clinicians often see patients who claim to be blue, depressed, anxious, sad, or overwhelmed with guilt, but do not know why. Or the reasons they put forward do not seem in any way commensurate with the power of the affect that has overcome them. Affect often remains when the thought related to it is repressed, and the troubled individual tends spontaneously to seek ad hoc explanations for it, attempting to understand it in some way or other.[6] The "forgetting" of the thought, accompanied by persistence of the affect, is especially common in hysteria.

Quite common in obsessive neurosis is the case in which a thought—for example, the memory of a particular childhood event—is quite available to consciousness, but evokes no affect whatsoever. The obsessive recalls the event but not his or her reaction or emotion at the time. Repression operates in such cases essentially by breaking the link between the thought and the affect originally associated with it. In such cases, the analyst must rely on the patient to transfer the dissociated affect onto the here and now of the analytic relationship. This is brought about neither by suggestion nor by accusation, but by the analyst's playing the part of a blank screen as far as possible and taking the positive projections with the negative.

Freud, in his work with the Rat Man, for example, was convinced early on that the Rat Man had, as a child, harbored hateful feelings toward his father, but no such affect was elicited by any of his childhood memories. By embodying the "Man without Qualities," however, Freud allowed his analysand to reproduce those feelings in the analytic setting and heap abuse on Freud as an extremely patient stand-in for the Rat Man's father. Thanks to a displacement (from father to analyst), the affect was able to come to the fore.

The Return of the Repressed

Once a thought is repressed, it does not lie dormant. It connects up with other related thoughts and seeks expression whenever possible in dreams, slips, bungled actions, and symptoms. "The repressed and the return of the repressed are one and the same," Lacan tells us.[7] In other words, the idea that is repressed is the same idea that is expressed in a disguised fashion in the Freudian slip, the forgetting of a name, the "accidental" breaking of a vase, or whatever the form taken by the return (for example, disgust at a mother's caresses, revealing the child's repression of its desire for the mother). Indeed, our only "proof" of the existence of the repressed is its return, its manifestations in the form of disruptions or interruptions. The existence of a symptom—a convulsive movement of a part of the face, for example—is the only proof psychoanalysis has or needs of repression:[8] the tick may result from repressed hostile thoughts or a repressed wish to see more; in either case, some wish is being put down or pushed aside. "The neurotic symptom plays the role of the language [langue] in which repression can be expressed" (Seminar III, 72). It is a message to the Other.

In the case of conversion symptoms—that is, symptoms expressed in the body (which run the gamut from minor aches and pains, tightness in the chest, a tingling sensation, a burning sensation, and dizziness to migraines, paralysis, blindness, muteness, and deafness)—the medium the symptoms adopt is a body written with language, a body overwritten with signifiers. The inventor of the "talking cure," Anna O. (whose real name was Bertha Pappenheim and who was treated by Joseph Breuer),[9] developed an occasional stiffening of her right arm, because it was that arm that refused to protect her father when she believed (in a "waking dream") that he was being threatened by a snake. In other words, her physical, bodily symptom "spoke of" a relationship to her father and a possible death wish she had toward him that she was loath to admit to herself. She developed another symptom that defied all medical knowledge of nerve pathways in the body: she began to feel acute pain in a small area of her thigh—the same area, as it turned out, where her father would rest his foot on her leg while she took care of his podiatric problems.

It is commonplace to say that obsession is characterized by the return of the repressed in the mind, whereas hysteria is characterized by the return of the repressed in the body. While it is true that the obsessive is likely to be plagued by disturbing thoughts (thoughts that are seemingly nonsensical, compulsive, or even persecutory), and the hysteric by physical ailments that may change considerably over time, this is not a hard and fast rule and does not afford a reliable distinction between obsession and hysteria. It seems that obsessives are increasingly succumbing to physical ailments that are "stress related"— which is nothing but a modern medical buzzword for psychosomatic—and that are just as *telling* in the choice of the part of the body affected as the hysteric's psychosomatic symptoms ever were. Is it, for example, an accident that the obsessive's "somatization" shows such a strong predilection for the digestive and excretory tracts? (Consider the number of "stress-related" gastrointestinal troubles diagnosed in our day, as well as new "syndromes" like "irritable bowel disorder.")

In the end, it is not the different sites of the return of the repressed—in one's thoughts or in one's body, both dominated by language, thus both the "locus of the Other"—that can help us distinguish hysteria from obsession.[10] A *predominance* of conversion symptoms in a patient's clinical picture may suggest a diagnosis of hysteria, but one still needs to look further. Specific characteristics such as conversion are rarely determinant; like masochistic tendencies, conversion can be found in a number of different clinical categories.

Lacanian Subject Positions

The different "clinical structures" (that is, diagnostic categories) within the larger structural category of neurosis—all of which are defined by the mechanism of repression—correspond, according to Lacan, to different subject positions, not to different symptoms. American psychiatrists, psychoanalysts, and psychologists seem intent on introducing ever more classifications and diagnostic categories within neurosis (if they even recognize the larger category of the neuroses)—"depressive disorder," "bipolar disorder," "panic disorder," "hyperactivity," "hypnoid states," "dysthymia," "polysubstance dependance"[11]—but none of their categories does anything but tag a particular symptom or set of symptoms manifested by an individual at a given moment in time. Each such category represents but a micro-symptom or mini-pattern in a person's overall psychological makeup.

In Lacan's view, there are structures that are far more fundamental than those of "addictive personalities," "introverts," "extroverts," "women who love too much," "men who are afraid of intimacy," and "codependents." American psychology and psychiatry tend to deal only with what immediately meets the eye, abandoning the notion of "deeper" structures with which psychoanalytic investigation began. Thus, they often succumb to the banal simplicity of mainstream American scientific thought: *divide and conquer*— break every pattern down into its smallest isolable parts, give those parts new names, and attempt to treat them (with drugs whenever possible, or with specific "therapeutic techniques") as logically separate "disorders." Indeed, the categories from pop psychology are ultimately no better and no worse than those promulgated by "medical science," since they both take a syndrome-by-syndrome, symptom-by-symptom approach.

A woman who is anorexic can legitimately be categorized as having an "eating disorder," but then we already know this as soon as we are told she is anorexic. If, however, she is diagnosed as hysteric, we can begin to situate the role of her "eating disorder" within the larger context of her psychical structure. This may allow us to see, for example, that the same role played by her anorexia in her teen years may have been played by vomiting when she was a child, shoplifting when she was in her early twenties, and high-stress, high-volume trading as a stockbroker in her later years.

In Lacanian psychoanalysis, the diagnostic subcategories within neurosis are also structural categories; they are not based on a particular set of symptoms, for the same symptoms can be found in extremely different sorts of people.

The main diagnostic structures and the subcategories under neurosis are schematically represented below:

Main Categories:	Neurosis	Psychosis	Perversion
Subcategories:	Hysteria Obsession Phobia		

The question then is: How are these "deeper structures" within neurosis defined?

Hysteria and Obsession

In his early work, Freud makes a number of attempts to define obsession and hysteria on the basis of the highly specific way in which people react to early (primal) sexual experiences; one of the most striking of the definitions he proposes is that obsessives react with guilt and aversion, whereas hysterics react with disgust or revulsion.[12] For clinicians who continue to view sexuality, in its broadest Freudian acceptation,[13] as extremely important, the possibility of distinguishing among patients on the basis of a fundamental difference in their sexual stances is a diagnostic contribution of major proportions. For in real-life clinical work, the more superficial indicators of obsession and hysteria (compulsive rituals, somatic symptoms, and so on) do not always appear to be decisive: one finds what are usually considered to be hysterical traits (for example, conversion or psychosomatic problems) in otherwise generally obsessive people, and obsessive traits in those who seem otherwise predominantly hysterical. Indeed, in one case I supervised, a patient presented anorexic tendencies (usually associated with hysteria) brought on by guilt feelings (usually associated with obsession): the guiltier she felt toward her mother, the more severely she would restrict her consumption of calories.[14]

If therapists had a "true definition" of hysteria, they would, for example, be able to see beyond some of the compulsive phenomena in a patient's clinical picture to a more fundamental mechanism, one which is truly regulating the person's psychic economy. This would also allow them not to dismiss or neglect the "stray" traits characteristic of other clinical structures, but to situate themselves in the transference as a function of the patient's most basic mechanism.

It was clearly Freud's goal in the late 1890s to provide such a definition for hysteria—a single unequivocal definition—but he never felt that he was able to do so. In his letters to Fliess,[15] he declares his intention to write the definitive work on hysteria which would explain it all, but he never wrote the book in question. We are left with a number of provisional definitions of hysteria and obsession, which are not always internally consistent. These remain extremely useful to the practitioner, but the larger question is left open: Why are there two main neuroses, hysteria and obsession, instead of, say, four? Or six? Or seven? (There are actually three, since we include phobia.)[16]

Apart from the historical importance of the categories hysteria and obsession in the development of psychoanalysis, and in the absence of some sort of absolute definition, it is difficult to convey a sense of their importance to anyone who is not already working with such categories and seeing clinical experience in terms of them. For virtually any classificatory schema can take on a certain usefulness and significance for a practitioner over time, as he or she begins to see common characteristics among patients in the same category. One could argue for the greater validity of psychoanalysis' categories on the ground that they are more *useful* than other categories, providing clinicians with a good idea of how to orient themselves in the transference, what to be on the lookout for, and the range of features that, while perhaps not initially visible, are likely to surface in the course of therapy. One could argue—as I do in this chapter—that psychoanalytic classifications go beyond other diagnostic systems insofar as they help *orient* the practitioner's interventions with different patients.

But Lacan allows us to argue for psychoanalytic categories still more forcefully: he shows that they *can* be defined at a profound, structural level. In his lifelong attempt to formalize and extend Freud's work, Lacan provides the basis for a structural understanding of obsession and hysteria that Freud himself did not provide.

Structural Definitions

"Everything for the other," says the obsessive, and that is what he does, for being in the perpetual whirlwind [vertige] of destroying the other, he can never do enough to ensure that the other continues to exist.

—Lacan, Seminar VIII, 241

To grasp Lacan's most far-reaching distinction between hysteria and obsession, we must return to his notion of the fundamental fantasy, introduced in Chapter 5. In its most basic form, it is the relationship between the subject and the object: ($ ◇ a). *The structure of the fundamental fantasy in hysteria is, however, radically different from that found in obsession.* Most simply stated, the obsessive's fantasy implies a relationship with an object, but the obsessive refuses to recognize that this object is related to the Other. Though the object always arises, according to Lacan, as that which falls away or is lost when the subject separates from the Other (see Figure 8.1), the obsessive refuses to acknowledge any affinity between the object and the Other.[17]

To take the simplest Freudian and Lacanian example, the mother's breast is initially the infant's primary source of satisfaction (for those infants who are breast fed). In Figure 8.1, we can situate the child in the left-hand circle, the mOther in the right-hand circle, and the breast in the intersection between the two. At first, the infant considers the breast not as separate from itself but rather as part and parcel of "itself" (there being, at the outset, no sense of "self," no sense of where one person or object leaves off and another begins); experience takes the form of a continuum, not of discrete, separate entities. Once the infant becomes aware of itself as separate from its mother, however, the breast can never be "possessed" in exactly the same way, for the initial satisfaction it brought was tied to a time prior to the self-other, subject-object distinction.[18] The infant did not consider the breast to belong to another person (indeed, the concept of belonging or possession was as yet unknown), but in the course of weaning—a form of separation, loosely speaking—it is experienced as wrenched away, as lost. It is not so much the mOther the child loses in separation as the erotic object, the object that provided so much pleasure.[19] The child does not suffer this loss passively: it tries to make good or compensate itself somehow for the loss.

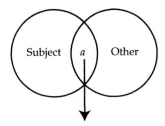

Figure 8.1

In the obsessive's fantasy (and I shall refer to the obsessive here as "he," since the majority of obsessives are male), separation is overcome or made up for as the subject constitutes himself in relation to the breast, which functions as the cause of his desire; unity or wholeness is restored to the subject by addition of the object. But the obsessive refuses to acknowledge that the breast is part of or comes from the mOther, or bears any relation to the actual woman who becomes the obsessive's sexual partner.

As schematically represented in Figure 8.2, the obsessive takes the object for himself and refuses to recognize the Other's existence, much less the Other's desire. The obsessive's fundamental fantasy can thus be adequately formulated using Lacan's general formula for the fundamental fantasy ($\$ \lozenge a$), as long as it is understood that the obsessive seeks to neutralize or annihilate the Other.[20]

On the contrary, in the hysteric's fantasy (and I shall refer to the hysteric here as "she," since the majority of hysterics are female), separation is overcome as the subject constitutes herself, not in relation to the erotic object she herself has "lost," but as the object the Other is missing. Separation leads the hysteric to grasp her own loss in terms of her mOther's loss, the falling away of the object she had been for her mOther. She senses that her mother is not complete as mOther without her child, and constitutes herself as the object necessary to make the mOther whole or complete (the object that plugs up or stops up the mOther's desire).[21] If this relationship does not become triangulated via the Name-of-the-Father, psychosis may result; but when it is triangulated, the hysteric constitutes herself as the object that makes the Other desire, since as long as the Other desires, her position as object is assured: a space is guaranteed for her within the Other.

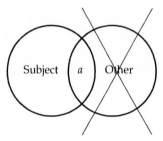

Figure 8.2

Rather than taking the object for herself, as in obsession, the hysteric seeks to divine the Other's desire and to become the particular object that, when missing, makes the Other desire. She constitutes herself on the subject side of the "equation" as object *a* (see Figure 8.3). The fundamental fantasy can be viewed as a response to separation. Here we see that the obsessive attempts to overcome or reverse the effects of separation on the *subject*, whereas the hysteric attempts to overcome or reverse the effects of separation on the *Other*.[22]

I will illustrate these rapidly sketched notions below, but first let us note that the hysteric's fundamental fantasy *cannot* be adequately formulated using

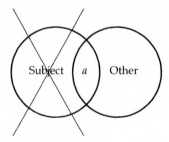

Figure 8.3

Lacan's general formula ($ \cancel{S} \diamond a$). In the slot to the left of the $\diamond$—the "subject slot," so to speak, the slot where the subject's position is indicated or where the subject is situated—the hysteric appears, identified with an object: object a. And the object with which she relates in her fundamental fantasy—indicated in the slot to the right of the $\diamond$, the "object slot"—is not the lost object, as in obsession, but the Other as lacking, which Lacan designates A (for Other, *Autre* in French) with a bar through it to indicate that it is divided or lacking: $\cancel{A}$. Hence, the hysteric's object or "partner" is not an imaginary other, a person she considers to be like herself, nor is it a real object that serves as her cause of desire (for example, the voice or the gaze). Rather, it is a symbolic Other or master: someone imbued with knowledge and/or power, whether male or female. The hysteric's fundamental fantasy could thus be written ($a \diamond \cancel{A}$).[23]

These formulas could be commented on at length, and will only take on meaning for the reader little by little here. The most important point to keep in mind from the outset is that, if we use Lacan's incisive (though complex) concepts—subject, object, and Other—*hysteria and obsession can be defined as radically different subject positions implying opposing relations to the Other and to the object.*

It should be noted that the formulas (or "mathemes," as Lacan calls them)[24] I have provided for obsession and hysteria are not exactly the same as the ones Lacan provides at different moments of his work. The formulas he offers date back to 1960 and 1961,[25] and appear to be superseded to some extent by his work in the 1970s. Since it is my purpose here to offer not a historical account of the development of Lacan's work but rather a summary of what seems to me of greatest value to the practitioner, I am deliberately leaving out many possible levels of commentary on Lacan's mathemes. I am doing so not because they are uninteresting but simply because they would weigh down my exposition.[26]

It should also be noted that the structures in question here are not superficial "patterns" which one is likely to detect upon casual observation (though at times they may be extraordinarily visible) or which are likely to be reported in the first sessions of analysis. The experienced clinician may see telltale signs of one structure or another after a very short period of time, but often many sessions are required to arrive at a reliable diagnosis.

Being in Thought (Obsession) versus Being the Cause (Hysteria)

Lacan views the fundamental question involved in neurosis as the question of being: "What am I?" As I indicated in Chapter 5, this question is reflected above all in the child's investigation of its parents' (the Other's) desire: "Why did they have me? What do they want from me?" These questions have to do with the place the child has in the parents' desire. When the child raises these questions directly to the parents, the answers are rarely convincing ("Mommy and Daddy loved each other very much, and then you came along . . ."), and the child is left to ponder the why and wherefore of its existence via the inconsistencies in its parents' discourse and deeds. The answer is provided in the fundamental fantasy.

The obsessive and the hysteric come to grips with the question of being in different ways, for the question is modulated differently in hysteria and obsession. The hysteric's primary question related to being is "Am I a man or a woman?" whereas the obsessive's is "Am I dead or alive?" The obsessive is convinced that he is, that he exists, only when he is consciously thinking.[27] Should he lapse into fantasy or musing, or stop thinking altogether, for instance during orgasm, he loses any conviction of being. His attempt to come into being or continue to be involves the conscious, thinking subject—the ego—not the divided subject who is unaware of certain of his own thoughts and desires. He believes himself to be master of his own fate.

The obsessive, as conscious thinker, deliberately ignores the unconscious—that foreign discourse within us, that discourse we do not and cannot control which takes advantage of the ambiguities and multiple meanings of words in our mother tongue to make us say the opposite of what we consciously meant, and do the opposite of what we consciously intended to do.[28] The obsessive cannot stand the idea of sharing his mouthpiece with that foreign voice, and does his best to keep it down or at least out of earshot. He acts as if it did not exist, all proofs to the contrary notwithstanding. In the classroom, the obsessive is the student who refuses to accept the idea of the unconscious in the first place, affirming that slips of the tongue have no meaning, that he is aware of all his thoughts, and that he does not need anyone else to help him become aware of them. If he comes to change his mind, he does so grudgingly and only when he sees a prospect of remaining at the level of psychoanalytic theory alone.

The obsessive thus views himself as a whole subject (designated by the letter S without a bar through it), not as someone who is often unsure of what he is saying or what he wants—in other words, not as someone subject to lack. He fiercely refuses to see himself as dependent on the Other, attempting to maintain a fantasmatic relationship with a cause of desire that is dependent on no one—hence his predilection for masturbation, in which no other person is involved. The obsessive is complete unto himself. In this sense, we can even remove the bar on the subject in his fantasy, rewriting it as (S $\diamond$ a). Hence also his predilection, if he is sexually involved with others, to equate them all as contingent "containers" or "media" of object *a*: each partner is fungible or exchangeable for any other.[29] He is led to annihilate any actual partner, ensuring that he or she not become an elective cause of sexual excitement. Instead, the human partner is often transformed in his mind into a mother figure—a provider of maternal love and a proper object of filial devotion. This is related to what Freud calls the "debasement in the sphere of love" (SE XI, 179ff.), wherein the obsessive creates two classes of women: the Madonna and the whore, the mother figure who can be loved and adored versus the exciting woman who embodies object *a*, who cannot be transformed into a maternal love object.[30]

The hysteric, on the other hand, emphasizes the partner or Other, making herself into the object of the Other's desire so as to master it. The Other is the desiring subject in the hysteric's fantasy—usually a partner (lover or spouse) who desires when and how the hysteric as object sees fit. Indeed, the hysteric orchestrates things in such a way as to ensure that the Other's desire remains unsatisfied, leaving the hysteric a permanent role as object. The Other as desiring subject here is but a puppet: it is the Other whose desire is kept unsatisfied by the hysteric in order for the hysteric to be able to maintain her role as desired object, as desire's lack. We shall see that the hysteric is also characterized by the better-known "desire for an unsatisfied desire" of her own; Lacan goes so far as to define the hysteric's stance by saying that hysteria is characterized by an *unsatisfied desire* (Seminar VIII, 425).

Unsatisfied Desire (Hysteria) versus Impossible Desire (Obsession)

> The crux [of desire] is essentially found in impossibilities.[31]
>
> —Lacan, *Ecrits*, 852

In sharp contrast to the hysteric, the obsessive is characterized by an *impossible desire* (Seminar VIII, 425). Let me borrow an example here from Colette Soler that nicely illustrates this.[32] An obsessive man meets a woman who attracts him greatly, seduces her, and makes love to her regularly. He sees in her the object that causes him to desire. But he cannot stop himself from planning when they will make love and asking another woman to call him at that exact time. He does not just let the phone ring, or stop making love when he answers the phone. Instead, he answers the phone and talks with the caller *while* making love with his lover. His partner is thus annulled or neutralized, and he does not have to consider himself dependent on her, or on her desire for him, in any way.[33] Orgasm usually leads, at least momentarily, to a cessation of thoughts, to a brief end to thinking;[34] but since the obsessive continues to talk on the phone with this other woman, he never allows himself to disappear as conscious, thinking subject even for so much as a second.

Few obsessives take the maintenance of thought to this extreme, but the annulling or negating of the Other (here of a woman as the Other for the obsessive) is omnipresent in obsession—though, as we shall see in the discussion of a case of obsession further on, this is often far easier to see in the obsessive's concrete actions related to a woman than in his conscious beliefs about his relationship with her. While making love, the male obsessive tends to fantasize that he is with someone else, thereby negating the importance of the person he is with.[35] _Desire is impossible in obsession,_ because the closer the obsessive gets to realizing his desire (say, to have sex with someone), the more the Other begins to take precedence over him, eclipsing him as subject. The presence of the Other threatens the obsessive with what Lacan calls "aphanisis," his fading or disappearance as subject.[36] To avoid that presence, an extremely typical obsessive strategy is to fall in love with someone who is utterly and completely inaccessible or, alternatively, to set standards for potential lovers which are so stringent that no one could possibly measure up to them.

In the hysteric's fantasy, it is the Other ($\cancel{A}$)—generally the hysteric's partner (for example, husband or boyfriend in the case of a heterosexual couple)—who desires. It thus seems, at first glance, that the hysteric herself occupies no position of desire, and is simply an object of a man's desire. Indeed, certain feminists claim that psychoanalysis, like society at large, assigns women no place as desiring subjects—that it objectifies them. But _Lacan is describing, not prescribing:_ his first claim is that clinical experience teaches us that hysterics _adopt_ a certain stance as objects. Whether or not they do so in large part due to women's social position is a moot point in this context, since Lacan's aim is neither to condemn nor to approve; he is simply saying that this is what clinicians see in analysis day in and day out. He is certainly not claiming that obsession is better than hysteria (if anything, the contrary!). As I have argued elsewhere, it seems to me that Lacan's point of view regarding women's association with the object is quite profound, involving the very nature of the symbolic order (signifiers, language) and its material medium.[37]

What must be stressed here is that the hysteric's stance as object is but one side of the story; for the hysteric also identifies with her male partner, and desires _as if she were him._ In other words, she desires as if she were in his position, as if she were a man. When Lacan says that "man's desire is the

Other's desire," one of the things he means is that we adopt the Other's desire as our own: we desire as if we were someone else. The hysteric desires as if she were the Other—her male partner, in this case.

To illustrate this, let's consider the example of the butcher's wife—a case that Freud describes in *The Interpretation of Dreams* (SE IV, 146–51) and that Lacan takes as a paradigm in "The Direction of the Treatment."[38] Freud's patient (whom he perhaps tellingly identifies only as "the butcher's wife") notices that her husband, while very much enamored of her and seemingly very satisfied with their relationship in every respect, is nevertheless some-what interested in a woman who is not at all his type (she is very skinny, and he is generally attracted only to plumper women like his wife). In the dream she recounts to Freud (a "counter-wish" dream, which she tells in order to disprove Freud's theory that every dream fulfills a wish), she identifies with—that is, literally puts herself in the place of—the skinny woman desired by her husband. In other words, she detects a previously unsuspected desire in her husband, and attempts to become its object (via identification). This gives her a sense of being, of being something—namely, the object that the Other is missing, the object required to complete the Other.

There is, however, a further element: by way of identification with her husband, she herself desires her female friend. Since "man's desire is the Other's desire," her desire becomes identical to his: she desires just as he desires and the same thing he desires. His desire points the way for her own. The "other woman," often referred to in discussions of hysteria, is a woman desired by the Other: the complex "love triangles" (see Figure 8.4) which the hysteric creates or thrives on all revolve around a man. The hysteric's position as a desiring subject is dependent upon the Other's desire; in other words, it involves a detour via a man.[39] She desires like a man, here.

Lacan characterizes hysteria with the formulation, "L'hystérique fait l'homme" (Seminar XX, 79), which can be understood in two ways, both of which are intended: the hysteric makes the man, and the hysteric plays the part of the man. She makes him what he is, bringing out his lack/desire; at

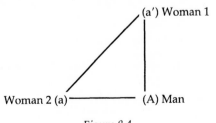

Figure 8.4

the same time she usurps his place or plays his role for him.[40] In the case of the butcher's wife, we see that she identifies *both* with her female friend, as an enigmatic object of her husband's desire, and with her husband, at the level of his desire for the female friend. Here we see the pertinence of the hysteric's question, "Am I a man or a woman?" Identifying with both positions—with the enigmatic object of desire and with the desirousness that seems enigmatic in view of her husband's apparent satisfaction—how is the hysteric to situate her own sexuality?

I do not mean to imply that the obsessive does not wonder about his own sexuality, for as Freud tells us in his *Introductory Lectures on Psychoanalysis* (SE XVI, 307) every neurotic has homosexual tendencies, and as he tells us in *The Ego and the Id* (SE XIX, ch. 3) children always identify in certain respects with both the male and female parent (when they are both present, of course). In other words, "Am I a man or a woman?" is a question for all neurotics. It is, however, more poignant or present for the hysteric, just as the question "Am I dead or alive?" is the more pressing or intrusive one for the obsessive.

Let's return for a moment to the case of the butcher's wife. We know from Freud's discussion that she seeks to keep a certain desire of her own un-satisfied; indeed, she tells Freud in no uncertain terms that she adores caviar, yet tells her husband not to buy it for her and "teases" him about it. In other words, she takes pleasure in simply being able to want it, and in depriving herself of it. (The pleasure derived from self-deprivation is significant in hysteria and should never be underestimated, given its important role in anorexia.)[41] She is quite well aware that she has a wish—that is, it is not an unconscious wish—for an unsatisfied wish. Lacan terms this a (preconscious) desire for an unsatisfied desire.

At the same time, in order to maintain her position with respect to her husband's desire, the butcher's wife must keep his desire alive, keep teasing and titillating him, not allowing him to garner too much satisfaction—for satisfaction squelches desire. As Lacan puts it, "Desire is sustained [in the person who incarnates the Other for the hysteric] only by the lack of satisfaction [the hysteric] gives him by slipping away as object" (*Ecrits*, 824/321).[42] Consider her maneuver with respect to the caviar: since she tells her husband that she would love to eat one caviar sandwich a day, she incites in him a desire to buy her the necessary caviar. But then she tells him that she does not want him to spend that much money on her ("she grudges the expense"). She first arouses a desire in him (a want-to-give) and then demands that he not satisfy it! Indeed, she teases him about it day after day, reminding him of his want-to-give, of the lack she has wrought in him.

The butcher's wife *detects* a desire in her otherwise so-very-satisfied husband for another woman, the wife's female friend, but she is also able to *create* one if she feels the need to. The hysteric finds a way, just when it seems her husband is most satisfied, to provoke a desire in him for something else, or even for someone else. In the case of the butcher's wife, another woman is ready to hand, so to speak; in other cases, however, the hysteric seems deliberately (though generally it is not consciously intentional) to seek out another woman with whom she can involve or ensnare her partner in a triangular *circuit of desire.*[43]

The Neurotic's Stance Regarding the Other's Jouissance

By orchestrating the circuit, the hysteric becomes master of the Other's desire— *the cause of his desire*—yet at the same time she attempts to avoid being the person with whom he satisfies his desire. She keeps his desire unsatisfied in order to avoid being the object of his jouissance. For Lacan, like Freud, the hysteric is someone who finds the Other's sexual satisfaction distasteful, and attempts to avoid being the object the Other gets off on. She refuses to be *the cause of his jouissance.* She wants to be the cause of his desire, but not of his jouissance.[44] This does not mean that she refuses to engage in all sexual activity with a man (although this sometimes happens); rather, when so engaged, she is inclined to imagine that some other woman is in bed with him, that she is someone else or somewhere else, or that he is a different man. In her mind, she is not the cause of his jouissance—someone else is, because, at least in thought, *she is not there.*

Imagine now, if you will, the obsessive and the hysteric together in bed: the obsessive refuses to fade as thinking subject when faced with a woman who incarnates the Other for him, and thinks of another woman or even talks to another woman while making love (he reduces the Other to the object *a* he sees in her and wants from her).[45] The hysteric refuses to be the cause of her male partner's sexual satisfaction, preferring to keep his desire unsatisfied, and imagines that some woman other than herself is in the bed. This can serve as a fine illustration of Lacan's oft-repeated claim, "There's no such thing as a sexual relationship." The obsessive relates to his object *a*, neutralizing the woman present, and the hysteric keeps her desire alive by mentally being somewhere else during sex. This is certainly not a "relationship" in the usual sense of the term![46]

The distinction between desire and jouissance is of the utmost importance here. We have seen that the female hysteric often requires a triangle involving a man to keep her desire alive and that she prefers to exclude sexual satisfaction from that circuit; she may nevertheless find great sexual satisfaction with women (the Other sex for both men and women, as Lacan says), in masturbation, in eating, in drug or alcohol use, or in other activities. The hysteric's inability to find sexual satisfaction and desire in one and the same relationship may be *structural,* not accidental, and the analyst must not in any sense take it as his or her goal to bring the patient to the point where the two can coincide.[47]

Lacan often criticized American psychoanalysts for believing that analysis could and should direct patients toward "normal heterosexual genital" satisfactions[48] and attempt to bring about a fusion of the patient's love object and sexual object; he faulted them for viewing the patient's neurosis as consisting precisely in the inability to find love and sexual excitement in the same partner. In contrast, Lacan suggests that love, desire, and jouissance are structurally different levels, and that—since the analyst directs the treatment for the analysand's greater eros, not for what he or she believes to be good for the analysand (Seminar VIII, 18)—the problem is not the analysand's inability to find love, desire, and sexual excitement all in the same place, but rather the fact that the analysand gives up the pursuit of desire and sexual excitement, say, for the sake of an ideal such as "the perfect love."

Neurotics are often so concerned with what those around them consider "normal" that the obsessive, for example, may seek to put out of mind any and all fantasies that do not involve his wife, and then wonder why he feels that his libido has shriveled up and died; and the hysteric may sacrifice the satisfaction she experienced on certain occasions with women because it does not fit in with her notion of what a love relationship with a man should be, and then wonder why her life seems so empty and restricted. The analyst must not adopt any pre-established notion of what is good or bad for the analysand, but simply encourage the dialectization of the analysand's desire and foster the analysand's separation from the Other's desire.

Returning to the hysteric's stance regarding jouissance (the fact that the hysteric refuses to be the cause of the Other's jouissance), let us note that the same is true of the obsessive. His sexuality is essentially masturbatory, the Other being annihilated; his strategy, like the hysteric's, can be characterized as a sort of "No jouissance for the Other!" Whereas the pervert, according to Lacan, devotes himself (at least in fantasy) to being the object the Other gets off on, the neurotic's motto is "The Other will never get off on me!"[49] Neurosis can thus be understood, in part, as a strategy regarding jouissance—above all, the Other's jouissance.[50] Both the hysteric and the obsessive refuse to be the cause of the Other's jouissance.

Ironically, Lacan nevertheless suggests that the neurotic's fundamental fantasy "takes on the transcendental function of ensuring the Other's jouissance."[51] The subject's position may well be one of refusal, but the fundamental fantasy nonetheless forms in response to the Other, "who passes this chain [the fundamental fantasy can be qualified as a chain or link] on to me in the Law"—that is, in response to the symbolic father or superego. We desire in accordance with the law: prohibition is what eroticizes and leads to the construction of the fantasy. Yet there is a *threshold* of sorts within fantasy itself, the point beyond which it turns to horror; this threshold is familiar to most of us from dreams in which we seem to be pursuing precisely what is most pleasurable, when suddenly what we most ardently desire turns out to be something else altogether, something absolutely horrible. The purity of desire veers in the direction of a kind of *obscene jouissance.*

I cannot go into the complex dialectic at work here, but it is related to Lacan's thesis (discussed in "Kant with Sade," for example) that the severity of the superego—while often reduced to the internalized voice of conscience—is actually a vehicle for jouissance: the obsessive's superego voices may command him to do certain things that are strangely exciting for him simply to think about. Indeed, Lacan formulates the essential imperative issued by the superego as *"Jouis!"*—a command directing the subject to enjoy, to obtain satisfaction. In the case of the Rat Man, for example, virtually every *command* the Rat Man tells Freud he hears consists of an order to do precisely what, at some level, he wants to do: be vindictive, aggressive, and so on. The superego commands us to satisfy our drives, oddly—and no doubt to some extent counterintuitively—commanding us to satisfy that sadistic Other within us, the superego. Obviously, we simultaneously satisfy "ourselves" in some sense, though certainly it is not at the level of the ego or self that we find it satisfying. When we obey such superego commands, it is as if we were obtaining jouissance *for the Other,* not for "ourselves."[52]

In a sense, the obsessive who lives for "Posterity" and not for today transfers all jouissance to the Other—that is (if he is a writer), to the whole set of future readers who will appreciate his writings and make him live on long after he is dead. The obsessive lives posthumously, sacrificing everything (all satisfaction in the here and now) for the sake of his name—having his name live on. The name—being the Name-of-the-Father, the name passed down from the father—is in some sense the Other who passes on the law and whose jouissance is ensured by the obsessive's accumulation of publications, titles, money, property, awards, and so on. This is but one illustration of how the neurotic, while positioning him- or herself in such a way as to avoid being the cause of the Other's jouissance, unwittingly sacrifices jouissance to the Other nevertheless. Whenever we force ourselves to conform to our ideals at the expense of our own satisfaction, we assure the Other's jouissance. In the case of hysteria provided below, we shall see one of the forms this may take.

A thousand details could be added to fill out this brief outline: virtually all of psychoanalysis' major concepts—transference, compulsion, symptom formation, the drives, and so on—can be usefully examined in terms of the hysteria-obsession divide. Since this is an introduction, and a clinical introduction in particular, I will discuss hysteria and obsession here only in terms of one of those major concepts: transference.

Obsession and Hysteria in Analysis

The obsessive attempts to neutralize the Other. The more obsessive he is, the less likely he is to go into analysis. For to go into analysis is to enlist the help of another person, someone generally considered to have specialized knowledge—in short, a symbolic Other. The obsessive is the one who, after attending weeks of classes on Freudian theory and practice, continues to say, "I still think people should be able to work out their problems on their own." He may, intellectually, come to accept the existence of the unconscious, but not the notion that it is inaccessible without someone else's help. He realizes he has problems, but engages only in "self-analysis," keeping a journal, writing down his dreams, and so on.

In more everyday situations, the obsessive refuses to be helped by other people: "I can do it *myself*," says Tim ("the Tool Man") Taylor on *Tool Time*, even though he always needs help—indeed, professional help. "Why would I call a specialist when I can install this heating unit myself?" asks the main character on *Coach* as the six-hundred-pound unit comes crashing through the ceiling into his living room from the attic. The perfect obsessive is the Ayn Randian "self-made man" who believes he doesn't owe anyone anything and that he made his fame and fortune in a completely ahistorical context, independent of any particular economic system, government, industry, or persons. More typically, the obsessive lives out his life in rebellion against one or all of his parents' wishes, but denies any relation whatsoever between what he does and what his parents wanted him to do or be. His whole life may be a protest against the Other's ideals, but he is likely to cast what he does in autonomous terms: "I do this because I believe in x, y, and z," not "My parents tried to force me to do p and that's why I'm doing q."

The obsessive's fiercely expressed independence from the Other makes him an unlikely subject for analysis. Generally speaking, it is only when something very specific (in analytic terms) happens that he truly goes into analysis. Many obsessives come for a few sessions, asking for help of a minor sort, or because their significant others have pushed them into therapy, but they do not stay. Those who do stay have usually had an unexpected encounter with the Other's desire, an encounter with the lack in the Other that generates anxiety (perhaps for years thereafter) and rocks the obsessive's world. It may be the Rat Man's encounter with the "Cruel Captain" (SE X, 166–169), who doesn't mince words about his desire to inflict punishment on others; or it may be the obsessive's sudden realization that one of his parents has become involved in a passionate love affair shortly after the death of the other parent. The obsessive is shaken up by such manifestations of the Other's desire, and can no longer successfully nullify or neutralize the Other and his dependence on the Other.

Such an encounter is usually at the origin of an obsessive's request to begin an analysis, and it results in what seems to be a certain openness or attentiveness to the Other. In other words, such an encounter makes the obsessive a bit more like the hysteric, the hysteric always being attentive to the Other's wants. The obsessive has become "hystericized," to use Lacan's term—has opened up to the Other.

The problem is that "hysterization" is fragile and short-lived: the obsessive often reverts quite quickly to shutting out the Other and denying any kind of dependence. If analysis is to have any effect on the obsessive, the analyst must foster hysterization; cast in the role of Other by the analysand, the analyst must continually bring to bear his or her desire (regarding all things analytic, as enumerated in Chapters 1–5) in order to thwart the otherwise inevitable "obsessionalization" or shutting off of the obsessive.[53]

Thus, the first and ongoing "maneuver" required on the analyst's part is to ensure that the obsessive is regularly confronted with the analyst's desire. Analysts who work with obsessives are quite familiar with the obsessive's tendency to talk on and on, to associate and interpret all by himself, paying no heed to the analyst's punctuations or interpretations. Indeed, the analyst often has to make a considerable effort to stop the obsessive from bulldozing right over his or her intervention: the obsessive gives the analyst the impression that he or she is intruding, getting in the way of what he wanted to say. The obsessive would prefer that the analyst remain silent, or play dead if not actually be dead. Every sound the analyst makes—moving in his or her chair, even breathing—is too much, reminding the obsessive of the analyst's presence that he would so much rather forget.

Many analysts respond by playing dead, remaining silent and trying not to intrude into the chain of the patient's endless associations, but it is only by intruding and reminding the obsessive of the Other's presence and the presence of the Other's desire that hysterization is maintained. The analyst must not conform to the obsessive's fantasy in which the Other is glossed over or annulled, but must try to foil the obsessive's attempts to repeat it with the analyst.

Given this portrait of the obsessive, one might be inclined to think that the hysteric must be the ideal analysand from the analyst's point of view. She is, after all, extremely attentive to the Other's desire, since she derives her being from it ($a \diamond \cancel{A}$). But in addition to expecting being from the Other, she also expects knowledge: she looks to the Other to fill her lack of being (or want-to-be) and lack of knowledge (or want-to-know). This is what makes it easy for her to request the analyst's help—she recognizes her dependence on the Other—but makes it difficult for her to work once she is in analysis. Just as she seeks out and provokes, if need be, lack/desire in her partner, seeking to know what she is as an object of desire, so too she seeks knowledge about herself— "What do I have, doctor? What is the matter with me?"—and expects to receive that from the analyst as well.

Should the analyst comply, and many do, attempting to supply the hysteric with knowledge about herself, this knowledge (which is, in any case, likely to miss the mark in the early stages of analysis) is only momentarily gratifying to the analysand. It is almost immediately questioned, examined, scrutinized, and evaluated by the hysteric seeking the lack in the analyst's knowledge, the lacuna or gap; for this gives her the role of the exception, living proof that she can supplement or complement the analyst's knowledge. Analysts often find hysterics very challenging to work with, having the sense that they are never far enough ahead of the hysteric's understanding of the situation, that they never have enough new knowledge with which to appease the hysteric's insatiable appetite. Analysts who play the game of feeding knowledge to the analysand sooner or later learn that it is the hysteric who always wins that game: she becomes the master of the analyst's knowledge, making the analyst produce that knowledge as fast as he or she can. Should the analyst succeed, through interventions and interpretations, in getting the hysteric to give up one symptom or in "resolving" one symptom, the hysteric is likely to report new symptoms at the next session.[54] In her position as the one who points out or demonstrates the lack in the Other's knowledge, she becomes a living exception or enigma, always one step ahead of any known theory or technique.

The hysteric makes herself the master of the analyst's knowledge and, indeed, of his or her desire as well, laying out the terms of the therapy and telling the analyst what he or she must want from the analysand. Thus, in work with hysterics, the maneuver required of the analyst is to turn the tables. Whereas the hysteric asks, "Tell me about myself, doctor. What is the matter with me?" the analyst has to direct the question at her: "What do *you* want?"

This transition is formulated by Lacan as the shift from "the hysteric's discourse" to "analytic discourse." Here, I will merely reproduce Lacan's formulas for those discourses and mention a few points, since I have discussed them at length elsewhere.[55]

Hysteric's course: Analytic discourse:

$$\frac{\$}{a} \rightarrow \frac{S_1}{S_2} \quad \Rightarrow \quad \frac{a}{S_2} \rightarrow \frac{\$}{S_1}$$

The hysteric's discourse is the discourse spontaneously adopted by the hysteric (as barred subject, $\$$): the hysteric addresses (the addressing being designated by the arrow, $\rightarrow$) a master (S_1), in this case the analyst, and tries to get him or her to produce knowledge (S_2).[56] In analytic discourse, the hysteric or hystericized analysand ($\$$) is put in the position of the worker (the upper right-hand position is the position of production or work), and it is the analyst's enigmatic desire (a) which is the agent that sets the discourse in motion (the upper left-hand position is the position of agency).

Thus, whereas the obsessive must be hystericized at the outset and throughout the course of his analysis, the hysteric must be made to *change discourses* and stop expecting or waiting to receive knowledge from the Other.[57] The different neuroses thus require different stances on the part of the analyst. When the analyst mistakes a hysteric for an obsessive, he or she may grant a request (never a good idea, in any case)—to use the analyst's bathroom, have a drink of water, change a session time, stand instead of sit, delay payment for a week, or whatever—only to find that the analysand's requests increase tenfold, one demand leading to a multitude of demands. Should the analyst then stop granting requests altogether, or draw the line somewhere in the attempt to put a stop to past indulgences, he or she is likely to be accused of being inconsistent. "Why can't I do *x* now, when you let me do it before?" "Did you make a mistake when you let me do it the first time?"

This kind of testing behavior, well known to analysts, is related to the hysteric's attempt to sound the analyst's desire and knowledge. The hysteric tries to discern the Other's desire in order to be able to position herself in such a way as to become its lack or cause. Is she going to be able to master the analyst's desire, to incite and then frustrate it? How far does she have to push the analyst before he or she will express his or her desire? She needs such expressions in order to situate herself, and if they are not forthcoming, she provokes them—perhaps subtly, perhaps not so subtly.

When an analyst mistakes a hysteric for an obsessive, he or she is also likely to direct the analysand to the couch too soon. In America, analysts and psychiatrists have a tendency to put everyone on the couch right from the outset, eliminating any distinction whatsoever between the preliminary meetings and "analysis proper," between the vague malaise with which patients often come to analysis and a genuine wondering about the why and wherefore of certain actions, symptoms, and pleasures. Assuming the analyst has grasped the distinction between the preliminary sessions and the later stage at which the "person" of the analyst (the analyst as an individual) progressively fades into the background, he or she must then consider that face-to-face sessions are of greater importance to the hysteric than to the obsessive. Attuned as she is to the Other's desire as embodied in a specific person, the hysteric cannot easily bear to speak to a blank wall (or even a wall with paintings or diplomas), needing to feel the Other's gaze upon her, needing to feel supported in some way. She finds it extremely difficult to explore the arcana of her circuits of desire without knowing whom she is talking to and the effect her words are having.

The obsessive, on the contrary, couldn't care less. Since he would just as soon be alone in the room, preferring that no one embody the Other for him, he is likely to find the couch a more convenient arrangement than face-to-face meetings—indeed, too convenient an arrangement at the outset, if we consider the importance of keeping him hystericized. The real presence of the analyst in the room must be emphasized from the beginning, if the obsessive is to be coaxed out of his solipsism. Once a certain openness to the Other's desire is ensured, he can be directed to the couch so that that Other becomes blank enough to support any and all projections.

I am not suggesting that every single hysteric openly tests her analyst and that every obsessive blatantly shuts his analyst out. These are general tendencies based on differences in psychical structure, and may vary in their expression to a *very significant degree*. They are, however, tendencies the analyst should always keep in mind.

It should be noted that, although I have been referring to the obsessive as a he and the hysteric as a she, there *are* female obsessives and male hysterics. They often confound modern psychiatry, which tends to place them in the twentieth-century catch-all category "borderline." (As I mentioned in Chapter 6, Lacan rejects this category outright as a simple throwing up of one's hands and saying, "I don't know what I'm looking at.") From my own experience, I would suggest that a certain number of male homosexuals and heterosexuals can be viewed as hysterics, and Freud describes a number of women he seems to consider obsessive (*Introductory Lectures on Psychoanalysis*, ch. 17). The complications that can arise in this kind of crossing over of typical categories are further compounded by Lacan's distinction between masculine structure and feminine structure, which, according to him, correspond neither to biology nor directly to obsession and hysteria, though there is a great deal of overlap (Seminar XX).

But rather than introduce more theory,[58] I will now provide some in-depth illustration of the mass of theoretical work that has been outlined in this chapter. I will present two of my own cases, one of obsession and another of hysteria, supplying first some of the general case material and then a detailed commentary. Neither case is in and of itself exemplary, but in both it was particularly easy to protect the identity of the patients.

A Case of Obsession

For about a year I saw a man in analytic therapy, at a frequency of two sessions a week at the outset, then three, and then four sessions a week by the end. The patient was from another country, and his therapy—which never, in my view, went beyond the stage of preliminary meetings—came to a premature end when he returned to his homeland. The material that came out in the course of this relatively short treatment was ample, but not so copious as to preclude giving the reader a reasonable idea of the clinical picture in a few pages. Names and certain biographical details have been changed to protect the identity of the patient.

The patient, whom I will call Robert, was thirty years old and worked as a troubleshooter in the area of high-tech equipment. He had been thinking of going into therapy for some time, and finally decided to do so at a moment of crisis that involved a number of factors, the most salient of which was that the company he had set up with a friend was foundering—due, he felt, to his own inadequacies and inertia. He had resigned as codirector the very day he first came to see me, had accepted the idea that he would henceforth have to work as his friend's subordinate, and was, in Robert's own words, "finally getting what [he] deserved." According to him, he had coasted through life without ever committing himself to anything and without ever really working at anything; he was a "fake," a "pretender" who had been found out, someone who had had a "free ride" and who was now in over his head. He had always managed "to pull the wool over people's eyes," but now he was being "called to account" by his friend.

Though initially shaken by this experience, two weeks later Robert described himself as "gleeful" about finally being held liable for his actions: "I won't get away with it for the first time," he crowed. "If my salary is cut off, I'll be forced to start from scratch, and everything will be truer. It'll be due to my own effort and not to luck." Robert hoped that no one would be there to pick up the pieces—that is, to help him out of his jam—and he would finally be obliged to do something for himself. His parents would try to interfere, he worried, but he did not want them "to bail [him] out." When fate did not fulfill his fantasy (no one cut off his salary and forced him to start anew), Robert considered other ways of tempting fate. Afraid to ask his boss for time off from work, for example, Robert waited until two days before his scheduled (and prepaid) trip to another continent to ask for vacation time, hoping that the request would lead to a confrontation and to his getting fired.

He said that his inability to work dated back a long time. "As soon as anything is even so much as cast in terms of involving *effort*, it's already too late." To try was to expose himself to the possibility—indeed, the virtual certainty—of failure. If someone else "spoon-fed" him what he needed to know, everything was fine; if not, he merely tried to fake his way through. What he already knew about his business was "trivial and boring"; what he didn't yet know was "impossible": "I'll never know it, I'll never figure it out."

Initially, he demanded that I help him stop procrastinating and get to work; he wanted me to give him small projects to work on, projects which, after a month of sessions, he described as "doing the dishes, cleaning up, tidying my desk," and so on. He wanted me to tell him to do such things so that he would have to be accountable to someone and report back on his achievements. Naturally, I did not provide any such assignments, requesting instead that he tell me what was on his mind and recount his dreams, fantasies, and day-dreams. Two months later Robert told me that he would feel like an "automaton" if he simply had lists of things he was supposed to do and followed through on them—he wouldn't have his "freedom."

Robert suggested that his inability to take action was also a longstanding problem. When in love with a girl during his school years, he could not bring himself to tell her; indeed, he still often waited for women to initiate conversation and intimate contact with him. He could never be sure a woman was "the right woman," and in an association to a dream—a dream in which he was with a prostitute and two other prostitutes were looking on and perhaps joining in—he said it seemed "as if one weren't enough." There was an "endless number of possibilities" (he said this about women and about life in general) and he couldn't choose among them, for he felt that if he did he would be missing something. "I can't devote myself to one activity without thinking about others I could be doing." He also expressed the "need to consider all the ramifications before acting," which is patently impossible and led to inertia on his part. It was "very displeasing" to him to consider that he had limits. He wanted to think "I can have any girl I like."[59]

His love life at the time consisted of short-lived relationships with women who resided in different countries and who visited him or whom he visited for a week now and then. Often there was no one in his life, but just as often there were two or three occasional lovers concurrently. Though this was not mentioned during the first few sessions, it turned out that, just prior to begin-ning therapy, Robert had begun to have repeated trouble achieving an erec-tion, and that this was an almost constant torment to him in his most recent relationship with a woman I will refer to as Sandra. Sandra was his sister's best friend, and Robert considered her the kind of woman he would like to settle down with. As it turned out, the most "suitable partners" were the ones with whom he was most often impotent, whereas when he went out with a woman who was "virtually punk," he had no such difficulty.

After spending a week with Sandra, Robert said that she was "no longer intact"; he had "violated" her; she was missing something; she no longer had what she had had before. She had seemed more whole, more perfect before he had gotten involved with her. It seemed as if he had taken something from her. Sandra, like his former long-term girlfriend from college, had become "too easy"; there was no longer any need for him to be seductive, and he lost interest in sex. When he did engage in it, he always took a shower beforehand and asked his partner to do the same.

In doubt about whom to love (about who was "the right woman"), Robert often fell for and fantasized about "another man's woman." Such women, though involved with his best friends, were considered sacrosanct and were idealized by Robert. Since they were inaccessible, he was free to daydream about them without ever having to worry about "violating" them in deed; in his dreams, however, they succumbed to the same fate as Sandra.

He recounted a dream in which he was walking down the street and saw a man pulling a drunk girl along in the opposite direction. Her "shirt was loose and a breast was exposed"; he grabbed it, and fondled it a few moments. In his associations to the dream, he said that he would normally resist that urge, but as she was "someone else's girl" she seemed more exciting, and as she was in a state of drunken passivity her breast seemed "available." He disliked it intensely if a woman was active or assertive, and sought to "possess" a woman, to overpower and immobilize her. Part of his typical sexual activity was to "pin a girl down, and squeeze her so tightly she can't move." He regretted that he often needed her collusion: he needed her to play along, since he didn't have the physical strength to immobilize her unassisted. "Complete control" was what he wanted.

This concern for control always arose with women he loved and cared for. With the "virtually punk" woman, on the other hand, he felt no such need. Though he had been sure at the outset that the relationship with her would not last, due to "her lower-class background," they continued to see each other for two years and he experienced no notable control or potency problems with her; their relationship was, in his mind, "mostly sexual." One day, after they had split up, he ran into her and started trying to seduce her. But when she eventually began to push him away, he went "out of control"; he told me he had been tempted to rape her, though he did not do so.

In another dream, he was "stoning a figure cloaked in black and huddled over"; it seemed to be a woman. And indeed, the first woman who came to his mind was an idealized woman who lived with one of his male friends. He was "horrified" by the violence of the act of stoning depicted in the dream, and was "amazed" that he could have been involved in it, that he could have gone along with the others who were stoning her. The look on his face as he talked about it nevertheless suggested that there was something strangely satisfying about it to him.

Despite all of his talk about relationships with women, his mother was rarely mentioned; instead, he always alluded to his sister as the model for all his "suitable partners." He described his relationship with his sister as "almost incestuous," but that seemed to be due to the frequency with which he made love to her in his dreams. His mother was characterized as "underhanded." When she disapproved of something he did or wanted to do, nothing could be discussed; she simply made "disapproving gestures and faces"—there was nothing he could argue with, nothing they could "banter back and forth." She wanted "total control," in his view, and the only way he could "rebuke" her was to disobey—that is, to do what he had wanted to do in the first place.

His father, a strict Catholic with high moral and educational ideals, was, according to Robert, very disapproving of him, but never hit him or even "got really angry" at him. Robert said that his father "kept it all inside" and didn't even understand anger because he couldn't feel it or express it. His parents maintained "a conspiracy of silence," admonishing him nonverbally.

Robert felt that in his inability to force himself to do things—to study, work, clean, and so on—he was "putting up resistance to some sort of internal authority," and that it was a "point of honor not to give in." This internal struggle manifested itself in Robert's relationship with me: he was always quick to hear a critical tone in my voice when none was (at least consciously) intended on my part, and confessed that he was trying at some level to provoke me, to get me to reprimand him. He felt that he had sometimes intentionally overslept to arrive late at sessions, which also made it difficult for him to stop off at the bank and pick up money with which to pay me. Very often he found himself leaving the house late and then rushing like mad to my office only to arrive late, engaging in a form of "brinkmanship," as he called it. He said he realized he was courting punishment in this way, but said that he derived pleasure from it.

Robert solicited criticism from many sources, including colleagues at work and women friends, and his usual strategy was to provoke it, quickly admit to being in the wrong to "disarm" the person and "escape the brunt of [his or her] pent-up anger," and then adopt a confessional stance allowing him to "cleanse [himself] of [his] sins." A great many military metaphors were employed in his description of this strategy; for example, he said that the "battle of will against will" brought out the "fighter spirit" in him. Provoking criticism in this way was thus "threatening but exciting."

Robert was sure I must resent him because he had asked me to reduce his fee at a certain point; he felt guilty, as if he had "unduly challenged [my] authority," opposing his desire to mine. I reminded him that we had agreed to a lower fee because he was now coming to see me four times a week instead of three, but he nevertheless expressed a nagging regret that if only he'd "accepted the original price, things would have proceeded more analytically, more professionally." He had the sense that he was "failing his analysis"—for he still couldn't manage to force himself to work—and that it was his fault. If our sessions were of variable length, it must be because he was paying me less than he was supposed to. I reiterated that I ended sessions on particularly important points, and that the length of a session had nothing to do with how much he paid me.

This led to quite another level of reproaches toward me: I was rejecting his "feminine side," and he was sure that if he cried during a session with me, I would cut it short and send him "packing." He needed "to cry it all out" and felt he would never be able to do that with me. With certain women he could show his weaknesses and cry, but felt that he had "to keep up a front for [me]," had to act "like a responsible thirty-year-old man." I did not accept or reject the notion that I disapproved of his "feminine side," nor did I immediately suggest that he was the one who didn't truly accept it in himself. Instead I asked, "Men don't approve of your feminine side?" He responded by saying that his father disapproved of all weakness, all imperfection. He went on to say that one of his former lovers had told him she believed he had a "male side" somewhere, but didn't show it much.

As a boy, he had viewed his father as a powerful figure; whenever someone mentioned that his father was at work, he would imagine "a Canadian lumberjack rolling logs on a river, jumping from one to another, and keeping them away from the banks." As an adult, however, he described his father as "incompetent, impotent, and ineffective," and claimed to be like him in many respects. Had his father been more authoritarian with him, Robert wouldn't, he felt, be so undisciplined. Had his father given him "more direction" and stated more openly what he believed, Robert could have rebelled in a more definitive manner. He had been pained, but also secretly pleased, when one day his college lover had gotten into an argument with his father, for she had made his father appear "vulnerable, exposed, and openly stupid."

In the early months of the treatment, Robert described me as "like a rock" for him. He associated me with a figure in a dream: "a priest with his legs spread apart, standing firmly on the ground, wearing a brown habit, the wind blowing through his cassock; he is unflinching, leaning into the wind." He thus viewed me as an ideal, phallically powerful figure, a rigid, unbending authority, yet at the same time as someone to whom he could confess his sins and from whom he could expect absolution. As the year went on, his view of me changed, and I became someone he could provoke and deliberately try to anger without jeopardizing his analysis. As the time of his return to his own country drew near, I encouraged him to continue therapy once he was home, and have reason to believe that he did so.

This short and obviously incomplete case discussion illustrates many general features of neurosis, as well as many particular features of obsession. Robert quite clearly came to therapy in a crisis with at least two components:

First, he had had a confrontation with someone who, though initially a friend, had become an "authority figure" for him: his business partner. As Robert remarked, "It [was] his approval which [was] in question." Through his inertia, Robert had provoked an expression of this Other's desire, and now this Other wanted him to step down, make amends, and put his nose to the grindstone. While upsetting for Robert, the experience was simultaneously titillating; he became positively "gleeful" at the thought that he would be forced to give up something, lose something: his salary. In Robert's mind, the Other wanted him to make the necessary sacrifice, wanted to castrate him symbolically.[60]

Second, he had had an encounter with a "suitable woman" (his sister's best friend, Sandra, an idealized feminine Other for him) who openly expressed her desire to have a relationship with him and her eagerness to have sex with him; this led to impotence on his part, clearly constituting a kind of "satisfaction crisis."

One of his primary internal conflicts revolved around a highly developed set of ideals and moral principles regarding what he should do and be—that is, a punitive superego or ego-ideal—which he wanted to live up to, yet could not act on.[61] Many obsessives strive for "the one truth," "the one true path," "the right woman," and so on, and their ideals are so lofty as to be unrealizable, no humanly possible effort seeming grand enough to constitute a genuine step in the direction of the ideal; hence, they do nothing. Robert's ideals seemed less grandiose than those expressed by certain obsessives, but the same characteristic inertia resulted from his rebellious stance toward them. He had all too clearly internalized his parents' ideals and moral values (in other words, the symbolic Other had plainly been instated), but had never made them his own. Like the parents he could never bring himself to openly rebel against, he danced around their ideals, paying them lip service yet at the same time resisting them.

A good deal of Robert's energy was tied up in that "dance," and this is what made the provocation of criticism from others so "threatening but exciting" to him. The obsessive is happy to be able to externalize the exhorting and criticizing voices in his own head, if only for a moment; the process gives him an external enemy to focus on and *brings him back to life*, so to speak, brings out his "fighting spirit" in the "will against will" Robert referred to. For the obsessive's internal conflict is so all-engrossing that it leaves little vitality for other activities—which is why the obsessive feels dead so much of the time. In Robert's case, it was only when an external authority figure could be found, whether business associate or analyst, that some verve appeared.

Robert's provocations of people he viewed as authority figures should not be confused with the *attempt to make the Other exist* that is characteristic of perversion (as we shall see in the next chapter). The law exists only too evidently in obsession, weighing the subject down and oppressing him or her. Robert had come into being as *a stance with respect to the law*, which is precisely how Lacan defines the subject in his early work.[62] Robert's provocations were designed to give him some concrete misdeed to which he could attach his ever-present guilt, guilt that no doubt went back to an Oedipal conflict leading to hatred of his father (and doubtless of his mother as well). The therapy did not go far enough to verify the wellsprings of his guilt, but it was clear that by provoking punishment, he could feel guilty for specific "crimes" carried out more or less intentionally, confess his sins, and thereby assuage his guilt, albeit temporarily.

Guilt was the dominant affect in Robert's life at the time; it was usually articulated in terms of his failure to do what he was supposed to do at work, and his more everyday failure to "make his bed," "tidy up his room," and so on.[63] Though he complained that his parents had not given him specific rules and principles, something he could argue with them about, resorting instead to criticizing him with gestures and facial expressions, certain injunctions had obviously been formulated. Indeed, one can easily see a certain hint of anality in the things Robert felt he was supposed to do, a hint that is confirmed by his characterization of his obstacle in life: "a big black boulder blocking a narrow path, the black shining a bit here and there; the boulder is roundish and thus 'rollable'—it could fall into a nearby stream and be washed downstream." Spoken after almost a year of analysis, this description also resonated with the earlier view he had expressed of me as being "like a rock"; perhaps I was, by that point in time, associated with his obstacle in life, the uncomfortable cause of his need for some kind of evacuation.[64]

As regards Robert's relations with the opposite sex, it was quite obvious that he was caught up "in the perpetual whirlwind of destroying the other" (Seminar VIII, 241), in the constant negation, neutralization, or annihilation of Woman as Other. He idealized certain women in his conscious thoughts, only to violate them in his dreams and reduce them to passive, lifeless, desireless objects, like the breast of the drunk girl being pulled down the street in his dream. Women (in his conscious thoughts) were either pure, sacrosanct, and Madonna-like—on the model of his sister (whose name contained the same first syllable as an important signifier in his religious background)—or "sluts and whores." This is the classic obsessive division,[65] and the way Robert knew that a woman was worthy of idealization followed a common obsessive schema: she had to be anOther man's woman. His own judgment regarding women was "clouded by doubt"; hence, he had to look to other men to know which woman to love. Just as his mother had probably been idealized early on, insofar as she was the Other's (his father's) wife and thus inaccessible, Robert idealized women in his entourage who were involved with men he considered to be strong and hardworking. One woman he talked about incessantly was living with a writer he was friendly with who knew how to say no when Robert tried to distract him from his writing. Such a man was a kind of father figure who could set limits.

This kind of triangle is a bit different from the hysteric's triangle. As is true of the hysteric, the obsessive's desire is also the Other's desire, but here the Other is of the same sex: Robert desired the same thing as that "manly man," the latter's desire pointing the way for his own. We might even go so far as to say that he desired "as if he were the Other man," a formulation that finds curious confirmation in a sexual fantasy that regularly accompanied Robert's masturbatory activity: "I, or *someone like me*, is penetrating a woman with an object—a pole or a dildo. I am often looking on while this happens. Sometimes it's even a mechanical device that's doing it" (emphasis added). The voyeuristic note in the fantasy contrasted markedly with Robert's concrete sexual activity, and suggested not a different diagnosis but simply the presence of "perverse traits"—in other words, traces of perversion that are almost invariably found in neurotics' fantasies.

Robert's fantasy suggests at least a twofold positioning of the subject in relation to the Other's woman: Robert is both executor (the penetrator, who, while sexually indeterminate here, should probably be understood as a father figure, since the women in these fantasies were usually the partners of such authority figures) and onlooker or witness. As executor or, indeed, executioner, he penetrates a woman who seems to be utterly passive and submissive (dead?) with a detachable, artificial erection, a phallic object that can never go limp. He is preserved thereby from both impotence and castration, and never loses himself as subject present to himself: he remains "in control." (As we shall see in a moment, when he lets go, it is as a woman.)

We may well get the sense here too that Robert established a relationship to the father figure via woman, suggesting an alternatively submissive and rebellious homoerotic tension of sorts. Fantasizing, as he did, about his male friends' women, he was, as it were, ripping off a certain jouissance right under those men's noses. The titillation of the masturbatory activity thus derived in part from his provocative stance with respect to the father figure.

There is, no doubt, yet another position Robert adopted in this fantasy: that of the woman being penetrated by one man and watched by another. This interpretation is lent credence by Robert's statement that, in the fantasy, "when the woman comes, I generally do too." In this respect, Robert *fait la femme:* he plays the part of a woman, submitting to penetration and having no apparent control over the remote-controlled situation. Jouissance happens.[66] It is independent of her will, and of his as well. It is only insofar as he plays the part of the woman here that he can relinquish control and reach orgasm.

This seems to add a hysterical note to the fantasy, and reminds us of the extent to which fantasies are like dreams: they are extremely complicated and overdetermined, and their analysis has no ascertainable endpoint. A feminized relation to a man is, nevertheless, a very common feature of obsession; it is quite visible, for example, in the Rat Man, whose sexuality was inextricably bound up with his relationship to his father. Such feminized relations seem to stem from a father-son relationship which can never be entirely free of imaginary elements that libidinize it. In other words, we may understand them as related to the father as punitive—that is, to the "obscene jouissance" that seems to accompany his enunciation of the law (see Chapter 9). Insofar as his criticism is both painful and innervating, the relationship to him (even once internalized in the form of the superego) is eroticized.

A great deal more could obviously be said about Robert's masturbatory fantasies,[67] but let us now turn to his actual relationships with women. We see that Robert made certain women into mother figures by idealizing them, rendering sexual satisfaction with them impossible (the relationships smacked too much of incest). This did not always stop him from ardently desiring them; indeed, it often made it possible for him to go on desiring them, whereas otherwise his desire would disappear due to sexual satisfaction (what Freud refers to as the "devaluation" of a partner after the sexual act). It was only with the "virtually punk" woman that he was able to pursue his sexual drives, leaving behind, to some extent, desire with all its highfalutin ideals and values. (The way in which desire, replete with such ideals, inhibits the satisfaction of the drives will be taken up in detail in Chapter 10.)

Since Robert virtually never talked about his mother (except to say that she was "underhanded" and wanted "total control"—like him, as we have seen), little can be said regarding the origin of his simultaneous desire for and aggression against women. We might speculate that he was extremely attached to her as a young child, and could not bear the greater distance she maintained between them after the birth of his younger sister. Her demands that he do certain things and not others, and that he act toward her in a respectful manner, might have been acceptable to him when he had her more exclusive attention, but perhaps grew unjustifiable and unbearable to him when he received far less. Indeed, he may well have felt that his mother preferred his younger sister to him, and forced him to care for her "as a loving older brother should." None of this, however, was in any way corroborated by Robert's still incomplete account of the major turning points in his life.

The particular challenge I faced in the treatment was that of bringing Robert to the point of formulating a question of his own—that is, of problematizing his own motives for his actions—and this was never fully achieved. His demands for me to "enlighten" him and tell him what he should do returned periodically, and even at the end of our work together he regretted that he had not learned to "push himself" as he had hoped at the outset. I never granted his demand for concrete assignments, nor did I take at face value his talk about "termination" after six weeks of therapy; I thereby refused him what he had explicitly been asking for, with the aim not of frustrating him but of opening up the space of desire. When confronted with direct demands, I skirted the issue by asking him to tell me more about a particular dream element he hadn't yet elucidated or a fantasy to which he had not yet associated, letting him know that I had been listening to him attentively and taking his words seriously. Never suggesting that his demands were "inappropriate" or "invalid," I instead offered him something else: my ear, presence, and speech, the latter in the form of punctuations and expressions of my desire that he continue to come to see me.

When he would attribute harsh views to me—as when he believed that I would be critical of his "feminine side"—I avoided defining myself as either accepting or rejecting, allowing him to continue to project his internal critique onto me and rebel against me; in this way I hoped to encourage him to relive certain affects with me in the controlled environment of the therapy setting, not in order to "let it all out" but in order to reconnect thought and affect. The connections between thought and affect are, as I indicated earlier, often dissolved or forgotten in obsession, and the obsessive must be brought to the point of, say, getting angry with the analyst for rejecting his weaknesses and then connecting this with his father's severe attitude toward him (thanks to a question or interpretation by the analyst). Repression, in Robert's case, consisted at least partly in the breaking of the association between his rebelliousness and his father's early admonitions, between his hatred of his father and the latter's disapproval (of his weaknesses and of his "feminine side," for example). The work of "destroying his father," not in effigy but in the relationship with the analyst, was initiated but not completed in the course of our work together.

The fact that Robert's demands resurfaced at different times did not mean that his desire had not at all come to the fore; it suggested that it was easier for Robert (as for all neurotics) to deal with the Other's demands than with the Other's desire, since the latter is, after all, never explicit and always open to interpretation. To have given him specific tasks would have amounted to telling him what he needed to do to be lovable in my eyes—allowing him to strive to become lovable or anathema to me—and would have spared him the more anxiety-provoking question: "What does he want of me?" If I did not berate him for coming to sessions late and without money, if I merely asked him to talk about his lapses instead of exacting punishment, there must have been something else I was looking for, something else I was wanting. But to ponder that was to throw into question the fundamental fantasy . . .

A Case of Hysteria

A thirty-seven-year-old Frenchwoman was in analytic therapy with me for about three and a half years, at a frequency of one session a week at the outset, increasing to two sessions a week by the end. She had previously been in therapy in France for about two years with someone who had never asked her to talk about her fantasies or dreams, and she had recommended therapy about six months after moving to the United States, her husband having been transferred by his company. The intensity of full-fledged analysis was not achieved until the last year of our work together, and most of the sessions were conducted face-to-face. The treatment was, in my view, by no means complete by the time she left the United States. My account here is highly selective and has been considerably condensed in the attempt to give the reader a reasonable idea of the clinical picture in a few pages; many questions have had to be completely left aside. As in the previous case, names and biographical details have been changed to protect the identity of the patient.

Jeanne (as I shall call her) initially entered therapy due to severe marital problems, culminating in her engaging in an extramarital affair and constant thoughts of divorce. She had met another man through work—her job involved planning lectures, conferences, and other events—and felt that things in her life had become explosive. A mother of two young children, holding down a full-time job, she did not feel that divorce was the best solution.

Jeanne seems to have used her first therapy as a crutch with which to keep her marriage hobbling along. Indeed, she said she "stayed with [her] husband because of that bearded psychologist" (her first therapist). The same was true of her early work with me, in which she was never willing to have more than one session a week. This seemed to allow her to vent her anger toward her husband and articulate some of her pain without ever truly rocking the boat. Only after two and a half years of therapy did she agree to two sessions a week, despite my repeated requests earlier on that she see me more often.

A good deal of family history came out in the course of Jeanne's treatment. The second of four sisters, she grew up in the French provinces, where her father and mother lived under the same roof until Jeanne was about seven (there was some question about her actual age at the time, however, since certain memories suggested that her parents stayed together only until she was around four). At about that time, her father went bankrupt, despite considerable borrowing from the mother's family. He abruptly left the country, leaving his wife and three daughters no forwarding address. The family was forced to move in with the mother's parents, and only after a year did the mother manage to locate and contact the father.

After that, Jeanne, her sisters, and their mother lived in France in near poverty and constant uncertainty. The father slowly rebuilt a business in North Africa, but sent his family little money at extremely irregular intervals. He spent quite lavishly on himself—and, as Jeanne came to realize during her analysis, on his mistresses—but allowed his family to languish. Once a year, he had the family come spend a month with him in North Africa during the summer, but always waited until the last minute to let them know when they could come.

Jeanne's memories of North Africa involved being ogled and harassed by men; she said that a man had even tried to kidnap one of her sisters in the building in which they lived. In that environment, the father continued to treat his wife and daughters as he always had: violently jealous of any male attention paid to them, extremely protective of all four of his "women," drunkenly abusive to the mother, foul-mouthed and foul-tempered. Jeanne depicted her father as domineering, explosive, and never offering a kind word. He bullied his wife, kept her at his financial mercy, vented his venomous rage at her, and cheated on her—indeed, when he was on his deathbed it came out that he even had a mistress and a daughter out of wedlock in France.

Jeanne considered herself to be her father's favorite, since she was the best of the four sisters in school. This provided one of the bases for her identification with her father, one of the only educated people in their circle. She said that her father had never hidden the fact that he wanted a son, and during sessions she occasionally slipped when speaking of herself as a young child, saying "quand j'étais petit" ("when I was little," using the masculine form of the adjective) instead of "quand j'étais petite." She was, in some sense, the son her father never had. It should be noted that only one letter separated Jeanne's real first name from a boy's name, the same letter she elided in the slip between "petite" and "petit."

Jeanne's mother vigorously criticized the father whenever he was away (that is, most of the time after Jeanne turned seven), attempting to make her daughters despise him. She was largely successful, since the daughters very often took her side and felt sympathy for her (this laid down one of the bases for Jeanne's identification with her mother). The mother tirelessly complained that the father promised money but never sent it and that she would love to get divorced but for the children. She nevertheless allowed this abusive relationship with her mostly absent husband to continue, got pregnant by him with their fourth daughter on one of the summer trips to North Africa, and stayed with him long after all the children were grown and gone. She was aware of his vicious temper, yet seemed to deliberately provoke him to harsh words and arguments.

When Jeanne was around seventeen, her father returned to France for good, uprooted the family from one part of France to another, and told Jeanne he was going to take the steps necessary to ensure her "a fine future." She waited three weeks for him to do something, during which time "he went out gallivanting." It seems that she first began to masturbate at this time (at least, this was the only period during which she remembered having masturbated).

He finally took some initiative and, twisting a few arms, enrolled her in the business school he himself had formerly attended. He knew full well that she preferred art and had no interest whatsoever in business, but he insisted that she would never succeed as an artist. Jeanne moved to the town where the business school was located, but she never studied, spending instead "the whole first year with a boyfriend." She visited her family from time to time, but her father never gave her the money that he promised. Consequently, she was often in trouble with the bank and with her landlord because she could not pay her bills on time. Once, when she was driving somewhere with her father at the age of eighteen, she went so far as to jump out of the moving car in protest of his callous attitude.

The father made terrible scenes whenever his teenage daughters began to date anyone. Jeanne recalled a memorable occasion at a hotel in North Africa where her older sister, who had met a boy there, was called a whore by the father in front of a great many people. He would rant and rave, use extremely foul language, and publicly humiliate all of his daughters.

Jeanne said that, as a teenager, she was uninterested in most of the boys who were interested in her; their love was worth nothing as it was so easy to win, and it did nothing for her—it did not arouse her interest in them. She was merely flattered, and "enjoyed jerking them around." There was one boy who managed to inspire great passion in her for a while, until the day he declared his love for her in a letter. She claimed that, from the moment she read the letter, she was no longer interested in him. But she was immediately attracted to a man I will refer to as Bertrand, the first man her own age who treated her more indifferently, more callously. *That* turned her on.

A struggle for the upper hand ensued between her and Bertrand in a tempestuous relationship that turned into marriage. If they were fighting and she wanted to leave the house, Bertrand would physically block the door; if she was mad at him and left town, he would call everyone they knew until he found her and then come and get her. He eventually gained the upper hand, according to Jeanne, and, when he did, her initial passion turned to revulsion: she could no longer bear to let him touch her. She began to suspect him of all kinds of things of which her father had been guilty, such as womanizing and spending all of the family's money on himself. She dreamed of leaving him but never did, claiming that it was "impossible" for her to do so.

Physical symptoms began to appear, some of which seemed to have antecedents in adolescence, but many of which seemed to grow out of her identifying her husband with her father (aided, no doubt, by the fact that the husband and the father got along well). She spoke of back pains, shoulder pains, jaw pains, tongue pains, chest pains, throat pains, and stomach pains, and went from gastroenterologist to chiropractor to herbal healer to acupuncturist, all to no avail.

Right from the beginning of Jeanne's therapy with me, the primary conflict seemed to revolve around her father and husband. Nevertheless, she devoted a good deal of time in early sessions to recounting rivalries with her eldest sister, whom she had often made fun of as a child and apparently outshined. Rivalrous identifications with her sisters were largely worked through within a year or so, it seemed, and receded into the background. The father/husband then monopolized her thoughts. Transferentially speaking, she never seemed to place me in the position of an other (person) like herself, despite the fact that we were very close in age; indeed, her imaginary relations seemed more or less confined to women. From the outset, I seemed to be identified with the one who knows: the symbolic Other. Virtually none of the anger or recriminations expressed toward her father during the sessions, or even later toward her mother, was reflected in her transferential attitude toward me; only occasional elements in dreams ever suggested possible anger toward me. A sort of good-father (me) bad-father (Bertrand) dialectic evolved that did little to accelerate our progress.

An important turning point came when, after two and a half years of my urging, Jeanne agreed to shift to two sessions a week. Her willingness to do so was no doubt overdetermined: her husband was away on business more and more, and, according to Jeanne, he was the one who opposed her seeing me (he did not believe in psychotherapy and did not wish to spend money on it); they had become somewhat more affluent, and Jeanne perhaps felt she could more easily hide the extra expenditure from her husband; and, perhaps most important, her symptoms had become more oppressive. The first two reasons were lent support by the fact that when her husband finally examined the family accounts eight months later, he made a big scene about her seeing me twice a week, and she went back to once a week, not being willing to challenge or disobey her husband on this point. Perhaps she had been willing to risk h wrath only when her suffering was most acute.

The intensification of her troubles was marked by the appearance of a new symptom: when her husband was away, she occasionally started feeling cold all over, so cold that taking a hot bath could not warm her up. It was her associations to this symptom, verbalized very quickly after the resumption of the therapy after a summer break, that tied together much of the unconscious material elicited over the years and that evoked a sort of "primal scene."

The feeling of coldness she was experiencing preceded the recollection of a scene presumably witnessed at the age of seven or eight; she seemed thus to be re-experiencing something that she could not at first remember.[68] In North Africa, her bedroom (which she shared with her older sister) adjoined her parents' bedroom. There was a door between the two rooms, but it was always kept closed. Her bedroom there was the scene of many dreams she had during the course of her analysis, and it became clear to Jeanne that she had often overheard her parents arguing in their bedroom.

She could easily talk about their fights, and said that she often "held her breath, trying to stop breathing, in order to listen," in order to hear what was going on in the next room. Often she could not go to sleep "until *it* was over," and "had to stay very still in order to hear *it*." She seemed very close to saying what that *it* was on numerous occasions, but circled around it every time as if she were unable to speak it. On one such occasion, after she had said that she would listen during their fights until *it* was over, I added a few words to the effect that her parents would end up making love.

This was obviously a construction on my part ("construction" in the sense found in Freud's article "Constructions in Analysis," SE XXIII, 257–269), a construction based on years of listening to Jeanne's discourse about her parents' tempestuous relationship. I cannot affirm with certainty that Jeanne had been conscious or preconscious all along of the thoughts she expressed after this intervention and had simply been loath to speak them; for it is also possible that my intervention led to a reconstruction of childhood scenes that she had never quite understood.[69] In any case, it led almost immediately to her saying that she believed she had heard her parents conceive her youngest sister, born nine months after their first summer trip to North Africa. During the next session, she told me that, one night in North Africa, she had gone out into the hall, where the ceramic floor tiles had felt *cold* under her feet. The door to her parents' bedroom had been ajar and she had looked in and seen her "father on top of [her] mother, his penis erect." According to her, she had been shocked, horrified, and disgusted.

The nocturnal feelings of coldness went away after she recounted the scene to me, and another symptom—tightness or pain in the chest—went away when she added another detail: from the angle from which she had observed the scene, it looked as if her "father had his knee on her [mother's] torso."

When listening to her parents' arguments and lovemaking from her room, Jeanne would not only try to stop breathing (the better to hear)—she would also tense up or stiffen, as if to protect herself against the expected blows (verbal and/or physical), to protect herself from being "wounded." In a sense, she put herself in her mother's shoes, imagining herself being beaten and made love to by her father. Many of her back, shoulder, and neck pains seemed clearly related to this stiffening while listening, but our work together did not go far enough to elucidate all of the material necessary to alleviate them entirely.

Although Jeanne devoted the first years of her therapy to detailing her father's atrocious behavior, her mother's role was only occasionally thrown into question. Her mother was at that time depicted as a victim, purely and simply; she had made a mistake marrying such a man, but had attempted to make the best of it "for the children's sake." During the last year of the therapy, however, Jeanne turned her attention to her mother's less obvious motives.

Her mother was now described as passive and self-indulgent, and as having made her daughters do all the housework. She was viewed as being interested only in her friends, and as having deliberately attempted to make her daughter despise the father. Though this attempt forced Jeanne to cover over her fonder feelings for her father and to hate him in certain respects, it also convinced her that her father was in some sense being victimized by the mother and was thus unloved. Jeanne recalled that her mother had loved dancing with men: indeed, Jeanne said her mother loved "all men except my father." Jeanne claimed that she herself was the exact opposite: she had "never loved any man except [her] father." She began to hate her mother for having *prohibited* her from loving her father, or at least from feeling it, being aware of it, and showing it.

Jeanne had nevertheless remained faithful to her father at some level, convinced that he really did love her even though he never expressed it, "never knew how to express it." In her everyday life, she had remained faithful to everything he said: he had told her she would never amount to anything, and so she sabotaged things in such a way as to fulfill his prophecies. For example, in her mid-thirties she began painting, drawing, and making ceramics—activities she had not engaged in since high school—and was often complimented on her talent. After a small exhibition of her work, she began having problems associated with her eyesight *(la vue)*[70] and associated them with her father's predictions: if she could not see well, she could not paint and thus could never amount to anything. He said that her life would be a disaster, and she felt she unwittingly confirmed this. For to succeed in life was to betray him, not just outwardly but inwardly as well.

Thus, in the course of Jeanne's analysis, there was an almost complete reversal of perspective. At first, she viewed her father as the cause of all of her problems in life, while solidarity with her mother seemed virtually complete. Later she came to see her father as her one true love and her mother as the villain. Jeanne proceeded to kill her mother in a dream, and began to think that her own daughter, who was then about thirteen, wanted her dead. Jeanne began to blame her mother for all kinds of things. For example, the mother would leave her daughters home alone in North Africa when she went out with girlfriends, warning them "not to breathe in her absence"; she would criticize her daughters' grades but do nothing to help them; she was "gratuitously mean to her daughters."

Jeanne also recalled that her mother would bring her daughters to a park in North Africa, and would talk absorbedly with a friend while her daughters wandered about the park unsupervised; on one occasion, Jeanne and her older sister had been led into a storeroom by a park guardian, who had proceeded to show them his penis. Jeanne complained that she had not been protected by her mother. (Indeed, within several months Jeanne said that the only thing her mother had ever done for her daughters was to stay with her "infernal husband.") The father was "insanely" overprotective, but at least he was protective.

In the course of this return to the father, Jeanne recounted a dream in which it seemed that she would rather imperil herself, following her father up a narrow, windy mountain path, than "passer par la mer/mère," "follow the path near the sea/mother" (*mer*, "sea," is pronounced exactly like *mère*, "mother"). The father might be dangerous, but the mother was worse. In another dream, Jeanne saw her own "two children in the sea *(mer/mère)*, and a big wave came toward them and engulfed them. They were okay and washed up on shore." According to her, the wave was her father, a tidal wave smashing everything before it, even Jeanne's mother *(mère)*, for the children were swept away from the sea up onto the shore, where they were safe. He saved the children, and thus Jeanne had them or was allowed to keep them thanks to him; in that sense "they were his." Her own father was thus, in some fantasmatic sense, the father of her children.

In yet another dream, she had "three new children—boys, all with brown eyes. At first it's not entirely clear if the third is a boy, but seems to be one in the end." In her associations to the dream, "brown," which at first elicited nothing, reminded her that she had recently seen a picture of her father's illegitimate daughter; the latter had brown eyes, like Jeanne's father. She said that the children in the dream could not be her husband's, since he had blue eyes . . .

She had thus remained eternally faithful to her father, despite everything,[71] and her relations with her husband suggested continued fidelity to her father. Though she had become aware that she tended to project paternal faults onto her husband, this was still a dominant theme in their relationship. In one instance, while he was away on business, she found some credit card bills and became enraged when she saw the huge expenditures he was making. It turned out that they were all business expenses reimbursed by his company, but she had immediately equated her husband (whom she sometimes described as a devoted family man) with her freewheeling, inconsiderate, spendthrift father.

In her own marriage, Jeanne viewed herself as like her mother: abandoned (though she was not), cheated on (though this was by no means clear to her), and so on. In short, her husband was identified in her mind with her father, and she saw herself in her mother's shoes (that is, she was her father's wife), though at the same time she viewed herself as her father's son.

Her therapy with me ended when her husband was once again transferred by his company, and she returned with her family to France. I obtained the name and phone number of an analyst in the town in France to which she moved, and encouraged her to continue the work we had begun.

This brief presentation of Jeanne's therapy, incomplete though it is, illustrates certain important characteristics of hysteria.

To begin with, Jeanne's whole way of talking about herself and her life involved other people—significant others. Her discourse contrasted sharply with Robert's discourse, which revolved almost exclusively around himself, an obsessive wrapped up in his own world and viewing himself as an island unto himself. Jeanne's world was peopled, and Jeanne defined herself in relation to people.

Jeanne's fundamental stance was that of completing the Other: becoming the son her father never had; becoming a faithful wife to her father, since his wife betrayed him by preferring the company of all other men to his (when dancing, in particular); and even becoming a kind of husband substitute for her mother when her mother tirelessly complained, in the early years after her husband left the country, of being abandoned and ill-treated by her husband. In the latter case, Jeanne tried to "give [her] mother what [her] father didn't give her," to make her life as easy and happy as possible, do many of the household chores, impose on her mother as little as possible, and perhaps even eat very little to save her mother money. Jeanne sought to detect what it was the significant Other in her life wanted, lacked, or was missing, and to become it.

Her sexual position was perhaps even more complex than Robert's, which was already multilayered. She identified with her mother, but with her father as well. In her marriage, she was an abandoned, mistreated, and misunderstood woman like her mother. In her many psychosomatic symptoms, she put herself in the place of her mother being abused and made love to by the father. In a certain sense, she viewed herself as the faithful wife her father never had, yet simultaneously as the son he never had (she described herself as a tomboy, "un garçon manqué"). She was like the father intellectually, considered herself strong-willed and stubborn like him, and cast herself in a masculine role in certain dreams and slips. In recounting one dream, for example, she slipped and said that "a number of men were falling in love with [her]," but instead of saying amoureux ("in love"), she said amoureuses, using the feminine form of the adjective. The slip turned the men into women,[72] reflecting, it seems to me, the fact that she was putting herself in the place of a man like her father, the seducer, the one who had "women falling all over him."

Jeanne's sexual identity was thus partly based on her mother and partly on her father—conventionally speaking, it was partly feminine and partly masculine.[73] Her sexuality, which remained largely unelucidated, seemed to be dominated by disgust, revulsion, and the refusal of direct, physical, sexual satisfaction; as an adult, she said that she almost never accepted her husband's overtures, never masturbated, and had had but one fleeting affair. Even the early tempestuous period with her husband seemed, according to her descriptions, to have been characterized by the passion of desire growing out of a (very serious) game of seduction and power struggle, rather than by the fulfillment of some corporal longing or lust of her own. Indeed, it seemed that, for her, sex was no more than a weapon in the battle with Bertrand. The very idea of sexual activity (with a man) evoked, in her discourse, every imaginable metaphor from the realm of food and digestion: it was "disgusting," "revolting," "nauseating," "sickening," and so on. In one dream, for example, her husband refused *her* sexual advances; in her associations to the dream, it seemed that being turned down, and thus being able to go on wanting, excited her more than sexuality itself. The dream thus seemed to fulfill her desire for an unsatisfied desire.[74]

In another dream she slept with one of her husband's friends, who, she had just heard, had cheated on his wife. She found the man disgusting in real life, but dreamed of "sleeping with him" (there seemed to be no representation in the dream of the sexual act itself). It seemed that she had, in the dream, put herself in the position of the mistress with whom a man might cheat on his wife, with whom a man like her husband might be unfaithful. She was interested in knowing why a man might cheat on his wife—"How can another woman be loved?" as Lacan formulates the question of the butcher's wife in *Ecrits* (626). She put herself in the shoes of the other woman and imagined the man's desire for her. Though she did not explicitly evoke her identification with her father (or, more generally, men) in her associations to this dream, there may also have been a sense in which she saw herself in her husband's friend, and imagined what it would be like to sleep with the other woman (a role she herself played in the manifest content of the dream).[75] This is an example of what I referred to earlier as the hysteric's complex "circuit of desire."

Jeanne closely scrutinized her husband's desire in the attempt to detect an interest in other women. Though he had, according to her, apparently been faithful throughout their fourteen years of marriage, she could not stop herself from imagining that he was having an affair with someone whenever he was away on business, and she was always on the lookout for clues. She would not hesitate to go through his personal effects, papers, and records, or call him at all hours at his various hotels; consciously "afraid" he was cheating on her, she nevertheless seemed to wish to discern a desire on his part for another woman.

Such a wish would, of course, have been overdetermined: were he to be having an affair, this would confirm her sense of being abandoned like her mother by a man like her father; but it would also provide a new possible circuit for her desire via the other woman. Recounting one of her dreams, Jeanne said, "Bertrand has a mistress; I catch him on the phone with her red-handed saying 'I love you.' I say to myself, 'Now I can get divorced, now I have the necessary proof. But I cannot. He will stop me from leaving!'" At least one level of interpretation of the dream elicited the idea that his desire for another was enraging, yet somehow seemed necessary to her.

The jealous scenes Jeanne made based on her suspicions appeared to have kept her husband's desire alive, in certain respects; the passionate struggle between them had never completely subsided. She perhaps also kept his desire in play (not necessarily deliberately) by frustrating most of his demands—demands that she take care of certain household business in his absence (cleaning, organizing, bill paying, and so on) and demands for sex. Seeking to be the cause of his desire, she nevertheless refused to *satisfy* his desire, refused to be the object of his sexual satisfaction. Unsatisfied desire is found on both sides in hysteria—in the hysteric and the partner. The hysteric keeps her partner unsatisfied, since it is the partner's desire that is so important to her in defining her being. Jeanne seemed to sense that if she allowed her husband to satisfy his sexual urges with her, his lack or desire would at least temporarily disappear.

Nevertheless, after three years of analysis Jeanne said she was "sick of [her] own behavior"—sick of refusing to have sex with Bertrand and being aggressive with him all the time. It seemed that, in denying herself what she wanted, she was doing so at least partly out of "solidarity" with her mother. For Jeanne's mother had repeatedly told Jeanne that all other couples were happy and united; only Jeanne's mother and father were not. By getting married yet preventing solidarity with her husband, Jeanne seemed to identify with her mother at the level of dissatisfaction, lack of satisfaction, or unhappiness.

Corroborating Jeanne's identification with her mother at this level was one of Jeanne's long-standing psychosomatic symptoms. She had developed a problem with the sciatic nerve after her father had thrown a memorable jealous fit when her mother had received anonymous flowers from someone at Christmastime. The father was convinced they had been sent by the mother's employer, a male chiropractor he believed she must be having an affair with (in fact, they had been sent by an aunt). Ever since then, Jeanne had frequently gone to chiropractors for pains related to the sciatic nerve—a problem her mother had described to her—and a whole variety of other complaints. She would fall "ill" so that she would have to come into contact with the kind of man her mother (according to her father) desired, even though that desire had never been fulfilled. The chiropractor had, in a sense,

come to represent her mother's unsatisfied longing for a different man, perhaps a better man (the chiropractor had also become associated with her
father's upsetting yet thrilling, annoying yet stimulating, jealous rage).

By stating that she was "sick of [her] own behavior," Jeanne nevertheless
suggested that *she was not satisfied with unsatisfied desire*—in other words, that
desire was not the whole story. "Woman does not live by desire alone," she
seemed to be saying, suggesting that she was not uninterested in satisfaction
at every level. At what level was she interested? While certain hysterics play
the game of desire with men but satisfy their sexual drives with women, no
homosexual current ever clearly manifested itself in our work together. But
another current showed itself when, after seeing the film *Indecent Proposal*,
starring Robert Redford, Jeanne had a dream which she recounted as follows:
"Bertrand agreed to do something in order to make $450 million. Though
worried about making money dishonestly, I eventually said okay." Jeanne
commented that, in the movie, a man agreed to let his wife sleep with Robert
Redford for a considerable sum of money. Jeanne said she disliked the idea of
making money in any sort of "dishonest way" ("de manière malhonnête"), but
her choice of words suggested something a bit different, since *malhonnête* can
also be heard as *mâle-honnête*, an "honest male."[76] There was perhaps something about "an honest to goodness male" like Robert Redford that could
make her turn a blind eye to certain scruples (that is, inhibitions); but she also
said she had the sense that "it would be impossible for [her] to refuse to help
her husband out for such a large sum."

Rather than immediately interpreting this as some sort of profound desire
on her part to become a prostitute—that is, to receive money for sex—we
should see in it a very general characteristic of hysteria: the inhibitions blocking sexuality must be overcome by a powerful force, often outright coercion,
in order for sexual satisfaction to be considered something other than reprehensible. Uninhibited sexual enjoyment seems possible only when forced
or obligatory—when it is beyond one's power to stop it. If prostitution fantasies arise so often in analysis with hysterics, it is because prostitution is
commonly associated in the public mind with utter destitution and compulsion—for example, an abandoned mother must walk the streets in order to
feed her children; or a young woman with no education, from an extremely
poor but honest background, must sell her body because she has younger
brothers and sisters to feed and invalid parents to care for.[77] We find a similar
motive at work in the rape fantasies that are so common among hysterics,
the essential idea being that *the woman has no choice but to engage in sexual
activity.*

This suggests that the part played by inhibitions in hysteria is extremely important. In Jeanne's case, we see that some of the inhibitions were related to solidarity with her mother. To actually enjoy sex (and not simply obtain jouissance from her conversion symptoms, associated with her mother's sexual activity) would be to betray her mother. The question of betrayal, whether it involves one's mother or father, is always a question of values, principles, and ideals—in other words, of the ego-ideal or superego. Although Jeanne may not seem to have been driven by impossible ideals in the way Robert was, contradictory ideals were nevertheless very much present in her mind: what she had been told a woman was supposed to be, what she, as her father's "son," was supposed to accomplish, and what she, as her mother's daughter, was responsible for giving her mother and could later expect from marriage.

Freud tends to view revulsion toward sexuality as virtually structural or a priori in hysteria, and the ego-ideal as far more developed in men than in women; but we might do better to consider revulsion as the *product* of a more typically feminine ego-ideal (typical for Western culture), and guilt as the product of a more typically masculine ego-ideal. For revulsion and guilt seem to be attitudes toward the satisfaction of the drives, attitudes that are imposed on us in the course of socialization; in other words, they are stances adopted at the symbolic level (that of ideals, values, and principles)—at the level of desire—with respect to the satisfaction of the drives. They are not necessarily characteristics of the drives themselves.[78] Freud seems to be misled into viewing women as having less highly developed ego-ideals because his notion of what constitutes an ideal is overly narrow: it includes only widely accepted social, economic, political, intellectual, and artistic ideals—the kinds of ideals hitherto inculcated primarily in men in Western societies. But an ideal is any kind of articulated entreaty or injunction which may be universalizable (for example, "A daughter is always respectful toward her mother") or may not be (for example, "Your father treats us all like dirt! All we have is each other, so we must band together"). The weight of particular, context-specific entreaties may be just as great as, if not greater than, that of more universalizable value judgments like "These days, you have to go to college if you expect to be anyone." A useful rule of thumb might be: "If it produces inhibitions, it's an ideal."[79]

It should be further noted that the structural difference between hysteria and obsession—in the former, the overcoming of separation through completion of the Other, and, in the latter, through completion of the subject—is grounded in social and sexual ideals, many of which are not terribly difficult to divine. Hysteria and obsession are "structures" that, in a Western societal context, constitute a sort of great divide in subjective positions, but they are not universal, transcendental necessities. They are contingent structures based on a particular (but quite widespread) form of society.

Turning now to the treatment, I wish to comment briefly on a particular intervention I made, the one I qualified earlier as a "construction." As I said, I cannot be sure that Jeanne had been conscious or preconscious all along of what she said after my intervention, and had simply been loath to say it; my impression, in fact, was that the intervention led to a reconstruction of scenes from the past that she had never quite understood. If this is the case, the intervention would constitute an example of interpretation "hitting the real" (as discussed in Chapter 4). The real is that which has not yet been symbolized, not yet put into words; it is what, at a certain moment, is unspeakable (the "impossible to say") for the analysand but not necessarily for the analyst. By naming what Jeanne had heard and seen as a young child, prior (apparently) to having learned about sex, I began the process of neutralizing it—that is, draining away its heavy affective charge—through symbolization. As long as it remained unspeakable, it fixated her. Once spoken, the fixation began to give way.

Insofar as interpretation hits the real, *it does not so much hit the truth as create it.* For truth exists only within language (it is a property of statements), and thus there is no truth of that which cannot yet be said. Truth is not so much "found" or "uncovered" by interpretation, as created by it. This does not mean that interpretation is free to invent as it pleases; the approach I adopted with Jeanne, listening to her attentively for two and a half years once a week prior to venturing such an interpretation, contrasts sharply with the "wild interpretations" made by so many psychologists and psychiatrists nowadays based on a ten-minute conversation or a handful of sessions with a patient. Jeanne had done everything but say what I said, circling around the notion in several sessions, and was obviously prepared to hear it.

Consider the difference between the subjective validity of such a construction for Jeanne, witnessed by the material she brought forward in the sessions that followed it, and the effect of an interpretation made by a psychiatrist with whom I am acquainted. A patient, who had been in therapy for two years with a psychologist I supervise, saw this psychiatrist every few months regarding his medication. On one occasion, the patient mentioned that he had suddenly recalled that he had been sexually abused three times as a child; the psychiatrist seized the opportunity to say, "You must have enjoyed it." The patient was quite shaken by the interpretation and almost left therapy altogether because of it.

One might argue that, based on psychoanalytic theory, what the psychiatrist said was true in numerous cases, since many people enjoy such sexual experiences in some, perhaps not so obvious, way; but it completely ignored the experience of the individual in question, and had little or no subjective validity for him. If *interpretation creates truth*, the ground has to be prepared for it (as for a plant, if we expect it to take root and grow): the surrounding material has to be elucidated and the relationship with the therapist has to be solid. Otherwise it has no more than shock value (at best). Shocking statements may be appropriate at times in teaching, if one's aim is to shake students out of their habitual ways of thinking, but they have little place in therapy.[80]

As I indicated in Chapter 4, the kind of interpretation I made with Jeanne, which is not "oracular" in nature—not ambiguous, polyvalent, or essentially evocative—should be reserved for a relatively advanced stage of an analysis, when the analyst's knowledge of the analysand is quite extensive and the analysand is quite open to the effect of the analyst's interpretation. Such interpretation provides a particularly clear illustration of what Lacan means when he says that interpretation is "apophantic" (*Scilicet* 4 [1973]: 30). "Apophantic" (from the Greek *apophantikos*) means "categorical," "declarative," or "assertive." Interpretation, in Lacan's sense, whether oracular in nature or a construction, is not presented in the form of a question or as possibly being true; it is declaratively stated by the analyst.

Jeanne's treatment was obviously far from complete by the time she returned to France. While Jeanne had begun to blame her father and mother somewhat less for her problems, she had by no means separated from them; at some level, she still sided with her mother against her father, simultaneously remaining faithful to her father by fulfilling his prophecies (that she would amount to nothing, for example). The therapy never attained the intensity necessary to "destroy" these parental figures—in other words, the power of their prohibitions and ideals that led to Jeanne's inhibitions—through the transference. Jeanne remained loath to become "overly dependent" on me, and I was unable to intrigue her sufficiently to overcome both her own resistances and her husband's. Though the frequency of sessions finally increased in the last year, the scene Bertrand made when he discovered that she was seeing me twice a week put an end to the greater intensity of our work together.[81] Jeanne felt she could not oppose him on this point.

Jeanne had begun to glimpse the sense in which she had made choices and adopted stances toward her parents—even if it seemed, at the outset, that her position had simply been thrust upon her—but had not yet been able to affirm that she had done so because of what *she* had wanted at the time. Subjectification—the process of bringing the subject into being where the Other is considered the responsible party—thus was not fully achieved. Although in certain respects she moved away from her father's ideals—for example, in her last year of therapy, Jeanne rekindled her long-stifled passion for art, which her father heartily disapproved of—she felt that he nevertheless continued to interfere in her pursuit of recognition as an artist. His values continued to inhibit her: she had not yet come into being as subject where his values had been—they had neither been destroyed nor become her own. She was held in limbo, suspended between rejecting his ideals and punishing herself for rejecting them.

Prior to Jeanne's analysis, her love for her father had been repressed, and this repression was evident in the extreme hatred she relentlessly expressed toward him. Her hatred was—as analytic theory would lead us to expect—directly proportionate to his importance to her, to the love she felt for him. The hatred represented *the return of the repressed* in a disguised manner, here in the form of a simple inversion, hate appearing in the place of love. Similarly, prior to her analysis, her repressed anger toward her mother manifested itself (in other words, returned) in the form of an exaggerated belief in her mother's saintliness and perfection. Although these repressions lifted in the course of her analysis, her repressed Oedipal longing to take her mother's place as the object beaten and made love to by the father—a longing that was fueling most of her somatic symptoms (for in those symptoms, she put herself in her mother's shoes)—remained barely broached, touched upon only in a few dreams (for example, that of the whale with the long trunk). Her fundamental fantasy seems to have been to be the object that is abused and made love to by a man like her father. While that fantasy came into view in the course of her analysis, it was far from reconfigured or traversed.

Etiological Considerations

The two preceding case studies have provided concrete illustrations of many of the facets of neurosis discussed in this chapter, and have, I hope, given the reader a clearer sense of what "modern-day" obsession and hysteria may look like in individual cases. There is no "pure" case of obsession, free of hysterical or perverse features, just as there is no "pure" case of hysteria. Each case confirms certain things we have already learned about neurosis and, if we are open to hearing what is not yet explicable within a particular theoretical system, teaches us new things as well. Robert's case brought out something that may turn out to be of general value—the importance of the Other man's woman—and Jeanne's history shed light on the why and wherefore of her revulsion, perhaps suggesting something about the origins of revulsion and guilt in the first place. As Lacan says, "The most particular cases are those whose value is the most universal" (Seminar VI, February 11, 1959).

The following table summarizes what I have been referring to thus far as the "defining characteristics" of hysteria and obsession.

	Hysteria	Obsession
Question	"Am I a man or a woman?"	"Am I dead or alive?"
Status of desire	Unsatisfied	Impossible
Stance toward sexuality	Revulsion	Guilt
Primary zone affected	Oral	Anal
Strategy with respect to being	Being the cause of the Other's desire	Being in thinking
Strategy for overcoming separation	Complete the Other	Complete the subject
Fundamental fantasy	$(a \lozenge \cancel{A})$	$(S \lozenge a)$

It should be quite clear that these "defining characteristics" are not etiological in nature; I have not sought to answer here the question of *why* someone becomes hysteric or obsessive (except parenthetically in my commentaries on the preceding cases), confining my attention to the *what* of hysteria and obsession. I have sought to use Lacan's most far-reaching distinctions to indicate what hysteria and obsession are and how they differ from each other.

Freud was clearly seeking etiological definitions at an early stage in his work. In his letters to Fliess, Freud hypothesizes that obsession is *caused* by an early sexual experience resulting in too much pleasure (and a subsequent feeling of guilt, which in turn leads to avoidance behavior—guilt and avoidance being later understood as the retroactive effects of a second experience in which the person learned the social/sexual meaning of the first event). Freud was seeking to explain *why* a particular person became an obsessive, and his early "definitions" concern "first causes." But even in the case of Freud's causal explanations, one can always ask why: "Why did one person experience too much pleasure, and another too little?" To explain this by saying that the former was imbued with an excessive desire for his or her "seducer," whereas the latter had too little or was disgusted by him or her, merely allows us to repeat the question at one remove: "Why an excessive desire?[82] Why too much desire in one case and too little in another?"

What seems most important in Freud's characterizations is the fact that clinicians are, indeed, presented with patients whose sexuality is dominated in one case by guilt, and in another by revulsion. Not that guilt never appears alongside revulsion, but in the overall clinical picture one or the other tends to predominate.

Lacan does not share Freud's concern with first causes, devoting his attention to logical processes instead. Since repression is the main mechanism in neurosis, repression must lead to different results in the different cases. If repression means that the subject becomes split into conscious and unconscious (that is, ego and subject) at a certain moment—not necessarily chronometrically definable—the split must occur somewhat differently in obsession and hysteria (the obsessive and the hysteric are "alienated" differently). Since it is signifiers that are repressed, differential splitting implies that the hysteric and the obsessive have different relations to language, and different relations to knowledge.

But such considerations do not tell us *why* repression or splitting takes one form in hysteria and another in obsession, or why one person becomes hysteric and another obsessive. They do not explain (as I tried to with my social-psychological explanation in an earlier footnote) why one person comes to negate the Other and another doesn't. Freud, with his well-known dictum "Anatomy is destiny," seems to suggest that it all depends on whether one has a penis or not: when you have it you cannot *be* it (that is, be the phallic object of desire for the Other); when you do not, you can embody it for the Other. Lacan repeats such Freudian formulations in his early work (for instance, "Intervention on Transference," from 1951), but problematizes such a schematization in his later work. His later discussions—revolving around the fact that in Western culture there is no signifier for Woman, whereas the phallus is the signifier for Man—take us further into the *dialectic* between anatomy and language, where biology does not have the last word. I cannot go into such a discussion now, however, as it would take us into complex questions about the nature of language that I have not laid the groundwork for here.[83]

Another question that is beyond the scope of this chapter concerns the possible social causes of two such highly distinct structures as hysteria and obsession. I have not in any way suggested here that these structures correspond to the way things should be. Lacan would not, I suspect, have considered these structures to be universal; rather, he would have seen them as dependent on a certain typically Western organization of society wherein the phallus is the predominant signifier of desire. All efforts to change women's and men's roles notwithstanding, as long as the phallus remains the signifier of desire, these different structures seem unlikely to disappear. If we look only at the different kinds of ideals at work in obsession and hysteria and the different ways in which they are inculcated in a specific family context (as I did in my commentary on Jeanne's inhibitions in sexual matters), we leave unanswered the larger social questions Lacan also attempts to address.

Phobia

The mainspring and the reason for phobia is not, as those who have but the word "fear" on their lips believe, a genital or even a narcissistic danger. What the subject is afraid of encountering is a certain sort of desire—linked to certain privileged developments in the subject's position vis-à-vis the Other, as is the case in little Hans' relationship to his mother—that would immediately make all signifying creation, the whole signifying system, fall back still further into nothingness.

—Lacan, Seminar VIII, 305

Before moving on to perversion, we must say a few words about phobia. While Lacan sometimes considers phobia to be a separate diagnostic category, it represents, according to him, "the most *radical* form of neurosis" (Seminar VIII, 425), in the sense that it is a response to a problem with the establishment of the paternal metaphor. In other words, phobia is not so much "in between" hysteria and obsession or a third independent structure, as in some sense prior to the other neuroses.[84] Whereas hysteria and obsession presuppose the instating of the paternal metaphor (and thus of primal and secondary repression), the phobic is able to instate the paternal metaphor only by canceling out the mother with something other than the father's "No!" or name.

The child's separation from its mother is rendered extremely difficult in phobia, due to the relative weakness of the father or father figure—that is, of the paternal function. Lacan shows, for example, that in Freud's well-known case of "little Hans" (SE X, 1–149), the refusal by Hans' father to separate his son from the boy's mother leads to a build-up of anxiety in his son; Hans' anxiety is clearly related to his mother and to the desires he attributes to her (engulfment, incorporation, and so on). The development of Hans' phobia coincides with an abrupt decrease in anxiety: the latter is bound temporarily when Hans takes the signifier "horse" as a sort of father substitute (a stand-in for the father, for the father's name or "No!" in the paternal metaphor; see Seminar IV).[85]

Phobia can thus be viewed as a strategy that the individual adopts in order to *shore up* a crucial element of the Other (this element being the Name-of-the-Father) which, though not altogether lacking, has a precarious status. Phobia cannot be situated on the "borderline" between psychosis and neurosis, for it is *a successful shoring-up:* it successfully instates the paternal metaphor. It allows "ordinary repression" to operate—that is, secondary repression and the return of the repressed. It does not, it seems, have a full set of defining characteristics of its own, like those provided in the table above summarizing the essential characteristics of hysteria and obsession.

Rather, phobia appears to be closely related to hysteria, since the hysteric constitutes herself initially as the object suitable for plugging up the lack in the mOther. Through triangulation (the intervention of the Name-of-the-Father), the hysteric is able to go beyond constituting herself as the imaginary object of the mOther's desire, to constitute herself as the "symbolic object" of the Other's (usually the father's) desire.[86] The phobic, though initially an imaginary object for the mOther, has to prop up the Name-of-the-Father. As we shall see, this suggests certain affinities between phobia and perversion, though one should keep in mind that the phobic's propping-up is successful, supplying a kind of permanence that the pervert's attempted propping-up is unable to supply.[87]

9

PERVERSION

Desire is a defense, a defense against going beyond a limit in jouissance.

—Lacan, *Ecrits*, 825/322

Most clinicians do not see many patients who can accurately be qualified as perverts, psychoanalytically speaking. A number of contemporary American analysts seem to believe that perverts in therapy are a dime a dozen, but when evaluated in terms of the Lacanian criteria I have been presenting in this book, the vast majority of the people commonly referred to as perverts in fact turn out to be neurotics or psychotics.[1] Modern psychiatry, for its part, has not in any way expanded our understanding of perversion. Doing what Freud tells us it does best, giving new "names to different [behaviors] but saying nothing further about them" (SE XVI, 260), psychiatry has simply provided a panoply of new terms to describe the particular objects that turn people on: pedophilia, frotteurism, toucherism, transvestic fetishism, and so on.[2]

Lacan, in contrast, is able to help us better understand the nature of perversion with his crucial distinctions between the imaginary, the symbolic, and the real, and between desire and jouissance. If neurosis can be understood as a set of strategies by which people protest against a "definitive" sacrifice of jouissance—castration—imposed upon them by their parents (attempting to recover some modicum of jouissance in a disguised manner) and come to desire in relation to the law, *perversion involves the attempt to prop up the law so that limits can be set to jouissance* (to what Lacan calls "the will to jouissance"). Whereas we see an utter and complete absence of the law in psychosis, and a definitive instatement of the law in neurosis (overcome only in fantasy), in perversion the subject struggles to bring the law into being—in a word, to make the Other exist. As usual, Lacan's work here grows out of Freud's, and thus I shall begin my discussion of perversion here by taking up some of Freud's distinctions.

The Core of Human Sexuality

If we begin with Freud's early assertion that any sexual activity engaged in for a purpose other than that of reproduction is perverse, then we have to accept the fact that the vast majority of human sexual behavior is perverse. Indeed, perversion lies at the very core of human sexuality, as we all begin life "poly-morphously perverse"—that is, as pleasure-seeking beings that know nothing of higher purposes or appropriate objects or orifices—and continue through-out our lives to seek pleasure for its own sake in forms other than those required for the reproduction of the species.

If we begin with the notion that "normal" sexual activity is directed toward a "total person," a partner who is desired for him- or her-"self," not for any particular attribute he or she may have or embody, then we once again must accept the fact that the vast majority of human sexual behavior is perverse. As we saw in the last chapter, the obsessive reduces his partner to object *a*, neutralizing the partner's Otherness, and the hysteric does not so much desire her partner as desire *via* her partner and wish to be the object he is lacking. The sexual partner is not considered as "an end in himself or herself"—in the Kantian sense of something pursued for its own sake, instead of for some other "selfish" purpose like achieving pleasure, feeling loved, or the like—but is pursued because he or she *has* something (even if it is but a lack that engenders desire) which does something for us. Indeed, as Lacan says, object *a* has something inherently fetishistic about it.[3] As we also saw in the last chapter, the object that elicits love from us is not necessarily the same as the object that elicits desire or that can bring us jouissance.

If we begin with either or both of these notions (or notions similar in kind), we are ineluctably led to qualify virtually all human sexuality as perverse. Given the way in which the terms "pervert," "perverse," and "perversion" are used by certain people to stigmatize those whose sexuality seems different from their own, it will no doubt seem politically expedient to certain readers to simply affirm that *all human sexuality is essentially perverse in nature*, and leave it at that. Indeed, Lacanian psychoanalysts view the perverse nature of sexuality as a given, as something to be taken for granted—in other words, as "normal."

What Lacanian analysts are concerned with, however, is a specific mecha-nism of negation—"disavowal" (Freud's *Verleugnung*)—characteristic of very few of the people considered in the popular mind and by most contemporary psychologists to be perverse, a mechanism that can be clearly distinguished from repression (at least, that is what I hope to show in this chapter). It is evidence of the functioning of this mechanism—not this or that sexual behav-ior in and of itself—which leads the analyst to diagnose someone as perverse. Thus, in psychoanalysis "perversion" is not a derogatory term, used to stig-matize people for engaging in sexual behaviors different from the "norm." Rather, it designates a highly specific clinical structure, with features that sharply distinguish it from neurosis and psychosis. The analyst can agree that *all* human desire is essentially perverse or fetishistic in nature, but nevertheless maintain an important theoretical and clinical distinction between neurotic structure, say, and perverse structure. In psychoanalysis, perversion is not to be viewed as a stigma but rather as a structural category.

Disavowal

In a number of different texts, Freud describes a process that he refers to as *Verleugnung*, a term that has been rendered in English as "disavowal," though in many ways the English term "denial" is closer to the German (indeed, the French have preferred the term *déni*, close in meaning and use to "denial").[4] Freud develops the notion to account for a curious attitude he detects in certain young boys who, when confronted with a girl's genitals, deny that the girl does not have a penis and claim that they in fact see one. Little Hans, for example, watching his seven-day-old sister being given a bath, says: "Her widdler's still quite small. When she grows up it'll get bigger all right."[5]

Freud formulates this by saying that, in such cases, the perception or sight of the female genitals is disavowed. He notes that in certain older male patients, one finds a twofold attitude regarding the fact that women do not have penises: they disavow the perception, maintaining a belief in what Freud terms the "maternal phallus," but develop symptoms which seem to indicate that this perception has nevertheless been registered at some level. It is not as if the memory of a specific perception had simply been "scotomized"[6] or in some way excised from the men's minds (as we might very loosely think of foreclosure); we know it is still *there* because it has effects—it generates symptoms—but it is nevertheless denied. In his article "Splitting of the Ego in the Process of Defence," Freud mentions two examples of such symptoms: a man's fear that his father will punish him (for continued masturbation), and "an anxious susceptibility against either of his little toes being touched" (SE XXIII, 277–278).

Described in this way, disavowal seems very similar to repression: the pushing of a memory out of consciousness, and the return of this memory in the form of symptoms. Indeed, Freud at first tries to devise a clearer distinction between repression and disavowal by proposing that what is repressed is affect, whereas the idea or thought related to it is disavowed (SE XXI, 153). Yet this first attempt contradicts Freud's more rigorous and oft-repeated assertion that only an idea or thought can be repressed. In neurosis, an affect and the thought related to it (its "ideational representative," as Strachey translates Freud's term *Vorstellungsrepräsentanz*)[7] become dissociated; for example, the thought representing a sexual impulse that the ego or superego considers incompatible or unacceptable is repressed, while the affect associated with it is set free to be displaced. In the description Freud provides in "Splitting of the Ego," disavowal and repression seem to collapse into one and the same process.

In an article from 1938, Freud makes a second attempt to distinguish repression from disavowal by saying that in repression one of the patient's own sexual impulses ("an instinctual demand from the internal world") disappears, whereas in disavowal it is "a portion of the real external world" (SE XXIII, 204) that disappears. To state this more rigorously: in repression, the *thought* associated with one of the patient's own drives[8] is put out of mind (the quantum of libido or affect associated with the drive being set free to drift or be displaced), while in disavowal a perception of the "real external world" is put out of mind.

This only makes matters worse, however, because the "portion of the real external world" in question is, Freud says, the "lack of a penis."[9] It should be clear that, strictly speaking, one never *sees* or *perceives* the lack of anything: one sees what is there to be seen, not what is absent. The *lack* of a penis (or of anything else for that matter) is not a question of perception: there is no lack at the perceptual level—there the world is full.[10] *One "sees" nothing only if one is expecting something in particular* and mentally notes its absence. Except in a totally dark room, one always sees something; there are always photons striking the rods and cones of the eye. "Nothing" exists only at the level of thought.

Thus, what is involved here is not perception per se—as Freud says, it is not as if there were a scotoma or black spot on the retina, impeding the fetishist from seeing what is there to be seen, stopping him from receiving certain photons—but a thought related to a particular perception. Seeing is not believing.

Freud's 1938 distinction between repression as related to the internal world and disavowal as related to the external world is reminiscent of his 1924 distinction between "neurotic anxiety" and "realistic anxiety." Neurotic anxiety stems from an internal danger—that is, an impulse within the patient that is considered inappropriate by the patient's own ego or superego—whereas realistic anxiety (which Freud also refers to as "fear") stems from a real external danger (SE XXII, 81–89). Insofar, however, as disavowal clearly involves a *thought* related to a perception—that is, something generally considered to be *inside* the subject, part of his or her *psychical* reality—not a perception alone,[11] the internal-versus-external distinction breaks down.[12] Both repression and disavowal involve thoughts, not perceptions.

Having criticized Freud's internal/external division, let us also note that Freud's view of disavowal as the putting out of mind of a perception of the *"real* external world," like his definition of realistic anxiety as stemming from a *"real* external danger," rests on a naive belief in objective reality. Let us accept, for the sake of argument, that a particular "danger" is external—say, the visible and audible presence of a brown bear in the vicinity of one's campsite in the mountains. What can we say about the supposed "reality" of the danger? The seasoned camper may believe (based on long experience) that the bear is interested only in the food carefully hung in the trees a hundred yards off, whereas the novice may believe that bears are vindictive and likely to attack humans without provocation. But the seasoned camper may turn out to be wrong one out of a hundred times. Are we then going to say that the novice's apparently neurotic anxiety is in fact realistic?

Let's shift the example to New York City. Suppose we know that one out of a hundred women who walk down a particular back alley gets raped. Won't most of us say that a woman's fear of walking there is realistic, not neurotic? Who is to say what a "real danger" is? Is the analyst the one who decides whether the "external danger" is real or not—in other words, whether it is a danger or not? The appeal to reality is always problematic. "Realistic versus unrealistic" and "real anxiety versus neurotic anxiety" are distinctions of dubious value at best, and become all the more doubtful when coupled with the spurious internal/external distinction.

Having discussed the overriding importance of psychical reality and the social/linguistic constitution of reality compared to some sort of objectivist view of reality, I will restate Freud's distinction as follows: in repression, the thought associated with one of the patient's own drives is put out of mind, whereas in disavowal a thought, or complex of thoughts—related to a perception of the female genitals, to the father's supposed castration threat (issued to keep the boy away from his mother and to keep him from masturbating), and to the patient's narcissistic attachment to his penis—is put out of mind.

A First Symbolization

One of the important things to note here is that, if what is put out of mind is a thought, then at least a first symbolization has taken place: in perversion, something related to the father and his will to separate his son from the mother is symbolized, and thus, in contrast to psychosis, an initial acceptance or admission *(Bejahung)* of the father as symbolic separator takes place. Basing our theorization on Freud's clinical observations about the perverse patients he treated, we can assert that the father is symbolized to at least some extent because of the castration-related symptoms that form.[13] Yet this symbolization is not as complete as that achieved in neurosis.

Since my goal here is not to provide an exhaustive critique of Freud's inconclusive definitions of disavowal as a mechanism that clearly differs from repression, I will first indicate what I think we *can* take disavowal to refer to in the context of Lacan's thought (though to the best of my knowledge Lacan never formulates it as I am going to) and then try to translate some of Freud's discussions into Lacanian terms—that is, in terms of the Other and the sacrifice of jouissance. My claim here is that disavowal is a mechanism that *can* be clearly distinguished from repression, though not in the way Freud attempts to do so.

Like foreclosure and primal repression, *disavowal concerns the father:* the father's desire, the father's name, and the father's law. *The three mechanisms that constitute the three essential psychoanalytic categories—neurosis, psychosis, and perversion—all concern the paternal function* (typically fulfilled by a child's father in our society). This point is not nearly as clear in Freud's work as it is in Lacan's, and thus Lacan can be seen to have systematized Freud's work in this respect.[14]

As we saw in Chapter 7, whereas Freud maintains that paranoia (one of the psychoses) results from a defense against homosexual urges (SE XVI, 308), Lacan says that homosexuality is not irrelevant to the understanding of psychosis but rather a *consequence* of the foreclosure of the Name-of-the-Father. The defense against homosexuality turns out to be a *byproduct* of foreclosure, not the cause of psychosis. Similarly, Freud's notion that the fetish object is related in the fetishist's mind to the so-called maternal phallus is not irrelevant from a Lacanian perspective, but is, rather, understandable in terms of the father, his desire, and his law. Belief in the maternal phallus suggests, as we shall see, that the mother's desire-engendering lack has not been canceled out or named by the father, as it is in neurosis.[15] In other words, Lacan does not consider Freud's observation irrelevant but subsumes it within a larger theoretical framework.

From a Lacanian perspective, the apparent contradiction inherent in disavowal can, it seems to me, be described as follows: "I know full well that my father hasn't forced me to give up my mother and the jouissance I take in her presence (real and/or imagined in fantasy), hasn't exacted the 'pound of flesh,'[16] but I'm going to stage such an exaction or forcing with someone who stands in for him; I'll make that person pronounce the law." This particular formulation applies better to the masochist than to the sadist or fetishist, as we shall see, but suffices to indicate that *disavowal implies a certain staging or making believe regarding the paternal function.*

Refusing the Sacrifice

The notion of sacrifice or exaction is certainly not absent from Freud's work on perversion, and one of the places we see it most clearly is in Freud's discussions of the "splitting of the ego." A splitting of the ego, Freud postulates, occurs in perversion, not in neurosis. In neurosis, contradictory thoughts are situated at different levels, in different agencies. For example, "I want to sleep with my sister-in-law" is repressed and persists in the unconscious, while the idea "I *don't* want to sleep with my sister-in-law" is what becomes conscious.[17] In perversion, on the other hand, the ego itself splits (SE XXIII, 204), and contradictory ideas—a woman both does and does not have a penis—are maintained side by side in the same agency.[18] Freud refers to this as a partial "turning away from reality" (SE XXIII, 277) by the ego, a procedure he would prefer to reserve for psychosis. Yet the description he provides of the case on which he bases his notion of splitting (SE XXIII, 276–278) differs little from cases of repression; for in the former the repressed returns in the guise of two symptoms (the man's fear that his father will punish him for continued masturbation, and "an anxious susceptibility against either of his little toes being touched"). Symptom formation requires, as Freud says (SE XVI, 358–359), two different agencies that are at odds—ego and id, or conscious and unconscious—and we seem to have neither more nor less than the conditions of neurosis here: the splitting of the "I" *(Ich)* into conscious and unconscious due to repression.

But let's take a closer look at this supposed case of splitting, to see where renunciation comes in ("instinctual renunciation," as it is translated in the *Standard Edition,* though it is a question of renouncing the pleasure provided by the drives). A young boy, early "acquainted with the female genitals through being seduced by an older girl," takes pleasure in touching his own genitals after relations with the older girl are broken off. One day his nurse catches him doing it and tells him his father will "cut it off" if he does not stop. Freud tells us: "The usual result of the fright of castration, the result that passes as the normal [neurotic] one, is that, either immediately or after some considerable struggle, the boy gives way to the threat and obeys the prohibition either wholly or at least in part (that is, by no longer touching his genitals with his hand). In other words, he gives up, in whole or in part, the satisfaction of the drive" (SE XXIII, 277). This boy, however, continued to masturbate as if no threat had been issued. He refused to give up that jouissance *in the name of the father.* His nurse demanded that he give it up for his father's sake (otherwise his father would castrate him, Freud tells us), because his father would not approve, but the boy refused.

Faced with the possible loss of jouissance, the pervert and the obsessive react in different ways, Freud suggests. The obsessive submits to the loss, however reluctantly, however half-heartedly, and even if he never stops trying to get some of that jouissance back later.[19] He gives up that jouissance in the hope of gaining esteem, recognition, and approval—a symbolic equivalent. He loses one thing to gain another; we might say that he is induced to give up his narcissistic (imaginary) attachment to his penis—which Lacan refers to as the imaginary phallus, φ, the penis as invested narcissistically—and the autoerotic pleasure it gives him, to win something at the social, symbolic level. He gives up φ for Φ, the phallus as signifier, as the socially recognized signifier of value and desire. As Lacan says regarding Hans, a boy must, in some sense, hand over his little penis to get a bigger and better one from his father (Seminar IV). Often the latter is not considered bigger and better enough, in the end. Often it is considered totally inadequate, and the boy may feel he got a raw deal and hold it against his father forever. But some autoerotic pleasure is nevertheless yielded, given up, or handed over by the obsessive.[20]

The pervert, on the other hand, does not hand that pleasure over, does not surrender his pleasure to the Other. Freud insists again and again that the pervert *refuses* to give up his pleasure—that is, the masturbatory pleasure related (in his fantasies) to his mother or mother substitute.[21] Why does one boy surrender it and another refuse? Freud sometimes appeals here to constitutional factors in explaining this refusal: perhaps the pervert's drives are stronger than the neurotic's, and cannot be subjected and tamed the way the neurotic's can.[22] It seems, however, that a number of different explanations are possible. Consider the following:

Clinical work and everyday observation show that mothers are often dissatisfied with their husbands and look for satisfaction in their lives from their relationships with their children. It is also clinically attested that mothers are more inclined to take a male child as their all-encompassing complement in life than a female child, and we can only assume that that is due to the child's sex (and the sex's social meanings, of course).[23] Now, a mother's interest in her son's penis always contributes to the localization of jouissance in the male sexual organ; and in cases in which a mother places great value on her son's penis, he may become extremely attached to it, narcissistically speaking, his whole erotic relation to his mother revolving around it. Often, such a son energetically resists any kind of perceived demand that he stay away from his mother, and the struggle is likely to center around his penis, even if no direct threat is made to it (though such direct threats still are made more often than many think).[24]

Insofar as mothers do not often take their daughters as their complement to the same extent, look to them for such intense satisfaction in life, or take such great interest in their genitals, the mother-daughter relationship is rarely eroticized to the same degree,[25] jouissance is not usually symbolically localized for females in the same way, and the struggle with the father over separation from the mother generally does not come to a head in the same way or focus on a specific organ.[26] The father often has an easier time separating his daughter from her mother (though he may not find it as important to do so, not feeling that he is in competition with his daughter as he is with his son); nevertheless, the result is likely to be either hysteria with traits of perversion when the father is not forceful, or psychosis when the father refuses to intervene at all.

This explains, in part, my use of masculine pronouns alone when talking about perverts. In psychoanalytic terms, perversion is virtually an exclusively male diagnosis. Indeed, Lacan goes so far as to say that "female masochism is a male fantasy,"[27] and qualifies lesbianism not as a perversion but as *"heterosexuality"*: love for the Other sex—that is, women. Homosexuality—*hommosexualité*, as Lacan spells it, including the two m's from *homme*, "man"—is, in his terms, love for men (Seminar XX, 78–79).[28] Lacan's statement that males are "the weaker sex with respect to perversion" (*Ecrits*, 823/320) should certainly give us pause for thought, and warrants more explanation than I can provide here.[29]

To return to the question of why one boy might agree to give up pleasure while another might refuse, we see that in cases in which there is a very close bond between mother and son, a father—in order to bring about a separation—has to be quite forceful in his threats and/or quite convincing in his promises of esteem and recognition. But the very fact that such a close bond has been able to form suggests that the father either is incapable of fulfilling the paternal function or does not care to interfere (perhaps happy to be left alone by his wife, who is now preoccupied with her son). The father, while avoiding the rivalrous ferocity of certain psychotics' fathers, does not forcefully put himself in the position of symbolic separator (the one who says, "This is mine and that is yours"—in other words, the one who gives the child a symbolic space). And even if he does try to do so, he may be undermined by the boy's mother, who, the moment the father's back is turned, winks at the boy, letting him know that their special relationship will secretly remain unperturbed.

It seems to me that we have to shift our focus from the kind of father Freud often seems to have *presumed* to exist—that is, the father who forcefully enunciates his will to separate his son from the boy's mother (the pervert being the son who obstinately refuses)—to the all-too-common contemporary father who is a much weaker figure and is often confused about his role.[30] In cases where there is a strong mother-son bond and a weak or indifferent father, the paternal function, though not altogether absent, may well stand in need of a boost. As I mentioned at the end of Chapter 8, in an early childhood phobia such as little Hans', appearing around age four, the object that becomes central in the phobia (in Hans' case, the horse) serves as *a* Name-of-the-Father that contributes to the separation of mother from child. Hans attributes certain characteristics to the horse—above all, anger—that he would like his father to manifest regarding Hans' special bond with his mother ("You're cross. I know you are. It must be true." [SE X, 83]), but that he can never get his father to admit to. Perversion, like early childhood phobia, results from a partial failure of the paternal function, the latter requiring supplementation in order to bring about separation. Rather than emphasizing, as Freud does, the pervert's refusal to sacrifice jouissance, and his attempt to maintain the jouissance he obtains from the relationship with his mother or mother substitute (a fetish, for example), we need instead to stress *the inadequacy of the paternal function.*

While disavowal could be described as a defense mechanism, a defense against the father's demand that the child sacrifice jouissance, we could instead view it, like Hans' phobia, as not simply evasive but as an attempt to prop up the paternal function (expressed in the father's law)—an attempt to make the Other *pronounce* the law, or to indicate oneself the place of the law—so that the anxiety-relieving separation can come about. In a Lacanian perspective, separation from the mOther may be anxiety producing in certain respects (the object becomes lost or falls away at the moment of separation), but is generally relieving at a more profound level—that is, at the level of being. Hans, at the conscious level, is "afraid" that his mother will go away, but unconsciously wishes she *would* go away and allow him to have desires that do not involve her. His "separation anxiety" reflects a wish to continue to "coax" with his mother—in other words, to obtain certain pleasures with her—but a simultaneous wish for an end to be put to that "coaxing," to that jouissance, since the latter engulfs him and stops him from coming into being as a desiring subject.[31] Thus, his "separation anxiety" is actually indicative of a wish for separation—separation from his mother.

Jouissance is simply overrated. It is not so wonderful that everyone really wants it, the pervert supposedly being the only one who refuses to give it up and who is able to go out and get it.[32] As we saw in previous chapters, the psychotic suffers due to an uncontrollable invasion of jouissance in his or her body, and neurosis is a strategy with respect to jouissance—above all, its avoidance. Perversion, too, is a strategy with respect to jouissance: it involves the attempt to set limits thereto.

Being and Having, Alienation and Separation

The whole problem of the perversions consists in conceiving how the child, in its relationship with its mother—a relationship constituted in analysis not by the child's biological [vitale] dependence, but by its dependence on her love, that is, by its desire for her desire—identifies with the imaginary object of her desire.

—Lacan, *Ecrits*, 554/197–198

Freud reveals to us that it is thanks to the Name-of-the-Father that man does not remain bound to the sexual service of his mother.

—Lacan, *Ecrits*, 852; *Reading Seminars I and II*, 418

One way to describe my essential thesis regarding perversion is to say that *the pervert has undergone alienation*—in other words, primal repression, a splitting into conscious and unconscious, an acceptance or admission of the Name-of-the-Father that sets the stage for a true coming-to-be of the subject in language (unlike the psychotic)—*but has not undergone separation.*[33] How can we characterize the pervert's alienation here? As Lacan tells us, we come into the world offering ourselves up as partial objects to the Other's desire (*Ecrits*, 582/225), hoping to be the object of the Other's desire, to win the Other's desire; and the pervert—whose father's desire is not terribly pronounced, it would seem— "identifies with the imaginary object of [his mother's] desire, insofar as she herself symbolizes it in the phallus" (*Ecrits*, 554/198). In other words, the imaginary object of the mother's desire here is the phallus—not as a displaceable symbol, in the sense that the mother might desire, say, all the trappings of status, all socially valorized objects, or a husband (or boyfriend or whatever) who resembles socially accepted images of "real men," sometime "possessors" of the phallus, but as an unsymbolized, nonfungible, undisplaceable object—and the child attempts to become it for her. He attempts to be her little prized possession, her little substitute penis, as Freud might have put it; and the father often does not care to interfere (perhaps preferring to be left alone) or is ineffectual in his attempts to interfere.

Using the kinds of schemas introduced in Chapter 8, we can represent the pervert's situation as shown in Figure 9.1. When we compare this configuration with that of neurosis, we see that the pervert's "subject position" does not entail something outside or beyond the Other. Instead the pervert, as subject, plays the role of object: the object that fills the void in the mOther. A first division in the Other has occurred for the pervert, graphically speaking: the Other is not whole; his mOther is lacking in something, wants for something. To the question "What am I?" the pervert responds, "I am that," that something she is lacking. Thus, for the pervert, there is no persistent question of being—in other words, no persistent question regarding his rai-son d'être.

To separate the boy from his mother here would entail forcing him to stop *being the phallus* so he can have it, stop being the imaginary phallus in order to obtain a symbolic one (through the father's recognition and esteem, through social, symbolic channels). If he *is* the phallus for his mother, he will never accede to a symbolic position—that associated with symbolic castration. Rather than becoming someone the mother can be proud of, he remains someone she cuddles with, strokes, and perhaps even reaches sexual climax with. He cannot go off to "make a name for himself" in the world, for it is not symbolic stature that he is able to seek.[34] He remains stuck at the level of serving as his mother's be-all and end-all.

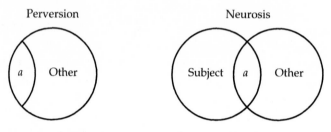

Figure 9.1

Primal repression allows the subject to come into being, but the child is then left to ask, "What *am* I? What am I to my parents?" The pervert constitutes himself as what is lacking in the mOther; making himself into the object of her desire, he constitutes himself as her object *a*. He becomes what she is missing (her penis/phallus) and what she wants. He plugs up her lack with himself. The Other's desire/lack is, as I explained at length in Chapter 5, anxiety producing, insofar as it is not named; the pervert's solution to this anxiety is to become the object that can stop up the desire by providing the Other with jouissance, with the kind of satisfaction that squelches desire (albeit temporarily).[35]

This explains why it is so difficult to do analytic work with perverts: the pervert casts himself in the role of object *a*, expecting to play the part of the object that can satisfy (plug up) the analyst's desire. The analyst may be hard pressed to maneuver the transference in such a way as to become the cause of the perverse analysand's desire, when the latter works so hard to occupy the position of cause of desire. The pervert would rather serve as the cause of the analyst's anxiety and desire than let the analyst become the cause of his own musings. It is thus quite difficult to do genuinely analytic work with perverts, to get them intrigued by unconscious formations and by what the analyst underscores in them, and to get their desire in motion. As Lacan says, object *a* must be situated by the subject in the Other, the Other as analyst here, in order for transference to be possible (Seminar X, July 3, 1963).[36]

In order to articulate the pervert's position more rigorously, however, it must be emphasized that *the pervert deals not so much with the mOther's desire as with her demand*. As long as the desire/lack a child's mOther "has" is not named or put into words, the child is confronted with her demand alone. Strictly speaking, we cannot even say that he is confronted with her lack or desire, since lack does not exist outside a symbolic system. Lacan's oft-repeated illustration of what constitutes lack is the example of a book that is *not present* on a library shelf. From the perspective of perception, we cannot say that the book is missing because we see only what is there, what is present, not what is not there. It is only because of a symbolic grid—for example, the Dewey decimal system or the Library of Congress book classification system—which provides the book with a designation or name (such as "BF 173, F23, 1899, v. 2") that we can say the volume is not in its place or is missing (volumes 1 and 3 being there, with no space between them). Nothing can be thought of as missing except when there is a signifying system in which certain spaces or places are laid out or ordained. We cannot think of something as missing without language, without some kind of symbolic order.

What this implies is that *we cannot even speak of the mother as lacking* (so far as her child is concerned) *until she is* said *to be wanting in some respect*—until she herself verbalizes a longing for something or someone or a desire for something or someone other than her child, or until someone else (typically the father) pronounces something about her desire (for example, that she is envious of so and so, wants a fur coat, wants to be promoted, would like the father to act like this instead of like that) or about her shortcomings. The child cannot be said to understand his mother to be lacking or to desire until her desire or lack has been formulated, put into words. Once it has been named, the weight of her demands (her real, physically unavoidable demands regarding the child's bodily functions, for example) lifts, and a space of desire opens up—a space in which her desire is articulated and moves, and in which her child can model his desire on hers.

Until "it" is named, there is no lack; the child is submerged in the mOther as demand and cannot adopt a stance of his own (a desire that constitutes a stance with respect to jouissance, a defense against jouissance).[37] The child here is confronted with what we can refer to as a *lack of lack*. Only the mOther's demand exists; she is lacking in nothing "to speak of," nothing that is symbolizable for the child.[38] Once named, however, the "real lack" (the lack in the mother's life—for example, her dissatisfaction with her husband, her career, her whole life—that she has been attempting to make good through her son, even though it has never been spoken) is neutralized to some extent. As Lacan says, the word is the death of the thing; the thing (the "real lack"), once named, comes into being as a word that can be linked up with other words, joked about, and so on. The word is far less dangerous than the thing it supposedly signifies or designates, for it actually annihilates the thing, drains away some of its oppressive force.

Once that which the mOther is missing is named, the *object* the child was for his mOther can no longer exist. For once desire is articulated in words, it does not sit still, but displaces, drifting metonymically from one thing to the next. Desire is a product of language and cannot be satisfied with an object. The naming of the mOther's desire forces the child out of his position as object, and propels him into the quest for the elusive key to her desire. What does she want? Something ineffable that seems to characterize the endless series of things her desire alights upon—what in Western society is known as the phallus. No longer the real object (the real organ) required to complete her, the child can go on to seek to possess what her desire points to, connotes as desirable, as phallic.

The mOther's lack has to be named or symbolized for the child to come into being as a full-fledged subject. In perversion, this does not occur: no signifier is provided that can make this lack *come into being at the level of thought*, easing its real weight. Neither the mother nor the father provides the articulation necessary for symbolization. As we see in Freud's work, the question of the mOther's lack often centers, in perversion, around the mOther's genitalia, her sexual difference from her son. Later in this chapter, we shall see a detailed illustration of the importance of nomination (that is, naming), discussed thus far in rather abstract terms, in a case that revolves around the mother's sexual organs.

In Chapter 7, I suggested that there are two moments of the paternal metaphor. This naming of the mOther's desire/lack is the second (logical) moment. If the first moment of the paternal metaphor is the father's *prohibition* of the child's pleasurable contact with its mother (prohibition of jouissance), *le Nom-du-Père* taking the form of the father's "No," the second moment involves the symbolization of the mOther's lack—that is, *its constitution as lack* due to the fact that it is given a name (here we see *le Nom-du-Père* as the name provided by the father, or the father himself as the name of the mOther's desire).

The two substitutive moments can be represented schematically as follows:

Father's "No!"	Father's name
Mother as jouissance	Mother as desire

Only the second moment can be considered genuinely metaphorical, since it is only in the second that language operates in a full-fledged manner by naming. These two moments correspond precisely to the two schemas provided in Figure 9.1: the first moment leads to a division within the mOther, whereby the child comes into being as the object with which the Other obtains satisfaction, while the second leads to the advent of a desiring subject (separate from the Other as source of jouissance). The first corresponds to what Lacan calls alienation, the second to separation. The first may also be fruitfully associated with what Freud calls primal repression, the second with secondary repression.

As I said earlier, my essential thesis here is that, although the pervert has undergone alienation, he has not undergone separation. The psychotic has undergone neither, while the neurotic has undergone both. This can be schematically represented as follows:

	Alienation		*Separation*	
Psychosis	$\dfrac{\text{Father's "No!"}}{\text{Mother as jouissance}}$	Perversion	$\dfrac{\text{Father's name}}{\text{Mother as desire}}$	Neurosis

Primary repression	*Secondary repression*
Prohibition of jouissance	*Naming of lack*

$$\varphi \qquad\qquad\qquad \Phi$$

Demand	*Desire*

If psychosis can be understood as owing to the absence or failure of paternal prohibition, perversion can be understood as owing to the absence or failure of symbolization.[39]

From Jouissance to Separation

In discussing perversion, Freud almost always emphasizes the subject's refusal of the law, his obstinate refusal to give up satisfaction; thus, in a sense, Freud considers perversion almost exclusively from the perspective of the satisfaction the pervert continues to obtain.[40] Lacan examines perversion in what might be qualified as a more classically Freudian manner: perversion, like every other activity, must be considered in terms of the satisfaction it brings (however indirect or unintuitive), but also in terms of the function it serves in relation to the law and separation. A neurotic symptom provides the patient with a certain substitute satisfaction, but it also forms *in order to bind anxiety;* so too, the pervert's activities serve a purpose that is not simply that of achieving direct sexual satisfaction.[41] Many neurotics think the pervert must be getting an awful lot more satisfaction in life than they are—indeed, many analysts fall into the same trap. This stops them from seeing what it is that the pervert's apparent "will to jouissance" (as Lacan calls it) is designed to do, is in the service of, and is covering over.

Turning our attention from the kind of father Freud often seems to have assumed to exist—that is, the father who has no reservations about separating his son from the boy's mother (the pervert being the son who obstinately refuses to let this happen)—to the all-too-common contemporary father who never worked out his own problems with authority, does not believe fathers should wield authority over their children, believes children are rational crea-tures and can understand adult explanations, prefers to let his wife discipline the children, wants to be loved not feared, and who (perhaps to boot) allows his wife to undercut his authority, we can begin to understand perversion from a rather different perspective.[42]

Perversion and the Law

One of the paradoxical claims Lacan makes about perversion is that while it may sometimes present itself as a no-holds-barred, jouissance-seeking activ-ity, its less apparent aim is to bring the law into being: to make the Other as law (or law-giving Other) exist. The masochist's goal, for example, is to bring the partner or witness to the point of enunciating a law and perhaps pro-nouncing a sentence (often by generating anxiety in the partner). While the pervert seems to be able to obtain a kind of "primal satisfaction"—transcend-ing his own subjective division as a subject of language (who, like the rest of us speaking beings, is not supposed to be able to obtain more than a mere pittance of jouissance: as Lacan tells us, "jouissance is prohibited to whoever speaks" [Ecrits, 821/319]), and finding a kind of wholeness or completeness neurotics can only dream of or fantasize about—anxiety in fact dominates the pervert's sexuality. The pervert's conscious fantasies may involve a kind of unending jouissance (consider the Marquis de Sade's numerous scenarios where the male sexual organ never manifests any limit in its ability to recom-mence sexual activity), but we must not confuse conscious fantasies with concrete activity, and the latter is designed to place limits on jouissance.[43]

Desire is always a defense, "a defense against going beyond a [certain] limit in jouissance" (Ecrits, 825/322), and the pervert's desire is no exception. For example, the masochist, in fantasy, seems to do everything for the Other and nothing for himself: "Let the Other get off on me, use me as he or she sees fit!" he seems to say. Beyond this fantasy, however, his aim is somewhat different: beyond this apparent altruism —"Nothing for me, everything for the Other!"—there is something in it for him. Desire as a defense appears in the pervert's fundamental fantasy that manifests his position with respect to the law.

The neurotic desires in relation to the law: the father says the child cannot have its mother, and the child thus unconsciously desires her. The pervert, on the other hand, does not desire as a function of the law—that is, does not desire what is prohibited. Instead, *he has to make the law come into being.* Lacan plays on the French term *perversion,* writing it as *père-version,* to emphasize the sense in which the pervert calls upon or appeals to the father, hoping to make the father fulfill the paternal function.

Some Structures of Perversion

To make this discussion more concrete, let's turn to the individual perversions. Since this book is an introduction, not an exhaustive description of each and every clinical structure, I will focus primarily on fetishism, sadism, and masochism, the perversions Lacan discusses most extensively (see "Kant with Sade," in *Ecrits* and Seminar X).

Fetishism: Analysis of a Case

> *If the Name-of-the-Father were to speak, it would say, "You are not the phallus!"*
>
> —Jacques-Alain Miller, "Donc," June 29, 1994

To illustrate some of the claims I have made about perversion thus far in this chapter, I will use a case that is quite contemporary, not one that dates back to Freud's time. While it is not one of my own cases, I have decided to introduce it here because it is readily available in English (though probably not well known), a mere fifteen pages long, and extremely provocative. It is entitled "Fetishization of a Phobic Object," and was written by René Tostain.[44]

The case is that of a man who, as a young child, has an extremely close bond with his mother, and whose father—though he lives at home with his wife and son—is effaced for most intents and purposes. The mother takes her son, Jean, as her complement in life, for her husband means nothing to her and does nothing for her. Jean becomes that which she is missing and which can make her whole. At first she cares for him when he is ill, but then begins to pretend that he is ill even when he is not (manually heating up the thermometer to make it seem he has a fever), so that he apparently needs a devoted mother's attention. One of the striking things in this case is that, by the kinds of medical treatments she subjects him to, she makes his whole body into a red, swollen, pus-discharging object that the patient himself can only describe years later as a kind of living dildo with which she does as she pleases. To her, he *is* the penis she wants; at the level of being, he *is* the real object she wants to make her whole.[45]

The father imposes no separation between mother and son, is clearly not an object of the mother's desire, and can in no way be considered to willfully instate any kind of triangulation at first. The mother displays no desire for anything other than Jean; there is no outside, no object that draws her toward something other than Jean, and thus Jean cannot *wonder* what it is his mother wants: he knows. She wants him to be her real, living complement. There is nothing symbolic about the position he has in her desire. For example, since he is an only child, he is not the second of three children, all of whom she might profess to love equally; nor is he second in line when the father makes demands upon his wife. There is no symbolic place for him at all. To be an object is the opposite of having a symbolic place. Certain important preconditions of psychosis are thus present in Jean's case.

At age six, however, Jean develops appendicitis, is rushed to the hospital, and wakes up to the sight of his father holding Jean's appendix in a jar, smiling radiantly at the excised organ. Jean never again plays along with his mother's "treatments," refusing henceforth to *be* the penis for her with his whole body, with his entire being. The father's presence at his bedside and approval of the organ removal seems to finally bring about a kind of displaced circumcision or loss symbolizing castration: a first division (or alienation) between Jean and his mother. The father "bars" or "cancels out" the mother here—in the sense briefly described in Chapter 7 in my discussion of the paternal metaphor—by exacting his due (the excised organ), and the paternal metaphor is instated. Jean does not become psychotic.[46]

Jean's mother nevertheless continues to view Jean as "my little man" and lets him know that his penis is inadequate to give her everything she needs: she refers to his penis as *ton petit bout*, "your little end or bit," the "little" suggesting "too little"; often, however, she simply calls it *ton bout*, "your end." She never stops looking for some sort of *real* satisfaction from him, however, and always asks him to come help her get dressed. He senses that his penis is truly at stake or involved in his relationship with her, for at the age of six he experiences (what he describes twenty years later as) a kind of abrupt and painful pleasure in his penis, a sort of orgasm, one day while helping her dress.[47] Jean is never praised by his mother for the speed at which he learns new words, songs, stories, and so on—in a word for his symbolic achievements as a child. He is valued only as an extension of herself, an extension that provides her with narcissistic and bodily pleasure.

One day Jean overhears his father refer, or so it seems to him, to the mother's genitals as her "button" (*bouton*, a simple inversion of the syllables contained in her euphemistic term for his penis: *ton bout*), naming her physical difference for the first time, putting a metaphorical name on her "lack." The naming is not done decisively, it seems (perhaps due to the son's uncertainty over what exactly it is the father is referring to, or the fact that it is not repeated in the mother's presence, and so on), and we see in the fetish Jean forms an attempt to supplement the father's act of naming: he comes to abhor buttons (the kind used on clothing) when they occur singly, but is turned on by many buttons of the same kind in a row—the more the better. It is not a "simple" button fetish, for he is aroused only by *rows* of identical buttons, and is compelled to follow only women who wear clothes that sport numerous identical buttons in a row. In the course of his analysis, he explains that the more buttons there are, the weightier his father's contribution (*la part du père*) becomes. The more buttons, the less he feels that his mOther's lack/desire is incommensurate (*démesuré*), overwhelming.

The name the father seems to have provided (and as I've already pointed out, the French term *Nom-du-Père* can also mean the name given by the father—that is, the term used by the father to name the mOther's desire) becomes more powerful the more buttons there are, and Jean can feel safer and more separate than at any other time. Hence, the perversion (that is, the fetish) serves to multiply the force of the father's symbolic action (putting the mOther's lack into words), to supplement or prop up the paternal function.[48] The name given by the father is a start, a first step, but does not go far enough. It needs support, it needs amplification.[49]

In Chapter 7, I illustrated the function of the father's name in the following substitution:

$$\frac{\text{Father's name}}{\text{Mother's desire}}$$

Since the mother's desire here seems to be for a real, anatomical penis (Jean's), we can rewrite the substitution as follows:

$$\frac{\text{"Button"}}{\text{Real penis}}$$

I put "button" in quotes to emphasize that it is the word "button" that is operative here, not the material object. The real penis is replaced by a word; Jean's real organ is thereby spared, and his mother's lack named. He need not hand his organ over to the mOther, nor suffer anxiety owing to the lack of lack in his relationship with her: her lack is named and thereby delimited ("It's only a button").

The problem is that "button" can accomplish this only in situations where he sees a woman wearing a multitude of identical buttons, and thus the anxiety-relieving separation (brought on by propping up the father's act of naming) has to be repeated again and again. It is never final and definitive.

It would appear that what is enjoyable for Jean in such situations is the fleeting separation itself. Strange as this may seem, we should bear in mind that separation is part and parcel of what Freud terms "castration," and that *there is a very intimate relationship between castration and jouissance.* There is a kind of jouissance in being separated from one's jouissance.[50] Jean, in a sense, is repeatedly led to attempt to complete his castration.

To talk about Jean in terms of disavowal, we could say that Jean's fetish suggests a twofold attitude regarding his father and his father's name: "I know full well that my father hasn't truly named my mOther's lack, but I will stage the accomplishment of that naming." Using somewhat different terms, we could say that Jean makes the Other exist—not the mOther, but the symbolic, law-giving Other. The pervert knows that his own father is not such an Other, but makes this Other exist via the perverse act. Having served as that which completes the mOther (as her complement), the pervert attempts to complete the Other as law.

It is this twofold attitude toward the father—involving the realization that he has not named or legislated, yet staging that naming or enunciation of the law—which is the very definition of the term "disavowal" as I am using it here.

The "Maternal Phallus"

> *Lack is graspable only by means of the symbolic.*
>
> —Lacan, Seminar X, January 30, 1963
>
> *The phallus is nothing but the site of lack it indicates in the subject.[51]*
>
> —Lacan, *Ecrits*, 877

What might Freud's theory of fetishism have to do with Jean? According to Freud, a fetish secretly represents the maternal phallus the pervert believes in, refusing as he does to accept the fact that his mother does not have a penis, because this would imply that she has been castrated and thus that he too could suffer the same fate. We can assume that Jean had, at one time or another, seen his mother's genitals, since she enjoyed having him watch and help her get dressed. And certainly the button fetish is strikingly related to the word Jean's father seems to have used to designate the mother's genitals—a word that turns out to include the same syllables as the term Jean's mother used to describe Jean's own genitals. Perhaps Jean believed that her button was essentially equivalent to his "end." We could then try to understand his fear of one button alone as follows: she has a penis of her own, does not need mine, and therefore there is no place at all for me in the world. But according to Freud's theory, it would seem that one button should turn him on, since it simultaneously represents the mother's never-castrated organ and his own (and thus represents the preservation of his jouissance), whereas in fact one button horrifies him, and a whole line of identical buttons excites him. How can we account for these clinical elements?

Note that no castration threat was ever made to Jean, and he was never asked (much less told) not to play with himself. Indeed, Tostain tells us that Jean continued to masturbate uninterruptedly from an early age. Thus, an important facet of Freud's theory of fetish-formation is missing in this case: there is no conflict here between the patient's narcissistic attachment to his penis and his father's castration threat. We cannot say that Jean's mother implicitly threatens to cut it off, since she seems quite content to simply use it, to employ it in her "sexual service."

I am not suggesting that Freud's notion of the maternal phallus is of no importance, since many of my own analysands and certain children have amply proven to me that they believe in it, at least at some level. What I am proposing is that it be seen within the larger Lacanian context of the naming of the mother's lack or desire. It is common to find phobics and perverts who believe that their mothers have a penis (or something along those lines), and the general reason for this belief is the father's inadequate naming of the mother's desire. Not every fetishist believes, at one level, that his mother has a penis, while at another level disbelieving it; but every fetish does revolve around the question of the mother's lack. Only Lacan explains this to us *in its full generality* via the function of naming—a putting into words.

On the Analytic Treatment of Perversion

This brief sketch of Jean's case history illustrates much of Lacan's theory of perversion. The case also raises the pressing question of treatment. It seems clear that, despite years of fruitful psychoanalysis, Jean does not change structures: he remains perverse. Indeed, as is generally true, structures seem quite irrevocable beyond a certain age. We see in Jean's case that a particular life event (his appendicitis at age six) and his father's reaction to it can probably be considered responsible for the fact that Jean becomes a pervert, not a psychotic. But coming to analysis at age twenty-six, Jean has little hope of becoming a neurotic: once again it seems that the paternal function must be operative by a certain age, or else . . . (ou pire).

This does not mean that Jean could get nothing out of his analysis; certainly a great deal of his anxiety and suffering abated in the course of it. Tostain does not tell us to what extent he himself, as Jean's analyst, was able to become Jean's cause of desire, leading Jean to adopt a different position, if only in the analytic relationship. We can only assume that this occurred to some extent and that Jean's fundamental fantasy was at least partly modified.

In certain cases that I myself have supervised, I have seen a gradual shift on the part of genuinely perverse subjects from positions in which they engaged in no wondering of any kind about their own actions, feelings, and thoughts— court orders or the hope of getting a rise out of their therapist seeming to be their only motive for showing up for therapy—to positions of true questioning. If there is never a loss of certainty about where jouissance comes from, there is at least a lessening of certainty about motives. This is accompanied by partial relinquishing of the role of object *a* to the therapist.

Masochism

> *The perverse subject loyally offers himself up to the Other's jouissance.*
>
> —Lacan, Seminar X, December 5, 1962

In the material that follows, I shall not present the elaborate four-term schemas of masochism and sadism Lacan provides in the *Ecrits*, since too much additional explanation would be required.[52] My discussions of these clinical structures should thus be viewed as partial. Nevertheless, with what has already been said about desire, jouissance, and the law, certain essential features of these structures can be outlined.

Though it may appear that the masochist devotes himself to giving his partner jouissance (the partner standing in for the Other here) while asking for nothing in return—in other words, that he sacrifices himself by becoming the instrument of the Other's jouissance, obtaining no enjoyment for himself— Lacan suggests that that is but a cover: the masochist's fantasy dissimulates the true aim of his actions. As we have seen several times, fantasy is essentially a lure that conceals the subject's mainspring, masking what truly makes the subject "tick." While the masochist would like to believe and to make us believe that he "aims to give the Other jouissance,"[53] in fact he "aims to make the Other anxious" (Seminar X, March 13, 1963). Why does he do so?

Like the fetishist, the masochist is in need of separation, and his solution is to orchestrate a scenario whereby it is his partner, acting as Other, who lays down the law—the law that requires him to give up a certain jouissance. A partner is not necessarily, however, immediately willing to legislate, give orders, make decrees, and so on in a relationship; a partner must often be pushed to some extent, bullied into declaring limits, into expressing his will that things be one way and not another, that things go no further. Often a partner must be pushed to the breaking point, to a point of intense anxiety, before he explosively expresses his will in the form of commands ("Stop!" for example).

"The masochist tries to bring something into being . . . by which the Other's desire makes the law" (Seminar X, January 16, 1963), and the Other must often first be made extremely anxious before he agrees to enunciate the law. Though the masochist seems to be single-mindedly devoting himself to "pleasuring" the Other, the Other cannot take it after a certain point: jouissance becomes unbearable, and the partner finally imposes limits on it. By making the Other anxious (by making himself into the instrument of the Other's jouissance), the masochist manages to get himself commanded (*se faire commander*, a formulation of the masochist's drive).

Thus, it is the masochist's own desire that leads the dance here: he *makes* the partner, as Other, lay down the law. Where the father's desire (to separate his son) is lacking, the masochist uses his own desire to push a father substitute to legislate and exact punishment. He pretends that it is the Other who is laying down the law, when he himself is the one pulling the strings. His own desire takes the place of the Other's desire as law, staging or enacting it, as it were, and propping it up.

This, it seems, is the specificity of disavowal as we see it at work in masochism. Separation, as part and parcel of castration, has not occurred, and the subject himself is compelled to bring about its completion. He is never altogether successful in doing so, and thus must reinitiate the enactment again and again.

Though it is often thought that the masochist is in search of pain, this is not what is essential; pain is merely a sign that the Other has agreed to impose a condition, limit, toll, penance, or loss upon him. Punishment may momentarily provide a form of relief to the masochist: it is the proof that there is someone who is demanding a sacrifice of him and who is exacting the pound of flesh. As one of my analysands said about a brief sexual encounter in which he played the slave, "It felt as if a great weight had been lifted from my shoulders." The problem is that the *symbolic space* in which the masochist can come into being is never supplied: the partner pronounces the law ("You've been a very bad boy, and now you shall be punished," or "You know you weren't supposed to do that") and exacts something, but provides no genuine separation in return. The masochist remains an imaginary object for his mOther's desire, never becoming someone with symbolic status who can see himself as valued for his social, cultural, or other symbolically designated achievements.

Failing all else, the masochist accepts here the vociferous father or mother who only in anger expresses desire for something to stop or change, the ferocious parent who gets off on imputing blame and inflicting pain. The masochist knows not the symbolic father who supposedly imposes limits "for the child's own good"; his experience teaches him that limits are merely expressions of the parent's desire. He knows not the father who yields his son a certain space of his own—that is, the father of the "symbolic pact" who says, "This is mine and that is yours," limiting his own jouissance at the same time as he limits his son's. The masochist knows only the father whose own jouissance is the sole limit imposed on the son's, the father who criticizes and limits without appealing to principles, but simply "because that's the way I want it."

Jouissance and the Moral Law

> *Jouissance . . . is indecently admitted to in its very wording.*
>
> —Lacan, Ecrits, 771

Certain moralists and ethical philosophers, such as Kant, would have us believe that moral principles are "rational" and objective, and that we can accept to live by them "rationally" just because they are "true." Freud suggests, however, that a principle is nothing in someone's psychical reality until a quantum of libido has been attached to it; in other words, a moral principle, like any other thought *(Vorstellung)*, has to be *cathected* before it can play a role in someone's psychical economy. And the psychical agency in which Freud situates moral principles is the superego, which takes pleasure in criticizing the ego—not simply reminding the ego of the law, but getting off on berating the ego for its failure to execute the law and enjoying a kind of vicious enunciation of the law. The superego, as the internalization of the criticism we receive from our parents, is a repository not merely of the moral principles our parents hand down to us, but also of the kind of harshness we sense in their voices when they lecture, scold, and punish us. The superego can be ferocious in certain cases, obviously taking a good deal of pleasure in badgering, berating, and bludgeoning the ego, but the important point here is that it is impossible—except in philosophical treatises—to divorce the statement of a moral principle from the libido or jouissance attached to its enunciation; it is impossible to divorce a precept taught us by our parents (for example, "Do unto others as you would have others do unto you") from the tone of voice in which it was pronounced.

The moral law, as it plays a role in our psychical lives, is *not* an abstract proposition, principle, or statement with universal or quasi-universal application: it is an enunciation, announcement, proclamation, or kerygma. The moral law—whether it goes by the name of the "voice within," the voice of conscience, or the superego—originates in parental voices, most typically in the voice of the father.[54] It is experienced by children as *an expression of the Other's desire.* The father who "lays down the law" for his children expresses, announces, and proclaims his desire for things to be a certain way and not another.[55]

The moral law is thus inextricably associated with expressions of the Other's desire and jouissance, and the masochist seeks to elicit that jouissance in lieu of the law. Since he cannot obtain the symbolic law as such, he seeks that which he somehow understands to be associated with it. The Other's desire or will is accepted by the masochist instead of the law, in place of the law, in the absence of the law. As Lacan mentions, the Marquis de Sade (better known as a sadist, but in this instance manifesting decidedly masochistic tendencies) pushes his mother-in-law, Madame de Montreuil, to the point where she expresses her will that Sade be punished. It is her desire or will that has to serve Sade as a law. Not *the* law, but *a* law.

The neurotic tends to be upset when the enunciation of the law is accompanied by jouissance on the part of the enunciator. The neurotic senses that there has been some kind of miscarriage of justice or abuse of power when a judge makes certain kinds of comments or adopts a certain tone in sentencing a criminal: "If it were up to me, Mr. Jones, given your heinous crimes, your sentences would run consecutively and you would be unable to even apply for parole until you were 140!"[56] For here "justice" becomes vindictive, exceeding its mandated role to act objectively and dispassionately. The neurotic implicitly grasps the notion and even clings to the *ideal* of the symbolic father who is fair, impartial, and disinterested, and who simply applies rules that govern everyone equally. "This symbolic Father, insofar as he signifies the Law, is clearly the dead Father" (*Ecrits*, 556/199)—that is, the father who can experience no jouissance, who cannot derive some sort of "perverse" pleasure from the enunciation of the law.

The pervert seems to be cognizant, at some level, of the fact that there is always some jouissance related to the enunciation of the moral law. The neurotic would prefer not to see it, since it strikes him or her as indecent, obscene. The symbolic law is supposed to be free of invocations of this kind. Indeed, it would seem that the pervert accepts the invocations in lieu of the symbolic law itself, unable as he is to obtain the latter. The criminal justice system, with its often vicious guards and wardens, certainly provides perverts who are subjected to it confirmation that vindictiveness and cruelty constitute the hidden face of the law.

Incarceration nevertheless continues to serve as an often sought-after form of punishment for the masochist, who wants some sort of substitute symbolic castration. As Lacan says, "Recourse to the very image of castration can come as a relieving, salutary solution to [*issue à*] anxiety for the masochist" (Seminar X, March 26, 1963). The subject in need of separation turns and returns for relief to whatever substitute castration can be had.[57]

Sadism

Sadism is not the inverse of masochism . . . The move from one to the other involves a quarter-rotation [in a four-term schema], not some sort of symmetry or inversion.[58]

—Lacan, Seminar X, March 13, 1963

In every movie in which a sadist is depicted, he does everything possible to generate anxiety in other people. His goal is not simply to harm them; indeed, often this is but a contingency, a mere byproduct of his concern with making them anxiously anticipate a horrible, painful death or torment. The importance to the sadist of the victim's *anxiety* is thus recognized by the popular mind as well as by the sadist himself; indeed, in his fantasies he views it as an absolute condition—that is, as absolutely necessary if they are to provide pleasure. But as we have seen, what is crucial in fantasies is no more than a screen.

That does not mean that the sadist must then be seeking to give the Other jouissance, as might be thought by simply reversing our earlier formulation regarding the masochist (apparently seeking to give jouissance, he is actually attempting to arouse anxiety). Sadism and masochism are not simple inversions of each other. What is covered over by the sadist's fantasies, Lacan tells us, is that *he is seeking to isolate object* a (Seminar X, March 13, 1963).

What does this mean? Let us consider the villain in a typical B movie. What does he do to the hero when he captures him? The villain ties him up in such a way that if he tries to free himself, his beloved falls into a pool of boiling acid. In this way, the hero is forced to contemplate the imminent loss of what is most precious to him: his cause of desire, the woman who for him embodies object *a*. In certain cases, the hero is not even aware that this woman is what is most important to him in the world until he sees her dangling by a thread over the boiling caldron: *an object becomes object* a *at the very moment one is threatened with its loss.* The breast becomes an object *a* for an infant when weaning is initiated, not before. It is when a certain will sets out to separate you from an object that this object manifests itself as the cause of your desire.

Object *a* comes into being due to the law—or the Other's desire or will standing in for the law—that is applied to it. According to Freud, anxiety arises as a "signal" indicating a danger.[59] Lacan suggests that the danger in question is "related to the characteristic of *cession* [the French here means yielding, transferring, giving up, or handing over to another person] at the moment constitutive of object *a*" (Seminar X, July 3, 1963). In other words, the danger that brings on anxiety is the subject's imminent renunciation of satisfaction derived from an object (the breast, feces, and so on). The parent, in making demands, lays down a law (of weaning or toilet training, for example) that isolates an object, cutting it away from its context or background, creating a foreground and a background: the breast is constituted as a separate object at the moment at which it is prohibited.[60] Anxiety, Lacan tells us, is not like fantasy, which can serve as a cover or veil; anxiety is never deceptive *(ne trompe pas)*: it always indicates that the object is about to be lost. Anxiety never lies. The sadist's aim thus is not anxiety itself, but what it attests to: the object to which the law applies.

A boy's penis may be an object of his narcissistic interest, but it is not until the father's law is enunciated that the boy's penis becomes isolated or engendered as an object that can be lost (castrated)—in other words, as an object *a*. It is the father's prohibition that, in the typical Oedipal scenario, isolates this object: the penis the father threatens to cut off unless the subject gives up the pleasure he gets from it in his (real or fantasy) relationship with his mother.[61] The sadist believes that it would be the symbolic Other's will to wrest the object from him, to take away his jouissance, if only the Other really existed. The sadist, for whom the law has not operated, plays the part of the Other in his scenario *in order to make the Other exist,* and seeks to isolate for his victim the object to which the law applies. Unlike the masochist, who has to orchestrate things in such a way that his partner enunciates the law even though he is the one pulling the strings, the sadist's own will can play the part of the law. In a sense, the sadist plays both parts: legislator and subject of the law, lawgiver and the one on whom the exaction or limit is imposed. To the sadist, the victim's anxiety over the isolation or designation of the object about to be lost is proof of the enunciation of the law, proof that the law requiring separation has been pronounced. It seems to be a moot point whether the law thus enunciated applies to the other or to himself, since at a certain level he identifies with his victim.[62]

As was true in the case of the masochist, this staging of the enunciation of the law by the sadist does not suffice to bring on any kind of lasting separation or to provide him with a symbolic place. He remains an object (imaginary or real) for the mOther's desire, never becoming someone who can see himself as valued for his symbolic achievements. Castration is never completed, and here, too, disavowal concerns the castrating or separating function of the father: "I know full well he hasn't required this of me, but . . ." It is the ever-repeated staging of castration that brings the sadist, like the masochist and the fetishist, a kind of jouissance. It is not some kind of "polymorphously perverse" jouissance that they obtain from every zone of their bodies; it is not a return to some sort of presymbolic stage where the body has not yet been written with signifiers. They get off on the enactment of castration.

Perversion and Jouissance

On the face of it, perversion is diametrically opposed to neurosis when it comes to jouissance. The neurotic says, "The Other must not get off on me!" while certain perverts seem to say, "Let the Other get off on me!" "Let me become 'the instrument of the Other's jouissance'" (*Ecrits*, 823/320). Nevertheless, as we have seen, this is not the whole story; indeed, it is but the screen. The pervert does not say to himself, "I'm doing all of this in order to be able to complete my own separation, my own castration; I've got to manage to make the Other exist and get the law pronounced!" Instead, he conceives of himself quite differently: as the object ready and willing to do anything to give the Other pleasure in masochism, as the instrument of the Other's anxiety in sadism, and so on.

What appears from the outside to be a no-holds-barred pursuit of satisfaction by the pervert himself is, in fact, a defense of sorts: the attempt to bring into being a law that restrains the pervert's jouissance, that bridles or checks him on the road to jouissance (Seminar X, February 27, 1963). The pervert's will to jouissance (pursuit of satisfaction) encounters its limit in a law of his own making—a law he makes the Other lay down, stipulate, mandate (even if, as in the case of sadism, the sadist himself plays the role of Other and victim simultaneously).[63]

Paradoxically, perhaps, he gets off on the staging of the very operation (castration) that is supposed to require a loss of jouissance. He derives satisfaction from the enactment of the very operation which demands that he separate from the source of his satisfaction.

Castration and the Other

What analytic experience attests to is that castration is . . . what regulates desire, in both normal and abnormal cases.

—Lacan, *Ecrits*, 826/323

Castration means that jouissance has to be refused in order to be attained on the inverse scale of the law of desire.

—Lacan, *Ecrits*, 827/324

We have seen that perversion differs from neurosis and psychosis in important ways. Whereas the psychotic may suffer from what is experienced as an invasion of jouissance in his or her body, and the neurotic attempts above all to avoid jouissance (maintaining an unsatisfied or impossible desire), the pervert gets off on the very attempt to draw limits to his jouissance. Whereas in psychosis the Other does not exist (since its principal anchoring point, the Name-of-the-Father, is not instated), and in neurosis the Other exists only too ponderously (the neurotic wishing to get the Other off his or her back), in perversion the Other must be made to exist: the pervert has to stage the Other's existence by propping up the Other's desire or will with his own.[64]

	Psychosis	Neurosis	Perversion
The symbolic Other	Is lacking, thus does not exist as such	Ineradicably exists	Must be made to exist

The pervert and the psychotic engage in an attempt to *supplement the paternal function* that brings the symbolic Other into existence—the pervert by staging or enacting the enunciation of the law, the psychotic by fomenting a delusional metaphor. Even certain phobias, in which a phobic object is put in the place of the Name-of-the-Father, involve a form of *supplementation of the paternal function.* Nevertheless, the psychotic's supplementation aims at alienation, while the pervert's and phobic's aims at separation.

Let us turn now to the mOther, the imaginary or real mother. In psychosis she is never barred by the Name-of-the-Father, and the psychotic never emerges from her as a separate subject; in neurosis she *is* effectively barred by the Name-of-the-Father, and the neurotic *does* emerge as a separate subject; in perversion the Other must be made to exist so that the mOther can be barred and the pervert can emerge as something other than an imaginary object of her desire.

	Psychosis	Neurosis	Perversion
The mOther	Never barred	Barred	Must be barred

Psychosis means there has been no effective prohibition of the child's jouissance in its relationship with its mother—that is, no inscription of the father's "No!"—due either to the father's absence or failure to impose himself as symbolic father, on the one hand, or to the child's refusal to accept that prohibition, on the other (or some combination of both). Perversion involves the inability to name something having to do with the mOther's desire (the father does not seem to be what she wants), to name or symbolize something having to do with sex—the mOther's lack[65]—the result being that the pervert is faced with a lack of lack that generates anxiety. Neurosis involves the inability to enjoy oneself, due to all the Other's ideals—that is, the inability to separate from the Other as language.

Neurotics are often very uncertain about what they want and what turns them on, whereas perverts are often quite certain. Even when neurotics do know, they are often highly inhibited in their ability to pursue it; perverts, in contrast, are generally far less inhibited in their pursuit. Neurotics may often have perverse fantasies in which they act in a very uninhibited manner, but this does not make them perverts, from a structural vantage point.

In *The Lacanian Subject*, I described three moments constitutive of subjectivity—alienation, separation, and the traversing of fantasy—that help us understand the three main clinical structures. These moments can be schematized as three substitutions or substitutional metaphors.[66]

Alienation	Separation	Traversing of fantasy
$\dfrac{\text{Other}}{\text{\$}}$	$\dfrac{\text{object } a}{\text{\$}}$	$\dfrac{\text{\$}}{\text{object } a}$

In alienation, the Other dominates, since the child comes into being as a subject of language (the child is, we might say, enticed into language, seduced into making the "forced choice" between pleasure and language, between the pleasure principle and the reality principle); this does not occur in psychosis. In separation, object a as the Other's desire comes to the fore and takes precedence over or subjugates the subject; this does not occur in perversion, for the pervert himself occupies the position of object a, not allowing the Other's desire to serve as cause of his own: he is the real object that plugs up the mOther's desire. In the traversing of fantasy, the subject subjectifies the *cause* of his or her existence (the Other's desire: object a), and is characterized by desirousness; this does not occur in neurosis.

In this sense, these three moments can be described as a sort of progression:

psychosis ⇒ alienation ⇒ perversion
perversion ⇒ separation ⇒ neurosis
neurosis ⇒ traversing of fantasy ⇒ beyond neurosis

Simply put, the difference between perversion and psychosis is alienation, and the difference between neurosis and perversion is separation. Without alienation, there is psychosis; alienation without separation leads to perversion; and alienation and separation without the traversing of fantasy leads to neurosis. The traversing of fantasy leads the subject beyond castration, beyond neurosis, into largely unexplored territory.[67]

In schematic terms, we can represent psychosis, perversion, and neurosis as shown in Figure 9.2. These graphical representations allow us to posit that, understood in terms of the mOther's desire, the psychotic's whole being and body are required to fulfill the mOther (the psychotic is engulfed within the mOther); the pervert's real penis is required to fulfill the same task; and the neurotic's symbolic achievements are required but never suffice for the same job: the neurotic's mOther always wants something else.

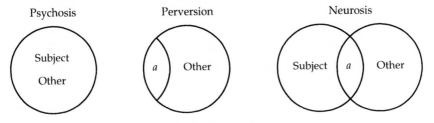

Figure 9.2

Meta-Considerations

Freud's whole investigation comes down to this: "What does it mean to be a father?"

—Lacan, Seminar IV, 204

To many readers, all of this talk about the Other, the law, the symbolic order, structure, language, and naming may seem quite odd. What could pathology, as we see it so concretely in the clinical setting, possibly have to do with making the Other exist? Readers familiar with Freud's work may feel that Freud at least stayed closer to the observable clinical features of cases, as far-fetched as his analyses may at times seem. Even when people find Freud's notions about the phallus and castration excessive or misguided, at least they feel that these notions are not so obscure—they have the sense that they understand what Freud is up to, and why he was led to introduce ideas that depart so significantly from the clinical facts at hand.

Yet with such notions—and with his myths of the primal father who keeps all of the women in the primal horde to himself, and of the sons who band together to kill the father, but who then impose the first egalitarian laws upon one another (see *Totem and Taboo* and *Civilization and Its Discontents*)—Freud goes beyond his own ability to provide explanations. We create myths to account for things we cannot explain otherwise, and though generations of psychoanalysts after Freud have simply regarded his myths as wild imaginings, they demonstrate the necessity of such constructions to Freud's thought. The father, the law, the renunciation of "autoerotic" satisfaction—all of these are absolutely crucial to Freud's way of thinking about individual cases and diagnostic categories, and it is Lacan who, benefiting from forty-five years of work in linguistics beginning with Saussure, recasts the Freudian myths in more scientific terms.

Psychoanalysis has not, with Lacan, completely moved beyond the stage of cosmology, of mythological thinking; indeed, at certain points, Lacan deliberately provides his own myths.[68] But his work on the relationship between words and the world (signifiers and "reality"), and on the movements and displacements within language itself (metaphor and metonymy), provides the necessary linguistic basis for understanding the crucial role of the Freudian father. The paternal function served by the latter is grounded in linguistics; his function is a symbolic one. His crucial role is not to provide love—as the politically correct popular mind is so likely to sustain to the exclusion of all else—but to represent, embody, and name something about the mother's desire and her sexual difference: to metaphorize it.[69] Serving a symbolic function, he need not be the biological father, or even a man. It is the symbolic function itself that is essential.

The Paternal Metaphor as Explanatory Principle

Understood as involving two distinct logical moments, and as instating the symbolic order as such, the paternal metaphor can be usefully understood as providing a subject with an "explanatory principle," an explanation of the why and wherefore of its having been brought into the world, an interpretation of the constellation of its parents' desire (and oftentimes grandparents' desire, as well) that led to its being born. To illustrate this, let us consider Freud's case of little Hans (SE X, 1–149).

Little Hans does not automatically understand what role the father plays in procreation. Indeed, his parents provide all kinds of nonsensical explanations about where babies come from—explanations that involve the stork and that obfuscate even the mother's role—but Hans is never completely duped: he sees his mother's stomach grow, hears her groans from the bedroom one day, and notices the simultaneous appearance of his sister Hanna and disappearance of his mother's large stomach. He grasps in his own way the mother's crucial role in bringing children into the world.

But his mother certainly does not prefer his father or Hanna to him—showing him in so many ways that he is the apple of her eye—and always gets her way, skirting the father's occasionally expressed displeasure when she allows Hans in her bed. Hans is aware of his father's displeasure (though he cannot get his father to admit to it) and is able to *raise* the question "What does my mother want?"—that is, he is not psychotic—but he is unable to answer it with anything other than himself: "She wants me." ("Me" here is a specific object; we are dealing with demand, not desire, strictly speaking.) He repeatedly asks his father what role the father played in his birth and whether Hans is his mother's child or also his father's child (SE X, 92 and 100), and the father bumblingly accords all procreative power to the mother (and to God, but God here is declared to go along with whatever the mother wants [SE X, 91]). The father never allows Hans to grasp the father's role in begetting children—a role which is not immediately graspable, which requires explanation and thus language—or the place a father might have in a mother's desire. Hans is thus left believing that he is the product of his mother's desire alone, not the product of their joint desires, contradictory and intertwined as they may be. Though he can wonder and even ask about his reason for being, the answer that presents itself is always the same: he was brought into the world to serve her.

Hans, who is never afraid of carts drawn by two horses—easily translatable as two parents, a father and a mother—but only of carts drawn by one horse alone (SE X, 91), is unable to find a place for his father, someone or something outside himself that serves as a relay of his mother's desire, an object of her desire that goes beyond him. There is no name for what she wants: there is only Hans as the object that can satisfy her demands. A first barrier has been erected between Hans and his mother, since Hans knows his father disapproves of their close relationship, but her desire is never named and thus never comes into being as such (in other words, as desire for something else, something other than Hans). Hans feels that all of him is required to keep her satisfied, and this is the true source of his anxiety. Once a first barrier has been erected, the subject does not simply rejoice in being the mother's sole source of jouissance; this role is both enjoyable (Hans' pleasure in "coaxing" with his mother) and threatening (for he senses that he can have no life beyond her). "Hans" is the only name of her desire.[70]

Hans' phobia is an attempt to put some other being (a certain kind of horse) into the father's place between mother and child, as shown in the figure. It is a being to which he can attribute pride and anger, the sentiments he believes his father feels when he sees Hans in bed with his mother (though the father denies any such sentiments, no doubt in part to conform to his and his wife's initial decision to raise the boy with the least possible coercion [SE X, 6]). The phobic object here binds or reduces his anxiety

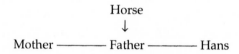

Horse
↓
Mother ———— Father ———— Hans

about being the sole object of his mother's affections for a certain amount of time (and takes on many attributes that I cannot go into here), yet it provides no permanent solution: the phobia dissipates when Hans finds a new solution. But the solution he finds is not a metaphorical one, whereby his mother's desire/lack[71] is named (indicating that she wants, say, status, wealth, a "real" man, advancement in a career, or recognition in an artistic or musical field—something beyond Hans that Hans would then have to grapple with, perhaps trying to help her achieve it or to give it to her through his own accomplishments). I would argue that it is a metonymic solution, whereby Hans simply hopes to have a child of his own whom he can offer up to his mother in exchange for himself. To get his mother off his back, he will follow his father's example: he will give her a male child to come between them, just as his father had Hans, who came between the mother and father:

Mother ——— Hans ——— Father ⇒ Mother ——— Child ——— Hans

This leads Hans to create an entirely new genealogy for himself, recreating the family tree—his symbolic lineage—in such a way that Hans marries his own mother and his father marries *his* own mother (Hans' paternal grand-mother). It may look Oedipal from the outside, but it is not at all the ex-pression of an Oedipal wish. Rather, in seeking some separation from his mother, he is required to give her another child to dote on; this is the only solution he can find to create a space of his own. Like Jean, Hans remains—at the end of his pseudo-analysis with his father and Freud—his mother's "little man." His hope—hardly a neurotic one—is to give her another son to suffocate.

Never having been enabled to name her desire (even falsely, and all names, by defining and delimiting, falsify to some degree, yet can be altogether effective in bringing about separation), Hans can never become someone who can set out to achieve symbolic status in order to win her praise and satisfy her desire in its unlimited displacements: strictly speaking, he is never con-fronted with her desire, since it is never named. He deals only with her demand, her demand for a specific object: him. Rather than glimpsing some-thing in her interests that goes beyond himself, all he can do is imagine giving her a substitute object, another child with which to coax.

Had Hans remained phobic, the paternal metaphor would have been suc-cessfully shored or propped up; an angry horse would have filled the fa-ther's shoes. Having taken on certain of the mother's attributes as well, however, the horse was perhaps never destined to do the trick. The result of the father's failure to provide any sort of an explanatory principle involving the father's will and the father's role in the mother's desire—and of Freud's failure to name the mother's demand and thus transform it into displace-able, enigmatic desire—left Hans in what it seems most appropriate to qualify as a perverse position. Indeed, Lacan's conclusion at the end of Seminar IV is that Hans becomes perverse, not (normally) neurotic, as Freud suggests.

For the neurotic, there is always some sort of explanatory principle; there is always a little story, vague and confusing as it may be, about why our parents wanted us, or perhaps didn't want us at first but grew to love us. This little story tells us something about the place we occupy in their desire—not the place we occupy in the universe as a whole, science seeming to provide us with such insignificant places in it (the universe contains, as Carl Sagan says, "billyuns and billyuns of galaxies")—and this space in their desire, however small, is our foothold in life.

But what are we wanted for? That is the question.[72] If we are wanted only as an extension of one parent, and expected to devote ourselves to that parent's "sexual service," trouble ensues. We must be wanted for something else, something perhaps extremely obscure: "We just want you to be happy," "We want you to achieve something important," "We want you to make us proud." As anxiety-producing as such parental desires often are to the neurotic, they are part of the price that must be paid to stave off the "worst."

The delusional metaphor constructed by a psychotic serves to make up for the lack of just such an explanatory principle. One patient (mentioned briefly in Chapter 7) came to therapy with the idea that a certain David she had once worked for, who had a predilection for reading Saint Paul's letters in the New Testament, had a sort of "cosmic connection" with David Letterman, the talk-show host. In the course of her therapy, she made all kinds of new connections: according to her, the first David was her half-brother, being the illegitimate child of her own father and the next-door neighbor; he was able to exert influence over all areas of her life, and was growing more powerful everyday due to his connections with prominent men like David Letterman; he was going to run for president, with God's help; and she herself played a role in his life as a fallen angel who, it seemed, might be raised up in the course of his ascent.

Her "connections" took on "cosmic" proportions: lacking a symbolic space in her own nuclear family, in her parents' desire, this patient set about recreating the world in such a way as to grant herself a special role in it, a place that would at last be truly hers. Her work is ongoing, and it is not clear exactly where she will fit into the cosmological scheme of things she is elaborating— not deliberately but spontaneously. What is clear is that she is slowly but surely generating an explanatory principle for herself; it is admittedly idiosyncratic, like Schreber's, and hardly likely to win adherents in a wider circle (though this sometimes happens), but if allowed to follow its own course, it should afford her far greater stability.

Like Hans' spontaneous recreation of his own family tree, of a new genealogy that would allow for a solution to his dilemma, the psychotic's delusions—when allowed to pursue their own course—move toward creating a world in which the psychotic is assigned an important place, a critical role. The psychotic's delusional cosmology serves to explain the why and wherefore of the psychotic's birth, and the purpose of his or her life on earth. Thus, it too attempts to tie word to meaning, like the paternal metaphor.

Consider the case of a very young boy I know whose mother had destroyed the boy's father, demanded complete loyalty from her son (never tiring of telling him that he would have trouble finding a wife later because of his special relationship with his mother), put him in her bed every night, and never revealed her genitals to him or said anything to correct his belief that both men and women had what he called "a ball" (his term for a penis). In order to have him, his mother had decided to get pregnant without consulting the father, a man she had just begun dating; she later told the boy his father had abandoned him because he didn't love him (when she had actually driven the father to suicide).

A therapist has a number of options in such a case. He or she can wait, and hope the child *articulates* something that will transform the mother's unbearable presence and demands (the mother as real) into a speakable, bearable reality (the mother's desire as named), but the therapist then runs the risk of abandoning the child to psychosis or perversion. Or the therapist can invent an explanation: "Your father very much wanted a little boy like you, and asked your mother to have his child. Since your father's death, your mother has been very scared and upset, and holds onto you as a reminder of her lost husband."[73]

This is not merely a construction—it is a calculated lie. But with such a lie, if it is introduced after a strong relationship has been established between therapist and child, and does not blatantly contradict too much of what the child has heard about the absent father, the therapist creates an important place for the father in the mother's world and thereby names her desire. In other words, if the therapist is successful in making this construction stick (and I have seen it work), the therapist transforms the mother's demand for the child to give her all of her satisfaction in life with the whole of himself—transforms it into a desire, a desire for something else, for the father or something about the father that the boy can then try to fathom.

This construction will contradict certain things the mother says, but the child will set about trying to understand what the mother says in the context of the construction: "She won't let go of me because she misses my father"; "She complains of his abandoning us because she is lonely." The contradictions do not uproot the construction or anchor the therapist has provided, but rather serve as the point from which everything else is interpreted. So although the mother's behavior and presence have not necessarily changed a whit, the therapist has enabled the child to *read* them differently. The child's experience of his mother has been radically transformed by the construction.

Later in life, the child may come to reject virtually all facets of the therapist's construction, coming to believe instead that the mother's motives were mostly malicious and self-serving, but *he will reject the construction from the standpoint of the construction*. In other words, he will have a point on which to stand that remains unshakable, a vantage point from which to cast doubt upon the accuracy of the construction. Prior to the construction, there was no place to stand, no ground, and thus no possibility of questioning or wondering. After the construction, the child can call everything into question without ever cutting out the ground from beneath his feet. He may, at the extreme, come to wish he had never been born, but at least there will be a place from which he can formulate that wish! This place is the subject, the Lacanian subject.

III

PSYCHOANALYTIC
TECHNIQUE BEYOND
DESIRE

10

FROM DESIRE TO JOUISSANCE

Only love allows jouissance to condescend to desire.

—Lacan, Seminar X, March 13, 1963

The preceding three chapters include a great deal of theoretical material that has taken us somewhat far from the clinical orientation I emphasized in the earlier part of this book. I would now like to reformulate some of the main thrusts of Lacan's approach to practice, incorporating the work on desire, jouissance, and language that has been introduced.

Beyond Desire: The Fundamental Fantasy Revisited

My emphasis on the importance of "opening up the space of desire" and "setting the analysand's desire into motion" might have given certain readers the impression that the ultimate goal of analysis, according to Lacan, is to dialectize the analysand's desire and then free it from the death grip of the Other's desire. It is true, in the early stages of analysis, that the dialectization of the subject's desire has certain salutary effects: a lessening of fixation and a decrease in anxiety ("Desire is a remedy for anxiety," as Lacan says in Seminar VIII, 430). And it is true that for many years (throughout the 1950s and into the early 1960s), Lacan himself viewed desire as the key to the successful resolution of analysis.[1]

This early stage of Lacan's work was marked by the belief that an analysis can come to a successful end via the symbolic order, desire being a phenomenon of language and there being no such thing as human desire, strictly speaking, without language. Lacan discusses at great length the way in which desire displaces and moves as a function of the symbolic order—that is, as a function of language. His well-known essay on Edgar Allan Poe's "The Purloined Letter" details how the desire of the different characters in Poe's story is determined by their position within a certain symbolic or signifying structure. He emphasizes the fact that patients' lives are determined by their "purloined letters"—the snatches of their parents' conversation (that is, of the

Other's discourse), often not intended for their ears, that were indelibly etched in their memories and sealed their fate. Patients bring those letters to analysis, and analysts attempt to render them legible to their patients, to uncover the hidden determinants of their desire.[2]

This is the Lacan who allows us to understand how it is that Jean's button fetish forms on the basis of a purely linguistic or literal connection between *ton bout* (his mother's term for his penis) and *bouton* (his father's term for his mother's genitals, as well as the everyday French term for button). This is the Lacan who stresses that analysts must constantly pay attention to the letter of what their analysands say, not to what they *mean to say*, not to their intended meaning, for they know not what they say: they are spoken by the signifiers (that is, the Other's discourse) that inhabit them. This is the Lacan who returns to Freud's insistence on the importance of the nonsensical concatenation of letters (what Freud refers to as "verbal bridges" [SE X, 213]) in the formation of symptoms; in the case of the Rat Man, for example, Freud tells us that the "rat complex" evolves from elements—*Ratten* ("rats"), *Raten* ("installments"), and *Spielratten* ("gamblers")—that link up not because of their meanings but because of the literal relations among the words themselves (that is, because they contain many of the same letters). This is the Lacan who demonstrates the extent to which we are subjugated by signifiers, by the discourse of our parents that determines our fate, and declares that through analysis we must come to accept that we are mortified by language, and thus, in a sense, the living dead (our bodies are overwritten, and we are inhabited by language that lives through us).[3] We must subjectify that mortal fate, make it our own; we must assume responsibility for the roll of the dice at the beginning of our universe—our parents' desire that brought us into being—bringing ourselves into being where their desire had served as cause of our own.

This is the Lacan who formulates the process of analysis as untying the knots in the analysand's desire, the goal of analysis as "no other than bringing to the light of day manifestations of the subject's desire" (Seminar VIII, 234), and the successful end of analysis as the development of a "decided desire" or "determined desire": a desire that does not allow itself to be put off by obstacles or swayed by the Other, a once unconscious desire that is no longer subject to inhibition, the kind of desire that—after an admittedly long period of analysis—can say no to the analyst's request that the analysand come back the next day for still more analysis, the kind of desire that no longer cares what the Other wants or says.[4]

This is the Lacan who formulates that the analysand must learn not "to give up on his or her desire," not "to give in when it comes to his or her desire," not to let the Other's desire take precedence over his or her own (for guilt results when we give in; see Seminar VII, 368/319). This is the stage of Lacan's work where desire is endowed with a certain utopian edge: it *can* take us where we want to go—that is, beyond neurosis.

From the Subject of Desire to the Subject of Jouissance

Desire comes from the Other, and jouissance is on the side of the Thing.[5]

—Lacan, *Ecrits*, 853

[There is] a certain link between the acephalous and the transmission of life as such—in other words, the passage of the flame of one individual to another in a signified eternity of the species—namely, that Gelüst [craving] does not involve the head.

—Lacan, Seminar VIII, 254

In the later stage of Lacan's work, it is not so much the general idea of what analysis wishes to achieve that changes but the terms in which those goals are expressed. The goal remains to separate from the Other, and to enable the subject to pursue his or her course without all the inhibitions and influences that derive from concrete others around the subject or the internalized Other's values and judgments.

Lacan comes to see that unconscious desire is not the radical, revolutionary force he once believed it to be. Desire is subservient to the law! What the law prohibits, desire seeks. It seeks only transgression, and that makes desire entirely dependent on the law (that is, the Other) which brings it into being. Thus, desire can never free itself completely of the Other, as the Other is responsible for desire's very being. Returning to the figures I used in earlier chapters to represent the subject's relation to the Other, we can say that desire remains inscribed, on the right-hand side, within the Other, while the subject is someThing else (see Figure 10.1).

What is that someThing else? If the subject is no longer to be conceptualized as the pure lack that gives rise to desire, as we see in Lacan's early work, what

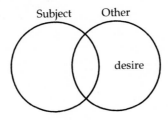

Figure 10.1

then is the subject? What is it that we can speak of as existing outside the Other, as independent of the Other? In Freudian terms, it is the id, the seat or locus of the drives, for the Freudian drives seem to be unsocialized, uneducated, and ungoverned, at least at the outset.[6] They pursue their own course without any regard for what is appropriate or approved of. In the words of Jacques-Alain Miller, to whom I owe this formulation of the early and later stages in Lacan's work:

> The drive couldn't care less about prohibition; it knows nothing of prohibition and certainly doesn't dream of transgressing it. The drive follows its own bent and always obtains satisfaction. Desire weighs itself down with considerations like "They want me to do it, so I won't," or "I'm not supposed to go that way, so that's the way I want to go, but perhaps at the last second I won't be able to do it anyway." . . .
>
> During a whole period of his theoretical elaboration, Lacan tries to prop up the life functions on desire. But once he distinguishes the drive from desire, a devaluation of desire occurs, as he emphasizes above all the "not" on which desire is based. What then becomes essential, on the contrary, is the drive as an activity related to the lost object which produces jouissance . . .
>
> What is essential to desire is its impasse. Its crux, says Lacan, is found in impossibilities, and we can say that its action essentially reaches a dead end. That is more or less what Lacan says in his "Proposition de 1967"[7]: "Our impasse [is] that of the subject of the unconscious." One might say: our impasse is that of the subject of desire. The crux of the drive is not found in impossibilities . . . The drive never comes to an impasse. ("Commentary on Lacan's text," 425–426)

In a word, we can say that Lacan shifts from identifying the subject (and when he says "subject" he means *what is most essential*) with unconscious desire to identifying the subject with the drive. What is most important about the human subject is no longer, in his view, the multifarious, metonymic movements of desire, but satisfaction itself: the Lacanian subject here is the headless subject (a sort of nonsubject, when thought of in traditional philosophical or psychological terms—Lacan uses the term "acephalous" in this context) which pursues satisfaction. This subject is, prior to analysis, hemmed in, kept down, and silenced as much as possible by the ego and the superego, by desire as it forms in language on the basis of the Other's discourse, which transmits the Other's desires, values, and ideals. In Lacan's earlier work, the subject was precisely the defensive stance that hemmed in, kept down, and silenced the drives' clamoring for satisfaction, the defensive stance adopted with respect to an overpowering experience of jouissance. Now, in contrast, with the subject viewed as drive, the aim of analysis in clinical work with neurotics (not psychotics or perverts)[8] is to transform the analysand's fantasy that props up his or her desire, for this desire impedes his or her pursuit of satisfaction.[9] The analysand must reconstitute him- or herself not in relation to the Other's demands or desires but in relation to the partial object that brings satisfaction: object a.

This implies that the drives themselves undergo a kind of transformation in the course of analysis, for as we saw in Chapters 4 and 5, the drives form as our needs are addressed to those around us (usually our parents) and as a function of the demands made upon us by those people (to eat, excrete, and so on). This is why Lacan, in his early work, provides a matheme for the drive that includes "D" for the demands we make on the Other and the demands the Other makes on us: ($\$ \lozenge D$). In response to the Other's demand for me to eat, I formulate my own demand that the Other demand that I eat.[10] Demand answers demand, demand counters demand, in a vicious cycle.

By Seminar XI (1964), however, Lacan's formulation of the drive changes: the drive goes around the object and encircles it, isolating it in a sense (that is, separating it). The drive is thus correlated with object a, not with the Other's demands or demands addressed to the Other. Conceptualized in this way, the drive continues to be grammatically structured (flip-flopping from the active to the passive voice, from the impulse to eat to the impulse to be eaten, from the urge to beat to the urge to be beaten)[11]—and as such is not totally divorced from the symbolic register, from the Other as language—but it appeals to no one, to no Other for guidance or permission. This might be understood as a change in Lacan's theorization of the drive itself (that is, one might think that by 1964 he believes that the drive is never related to the Other's demand, neither before nor after analysis), but I think it is better understood as the transformation the drive undergoes in the course of analysis: subjugated first by the Other's demands, and then by the Other's desire, the drive is finally freed to pursue object a.[12]

Note that this chronology of the drive's transformations corresponds precisely to Lacan's three logical moments—alienation, separation, and the traversing of fantasy—presented at the end of Chapter 9 in the form of three metaphors:

$$\frac{\text{Other}}{\$} \qquad \frac{\text{object } a}{\$} \qquad \frac{\$}{\text{object } a}$$

If we take $\$$ to designate the *subject as drive* or the subject as satisfaction, we see that the subject is first dominated by the Other (which we can take to be the Other as/of demand here: D), and then by object *a* as the Other's desire (which is the same as the subject's desire). Only at the end does the subject as drive come into its own, so to speak, in relation not to the Other but to object *a*. The three metaphors or substitutions can then be written as follows:

demand	desire	subject as drive
subject as drive	subject as drive	object *a*

Alternatively, or even simultaneously, we could talk about these three moments as three statuses of the subject: (1) the subject as constituted in relation to demand or the subject as demand, (2) the subject as desire, and (3) the subject as drive. The neurotic often comes to analysis stuck on the Other's demands, asking (as Robert did, in the case discussed in Chapter 8) the analyst to tell him or her what to do—that is, to make demands; by refusing to do so, the analyst seeks to open up a space of desire in which the analysand's desire comes to the fore in its subservience to the Other's desire; and by playing the role of object *a*, the analyst seeks to throw into question the analysand's interpretation of the Other's desire in the fundamental fantasy and bring about its transformation, such that it no longer inhibits the pursuit of satisfaction. We could say that the subject is these different modalities at each stage of the analytic process: as demand, the subject is stuck in the imaginary register; as desire, the subject is essentially a stance with respect to the symbolic Other; and as drive, there is a "subject in the real."[13] In this sense, the subject would have an imaginary, a symbolic, and a real face, each of which predominates at a certain point in the analytic process, and the aim of analysis would be to bring the analysand through these different moments to the point at which the subject as drive—that is, the subject as real—comes to the fore.

Furthering the Analysand's Eros

How can a subject who has traversed his most basic fantasy live out the drive [vivre la pulsion]? *This is the beyond of analysis and has never been touched upon.*

—Lacan, Seminar XI, 246/273

In referring to the goal of "living out the drive," Lacan is implying not that the "fully analyzed" subject becomes a kind of nonstop pleasure-seeking machine, but that desire stops inhibiting the subject from obtaining satisfaction. One of my analysands expressed the neurotic's predicament quite nicely by saying that he could not "enjoy his enjoyment," implying that his satisfaction was, in some sense, ruined or tainted by simultaneous feelings of dissatisfaction or displeasure. Perhaps one way of stating the configuration analysis aims at is to say that *the analysand is at last allowed to be able to enjoy his or her enjoyment.*

Lacan maintains that the neurotic in analysis must be brought not to the point of altogether jettisoning the symbolic constraints on the drives, jettisoning the ego and superego entirely, but to the point of *accepting, in a new way, the drives and the type of satisfaction they seek.*[14] As Miller says, this does not mean that satisfaction becomes mandatory or commanded (which would be tantamount to a return to the superego that commands one to enjoy, to satisfy the drives); rather, it becomes possible or permitted. One "gives permission" to the drives to go their own way, to pursue their own course;[15] one "permits their perversion," insofar as the drives always seek a form of satisfaction that, from a Freudian or traditional moralistic standpoint, is considered perverse. What the drives seek is not heterosexual genital reproductive sexuality, but a partial object that provides jouissance.

In this sense, we can fill in the blank spaces in Figure 10.1 as shown in Figure 10.2.

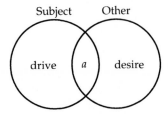

Figure 10.2

From the revolutionary character of unconscious desire, Lacan looks elsewhere: the revolutionary was, in fact, no more than a rebel against a very specific law, and as such utterly and completely dependent upon that which he or she rebelled against. The new configuration Lacan seeks is one involving a kind of "harmony" (though one hesitates to use such a term in talking about Lacan) between desire and the drives. Desire learns how to keep its mouth shut and let enjoyment prevail.[16]

In a sense, this evolution in Lacan's theorization does not represent a radical change in his general orientation, for in Seminar VIII (1960–1961) he had already stressed that analysis aims at furthering the analysand's eros.[17] What we can say is that from viewing eros in terms of desire, Lacan comes to view it more in terms of jouissance.

This distinction between desire and jouissance, or between the signifier (since desire is only articulated in signifiers) and jouissance, parallels the important Freudian distinction between representation and affect discussed in Chapter 8. The subject of representation can be associated here with the unconscious, and thus with the articulation and development of unconscious desire—Lacan's subject of desire or desiring subject—whereas the subject of affect or "emotive" subject is the subject of jouissance or "enjoying subject."[18] For as clinicians quickly learn, where there is affect, there is jouissance.

Technique beyond Desire

It is insofar as the analyst's desire, which remains an x, tends in the exact opposite direction from identification, that it is possible to go beyond the level of identification, via the subject's separation . . . The subject's experience is thereby brought back to the level at which . . . the drive can present itself.

—Lacan, Seminar XI, 246/274

In his seminars from the early 1950s, Lacan theorizes that the analysand must work through the imaginary interference in his or her symbolic relation to the Other. In those from the early to mid-1960s, Lacan proposes that the analysand's symbolic relation itself—the relation in which desire is deployed— must be worked through. From this latter perspective, the subject of (or as) unconscious desire has to be worked through, interfering, as it does, in the analysand's relation to object *a*, and interfering thus with the subject as satisfaction (see Figure 10.3). Desire here is a defense against satisfaction, and the subject as desire is thus a defense against the subject as drive: the former meddles and interferes with the latter's jouissance.

When analysis is theorized in terms of desire alone, the analysand is likely to end up modeling his or her desire on the analyst's, even if this is not what the analyst is deliberately aiming at. This is likely to be tantamount to certain

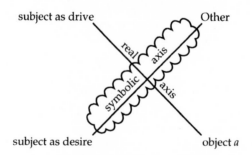

Figure 10.3. Modified L Schema

analysts' goal of having the patient's "weak ego" identify with the analyst's "strong ego": it is a solution via identification. But once Lacan formulates the notion of separation from the stranglehold of the Other's desire, desire is seen to be associated with language (the signifier), identification (which is based on language), and interpretation, whereas jouissance is outside language, has no ties to identification, and requires tools beyond interpretation.

Deciphering and interpreting the unconscious can be made into an endless process. They remain crucial in Lacan's latest conceptualization of analysis, but are not enough; they are not considered adequate for the kind of transformation Lacan is looking for. Analysis should not, according to Lacan, be an infinite process; instead it should involve a concrete move, a shift in subjective position—what he calls the traversing of the fundamental fantasy.

This positional shift is attested to in the institutional procedure known as the "pass," a procedure that Lacan developed in the late 1960s for his psychoanalytic institute, the Ecole Freudienne de Paris, and that is still implemented by the institute he founded shortly before his death, the Ecole de la Cause Freudienne. Lacan decided to implement such a procedure—which involve having an analysand extensively discuss his or her analysis with two oth analysands, who in turn communicate what they have heard to a group of experienced analysts—to gather information on what Lacan calls "the beyond of analysis," which has never been theorized or studied in any other context. Analysands willing to bear witness to their experience in analysis by going through the pass contribute to the greater understanding of the results of analysis—how "a subject who has traversed his most basic fantasy can live out the drive" (Seminar XI, 246/273), how he or she experiences the drive after his or her fantasy has, in the best of cases, been radically transformed or removed, or how and why analysis has been unable to bring the analysand to such a pass, so to speak. In this sense, the pass is a kind of verification procedure, a way of checking whether or not Lacan's wager—that analysands can be taken beyond the "bedrock of castration"[19]—is being confirmed through use of the techniques he developed.[20]

I have examined many of those techniques in the course of this book, and shall discuss one further technique in a moment. The majority of them were developed early on by Lacan—above all, the nonverbal interventions known as punctuation and scansion (the variable-length session), and the verbal intervention known as "oracular speech." The latter is obviously a form of interpretation, but aims at something beyond meaning effects; like the variable-length session, it confronts the analysand with the question of the analyst's enigmatic desire (the Other's desire), and continually demonstrates to the analysand that the Other's desire is not what he or she always assumes it to be. Insofar as the Other's desire plays the role of object *a* in the analysand's fundamental fantasy, it is by calling into question the Other's desire that it becomes possible to take the analysand to the next step—from the second to the third metaphor, as I have been presenting them here, from a situation in which the subject is subjugated by (his or her interpretation of) the Other's desire to a situation in which the subject as drive is no longer subjugated:

$$\frac{\text{Other's desire}}{\text{subject as drive}} \qquad \frac{\text{subject as drive}}{\text{object } a}$$

Laying Bare the Subject's Jouissance

[The analyst's desire] is to lay bare the subject's jouissance, whereas the subject's desire is sustained only by the misrecognition of the drive known as fantasy.

—Jacques-Alain Miller, "Commentary on Lacan's Text," 426

This next step requires a constant bringing into play of the analyst's desire—not just now and then but constantly, at the end of every session in the analyst's "I'll see you tomorrow," and perhaps within every session as well—not just to encourage the analysand to talk about what is important, but to "lay bare" the analysand's jouissance. When the therapist focuses on what the analysand wants, the analysand's "deepest desires"—which, as we have seen, are responses to (even if refusals of) the Other's desire—the therapist allows the analysand to gloss over the question of satisfaction. Very often, the analysand talks about activities that bring satisfaction, but is quick to express his or her own disgust or dissatisfaction with them. "There was only one lover I ever really got excited with, but I couldn't stand what she did for a living." "I got really turned on by the character in the movie, but that's not the kind of relationship I want for myself." If clinicians focus on what the analysand says he or she wants and doesn't want, they unwittingly confine their attention to the defense—to the stance adopted by the desiring subject with respect to jouissance.

Instead, the therapist must punctuate and emphasize the excitement, the turn-on, the disguised or systematically unrecognized/misrecognized pleasure. Even if the analysand is disgusted by his or her enjoyment, it must still be highlighted—not in such a way, of course, that the analysand feels that he or she is being accused of getting off in a particularly weird, perverse, or disgusting way. The analyst must stress those places in the analysand's discourse where jouissance is expressed, yet avoid disapproving (and "clear up" any misapprehension on the analysand's part that the analyst disapproves). The analysand's natural tendency—"natural" in the sense that fantasy blinds us to jouissance—is to forget or misrecognize satisfaction, to explain it away or not take responsibility for it. The analysand does not spontaneously proclaim, "Where there is jouissance (where it—the id—gets off), I must come into being as the subject of that enjoyment!"[21] By no means. The analysand spontaneously tries to pass that enjoyment off as something else—anxiety, for example. As Freud tells us, anxiety is the universal currency of affect, in the sense that every emotion can be converted into it. It signals an emotion—that is, a satisfaction—which is unwanted or disturbing at some level.[22]

When the analysand says, "A strange feeling came over me," the subject is relating a kind of unrecognized satisfaction. When the analysand reports suffering or great sadness, a disguised enjoyment is at stake. There is a kind of basic equivalence between affect and jouissance (in Freud's terms, between affect and libido or libidinal discharge)—an equivalence that is systematically misrecognized due to fantasy,[23] due to the ways in which we would like to see ourselves, and the analyst must not miss the occasion to point toward the satisfaction in what the analysand characterizes as "painful" affect. This involves overcoming the patient's resistance to seeing where jouissance really comes from, what it is that really turns him or her on; and it is only by overcoming that resistance that the analysand can then adopt a different position—a different subject position—with respect to this jouissance, with respect to the drives that provide satisfaction. It is only then that the analysand can stop inhibiting his or her "own" pursuit of satisfaction at the level of the id.

In the case of hysteria discussed in Chapter 8, Jeanne sometimes manifested dissatisfaction with her lack of sexual satisfaction, and seemed, in her dream related to the movie *Indecent Proposal*, to be looking for a reason to overcome her inhibitions. The goal in such a case would be to give voice to whatever sexual drive might be seeking fulfillment in the dream (not to the social stigmas attached to it), in the hope of bringing the analysand to the point of affirming, "I am *that*"—"I am that drive, that craving." Were the analyst to emphasize only the prostitution image of receiving money for sex, and the moral "indecency" surrounding it, this would be tantamount to suggesting to the analysand that she is the prohibition and its transgression—in other words, that she is desire and desire alone (which is what Lacan refers to as "analyzing the defense before the drive" [*Ecrits*, 599/238]). For her to recognize the drives as her own, on the contrary, is what Lacan calls subjectification: the coming into being of the subject where *it* was, where the drives (considered not to be hers) were. To subjectify them is to give them a place, and perhaps an importance, otherwise refused them. To see them as one's own is already a step toward allowing them expression, and this must be combined with the progressive interpretation of the why and wherefore of the symbolic constraints placed upon satisfaction—in Jeanne's case, the sense in which sex always implied *betrayal* of one of her parents or the other. Betrayal was a meaning grafted onto sex by Jeanne's interpretation of her parents' desire, and it was only by calling into question this interpretation (something which was only partially achieved in the course of her analysis) that she could experience sex differently.

A patient comes to analysis in the first place with a "satisfaction crisis," and clinicians must keep their sights set throughout the analytic process on the problem of satisfaction. The patient's satisfaction crisis consists in the fact that the satisfaction being obtained is waning or is considered to be of the "wrong kind." The question of satisfaction was always foremost in Freud's mind, and Lacan summarizes Freud's position by saying that "the subject is always happy"[24] in some respect, always getting off on something, even if it is on his or her own dissatisfaction. He or she is, in the words of Jacques-Alain Miller, "always happy at the level of the drive . . . so happy that the subject repeats that satisfaction, even if it seems to bring dissatisfaction" ("Donc," May 18, 1994). The subject always enjoys him- or herself even as he or she defends against enjoyment. Even though Lacan tells us at one point that "jouissance is prohibited to whoever speaks" (*Ecrits*, 821/319), he is referring there to a kind of immediate, "oceanic" pleasure before the letter, before language, before triangulation;[25] for we all obtain certain satisfactions, as counterintuitive as they may seem, from our symptoms, from criticizing ourselves, and so on. The subject of desire comes into being as a stance with respect to the satisfaction of the drive, as a defense against it; this subject sees itself in desire, not in the jouissance (of the drive). Lacan's approach, insofar as it can be characterized as a "handling of," an "interfering in," or even as a "rectification of" desire (Seminar X, May 22, 1963), involves bringing about a modification in the relationship between satisfaction and desire—that is, between the drives and their inhibition, between the subject of jouissance and the subject of desire.[26]

Rather than untying the knots in the analysand's desire so that he or she can pursue his or her own "true desire," we must untie the knots in the analysand's jouissance: the knots that form in the interrelationship between desire and jouissance.

This should not be taken to imply that analysis seeks to somehow *master* the analysand's jouissance: "The analyst's discourse . . . must be opposed to any will, at least openly declared, to master. I say 'at least openly declared' not because the analyst must dissimulate such a will but because it is, after all, always easy to slip into the discourse of mastery" (Seminar XVII, 79). Just as the analyst must abdicate the role into which he or she is often cast by contemporary psychology and psychiatry—as the master of reality, as the judge of what is real and what is not real—so too must the analyst abdicate the master's discourse in all its forms. For it makes the analyst genuinely hard of hearing, unable to hear the next thing that comes out of the analysand's mouth—the very thing that forces the analyst to revise his or her understanding not only of the case at hand, but of "reality" and all of psychoanalytic theory as well.

AFTERWORD

It is not without certain misgivings that I have prepared this clinical introduction to Lacan's work. I have taken Lacan's "antisystem," as I have referred to it elsewhere,[1] and presented its formal, system-like elements. I have taken a kind of "Gödelian structuralism"—for Lacan maintains the importance of structure while continually pointing to its necessary incompleteness—a constantly evolving work in progress, whose author continually exploded the emerging "orthodox" interpretations of his own teaching, and presented it as a finished product: as a doctrine.

This is a bold and perhaps foolhardy endeavor, and in attempting it I have no doubt exposed myself to criticism from all fronts. I shall be attacked for having oversimplified, and it is true: I have oversimplified many of Lacan's notions in order to present things in a manageable fashion, and I have left aside lengthy qualifications and alternate explanations that Lacan provides. But not everyone is willing to invest the time necessary to read the many volumes of Lacan's work without a little incentive, without a certain glimpse of what there is in Lacan's work that makes the effort worthwhile. I generally assume that a glimpse of the "spread" to come—in my graduate seminar, I refer to it as the "Lacanian smorgasbord"—whets the appetite and makes the ensuing intellectual challenge more palatable. In other words, I assume that the reader would like to be enticed or seduced into the complex world of Lacan's enigmatic formulations with a certain amount of "forepleasure."

This inevitably leads to "precipitated understanding,"[2] and my caution to the reader is simply this: Don't think that the book you have just read will allow you to grasp everything Lacan ever said or wrote, and be prepared to find numerous passages in his work that qualify, if not out and out contradict, what has been put forward here.

At the other end of the spectrum, I shall be criticized by beginners for having made their task overly difficult, for having introduced too many notions (the fundamental fantasy, alienation, separation, desire, jouissance, the symbolic order, the real, and so on) too quickly and in too sketchy a fashion. Indeed, this book no doubt bears a certain resemblance to Freud's *Introductory Lectures on Psychoanalysis*, starting out with apparent graceful simplicity, and ending with dense formulations that require a complete assimilation of every concept mentioned in the book. All I can say is that Lacan's clinical work cannot be understood without certain fundamentals of his theory, and I have done my best to work the theory in a little at a time so as not to overwhelm the reader. Nevertheless, I am well aware that the later chapters are far denser, theoretically speaking, than the earlier ones. The last several chapters may require some rereading and deciphering, and the references I make to other texts should be followed up.

I have provided a slice of Lacan's work, a "cut" that reflects what I myself have managed to glean from his writings and that I find most useful as a clinician. Other clinicians glean other things, and may feel that I overemphasize certain points and underemphasize others. This is unavoidable in the case of an opus that is as enormous as Lacan's, and so rich and varied that it has been giving rise to hundreds of publications a year the world over.

What I hope will be clear is that, even if I do not formulate psychoanalytic experience using terms Lacan introduces from each and every period of his work, I never dismiss his formulations offhandedly. It seems far more fruitful to read Lacan the way Lacan read Freud, adopting, in the words of Jacques-Alain Miller, his "entire theory, including the inner logic of its changing and sometimes contradictory expression."[3]

What is well conceived is stated obscurely.[4]

—Parody of Boileau

After reading my version of Lacan, the reader may well wonder: "If this is all he meant, why didn't Lacan himself just come out and say it?" This may give rise to justified suspicion of my reading ("How can Fink be believed when it is so difficult to confirm anything he says by reading Lacan's own writings?"), which I can only invite, challenging the reader to go on to verify or qualify what I have said on the basis of his or her own reading of Lacan's work.

On the other hand, it may give rise to justified suspicion of Lacan himself: "If what he says is so insightful, why is it written so damn obscurely?" I obviously cannot be held accountable for Lacan's style[5] or for the unreadability of many of the existing translations of his work, but the question is more far-reaching still: "Why is everything stated (even in French) in such an allusive, ambiguous manner?" In part, and this point has been mentioned by many people who have written on Lacan, he is seeking to have certain effects on the reader other than meaning effects: he is seeking to evoke, to provoke, to unsettle us—not to lull us but to jolt us out of our conceptual ruts. Related to this is his aim to put us to work, to remind us that in fact we do not understand what we think we understand (whether it is Freud's writings that are deceptively easy to follow, or our analysands' discourses), and that we may have to make numerous attempts to express or conceptualize something, and then our interpretation will still only be approximate: it will still miss the mark.

The ambiguities in Lacan's speech and writing are often very deliberate. Wholly un-American in spirit, Lacan's motto might well have been: "The more ambiguous and polyvalent, the better." Many will find that approach unpalatable, and a reflection of French intellectual snobbery—which is true, no doubt, at least in part. But I hope I have shown that there is far more to it than that.

A NOTE ON DOCUMENTATION

NOTES

RECOMMENDED READING

INDEX

A NOTE ON DOCUMENTATION

In referring to *Ecrits*, I provide the page number in the French edition followed by a slash and the page number in the current English edition, when the article in question is included in the latter. All page references to Seminar III are to the French edition, the pagination of which is conveniently indicated in the margins of the English edition (New York: Norton, 1993). References to other seminars that have been published include the French pagination and the English pagination, when available. Lacan's unpublished seminars are referred to by number and the date of the lecture being cited—for example, Seminar X, March 13, 1963. Virtually all references to Freud's work are to *The Standard Edition of the Complete Psychological Works of Sigmund Freud* (London: Hogarth, 1963), abbreviated here as SE, followed by volume and page numbers.

NOTES

1. Desire in Analysis

1. See Slavoj Žižek, *Enjoy Your Symptom! Jacques Lacan in Hollywood and Out* (New York: Routledge, 1992).

2. As Freud says, regarding the secondary gain a patient derives from his symptoms, "the patient's intention of getting rid of his complaint is not so entirely and completely serious as it seemed," SE VII, 43–44.

3. The value of calling patients who miss appointments is highlighted by the fact that patients occasionally leave therapy due to "simple" miscommunication or to a (symptomatic) misunderstanding. One patient, an obsessive man I learned about when supervising his therapist, missed an appointment with his therapist because he was ill, but felt guilty about it; when he called the center where the therapist worked to schedule a new appointment, he apparently misunderstood what the receptionist there told him, believing that the therapist was refusing to talk to him ever again—not just at that very instant. This fed into his guilt, and he never called back to reschedule, feeling that he was merely getting what he deserved. If his therapist had not repeatedly called him until she managed to speak to him personally, the patient would have left therapy (perhaps for good) believing that he was receiving "just punishment," rather than having the chance to work through his intense feelings of guilt.

4. The recommendation that the therapist always express a desire for neurotic patients to continue their therapy assumes that the therapist has been through extensive analysis, has the clear sense that the therapy has been moving forward (despite the patient's possible view that things are stagnating) and that it is not mired in the therapist's own countertransferential blocks (see Chapter 3), and is not dealing with a patient whose own desire has been fundamentally stymied at every turn by his or her parents. As I suggest in Chapter 2, analysis must essentially open up a space of desire, a space in which the patient can come to desire, and, in certain instances, specific expressions of the analyst's desire may be counterindicated, especially in the early stages of treatment.

My recommendation here, like all the other recommendations made in this book, is not a universal rule applicable to all contexts, all patients, all cultures, and all historical periods. It is, rather, a rule of thumb that should be of use to analytically trained therapists and to therapists-in-training under analytically oriented supervision. Like all of the other techniques recommended in the first five chapters of this book, it is *not* applicable to the treatment of psychosis (see Chapter 7) and is applicable only with certain caveats to the treatment of perversion (see Chapter 9). It grows directly out of Freud's recommendation that therapists manifest "a serious interest" in patients (SE XII, 139) and "prevail on [them] to continue their analysis" (SE XII, 130).

5. I am assuming here that a well-trained, well-analyzed analyst is able to put aside his or her antipathy or attraction to patients and not allow it to interfere in the work. If an analyst is unable to do so, my recommendation would obviously be that the analyst refer the patient to someone else.

6. See, for example, *Ecrits*, 824/322.

7. Cf. Freud's term, "psychoanalytic purification" (SE XII, 116).

8. As Jacques-Alain Miller puts it, "The most precious thing, the *agalma* [a term for object *a*] that keeps the patient coming, is the question mark—that is, the lack in the Other." "La Sortie d'analyse," *La Lettre mensuelle de l'ECF* 118 (April 1993): 30.

9. See, for example, SE VII, 194, where it is translated as "instinct for knowledge," and SE X, 245, where it is translated as "epistemophilic instinct." More generally, however, Freud (like Lacan) believes that "thirst for knowledge [is] inseparable from sexual curiosity" (SE X, 9).

10. See, for example, Seminar III, 21. See also Seminar XXI, where Lacan says, "Il n'y a pas le moindre désir de savoir" ("There isn't the slightest desire to know"). Virtually the same words are repeated in published form in "Introduction à l'édition allemande d'un premier volume des *Ecrits*," *Scilicet* 5 (1975): 16. See also the first page of Seminar XX, where Lacan qualifies his own path as involving a "je n'en veux rien savoir" ("I don't want to know anything about it"), as well as page 95 of the same seminar.

11. "Introduction à l'édition allemande d'un premier volume des *Ecrits*," *Scilicet* 5 (1975): 16. As we shall see, it is a will not to know the source of the subject's satisfaction—that is, not to know what the subject really and truly "gets off" on.

12. See, for example, Seminar III, 60: "The patient's resistance is your own." See also *Ecrits*, 595/235: "There is no other resistance to analysis than that of the analyst himself."

13. As Colette Soler says, "What does it take for a symptom to be analyzable? I propose the following: it must be losing jouissance, in the sense in which we say that something is 'losing speed.'" "Les fins propres de l'Acte analytique," in *Actes de l'ECF: L'acte et la répétition* (1987): 19; translated as "The Real Aims of the Analytic Act," *Lacanian Ink* 5 (1992): 57 (translation modified).

14. Consider Freud's remarks in SE XVI: "The kind of satisfaction which the symptom brings has much that is strange about it . . . It is unrecognizable to the subject, who, on the contrary, feels the alleged satisfaction as suffering and complains of it" (365–366).

15. In this book, I employ the French term "jouissance" more or less interchangeably with Freud's term "satisfaction." For those readers familiar with Freud's distinction between the pleasure principle and the reality principle, it may be helpful to indicate that "jouissance" and "satisfaction" (as I am using them here, and as Freud and Lacan generally use them) imply something other than the immediate "dis-

charge" of tension—that is, something other than pleasure "pure and simple." They involve the impingement of "reality," which I will interpret here essentially as the impingement of a child's parents (I begin with the child in order to keep things simple for the moment)—that is, as the demands they make upon the child to do this and not do that. *Jouissance (or satisfaction) is thus a pleasure beyond the pleasure principle*, for it already implies the existence of other people, their demands, injunctions, desires, and values—all of those things that tie pleasure up in knots, inhibiting it and impeding it.

In Lacanian terms, "jouissance" means (as we shall see in later chapters) that immediate discharge has become bridled by symbolic means: by the child's assimilation or internalization of the parents' (that is, the Other's) admonitions, values, prohibitions, and so on. When discharge comes, it already includes the Other in some sense. In certain cases, the resulting discharge may be greater, involving, as it does, the simultaneous *overcoming* of a prohibition; in other cases, the inclusion of the Other may lead to the diversion of discharge to specific realms of life (these two possibilities are by no means exhaustive).

Note that Freud's oral, anal, and genital stages are related to the *parents' interest* in the child's different organs and prohibiting actions and threats (including weaning, toilet training, and prohibiting of thumb-sucking and other forms of "self-gratification"); due to the parents' concerns, the "pure pleasure" the child originally procures from different zones (at some hypothetically initial moment) becomes *allo-erotic*. In other words, it begins to include those others, whether submissively, defiantly, lovingly, or whatever. The no-longer-pure pleasure the child takes in thumb-sucking now involves a relationship to those who have prohibited it, disapproved of it, made fun of it, and so on. It has become relational or social; it means something about the child's stance toward its parents, educators, and others. It is *that* transformation which marks the divide between pleasure and jouissance.

Let me add a word here on terminology. To use the various French conjugations of the verb *jouir* in English to talk about the process of obtaining jouissance would become extremely complicated, and the English verb "to enjoy" is often inadequate to render the notion of a pleasure beyond the pleasure principle. In this book I sometimes use the verb "to enjoy" where it seems suitable, but more often I use an expression that some readers may not relish: "to get off." In the colloquial American English spoken by many people of my generation, "to get off on something" corresponds quite closely to the meaning of *jouir* as I understand Lacan to use it, suggesting not a solely physical, corporal pleasure, but a "kick" someone may get from being cruel, inflicting punishment, embarrassing someone, living out a fantasy (regardless of its consequences for others), receiving a great deal of attention (a "narcissistic" pleasure), lecturing, writing, painting, making music, dancing, singing, and so on. When I talk about trying to determine what a patient "gets off on," I am essentially asking the same question Freud asks when he focuses on the source of a patient's "satisfaction" (usually a symptomatic "substitute satisfaction," according to Freud).

In French, *jouir* means "to come" (climax or orgasm) and "to enjoy," and *jouir de* means "to get off on," "to take advantage of," "to benefit from," and so on. For a fuller account of the term, in its many colloquial and juridical meanings, see Bruce Fink, *The Lacanian Subject: Between Language and Jouissance* (Princeton: Princeton University Press, 1995), chs. 7 and 8. See also Seminar XX, *Encore,* trans. Bruce Fink (New York: Norton, 1997). On pleasure, desire, and jouissance, see Bruce Fink, *Masculine/Feminine: Human Sexuality in the Twenty-First Century* (forthcoming; title tentative).

16. It should be pointed out here that *demande* in French, which I almost always translate into English as "demand," is not as strong in French as it is in English; in French it can often simply mean "request." This should be kept in mind when I talk about patients' demands, for in clinical work patients make a great many requests that we might not, in ordinary English, qualify as demands. "Demand," as I use it, should be understood as a technical term implying that *someone asks someone else for something.* It is defined in Chapter 4.

17. In his 1993–1994 seminar entitled "Donc" (unpublished), Jacques-Alain Miller astutely points out Freud's failure to bring to bear his desire as analyst in his work with Dora, pointing out the cold, noncommittal nature of Freud's response when Dora says, "Do you know that I am here for the last time today?" Freud replies, "You know that you are free to stop the treatment at any time" (SE VII, 105). Freud fails to take advantage of the opportunity to express his desire that Dora continue her analysis. The expression of his desire for her to stay in therapy might have swayed her faltering conviction, and perhaps have allowed Freud the time to change the way he was conducting therapy and interpreting with her; perhaps not. The reasons Freud gives there for not having expressed "the importance to me of her staying on"—"that there must be some limits set to the extent to which psychological influence may be used, and I respect as one of these limits the patient's own will and understanding" (109)—sound a good deal like rationalizations when compared with his remarks in SE XII, where he talks about his persistent attempts to "prevail on [his] patients to continue their analysis" (130).

The analyst's desire must come into play right from the beginning of therapy, not only at some isolated moments later in time. On shaking the analysand's hand at the end of the first session, the analyst expresses his or her desire to see the new analysand at the next session. Constraints of the analytic setting—often referred to in American psychology as "boundary issues"—are set not by appealing to some theory, institutional rule, or higher authority, but because that is the way the analyst wants it to be. Therapists are prone to responding to patients' invitations to go out for coffee or a drink together by saying things like "That wouldn't be appropriate" or "I'm sorry, but I can't do that," as if it were independent of their own will or as if they were obeying some higher power. That, of course, suggests to the patient that the therapist *would* go out with him or her *if he or she could*—that is, if the "powers that be" allowed it. The therapist need not, in changing tacks, be crude, saying something like, "No, I don't want to," but can certainly say, "No, *I* don't socialize with my patients." Some misguided therapists do go out with their patients, and patients are often aware of that. To appeal to a universal principle like "Therapists do not socialize with their patients" is to make a false claim and miss an opportunity to bring the analyst's desire to bear.

The analyst's desire must also be brought to bear as soon as a patient is late for a session or misses a session, or even calls to cancel. The analyst must always attempt to limit cancellations to the absolute minimum, and oblige the patient to reschedule missed sessions (simply making the patient pay for a missed session is often not enough; some patients would rather pay than come and talk). If the patient has not given me twenty-four hours' notice of a cancellation, I generally charge the patient *and* reschedule to make up for the session missed. The analyst has to use his or her desire to counter the analysand's resistance, and cannot accept any and all excuses for missing sessions. The analysand must be made to understand that the analyst expects analysis to take precedence over virtually everything else in the analysand's life; within certain limits, life gets organized around analysis, not vice versa (see Chapter 2).

It is extremely important not to let patients cancel appointments by leaving messages with answering services, answering machines, and other intermediaries unless the therapist calls them back, finds out the why and wherefore of the cancellation, and reschedules appointments. A number of clinics allow patients to cancel by calling a service or a secretary, and discourage therapists from calling those patients to reschedule. I, on the contrary, always encourage therapists to call patients—even when they are only fifteen to twenty minutes late for an appointment—to use the lever of their desire to get the patients to their sessions, and to get them there on time. If a patient cancels a session, and there is no other preset appointment time, the therapist may have to call the patient repeatedly in order to talk with him or her in person, perhaps even at odd hours, to be sure to catch the patient at home (early in the morning or late at night, even risking waking the patient). If the patient is resisting the process, which we assume he or she must at certain points, the therapist may have to be very persistent to get through the roommates used as screens, family members who do not transmit messages, answering machines used to screen calls, and so on to actually speak to the patient directly. We know the patient will resist changing, because that implies giving up certain satisfactions. It is the therapist's responsibility to keep the patient in therapy, even when the patient obviously does not want to be there at some level.

If the therapist has adopted this general orientation, he can then assess if and to what degree he deviates from it with a particular patient. When he finds himself being more lenient with one patient than with the others—that is, allowing one patient's resistance to run therapy, instead of refusing to negotiate with it—he has to ask himself why. What are the countertransferential issues that are leading him to act that way? Does he feel especially sorry for this patient? That this patient's life has been particularly rough? Even the best-analyzed analyst must continually associate to and reflect upon his own slips, daydreams, dreams, and fantasies to know what is leading him to make exceptions for certain patients. One of the main purposes of supervision, where the analyst talks about cases with another analyst, is to ensure that the analyst is clear about his own desire in work with specific patients, and not deluding himself about the why and wherefore of his interventions or failure to intervene. Supervision obviously also serves to help the analyst grasp things he has perhaps failed to grasp in a case, but often that very failure is due to resistance on the analyst's part (see Chapter 3).

2. Engaging the Patient in the Therapeutic Process

1. See the section entitled "The Person of the Analyst" in Chapter 3; reciprocity is part and parcel of imaginary relations.

2. Indeed, as Lacan says, we often see a consolidation, organization, or systemization of symptoms in the early stages of analysis; see Seminar X, June 12, 1963. Lacan suggests that such a systemization occurs in Freud's work with the Rat Man (*Ecrits*, 596/236).

3. Jacques-Alain Miller, "La sortie d'analyse," *La lettre mensuelle de l'ECF* 119 (1993): 34.

4. On the analyst as a mirror, see Seminar VIII, 435.

5. See Lacan, "Geneva Lecture on the Symptom," *Analysis* 1 (1989): 10. It is perhaps worth reiterating here that the approach to therapy outlined in the first five chapters of this book is not applicable in cases of psychosis; on the treatment of psychosis, see Chapter 7.

6. See Freud's comments in SE XII, 140–141. Freud's analysis of Dora (SE VII) might serve as a case in point here: Freud presents Dora with a plethora of interpretations that she is not ready to hear, especially from someone she still trusts so little. The ground for interpretation has to be carefully prepared, as if for a seedling. See my discussion of the preparation of the ground for interpretation in the section entitled "A Case of Hysteria" (Chapter 8).

7. See Lacan's use of this term in *Ecrits*, 313/98.

8. See SE XVI, 285.

9. See Lacan, *Ecrits*, 315/100.

10. From the verb "to scan," as in "to scan verse": to divide a line of poetry up into its metrical feet. The French *scander* would normally be translated "to scan" or "scanning," but I prefer to use "to scand" or "scanding" to distinguish the far more common contemporary uses of scanning (looking over rapidly, quickly running through a list, taking pictures of cross-sections of the body with a scanner, or "feeding" text and images in digital form into a computer) from Lacan's idea here of cutting, punctuating, or interrupting the analysand's discourse.

11. This error is made just as often by analysts as by patients. Lacan notes, "Some imagine that we have to totally restore the undifferentiated lived experience of the subject . . . But the continuity in everything a subject has lived through since birth . . . doesn't interest us in the least. What interests us are the decisive moments of symbolic articulation" (Seminar III, 111).

12. This is just as true later, when, for example, the patient, having localized a particularly problematic life event or a symptom, attempts to analyze it head on and refuses to move on to something else. The analyst is confronted, in such cases, with a conscious desire on the patient's part to understand and an unconscious will not to know. By not deftly changing the subject to a different but related point, the analyst allows the patient to become more and more frustrated at not being able to immediately understand, which will no doubt lead to increasing demands by the patient for the analyst to provide interpretations. If these are not forthcoming or are not immediately grasped by the patient, the patient is likely to reproach the analyst: "You're not helping me!"

We do not put stock in the patient's intentions regarding what is to be talked about and in what order. Rather, we put our faith in the unconscious: in the new material it produces and in the order in which it produces it.

13. On the pleasure derived from such blah, blah, blah, see Seminar XX, 53.

14. For Freud's comments on such neurotic strategies, see SE XII, 136.

15. Many therapists have, at one point or another, had patients who act in a somewhat seductive manner in therapy, and while in some cases it may simply be the patient's general style to act seductively, in others the patient is consciously or unconsciously testing the therapist: "Are you going to succumb to my charms? Are you going to fall into my trap, like everyone else? Can I pull the wool over your eyes? Are you just as fundamentally untrustworthy as all the others?" While tempting the therapist, demanding that the therapist reciprocate with love and perhaps sexual intimacy as well, the patient is all the while hoping the therapist *will* pass the test by refusing.

As we shall see, Lacan uses the terms "demand" and "desire" to formulate the difference between the patient's verbally or behaviorally formulated demands and what the patient wants at another level. "Demand" is what I *say* I want or clearly act as if I want, even though I do not necessarily really want it. Indeed, I would not know what to do if the analyst actually gave me the love that I so insistently demand!

16. This is precisely what Freud could be reproached for not having seen at the end of his work with Dora. Dora, if we are to believe Freud's account, slapped Herr K., manifestly refusing his proposition, but all the while hoping that he would return to their summer resort and openly declare his love for her, divorce his wife, and make of Dora an honorable woman. Herr K. did not realize that there might have been some other desire lurking behind Dora's explicit demand that he leave her alone; Freud, similarly, did not realize that behind Dora's explicit demand to end her therapy there might have been a reaching out, on her part—a solicitation or desire for Freud to manifest an interest in having her continue.

17. Freud's definition of "resistance" is very broad: "whatever interrupts the progress of analytic work is a resistance" (SE V, 517).

18. I am not suggesting here that the analyst should solicit all the details of an excuse from an analysand in order to "talk them through" or "interpret them." I have never found it to be of any value to indicate in any way to an analysand that he or she is putting other things ahead of our therapy. Instead, I recommend manifesting to the analysand, by always rescheduling, that you, the analyst, do not intend to let sessions be missed.

19. This is one of the reasons analysts must avoid giving advice. As Lacan says, "It's not simply because we know too little of a subject's life that we are unable to tell him whether he would do better to marry or not in such and such circumstances and will, if we're honest, tend to be reticent. It's because the very meaning of marriage is, for each of us, a question that remains open" (Seminar III, 152).

20. *Demain la psychanalyse* (Paris: Navarin, 1987), 66.

21. This, in and of itself, is already an ambiguous formulation.

22. Logical positivism, a philosophical movement that was in vogue in Vienna around 1900 and in England and America later in the twentieth century, tried to eliminate all ambiguity from language—that is, to construct an unambiguous philosophical language. That project was, it seems to me, doomed to failure from the outset, and was largely abandoned.

23. With the proviso that ideas formulated differently are never more than *approximately* the same.

24. Consciousness itself is not a unitary phenomenon.

25. See his paper "The Freudian Thing, or the Meaning of the Return to Freud in Psychoanalysis," *Ecrits.*

26. Indeed, Lacan maintains that "the structure of a neurosis is essentially a question" (Seminar III, 196), a question such as "Am I a man or a woman?" in hysteria or "Am I dead or alive?" in obsession (Seminar III, 193ff). See Chapter 8 below on these questions in neurosis.

27. I would argue that, despite all of the mistakes Freud makes in his work with Dora, Dora nevertheless does reach this stage of genuine engagement in her analysis. At one point, Freud tells us that "for some time Dora herself had been raising a number of questions about the connection between some of her actions and the motives which presumably underlay them. One of these questions was: 'Why did I say nothing about the scene by the lake for some days after it had happened?' Her second question was: 'Why did I then suddenly tell my parents about it?'" (SE VII, 95). The problem is that Freud bulldozes right over Dora's own questions, obsessed as he is with his own.

28. The term "unconscious formations" comes from Lacan's seminar of the same name (Seminar V).

29. To make a play on words, we could define "desire" as *Wanderlust:* lust that wanders, or the taking of pleasure in wandering/wondering. My brief remarks on desire here will be filled out below, especially in Chapters 5 and 8.

30. See Jacques-Alain Miller's comments on "dialectical negation" in "An Introduction to Lacan's Clinical Perspectives," in Bruce Fink, Richard Feldstein, and Maire Jaanus, eds., *Reading Seminars I and II: Lacan's Return to Freud* (Albany: SUNY Press, 1996), 245.

31. See Lacan's article "Subversion of the Subject and Dialectic of Desire," in *Ecrits.*

3. The Analytic Relationship

1. Such skepticism is part and parcel of the American character, and is one aspect of the independence fiercely expressed by Americans in all matters: there is no such thing as an expert, and nobody's opinion is any more valuable than one's own. This was nicely summarized by someone I knew when I was growing up—a certain Dr. Molinoff, who was fond of saying, "An 'expert' is just an ignoramus from the next town." While laudable in many respects, this typically American spirit leads to superficial readings of difficult yet profound thinkers.

2. See, for example, Seminar XI, ch. 18.

3. See, in this connection, Freud's remarks in SE VII, where he reminds us that in cases of suggestion, the patient "may be said to be cured not by the method but by the physician"—that is, not by free association and interpretation, but merely by the relationship with a therapist believed to be a great healer.

4. Not the patient's ego: the Lacanian analyst attributes little if any importance to the patient's preconceived notions about the why and wherefore of his or her symptoms. Indeed, Lacan confines the technical use of the term "subject" to the unconscious, that which is conscious being covered by the term "ego" (though the ego is not wholly conscious). This should not be taken to imply that Lacan makes the unconscious into a full-blown "agency," in the Freudian sense of the term. He

begins with the notion of something which *is* known unbeknownst to the ego, a knowledge which inhabits us and of which we are unaware, and says that we are inclined to attribute some kind of subjectivity to it. In a slight modification of his more usual expression, *le sujet-supposé-savoir* ("the subject-supposed-to-know"), Lacan suggests that we tend to assume there is a subject wherever there is knowledge: *le sujet-supposé-au-savoir,* "the subject (pre)supposed in knowledge." Indeed, it could be sustained that the knowledge of which the ego is unaware (that is, unconscious knowledge) has never been "subjectified," that it is knowledge without a subject and that the goal of analysis is to subjectify it, to bring the subject into being where that previously unsubjectified knowledge was (see, in Chapter 8, the remarks on the case study of hysteria; see also Bruce Fink, *The Lacanian Subject: Between Language and Jouissance* [Princeton: Princeton University Press, 1995], chs. 2 and 5). As Lacan says, "The subject is never more than supposed" (Seminar XXIII); we *presume* that a subject of some kind must exist wherever we find knowledge, but this is nothing more than an assumption we make. As Chapter 10 will show, Lacan in some sense shifts, in his later work, from identifying the subject with the unconscious to identifying the subject with the id.

5. Indeed, the analyst expresses surprise, curiosity, and interest regarding statements that the patient (and virtually everyone else in the "outside world") may consider self-evident.

6. See Lacan, "Intervention on Transference," in *Ecrits;* translated miserably in *Feminine Sexuality* (New York: Norton, 1982).

7. See Lacan's comments in *Ecrits,* 595/235.

8. In Lacan's work, the term "other" with a lowercase "o" almost always means someone with whom you have an imaginary relationship (someone similar to yourself, someone like you), whereas "Other" with a capital "O" generally refers to a person or institution serving a symbolic function (legislating, prohibiting, putting forward ideals, and so on), though it often designates the mother in a real or imaginary capacity. For clarity's sake, I try to use "Other" for the symbolic function and "mOther" for the mother as real or imaginary (the mOther need not be the biological mother or even a woman; the mOther is the primary caretaker).

It should be mentioned that there is another extremely important component of what Lacan calls "countertransference": he defines the latter as "the sum total of the analyst's biases [*préjugés*], passions, difficulties [*embarras*], and even inadequate information" (*Ecrits,* 225). The analyst's biases may be theoretical prejudices (the belief, for example, that a woman must, in order to achieve "normality," learn to obtain vaginal satisfaction from genital intercourse with a man—a bias that Freud certainly had, at least at one point in his career) that prevent the analyst from hearing what the analysand has to say, preoccupied as he or she is by what he or she believes the analysand needs to accomplish. This is especially important given the firm belief in many schools of psychoanalysis, psychiatry, and psychology that therapists somehow have a better grasp of "reality" than their patients. Lacan teaches us that *the therapist's view of reality is part and parcel of his or her own countertransference;* the therapist's belief that the patient is "blocking out" certain aspects of reality and refusing to "see things the way they really are" must thus be set aside, bracketed out, if the patient's *psychical reality* is to be attended to.

No matter how well trained, a therapist is not an arbiter or judge of what is real and what is not, what is possible and what is impossible. The all-too-common view that it is the therapist's job to lead the patient to see reality clearly is a colossal piece of ideology that instates the therapist as the *master of reality and knowledge* (usually designed to legitimate the therapist in serving some kind of "normalizing" function).

It is obviously impossible for a therapist to put aside *all* theoretical views, since theory allows us to see things we could not otherwise see, even as it blinds us to other things. The therapist must attempt to be open enough to hear what is new and does not fit in with his or her theoretical perspective, and then throw that perspective into question, open it up, jettison blinders, and so on. We cannot see anything without theory, but a strict adherence to already digested theory renders the therapist truly hard of hearing. The obvious conclusion is that countertransference is ineradicable, since our "information" and theories will always be incomplete and inadequate.

9. A very typical scenario for students with high standards is not to study at all for an examination, so that if they do badly, they have a ready excuse. If such students were to "give it everything they've got" and still not achieve the high grades they demand of themselves, they would have to face up to the fact that there are certain limitations to their abilities, something they avoid doing at all costs.

10. This is an extremely simple way of translating a far more complicated sentence found in *Ecrits:* "What the neurotic does not want, and what he strenuously refuses to do until the end of his analysis, is to sacrifice his castration [that is, his subjugation to or dependence upon the Other] to the Other's jouissance, allowing his castration to serve that jouissance" (826/323). This notion will be discussed at length in Chapter 8.

11. This model is also sometimes referred to as Schema Z; it can be found, for example, in *Ecrits*, 548/193.

12. Characterized by identification (of one ego with another) and rivalry.

13. Lacan's term here is *travail du transfert*, an expression he preferred to *perlaboration*, the standard French neologistic translation of Freud's *Durcharbeitung*. See, in particular, *Ecrits*, 596; see also *Ecrits*, 630, where it appears as *travail de transfert*. This expression is not included in the current English translation (235 and 265).

14. In Lacan's later work, the imaginary and the symbolic are conceptualized somewhat differently as equally important orders; there the question is not so much the *dissipation* of the imaginary, but the way in which it is linked to the symbolic and the real. See, in particular, Seminar XXII, *RSI*, 1975–1976, and the seminars that follow it. Lacan's later developments do not, however, negate the importance of working through imaginary identifications in analysis and clarifying and modifying relations to the Other.

As we shall see in Chapter 10, this early stage of Lacan's work was marked by the belief that analysis comes to a successful end via the symbolic order (a change in one's relation to the Other involving the assumption or taking responsibility for death or one's own being-unto-death), the resolution occurring at the level of desire. In his later work, analysis must go beyond a symbolic solution, a solution involving desire, to attain its goals. See, in this regard, Jacques-Alain Miller's fine periodization of Lacan's work in his 1993–1994 seminar, "Donc" (unpublished).

15. In the context of Lacan's discussion here, it seems quite clear that the analyst is the person "who interprets by taking advantage of transference"; the last choice is severely criticized in the passages that follow this quote in *Ecrits*.

16. Consider, in this regard, how Freud handles the Rat Man when the latter begins to heap "the grossest and filthiest abuse" onto Freud and his family (SE X, 209), vehemently expressing his anger while pacing around Freud's office. Freud does not say, "You're transferring anger onto me"; rather, his approach seems to be to say, "Something must have happened between you and your father in the past." He points, thus, not to the fact or existence of transference, but to its content or source. Lacan suggests that transference phenomena (e.g., displays of love or hatred for the analyst) manifest themselves when the dialectical movement of analysis falters or stagnates. The analysand, logically enough, blames the stasis on the only other person present, the analyst. "What then does it mean to interpret transference? Simply to replace the emptiness of this deadlock with a lure" (Ecrits, 225). This doesn't mean that the lure is never useful, for it may, at times, set the process in motion anew.

17. Indeed, as Freud says, "We look upon successes that set in too soon as obstacles rather than as a help to the work of analysis" (SE XVI, 453).

18. This should not be taken to imply that the analyst stops playing the role of a blank screen upon which the analysand can project thoughts, rage, love, and so on.

19. Consider, in this regard, the expression, "My tongue got in the way of my eye teeth and I couldn't see what I was saying."

20. As Freud tells us, positive transference—also known as "transference love"—can serve as a form of resistance just as much as negative transference can. See, in particular, "Observations on Transference Love," SE XII, 159–171.

21. As Freud says, the "simultaneous presence [of affectionate and hostile feelings] gives a good picture of the emotional ambivalence which is dominant in the majority of our intimate relations with other people" (SE XVI, 443).

22. Another way of saying this might be that there is always a quantitative factor involved: affect or libido.

23. See Studies on Hysteria, especially ch. 1, in SE II.

24. Just as one should interpret not the fact of transference but rather its content, one should avoid interpreting "resistance," transference being but one manifestation of resistance. Resistance, rather than being nothing more than an ego defense, is—in Lacan's view—structural, arising because the real resists symbolization; when the analysand's experience resists being put into words, he or she grabs onto, digs into, or takes it out on the only other person present: the analyst. Transference is thus a direct product of resistance, of the resistance the real (e.g., trauma) erects against its symbolization, against being spoken. What sense could it possibly make, then, to accuse the analysand of resisting? Of course the analysand resists—that is a given, a structural necessity. Interpretation must aim at the traumatic event or experience that is resisting verbalization, not the mere fact of resistance. On resistance and its "interpretation," see Ecrits, 332–336; on the symbolization of the real, see Chapter 8 below (discussion of a case of hysteria), and The Lacanian Subject, ch. 3.

4. Interpretation: Opening Up the Space of Desire

1. She could, for instance, be aware at some level that this request is a manifestation of her resistance to going any further in her analysis or of her fear of recent developments in her analysis.

2. He or she may also be understood by the analysand as having little interest in seeing the analysand more often.

3. The politician who attempts to set the record straight in the hope of achieving some sort of "genuine communication," or of at least clearing his or her name, often finds that the press and the public continue to "misinterpret" and "misconstrue" his or her statements. The politician learns thereby the hard-to-swallow truth Lacan teaches us: *the essence of communication is miscommunication.* In Lacan's own words, "The very foundation of interhuman discourse is misunderstanding [*malentendu*]" (Seminar III, 184).

4. A few words should be said here about Lacan's distinction between need, demand, and desire. "Desire" is not a given in human experience, something that is there from birth; neither is "demand." Biologically determined strivings (say, for nourishment) are referred to by Lacan as "needs." (He does not use the term "need" in the way it is used in popular American discourse, in which whatever we feel we cannot do without is termed a need, and in which something is said to be a need when it fits in with the kind of image we have of ourselves and of the life we would like to be leading.) We need to eat and to excrete; we need warmth and affection; up to a certain age, if we are deprived of the latter we may die. As infants we are unable to provide ourselves with most of what we need, and must appeal to others to attend to our needs. We call upon them to help us, and do so by crying. We make demands upon them: a demand is a need that is *addressed* to another person.

But since the infant's speech is quite inarticulate, people must interpret its crying. A baby cannot be said to *know* what it wants when it cries; the *meaning* of that act is provided by the parents or caretakers who attempt to name the pain the child seems to be expressing (for example, "she must be hungry"). There is perhaps a sort of general discomfort, coldness, or pain, but its meaning is imposed, as it were, by the way in which it is interpreted by the child's parents. If a parent responds to its baby's crying with food, the discomfort, coldness, or pain will retroactively be determined as having "meant" hunger, as hunger pangs. One cannot say that the true meaning behind the baby's crying was that it was cold, because *meaning is an ulterior product.* Indeed, constantly responding to a baby's cries with food may transform all of its discomforts, coldness, and pain into hunger. (Meaning is thus determined not by the baby but by other people—that is, by the Other.) Certain parents take every cry as an expression of biological need, reading every demand as based on need, pure and simple; the baby's cry (a demand addressed to another person) is thereby reduced to need.

Other parents read the baby's crying as sometimes manifesting a desire for something else, something less tangible, less related to immediate, biological needs—perhaps a desire for attention, to be held, for human contact, presence, or something still more imprecise, indiscernible. To reduce demand to need is to misrecognize or annul the *addressing of the Other* that is implicit in it—that is, the fact that the subject is addressing, calling upon, or appealing to the Other.

Just as a parent can reduce the baby's demands to need or open them up as desire, the analyst can take an analysand's demands at face value and grant them (give in to a request to reduce the number of sessions per week, for example), or see instead a manifestation of desire behind them, thereby bringing desire to light or to life.

In a sense, *desire is budding within demand; it can be nipped in the bud*—that is, flattened out, reduced to need—*or allowed to blossom.*

5. A psychotherapist once told me, with an obvious tone of triumph in his voice, that one of his patients, when she ended her therapy with him, had expressed her gratitude that he was *not* a Lacanian, because if he had been, everything she said would have been open to question instead of being taken the way she meant it. The story further confirmed my impression that the therapist was engaging in a kind of psychology of the ego, no more and no less: he was taking at face value the patient's statements which were intended by her to reflect nothing but her consciously accepted view of herself.

6. If utopia is a "place" where there is no want of anything, then there would seem to be no desire either, no reason or call/cause for desire. As David Byrne says, "Heaven is a place where nothing ever happens."
In Lacan's fine discussion of demand and desire in Seminar VIII (ch. 14), he says that "the crushing of demand in [the course of] satisfaction cannot occur without killing desire" (239). As we shall see, while satisfaction tends to bury desire, desire in turn tends to inhibit satisfaction (satisfaction of the drives specifically), no doubt in order to go on desiring.

7. Certain Lacanians use this type of interpretation with psychotic patients who are overwhelmed by the number and vividness of their thoughts and hallucinations. The goal in such cases is to *stabilize* the patient, to lay down a few provisional guideposts for the patient by establishing stable meanings. This process, like the process of meaning making in general, is referred to as *capitonnage,* derived from Lacan's model for the creation of meaning: the *point de capiton* or "button tie." (Russell Grigg, in his translation of Lacan's Seminar III, *The Psychoses* [New York: Norton, 1993], renders *capitonnage* as "quilting" and *point de capiton* as "quilting point"; see 293–305.) A button tie is a stitch used by an upholsterer to secure a button to fabric and stuffing; by analogy, in the case of meaning making, one attempts to tie a particular meaning to a particular statement or to particular words, thereby putting a stop to the endless series of meanings someone may attribute to a statement or event, or the ever greater dissociation a patient may manifest between words and their meanings. I shall discuss this kind of interpretation in greater detail in Chapter 7.

8. This also obviously introduces a kind of *mirroring* between analysand and analyst.

9. In Plato's *Symposium,* Agathon expresses the desire to be near Socrates so that the fullness of Socrates' knowledge will fill up his own emptiness or lack of knowledge, as in the familiar "communicating vases" phenomenon. The analyst does not adopt what is commonly known as the Socratic method, but does employ certain techniques used by Socrates in the course of the *Symposium.* See Lacan's extensive commentary in Seminar VIII, *Transference,* trans. Bruce Fink (New York: Norton, forthcoming).

10. As Lacan puts it, "an interpretation can be right only if it is . . . an interpretation" (*Ecrits,* 601/240).

11. On analytic interpretation as oracular in nature, see Seminar XVIII, January 13, 1971; *Ecrits* 106/13 and 588/228; *Scilicet* 4 (1973): 37; and *Scilicet* 5 (1975): 16.

12. "Interpretation bears on the cause of desire," as Lacan puts it in

"L'Etourdit," *Scilicet* 4 (1973): 30; the cause of desire is object *a*, which is real. Jacques-Alain Miller has discussed this notion at length in his unpublished seminars.

13. This is related to Freud's early work in *Studies on Hysteria*, where the associative links between one idea and others are broken, one idea being dissociated from the others. The link must be restored if the dissociated idea (or group of ideas) is to stop producing symptoms. As I argue in *The Lacanian Subject: Between Language and Jouissance* (Princeton: Princeton University Press, 1995), the subject is that link: the subject is that which comes into being in the linking up of the different ideas or thoughts (representations or signifiers), disappearing when the link is broken. See my long discussion of the real and the symbolic in *The Lacanian Subject*, ch. 3.

14. Akin to "the draining of the Zuider Zee" in Freud's formulation in SE XXII, 80; I owe this formulation to Jacques-Alain Miller's "Orientation lacanienne." The sketch of the Lacanian real I have provided thus far will be filled out little by little in later chapters. For a fuller discussion, see Fink, *The Lacanian Subject*, chs. 3, 7, 8, and 10. A further example of this kind of interpretation, and of the sense in which such an interpretation fosters construction—that is, the (re)construction of the analysand's never-before-symbolized experiences—is provided in Chapter 8.

5. The Dialectic of Desire

1. In other cases, the patient seems stuck on a particular object, not a cause. The patient has set her sights on something that she cannot attain or keeps falling short of attaining, whether it be a diploma, a promotion, an amorous conquest, or a relationship with a significant other. Often, the demand made upon the analyst in such cases is: "Help me achieve my aim!" The analysand does not wonder why she is so obstinate in her pursuit—that is, what makes the thing she claims to be pursuing so inescapable, so vital, so necessary. She would rather give up her life than give up the single-minded pursuit. Desire cannot be deflected onto other objects or people.

Although the person's desire seems fixated on a particular object (for instance, a diploma or marriage), it is, in fact, fixated on that which caused the person to desire that object in the first place—usually the Other's desire or demand.

2. See Freud's analysis of the dream by the witty butcher's wife in *The Interpretation of Dreams*, and Lacan's comments in "Subversion of the Subject and Dialectic of Desire" and "Direction of the Treatment" in *Ecrits*. See also Colette Soler's excellent commentaries (based in part on Jacques-Alain Miller's unpublished 1988–1989 Diplôme d'Etudes Approfondies Seminar) in "History and Hysteria: The Witty Butcher's Wife," *Newsletter of the Freudian Field* 6 (1992): 16–33; and idem, "Hysteria and Obsession," *Reading Seminars I and II: Lacan's Return to Freud*, ed. Bruce Fink, Richard Feldstein, and Maire Jaanus (Albany: SUNY Press, 1996), 257–264. I discuss hysteria and obsession in detail in Chapter 8 below.

3. As we shall see, it is the drives that seek satisfaction, not desire.

4. This does not imply that the "fully analyzed" subject becomes a kind of nonstop pleasure-seeking machine; rather, it implies that desire stops inhibiting the subject from obtaining satisfaction. One patient of mine expressed the neurotic's predicament quite nicely in saying that he could not "enjoy his enjoyment," implying that his satisfaction was, in some sense, ruined or tainted by simultane-

ous feelings of dissatisfaction or displeasure. Perhaps one way of stating the configuration analysis aims at is that of allowing the analysand to finally be able to enjoy his or her enjoyment. On these and related points, see Chapter 10 below.

5. It is also sometimes written "object (a)," "little a," "petit objet a," "objet a," "petit a," and so on.

6. Lacan himself, inclined as he was to double negatives, might well have said, "Desire is not without an object" ("Le désir n'est pas sans objet"), just as he did in the case of anxiety, but that object would nevertheless have been the object understood as cause.

7. Related, in certain respects, to what I referred to in Chapter 1 as a "satisfaction crisis."

8. As mentioned at the end of Chapter 3 above. Often the analyst even becomes the cause of the analysand's fantasies; many an analysand mentions that the analyst, the analyst's name, or appointment times and subjects discussed in the sessions "come" to the analysand's mind during masturbation.

9. This is an aspect of the noncontractual exchange (mentioned in Chapter 2) that occurs in the early stage of analysis: the analysand wants the fixation to work as it had before; the analyst offers a new fixation in its stead, one that entails deciphering the unconscious and taking the analyst as cause.

10. See Bruce Fink, *The Lacanian Subject: Between Language and Jouissance* (Princeton: Princeton University Press, 1995).

11. The reference here is to Lacan's dictum "Le désir de l'homme, c'est le désir de l'Autre," which we can also translate as, "Man's desire is for the Other to desire him" or "Man desires the Other's desire for him." As we shall see, it can also mean "Man's desire is the same as the Other's desire." On this point, see Fink, *The Lacanian Subject*, ch. 5.

12. This should not be taken to imply that the parents both desire the same thing, or even that each parent alone has a specific, unambiguous desire—in other words, that all of his or her desires are in some way coherent.

13. Here we seem to follow the often fallacious principle that the more we are like our parents, the more they will love us.

14. See his comments in *Introductory Lectures on Psychoanalysis:* "From this time [puberty] onwards, the human individual has to devote himself to the great task of detaching himself from his parents . . . By neurotics, however, no solution at all is arrived at" (SE XVI, 337).

15. According to Lacan, this diamond or lozenge designates the following relations: "envelopment-development-conjunction-disjunction" (*Ecrits*, 634/280), alienation ($\vee$) and separation ($\wedge$), greater than ($>$), less than ($<$), and so on. It is most simply read: "in relation to," or "desire for." Thus, "$\$ \Diamond a$" means "the subject in relation to its object," or "the subject's desire for its object." The terms of this latter formula are extremely polyvalent; we shall see some of their multiple meanings in subsequent chapters.

16. "Taken in this way, what is fantasy if not . . . *ein Wunsch*, a wish, a rather naive wish at that, like all wishes" (Seminar X, December 5, 1962).

17. This is what Lacan has in mind when he says that "one is always responsible for one's position as subject." See Lacan, "Science and Truth," trans. Bruce Fink, *Newsletter of the Freudian Field* 3 (1989): 7.

18. The actual quote I have in mind here is: "He asks me for . . ., due to the very fact that he speaks; his demand is intransitive, implying no object" (*Ecrits*, 617/254). See also Seminar VIII, where Lacan, talking of the analyst, says that "as soon as he speaks, [he] is no longer anything but a beggar, shifting to the register of demand" (430). The analyst is faced with a challenge, then: How can one make interpretations without slipping into the register of demand? Perhaps oracular interpretation allows the analyst to speak while at the same time maintaining, at least in part, his or her position of pure desirousness.

19. On this point, the reader is referred to Seminar VI, "Desire and Its Interpretation" (1958–1959). Seven sessions were edited and published by Jacques-Alain Miller in *Ornicar?* 24 (1981): 7–31; 25 (1982): 13–36; and 26/27 (1983): 7–44. The final three sessions, on Hamlet, were translated by James Hulbert as "Desire and the Interpretation of Desire in *Hamlet*," in *Yale French Studies* 55/56 (1977): 11–52. See also Bruce Fink, "Reading *Hamlet* with Lacan," in Richard Feldstein and Willy Apollon, eds., *Lacan, Politics, Aesthetics* (Albany: SUNY Press, 1996, 181–198).

20. The neurotic confuses "the Other's lack [that is, the Other's desire] with the Other's demand. The Other's demand takes on the function of the object in the neurotic's fantasy" (*Ecrits*, 823/321). The fundamental fantasy, which Lacan normally writes ($ \lozenge a$)—meaning the subject in relation to the object that causes his or her desire—is, in the case of the neurotic, written ($ \lozenge D$), the subject in relation to the Other's demand.

21. According to Lacan, the neurotic believes that the Other wants to castrate him or her. This, too, is exemplified in the case of obsession included in Chapter 8.

22. That is, not the Other of the "symbolic pact"; see Chapters 7 and 9 on this point.

23. Seminar X, class of November 14, 1962. This example is cited by Colette Soler in her article "Hysteria and Obsession."

24. It should be noted that Freud does not always equate the ego-ideal with the superego; see J. Laplanche and J.-B. Pontalis, *The Language of Psychoanalysis* (New York: Norton, 1973), 144–145.

25. I do not mean to suggest that the register of desire is utterly and completely foreign to them, for at least neurotics have come to be in language (see Chapters 7 and 8 below). Nevertheless, their desire is by no means "fully fledged"; see Fink, *The Lacanian Subject*, chs. 5 and 6; and idem, "Reading *Hamlet* with Lacan."

26. Expressed in the saying by the French king François I: "Souvent femme varie, bien fol est qui s'y fie."

27. On this point, see Chapter 8 below on hysteria and obsession.

28. In the words of the poet, desire is when you are "aching with some nameless need."

29. This lack or inadequacy in the Other can be viewed from the point of view of desire, but it can be viewed from the point of view of knowledge and power as well. For example, children often assert that their parents are the strongest, the best, and the most capable of all people: they can do anything. In the minds of children, their parents should be able to beat out anyone and take care of everything—it is a wish that the parents not be lacking in any way. Obviously, however, this is not the case, and a child senses that the parents' lack somehow has something to do with him or her, has ramifications for him or her. If my parents are not all-powerful and all-

knowing, then maybe what they tell me about myself is not true; perhaps I need to appeal to a higher authority. Perhaps they are wrong when they tell me I should be a lawyer, that I should marry and have children. How do I know that what they tell me is right? How do I know what I really should do or be?

The lack in the parents' knowledge may lead the child to seek out and question people perceived to be higher authorities (experts, teachers, religious leaders), and eventually philosophies and religions, hoping to find the ultimate justification for being this and doing that. The crushing realization that each system of beliefs is but one among many may lead to an existential crisis: the Other is lacking; there is no God, no ultimate being that can tell me who and what I should be. There is no word, no truth the Other can give me that tells me what I am and what I should do. As Lacan puts it, "There is no signifier in the Other that can . . . answer for [account for or take responsibility for] what I am" ("Il n'y a dans l'Autre aucun signifiant qui puisse . . . répondre de ce que je suis"); *Ornicar?* 25 (1982): 32. See my discussion of this point in "Reading *Hamlet* with Lacan."

30. The analyst's desire remains unknown partly due to the *nonverbal* nature of certain of his or her interventions (such as punctuation and scansion), to which a name cannot easily be attached.

31. See Freud's detailed example of deferred action in SE I, 353–356; also Lacan's numerous discussions of deferred action in *Ecrits* and his seminars (for example, Seminar V, "Unconscious Formations," unpublished).

32. These accounts are both personal and institutional. For personal testimonies, see comments by Colette Soler, Gérard Pommier, and others in Elizabeth Roudinesco, *Jacques Lacan & Co.: A History of Psychoanalysis in France, 1925–1985*, trans. Jeffrey Mehlman (Chicago: University of Chicago Press, 1990). Institutional testimony comes from the procedure known as the "pass," employed by the Ecole de la Cause Freudienne, and is documented in literally hundreds of articles; see, for example, the collection *Comment finissent les analyses* (Paris: Seuil, 1994), 163–210.

33. SE XXIII, 252. Lacan translates Freud's term as *roc* ("rock") and often speaks of the supposed "rock of castration." See, in particular, Seminar VIII, 269.

34. Like the later Freud, Lacan emphasizes fantasy: an imagined scene, a construct. But another way of understanding what Lacan has in mind when he speaks of the "fundamental fantasy" is what he calls one's "subject position," "subjective position," or "position as subject" (*Ecrits*, 856): the fundamental fantasy stages the position one has adopted with respect to an early experience that was sexually charged and experienced as traumatic. In that sense it encompasses Freud's early theory of trauma: the child experiences excessive sexuality, a surplus or overload of sexual feeling or pleasure, and is revolted by it (in hysteria) or later comes to feel guilty about it (in obsession). (Freud's term *sexual über* is translated in *The Origins of Psychoanalysis* [New York: Basic Books, 1954] as "surplus of sexuality" [163–164, letter dated May 30, 1896]; the French translate it as *excédent de sexualité* or *excédent sexuel*, that is, "excess of sexuality" or "sexual excess"; see *La Naissance de la psychanalyse* [Paris: Presses Universitaires de France, 1956].) Sexual sensations that are rejected or defended against constitute, as we saw in Chapter 1, the kind of pleasure that Freud refers to as "satisfaction" and that Lacan refers to as "jouissance": a kind of pleasure beyond the pleasure principle.

Here one can see that the subject's position is that of a defense against a certain kind of sexual satisfaction or jouissance. This defense is reflected in the fantasy that stages the fulfillment of or props up the subject's desire. Desire thus comes into being in place of satisfaction, as a defense against jouissance. This explains why desire, by its very nature, abhors satisfaction—real, sexual satisfaction. Desire finds a kind of pleasure in fantasy—"Fantasy provides the pleasure peculiar to desire," as Lacan says (Ecrits, 773)—the kind of pleasure that comes from hallucinating rather than taking steps in the "real world" or "external reality" to obtain something, the kind of pleasure that comes under the pleasure principle.

The human infant's first tendency, according to Freud (see The Interpretation of Dreams, ch. 7, and "Project for a Scientific Psychology" in The Origins of Psychoanalysis), is to obtain immediate satisfaction of a need for nourishment by hallucinating (that is, vividly recalling to mind a perception of) the face of the person who brings the bottle with milk in it and imagining itself sucking and swallowing the milk, rather than awaiting delayed gratification based on the taking of motor action in the world (such as crying) so that a real person will bring a real bottle, providing the baby with real nourishment. We derive a certain kind of pleasure from simply imagining satisfaction, a pleasure that is far easier to procure and far more dependable than the real forms of satisfaction that involve other people, with all the risks, perils, and uncertainties entailed.

Indeed, desire prefers the pleasure of fantasy to the satisfaction of the drives. Desire inhibits such satisfaction, reining in the drives, since the drives pursue a kind of satisfaction that is experienced as overwhelming or excessive and thus abhorred (satisfaction kills desire, smothers it). Desire here is tantamount to a defense. The subject, too—the subject as desire, as desiring—can be viewed here as little more than a defense: a defense against jouissance.

As we shall see, by getting the analysand to subjectify the cause (the Other's desire upon which his or her own desire depends), the analysand's desire is radically transformed and ceases to inhibit the pursuit of satisfaction/jouissance. The relation between desire and jouissance, whereby desire is but a defense against jouissance, is thereby altered. (See, in particular, Lacan, "On Freud's 'Trieb' and the Psychoanalyst's Desire," trans. Bruce Fink, in Reading Seminars I and II, 417–421; and Jacques-Alain Miller, "Commentary on Lacan's Text," ibid., 422–427. These points are discussed extensively in Chapter 10 below.)

In Freudian terms, the desiring subject can, in some sense, be thought of as the ego (partly conscious and partly unconscious), which defends against the kind of satisfaction the id strives for. The ego finds objectionable and threatening the id's pursuit of satisfaction, for the id pays no heed to social norms and ideals in its selection of objects and orifices, partners and practices. While it inhibits the id's pursuits, the ego nevertheless provides substitute satisfactions. But (wo)man cannot live on desire alone.

This translation into Freudian terms allows us to see a shift in Lacan's concept of the subject from the 1950s to the late 1960s. In Lacan's early work, the subject is equated with desire, usually unconscious desire, and the goal of analysis is to get the analysand to "stop giving up on his desire" (Seminar VII), to untie the knots in his desire, and to constitute a "decided" or "determined desire" (désir décidé). By 1965, however, the subject is more closely equated by Lacan with the id, with the "mindless" ("acephalous" is his term, literally "headless") pursuit of satisfaction characteristic of the drives that is thwarted by ego and superego inhibitions. This brief periodization of Lacan's work, borrowed from Jacques-Alain Miller, is expanded in Chapter 10.

35. On the relation between Freud's notion of the lost object and Lacan's object *a*, see Fink, *The Lacanian Subject*, ch. 7. Here it would seem that we are not so much a product of what we have or possess, but of what we have lost.

36. The object here is clearly related to the lost satisfaction. In some sense, it can be said to "contain" the jouissance lost due to the castration complex, that loss of jouissance being designated as (-φ) by Lacan (*Ecrits*, 823–826). The fundamental fantasy can then be written as follows:

$$\frac{\$ \lozenge a}{(\text{-}\varphi)}$$

A great deal more could be said about this formulation. See, in particular, Lacan, "Subversion of the Subject and Dialectic of Desire"; and idem, Seminar VIII, "Transference," chs. XV–XVIII. See also Chapter 8 below.

37. The parameters of the choice also reproduced a situation the Rat Man's father had apparently faced prior to marriage: he had been interested in a "poor girl" but had made the "right kind of marriage" by instead marrying the Rat Man's mother.

38. His "lady," the only woman he seems to have truly considered marrying, is apparently quite uninterested in his sexual advances.

39. It should be noted that Freud does *not* categorically claim in this article that analysis is *incapable* of taking the patient beyond the castration complex. Consider his closing statements: "It would be hard to say whether and when we have succeeded in mastering this factor [the protest against castration: either "penis envy" or the "masculine protest"] in an analytic treatment. We can only console ourselves with the certainty that we have given the person analysed every possible encouragement to re-examine and alter his [or her] attitude to it" (SE XXIII, 252–253).

In other words, Freud does not seem to rule out the possibility of the patient's adopting a different attitude toward castration. He says, "We *often* have the impression that" we can go no further (emphasis added), but does not assert that we can *never* take the analysand further.

40. As Freud puts it, "men have always found it hard to renounce pleasure; they cannot bring themselves to do it without some kind of compensation" (SE XVI, 371).

41. No longer assures the Other's jouissance (see *Ecrits*, 826/324).

42. See, in particular, "Constructions in Analysis," SE XXIII, 257–269.

43. The neurotic's complaint is always, "They did that to me," "They made me that way." The neurotic does not take responsibility for his or her actions, choices, or decisions; even certain obsessive neurotics, who seem perfectly willing to accept *blame* for anything and everything, do not view their lives as having involved a series of *choices*, compromises, and sacrifices they themselves made. The story told is that the Other did this, wanted this, expected this from me, and I *could not* refuse: it was impossible. Not "I wasn't willing" or "I didn't want to because of *x, y,* and *z*," but "They forced me," "I had to," "I couldn't refuse," and so on.

Subjectification means that the subject assumes responsibility—not in words alone, that is, consciously, but at some "deeper" level—for his or her fate, his or her past actions, decisions, and accidents. The subject comes into being where his or her life was determined by outside or impersonal forces: the Other's desire, his or her parents' desire that brought him or her into the world. "Where it was"—where my life was run by the Other's desire—"I must come into being" ("Là où fut ça, il me faut advenir," *Ecrits*, 524/171). This is but one of the ways Lacan translates Freud's "Wo Es war, soll Ich werden," from *New Introductory Lectures on Psychoanalysis* (SE XXII, 80). It is a sort of "Be there now."

6. A Lacanian Approach to Diagnosis

1. As Lacan mentions, "Every now and then we take prepsychotics into analysis, and we know what that produces—psychotics. The question of contraindications for analysis wouldn't arise if we didn't all recall some particular case in our own practice, or in the practice of our colleagues, in which a full-blown psychosis . . . was triggered during the first analytic sessions in which things became a little too heated" (Seminar III, 285). It should be noted that, later on, Lacan does not view psychosis as a contraindication for analysis—that is, does not recommend that psychotics be excluded from analytic therapy; he suggests, however, that the approach adopted by the analyst has to be quite different in work with psychotics. One psychotic patient I saw in therapy for some time came to me precisely because the analyst he had been working with before had been emphasizing the ambiguous meanings in his words—that is, treating him as if he were a neurotic. Had he stayed with that analyst, a psychotic break might well have been triggered.

2. See, for example, SE XIX, 153.

3. See, on this point, SE XIX, 143, and SE XXIII, 204 and 277. Freud's distinction is not always as consistent as one might like. Compare, for example, SE XXI, 153, where disavowal is said to be what happens to an idea when the affect attached to it is repressed, and SE XIX, 184, where Freud considers disavowal to be a "psychotic reaction."

4. See, in particular, *Gesammelte Werke* I (Frankfurt: Fischer Verlag, 1952), 72, where Freud uses the verb *verwirft*, translated by Strachey as "rejects" (SE III, 58).

5. This close reading can be found in Seminar II, and is carried out with the help of Jean Hyppolite, a notable philosopher and translator of Hegel's work into French. It is also discussed in *Ecrits*.

6. The first translation ("rejection") can be found in Seminar I, 54/43, the second ("foreclosure") in Seminar III, 361. Both are again mentioned in Seminar XXI, class of March 19, 1974.

7. SE XVI, 358. He makes the same point in greater detail further on in the *Introductory Lectures on Psychoanalysis*: "We cannot deny that healthy people as well possess in their mental life what alone makes possible the formation both of dreams and of symptoms, and we must conclude that they too have carried out repressions, that they expend a certain amount of energy in order to maintain them, that their unconscious system conceals repressed impulses which are still cathected with energy, and that *a portion of their libido is withdrawn from their ego's disposal*. Thus, a healthy person, too, is virtually a neurotic" (SE XVI, 456–457).

8. For the most part, Lacanians view patients who are classified as "borderline" by other therapists as neurotics who simply give clinicians a harder time than most

other neurotics. Viewed in historical perspective, there has always been a sort of basket category in psychiatry/psychology into which difficult patients have been placed; in the nineteenth century, it was "paranoia," today it is "borderline." Consider Lacan's remarks on the dominant view of paranoia in France and Germany prior to his own work: "A paranoiac was someone who was mean, intolerant, ill-tempered, prideful, distrustful, overly sensitive, and had an overblown sense of himself. That was considered to be the fundamental basis of paranoia; and when the paranoiac was overly paranoid, he would even begin to have delusions" (Seminar III, 13).

9. See Seminar III, 42: the "signature" here is a quasi-neologism the patient produced in French: *galopiner*.

7. Psychosis

1. See, for example, Freud, "Female Sexuality," in *Collected Papers* V, 256; Strachey translates it as "paternal agency" (SE XXI, 229). In Lacan, Seminar III, 230, and Seminar XX, 74, one finds the expression *fonction du père* ("father function" or "function of the father"). See my translation of Seminar XX, *Encore* (New York: Norton, 1997).

2. Note that *le nom du père* can also mean the name that is given to the child by the father—that is, the name that comes from the father or is handed down by the father. The father's *symbolic function* in no wise precludes or in any way suggests the superfluity of the father's function as a provider of love and encouragement, as certain feminist writers have argued.

3. Indeed, foreclosure is a function, and as such we cannot exhaustively describe all of the possible "environments," or family configurations, that give rise to it. Those who try to do so lapse into a kind of psychologizing, in which they "wander like lost souls from the frustrating mother to the smothering mother" (*Ecrits* 577/218), and when they do examine the role of the father ("the dominating father, the easy-going father, the all-powerful father, the humiliated father, the awkward father, the pitiful father, the home-loving father, the father on the loose" [*Ecrits* 578/218]), they neglect the role accorded the father's word and authority by the mother—in other words, "the place she reserves for the Name-of-the-Father in the promotion of the law" (*Ecrits* 579/218)—and the father's own relation to the law.

4. We are all familiar with families in which the father is weak and the mother domineering; indeed, that is the description of the stereotypical Jewish family. Nevertheless, that generally does not mean that the paternal function is not fulfilled in such families. A mother may dominate her husband, and yet lend him a certain weight simply by kvetching about him: if he is a source of so much tsuris, a thorn in the mother's side, then, if nothing else, he is still a force to be reckoned with. The annihilation of the father by the mother must generally be far more complete than this to preclude the paternal function.

5. "An Introduction to Lacan's Clinical Perspectives," in Bruce Fink, Richard Feldstein, and Maire Jaanus, eds., *Reading Seminars I and II: Lacan's Return to Freud* (Albany: SUNY Press, 1996), 242.

6. In some ways, it could be considered a "mere matter of semantics" to maintain that not all hallucinations are alike instead of maintaining that hallucina-

tion is not enough to justify a diagnosis of psychosis and that we have to look at other factors. It seems to me, however, more politically expedient, given the stigma of hallucination—namely, the automatic association in the public mind, as well as in the minds of many clinicians, of hallucination with psychosis—to provide a more careful description and explanation of hallucinatory phenomena, and psychoanalysis gives us the means with which to do so. As long as someone may be committed against his or her will because of "hallucinations" (something most French practitioners do not have to contend with), the semantic distinction between bona fide and nonpsychotic hallucinations will be of considerable import.

7. See, for example, Lacan's comments in Seminar XXII, *RSI:* "The difference is, nevertheless, clear between believing in the symptom and believing it. That constitutes the difference between neurosis and psychosis. The psychotic not only believes in the voices [he or she hears], but believes them as well. Everything hinges on this divide" (January 21, 1975; my translation). In English in *Feminine Sexuality,* ed. Juliet Mitchell and Jacqueline Rose (New York: Norton, 1982), 170. On this point, see also Colette Soler, "Quelle place pour l'analyste?" *Actes de l'Ecole de la Cause freudienne* 13, *L'expérience psychanalytique des psychoses* (1987): 30.

8. Indeed, Lacan suggests that we all see reality through the lenses of our (fundamental) fantasy. How, then, could the analyst possibly "know reality," "know what is real and what it not," better than the analysand? Lacanian psychoanalysis is certainly not a discourse of mastery wherein the analyst is considered some sort of master of reality. In the course of his or her own "training analysis," the analyst does not learn what is real and what is not, but learns something about his or her own fantasy (even as it is reconfigured) and how to prevent it from impinging on work with patients.

9. See, for example, Seminar III, 88. Consider also Lacan's remarks in *Ecrits* (576/216):

"The fact that a [collective] psychosis [involving belief in things like freedom and Santa Claus] may prove to be compatible with what is called good order is indubitable, but it does not authorize the psychiatrist, even if he is a psychoanalyst, to trust in his own compatibility with that order so as to believe that he has an adequate idea of the *reality* to which his patient seems to be unequal.

"Under such conditions, it would perhaps be better to eliminate this idea [reality] from his evaluation of the foundations of psychosis—bringing us back to the aim of its treatment."

10. As Lacan says, "Certainty is the rarest thing for the normal subject" (Seminar III, 87), in other words, the neurotic. Lacan tells a story of the proverbial "jealous husband [normal, by Lacan's account] who follows his wife right to the very door of the bedroom in which she has locked herself with someone else," and still wonders whether or not she is really and truly having an extramarital affair. The psychotic, by contrast, achieves certainty without requiring any such proof.

11. See, for example, Daniel Paul Schreber, *Memoirs of My Nervous Illness* (Cambridge, Mass.: Harvard University Press, 1988).

12. On fears covering over wishes, see SE X, 180.

13. See, for example, the case of the Rat Man in SE X; the Rat Man reported voices commanding him, for example, to slit his own throat.

14. See "The Mirror Stage as Formative of the Function of the I," in *Ecrits;* and

the later revision of the mirror stage theory in Seminar VIII, *Transference*, trans. Bruce Fink (New York: Norton, forthcoming).

15. See the detailed discussion of the ego in Bruce Fink, *The Lacanian Subject: Between Language and Jouissance* (Princeton: Princeton University Press, 1995). Lacan clearly associates this "running commentary on [one's] existence" with the alter-ego (Seminar III, 219).

16. In saying this, I do not mean to imply that the "self," as defined by all other theorists, is identical to the ego. What I do mean is that what, *in common parlance,* one refers to as one's "self" is more or less equivalent to the ego as understood in Lacanian psychoanalysis.

17. In *The Ego and the Id*, Freud provides at least four different glosses on the ego, two of which seem to define the ego as an object: (1) a projection of the surface of the body, and (2) a precipitate or sedimentation of abandoned object-cathexes— that is, of former identifications. The other two seem to define the ego as an agent: (3) the representative of reality, and (4) a part of the id that has been specially modified—that is, desexualized. It is by no means clear that these four characteristics could, in any sense, apply to one and the same "thing," and Lacan clearly considers the first two to be crucial to the ego, whereas the latter two are not.

18. Insofar as the coming into being of the ego requires language (see Seminar VIII), it is, not surprisingly, language that allows for the possibility of self-consciousness, not vice versa. Language is, after all, what allows us to talk about something as an object—to talk about talking, think about thinking, and so on. For a provocative discussion of "*self*-consciousness," see Seminar II, 62–69 / 46–52, where Lacan likens it to a camera taking pictures of a lake from morning till dark; see also Seminar III, 204, where Lacan discusses auditory hallucination in relation to the far more common experience of hearing ourselves pronounce words in our own minds.

My approach to self-consciousness here can be fruitfully compared with Julian Jaynes' theory of the origin of (what he refers to simply as) consciousness—a theory he presents in *The Origin of Consciousness in the Breakdown of the Bicameral Mind* (Boston: Houghton Mifflin, 1976; rpt. 1990). While feeling a need to locate everything in either the right or left hemispheres of the brain, and completely ignorant of Lacan's well-known work on the mirror stage, Jaynes nevertheless recognizes the importance of language (and even of metaphor) in the advent of consciousness in human history and in each child's ability to become self-conscious. Jaynes is also one of the few contemporary psychologists who realizes that in schizophrenia there is a loss of a sense of self (indeed, he provides ample clinical evidence of it on pages 404–426 of his book). Yet he never manages to connect the schizophrenic's problem sustaining an ego or sense of self with the schizophrenic's language disturbances, because, wanting to stay on some sort of supposedly firm scientific ground (and one can hardly imagine a less traditionally scientific book than his, which is reminiscent, in certain respects, of Freud's *Moses and Monotheism*), he relies on the absurdly simplistic theory that all hallucinations are due to stress: we supposedly hallucinate when stressed out, and some people cannot take as much stress as others because of genetic deficiencies. Yet Jaynes, like most of my readers, would surely agree that no matter how stressful the conditions to which we were subjected, we would never end up hallucinating in the way psychotics do. It does not happen to just anyone, because it *cannot* happen to neurotics! Our egos do not disintegrate when under stress; we may see and hear things, as when seriously sleep deprived, or may think we are going crazy due to visions and voices in our heads in solitary confinement, but we do not interpret like psychotics, our paranoia does not take on the same proportions, and we do not delusionally reconstitute the world (see my discussion of the "delusional metaphor" later in this chapter). If nothing else, the experiences of concentration camp survivors should once and for all refute any such theory that psychosis or hallucinations are due to stress.

19. This notion will be developed in the sequel to the present volume, tentatively entitled *Advanced Lacanian Clinical Practice.*

20. For a detailed account of the concept of alienation in Lacan's work, see Fink, *The Lacanian Subject,* chs. 1, 2, 4, and 5.

21. Samuel Beckett is an interesting author to consider in this regard: he rejected his native English in favor of French, and wrote many of his works in the latter language.

22. Little children, for example, endlessly reproduce commercials, jingles, and phrases of all kinds that they hear on TV, on the radio, at home, and elsewhere. What we hear on the news in the morning we pass on to those around us later in the day, using the same words, the same terms we heard—often verbatim.

23. See Fink, *The Lacanian Subject,* ch. 1.

24. See "The Mirror Stage as Formative of the Function of the I," in *Ecrits.*

25. See Seminar VIII, *Transference,* trans. Bruce Fink (New York: Norton, forthcoming).

26. Lacan's term is *entériné,* which has legal connotations: ratified or certified, as in the case of something which has been passed into law or recognized by the law.

27. "While images also play an important role in our field [that of human beings, as opposed to animals], this role is entirely reworked, recast, and reanimated by the symbolic order" (Seminar III, 17).

28. See his comments at the very end of Seminar III, and in Seminar IV.

29. SE XVI, 323.

30. This is similar to bodily phenomena seen in autistic children; in such cases, though one part of the child's body is engaged in an excretory function, there is no assistance provided by any other part of the body. (See, for example, Bruno Bettelheim's descriptions of Laurie in *The Empty Fortress* [New York: Free Press, 1967].) One muscle operates independently of the others. The body fails to operate as a whole, in a harmonious, unified manner. Without the anchoring point (internal parental judgment or ego-ideal), which allows a relatively coherent and stable self-image to form, no unified sense of self is possible in many cases of autism. In psychosis, this self-image may easily shatter under pressure: the individual's sense of self dissolves.

31. In *How Lacan's Ideas Are Used in Clinical Practice,* ed. and trans. Stuart Schneiderman (Northvale, N.J.: Jason Aronson, 1993), esp. pp. 19 and 40. The earlier edition of this collection is better known to many readers: *Returning to Freud: Clinical Psychoanalysis in the School of Lacan* (New Haven: Yale University Press, 1980).

32. In Guy de Maupassant's short story "Le Horla," an invisible force seems to be trying to take the narrator's place; often, however, it is a person much like the

248

psychotic. "Le Horla" can be found in *Oeuvres Complètes de Guy de Maupassant*, vol. 18 (Paris: Louis Conard, 1927), 3–48. For an English translation, "The Horla," see *The Life of Henri René Guy de Maupassant*, vol. 2 (New York: M. Walter Dunne, 1903), 1–35.

Julian Jaynes provides numerous examples of the blurring and breakdown of the ego or sense of self—or what he terms the "analog 'I'"—in schizophrenics; see Jaynes, *The Origin of Consciousness in the Breakdown of the Bicameral Mind* (Boston: Houghton Mifflin, 1976; rpt. 1990), 404–426. Making no distinction, however, between the multitude of voices one may hear—superego voices, the other (or alter-ego, *a'*) speaking in one's own mind, preconscious thought verbalization, and unconscious dreams and fantasies (that is, the Other)—Jaynes is led to absurdly associate schizophrenia with what he calls the "bicameral mind." Although psychosis was probably far more prevalent in "early man" than in humans today (due to the virtual nonexistence of the law as we now know it, and to the tenuous status of the paternal function), the "bicameral" attunement to voices is in no way coextensive with schizophrenia. Part of every analysand's experience in undergoing psychoanalysis—and I am talking here about "ordinary neurotics"—is to learn to hear the voices and verbalized thoughts that go through one's mind all the time. Freud calls them "preconscious" or "unconscious" thoughts, or "superego" voices ("admonitory" voices, in Jaynes' terms), and Lacan refers to them as "the Other's discourse." None of these have anything whatsoever to do with schizophrenia, and if "bicameral man" attributed them to God, he did so in the absence of any psychological understanding—just as religious people of many ilks continue to do even in our own day.

33. Another way of saying this might be that language never becomes symbolic in psychosis—it remains real.

34. For an excellent discussion of substitutional metaphors, see Russell Grigg, "Metaphor and Metonymy," in *Newsletter of the Freudian Field* 3 (1989): 58–79.

35. Though it is not yet repression proper, as we shall see in Chapters 8 and 9.

36. A child has to feel invited or be "seduced" into its mother's world and into language. When parents use language only to express hostility or to demand compliance with inflexible feeding and excretory schedules, and want their child to speak merely so that they can have the sense that it is an intelligent, precocious reflection of themselves, it is no wonder the child refuses to speak (though it often understands much of what is said around it).

37. Other children and other family members may, of course, get in the way as well.

38. The "moments" I am discussing are not so much developmental stages as what Lacan refers to as "logical moments"—moments which, while not always or easily discernible chronologically, must have occurred in order for the child to have reached its present clinical structure (neurotic as opposed to psychotic, for example). Very briefly stated, the second moment of the paternal metaphor might be understood as follows:

Once repression occurs, a certain transparency disappears: I no longer know myself as I did before, and I can begin to wonder what I want and what others want of me. Formerly, I did not ask myself, "What does my mother want?" but now it becomes a question for me. "Am I what is most precious to her? She seems to accept Dad's prohibitions while he is around, and sometimes even when he is gone, but aren't I still the apple of her eye?" Thus, the child is led to scrutinize the mother's behavior and speech insofar as it manifests desire, attempting to discern its place in her desire. Typically, the child is forced to realize that it is by no means its mother's be-all and end-all: the mother is perceived to leave the child's side when the father calls, to abandon the child to perform tasks for the father or be alone with him, and so on. To the question, "What does she want?" the child is forced to answer: Dad. Her desire points beyond the dyadic mother-child relation to the stereotypical Oedipal triangle.

The second moment of the paternal metaphor can, then, be understood as the answering of the question, "What does my mOther want?" "What is it that she desires that takes her away from me?" The classic response here is "the father": *the father is the key to the mystery of the mother's desire.* This second moment of the paternal metaphor results in the naming of the mother's desire—that is, its interpretation and delimitation.

Father's name

Mother as desire

The child generally does not stop there, but wonders instead what it is about the father that the mOther desires, and what it is about other men, other people, other activities, and other things that leads mom to desire them. If the child can figure out what it is she wants, it can go on to try to become *that*—not the object with which she obtains jouissance, but the object she esteems, desires, or praises. Whether it is wealth, status, or power she wants, it is, in the best of cases, something that situates the child's quest at the symbolic level, as a seeker of socially valorized positions (first place in sports, cooking, dancing, singing, music, or mathematics, or part of a team, group, or department engaged in recognized projects or endeavors).

The first moment of the paternal metaphor corresponds to what Lacan calls alienation, and the second to separation. These points are expanded upon in Chapter 9.

39. Figure 7.3 is based in part on a figure in Ferdinand de Saussure, *Course on General Linguistics* (New York: McGraw-Hill, 1959), 112. Saussure, however, places language ("the vague plane of sounds") on the bottom, and meaning ("the indefinite plane of jumbled ideas") on the top.

40. This suggests an important link between the paternal metaphor and the ego-ideal; indeed, the former can be understood to instate S_1, the master signifier, the imperative, just as the ego-ideal involves the instatement of the "unary trait," Lacan's earlier name for S_1 (see, for example, Seminar IX, "Identification"). If we borrow Corday's image of the self (or ego) as a balloon, the ego-ideal is the string (or thread) which ties the balloon shut and keeps it from deflating.

41. See *Ecrits*, 804–827. For detailed commentary, see Slavoj Žižek, *The Sublime Object of Ideology* (London: Verso, 1989), ch. 3.

42. In Seminar XX, Lacan says something very similar regarding Schreber's interrupted sentences (such as "Now I shall . . ." and "You were to . . ."): "We perceive here the requirement of a sentence, whatever it may be, which is such that

one of its links, when missing, sets all of the others free, that is, withdraws from them the One" (115), in other words, takes away the sentence's unity of meaning.

43. A Canadian photographer in a panicked state once came to see me at my office when I was practicing in Paris. He was in the midst of what he was manifestly experiencing as a serious life crisis. He said he had been hospitalized on a couple of occasions, had been in therapy for six years, and was considering voluntarily committing himself at a nearby psychiatric hospital. His other possibility, according to him, was to go back to Canada. He was quite disoriented and confused, and my first concern was to determine whether or not he was psychotic, and perhaps should be encouraged to allow me to accompany him to the hospital immediately. Inviting him to talk about what was going on that had put him in such a panic, I attempted to determine whether the conflict was situated at a strictly imaginary level or not. There was another photographer whom he described as trying to take his job away from him; but as we talked, it appeared more clearly that the conflict with this other photographer was subordinate to his desire to please their mutual boss, an older father figure. The use of these two axes alone, imaginary and symbolic, allowed me to assess the situation quite quickly, provisionally diagnose the patient as neurotic, and work out treatment arrangements with him that did not include hospitalization. (I am obviously not suggesting that all psychotics need to be hospitalized at times of crisis or that neurotics never do.)

44. According to Lacan, the origin of the ego in the mirror stage is such that there is a core of paranoia in all of us. The ego itself is essentially paranoid in nature, defining what is me and what is not me, and coming into being in a fundamental rivalry or competition with the other.

45. In *Studies on Hysteria* (SE II), Freud mentions numerous cases of anesthesia and hypersensitivity which were in no way, shape, or form regulated by the location of a particular nerve's endings in some part of the body, but which instead clearly obeyed popular notions about where a part of the body, as defined in common speech, started and stopped. While, for example, no particular nerve starts and stops in what we commonly refer to as the "wrist," it may become a site of psychosomatic anesthesia or hypersensitivity, since it is the general area where bracelets and watches are worn in Western societies. (The symptom behaves, says Freud, "as if there were no such thing as anatomy.") Each language cuts the body up or "covers" it in slightly different ways, and the body becomes written with signifiers; language is "encrusted upon the living," to borrow Bergson's expression. The body is overwritten/overridden by language.

46. And is even "channeled outside the body," insofar as object *a* is a locus of libido outside the body (*hors corps*).

47. See Freud, "Psychoanalytic Notes on an Autobiographical Account of a Case of Paranoia [Schreber]," SE XII, 9–82; Freud's study is based on Daniel Paul Schreber, *Memoirs of My Nervous Illness* (Cambridge, Mass.: Harvard University Press, 1988). Lacan comments on the Schreber case extensively in "On a Question Preliminary to any Possible Treatment of Psychosis," *Ecrits*, 531–583/179–225; and in Seminar III, *The Psychoses* (New York: Norton, 1993).

48. When the neurotic is effective, it is often unintentional or inadvertent on his or her part.

49. See, for example, Françoise Gorog, "Clinical Vignette: A Case of Transsexualism," in *Reading Seminars I and II*, 283–286.

50. See, for example, Seminar III, 74–75.

51. One of my patients said that his father wanted a girl, not a boy, and competed with his son in many areas: when there was cake, the father would take it all, and the mother would be forced to "split things half and half between them"; when my patient went to college, his father decided to enroll in the same academic program as his son. The mother's symbolic interventions were not sufficient to counter the father's rivalrous relationship with his son, and the latter began having psychotic episodes in his twenties.

52. Not by identification with the mother, as we sometimes see in cases of nonpsychotic male homosexuality.

53. I discuss some of the reasons for psychotic breaks in the course of my discussion of a case of psychosis further on in this chapter.

54. See, for example, Gorog, "Clinical Vignette."

55. In that sense, the paternal function might be said to "humanize" language itself, language being understood as a kind of autonomously functioning machine. On this perspective regarding language, see Fink, *The Lacanian Subject*, ch. 2, and apps. 1 and 2.

56. In Fink, *The Lacanian Subject*, ch. 8. See Lacan's extremely dense discussion of masculine and feminine structure in Seminar XX.

57. Lacan's term for such feminization is *pousse à la femme*, which is rather difficult to translate and which literally means "budding into a woman" or "growing into womanhood/womanliness"; less literally, "a surge to become like a woman." In a somewhat similar register, Freud emphasizes the importance of homosexuality in male psychosis; he also employs the term *Verweiblichung*, which might be rendered as "transformation into a woman," "transmogrification into a woman," or feminization. See *Ecrits*, 565/206.

58. Indeed, the delusional system fomented by the psychotic represents a spontaneous attempt to construct an imaginary system (that is, a system of meanings) capable of holding his or her universe together (of stabilizing the relationship between signifier and signified). Lacan refers to it as a "delusional metaphor" (*Ecrits*, 577/217); I discuss this later in this chapter in connection with a specific case and at the end of Chapter 9.

59. Originally published in *Scilicet* 2–3 (1970): 351–361. English translation by Stuart Schneiderman, in *How Lacan's Ideas Are Used in Clinical Practice* (Northvale, N.J.: Aronson, 1993), 184–194. Page references in the text are to the English edition, though I have often modified the translation.

60. Schneiderman translates the phrase "ça n'a pas de nom" literally as "has no name" (187). The connotation seems to me that there is no name strong enough to qualify his father, no epithet that can say how terrible he is.

61. "Je m'attacherais plutôt à un chien": Schneiderman translates this as "I'd rather be related to a dog" (187), but the French implies that the father would more easily grow fond of a dog than of his own son—would rather become devoted to a dog than to his own son.

62. In cases of adoption, remarriage, and so on, the biological father's identity may, of course, be thrown into question.

63. As the stereotypical Freudian father does, serving as a symbolic Other who separates mother from child.

64. All four places—ego, alter-ego, subject, and Other—are, loosely speaking, "found within" each "individual"; while the L Schema can be used to understand the imaginary and symbolic components of the analytic relationship, it also applies to each "person," mapping the "intrapsychic spaces," the "intrapersonal" structure. As we see, however, half of the L Schema is inapplicable to the psychotic (the L Schema is applicable to neurosis and perversion). Lacan provides a far more complex mapping of psychosis in its "terminal" phase: the R Schema (*Ecrits*, 571/212).

We can understand the subject here as that which is constituted by repression: the primal repression of the mother as desire. That repression gives rise to the positions of the subject and the Other.

65. The link here is even more direct in French: *marteau* means "hammer" and is also a slang term for "crazy."

66. When Lacan capitalizes *Un*, above all in his later work, it refers to the symbolic order insofar as it is totalizing—that is, inasmuch as it constitutes wholes or complete units (taking a perhaps amorphous and disparate set of things or events and counting them as one, as, for example, when we take a historical period composed of millions of heterogeneous occurrences and dub it the "Renaissance"). There it is juxtaposed to the "Other," understood as that which remains radically outside of or heterogeneous to the symbolic order—in other words, as that which resists symbolization (as in the "Other jouissance").

67. Akin to God the Father, the father who creates something, a subject, from nothing by naming it. See Chapter 9 on naming and creation.

68. He tries to contact the "professeur: c'est 'un nom.'" Schneiderman translates this literally, providing "the professor is a 'name'" (189), missing the idiomatic sense implied here.

69. "L'homme à la 203": Schneiderman translates this as the "the man in 203," but in French one does not say *à la* when referring to apartment or street numbers.

70. It seems likely that while certain drug treatments used with psychotics put a stop to delusional activity, they thus also impede the possible construction of a delusional metaphor. To maintain stability, then, the drug treatments must often be continued ad infinitum.

71. As Bruno Bettelheim once put it, "love is not enough" when it comes to raising children, and even the contemporary espousers of "tough love" do not usually grasp the distinction between setting limits and establishing the Law as such. Parents often set limits for their children simply because it is more convenient for them to do so, and the limits depend on nothing but the parents' own mood or whimsy. If I tell my children they have to go to bed by 8:30 P.M. every school night, and then I let them stay up until 11 P.M. on a school night because I feel like having company, I show them I consider myself to be the only limit to their jouissance. If I tell them they have to obey property rights and speed limits, and then proceed to steal little things from hotels and try to talk my way out of speeding tickets, I show them that I accept no law above myself, no legitimate limitations or restrictions on my own will and desire.

The law of the symbolic pact, on the other hand, applies to all parties, limits all parties. If I promise my child that Saturday afternoons are his to do with what he will, then I cannot arbitrarily decide that he has to spend all of this Saturday afternoon cleaning up the toy room, his bedroom, and his closet. *According to the symbolic pact, I am bound by my promises just as much as my child is.* If I make as many exceptions as I like, nothing remains of the rule, and the child—perceiving that I consider myself my own law—aspires simply to dethrone me and become his own law in turn.

A mother is just as likely (if not more likely) to grasp the importance of the law of the symbolic pact (or Law with a capital "L") as a father is, but both mothers and fathers, insofar as they are neurotic, are likely to have their own problems accepting the Law (as we shall see in the next chapter) and are more likely to criticize each other's breaches of the Law than to criticize their own. We find it far easier to detect capriciousness, selfishness, and inconsistency in another's speech and behavior than in our own. A single mother can, in theory, provide both a loving mother-child bond and appeal to a law beyond herself (whether Dr. Spock or the U.S. Constitution, either of which could serve as a Name-of-the-Father in Lacanian terms) that applies equally to mother and child, thereby introducing that necessary symbolic third term. So too, single fathers and gay couples could, in theory, provide both love and Law. Given how frequently the traditional family structure already fails, despite centuries of dividing love and Law between the sexes in considerably codified sex roles, what are the chances that both roles will be played by one parent alone or by two parents raised into similarly codified sex roles? Isn't the incidence of psychosis likely to rise in such cases?

Our relation to the Law is obviously a very complicated matter, and I have barely scratched the surface in these brief comments. For we can always raise the question of the injustice or immorality of the law (whether local, state, national, or international), and this has been done from Antigone to Thoreau, from the civil-disobedience tradition to the civil rights and women's rights movements, and takes myriad forms. In such cases, we appeal to a notion of right or justice beyond the particular laws of the land, questioning what it is that makes the law right or just in the first place and thereby raising the question of what Lacan calls the "guarantee"—that is, what legitimates or lends authority to the Other, to the Law itself. The problem being that *there can never be a guarantee*: there is no absolute justification of the Law (in Lacanian terminology, no "Other of the Other," no stable bedrock outside the Other that serves as the Other's foundation or anchor in truth, no outside point that guarantees the Other's consistency and coherence).

Contemporary novels and movies display a fascination not simply with the topic of the legitimacy or illegitimacy of a nation's laws (a topic debated since at least the time of Aeschylus and Plato, and spawning a social-contract theory tradition that extends from Rousseau to Rawls) but with the ineffectiveness of the enforcement, justice, and correction systems supposedly designed to implement the Law (since they fail to do their jobs, we the citizens are obliged to "take the law into our own hands") and with the generally illegal covert operations required to sustain the "rule of law" in "free" countries.

If the current legal system ties the hands of law enforcement officials regarding the procurement of evidence, lets known criminals off on procedural technicalities, puts convicted criminals back out on the street due to overcrowding in prisons, allows lawyers to stack the deck in favor of the client they are defending by eliminating all jurors who might be unfavorably disposed toward him or her, and permits politicians and military officials to be heard and judged by their peers instead of by the courts that apply to everyone else, then faith in the law is undermined. The law may sound good on paper, but is enforced unequally and often not at all. Hence the perceived importance of taking the law into one's own hands.

On the other hand—again according to popular novels and films—there are agencies (such as the FBI, CIA, Secret Service, National Security Agency, and Drug Enforcement Administration) in which agents seem to believe they are defending the rule of law (euphemistically referred to as "the American way of life") by breaking every known national and international law. Covert operations, kept secret from the president and Congress, are carried out to defend "American interests," but the president, Congress, and the people are considered "too naive" to realize the necessity of such operations. In other words, the view of such agency operatives is that the nice, clean-cut law can be upheld only by far messier, legally questionable, if not downright illegal activities. The notion here seems to be that *what guarantees the Other—in other words, the Other of the Other—is abominable atrocities.* Yet this secret can never be told.

The "legitimation crisis" runs deep: what was once allowed and even encouraged (the massacre of Native Americans, the enslavement of blacks) has become illegal. One of the most far-reaching events of our time—the assassination of John F. Kennedy, which called into question the foundations of the American government and legal system—remains shrouded in mystery. The "secret" bombings of countries in Southeast Asia that the U.S. had never officially declared war on were ordered by officials at the very highest levels of government. Many such events lead to suspicions of illegal dealings by the most visible representatives of the law on both the right and the left of the political spectrum.

I'm certainly not claiming that, in the past, the law and its representatives used to seem above reproach (the nostalgic's argument). But the more the law's representatives appear untrustworthy, the more the law itself can be thrown into question, and the less we are inclined to accept the sacrifices exacted by the law (that is, to accept limitation/castration). If we are to preserve some notion of a just Law above and beyond the particular laws of the land—given the current legitimation crisis of the legal, juridical, and executive branches of government—a just Law that is equitably and uniformly enforced, we must have an experience of Law at home which at least approaches that ideal to some degree. As rare as this experience may be in the stereotypical nuclear family, practices currently being advocated seem likely to make it rarer still. As Lacan once said, in a pessimistic vein, "I won't say that even the slightest little gesture to eliminate something bad leaves the way open to something still worse—it *always* leads to something worse" (Seminar III, 361).

8. Neurosis

1. Consider Lacan's definition of a genuine act: "An act is an action in which the very desire that is designed to inhibit it is manifested" (Seminar X, June 25,

1963). See also Lacan's year-long seminar entitled "L'acte psychanalytique" (Seminar XV).

2. See, for example, Seminar III, 20.

3. According to Freud, the unconscious results from a twofold process: primal repression and secondary repression. For a discussion of how Lacan translates this into his own terms, see Bruce Fink, *The Lacanian Subject: Between Language and Jouissance* (Princeton: Princeton University Press, 1995), ch. 5. Note that if there is no unconscious in psychosis, there is no being, no subject, and no desire, strictly speaking.

4. On "affirmation" *(Bejahung)*, see "Negation" in SE XIX, 236–239; also Jean Hyppolite's long commentary on this article at the end of Seminar II. Colette Soler has suggested that *Bejahung* be translated into French as *admission* ("admission" or "acceptance" in English); see Soler, "The Symbolic Order," in Bruce Fink, Richard Feldstein, and Maire Jaanus, eds., *Reading Seminars I and II: Lacan's Return to Freud* (Albany: SUNY Press, 1996), 52. I am very much indebted to her clinically oriented paper, "Hysteria and Obsession," which is included in that volume (248–282).

5. On repression as involving thoughts, not perceptions, see the beginning of Chapter 9 on disavowal.

6. In certain cases, when a thought is repressed, the affect attached to it is caught up in the struggle of forces which led to the repression of that thought in the first place; it is not felt, because it has been neutralized by opposing forces. When, for example, our aggressive impulse (thought or wish and affect) is countered by a moral judgment censoring such impulses, the anger or affect may be held in check, balanced, or zeroed out by the judgment. The neurotic, in such a case, professes not to be angry and shows little if any emotion. Many therapists I supervise believe such patients to be overly "cerebral" and "unable to express their feelings"; they take it as their goal to induce patients to "feel their anger"—in a word, "get in touch with their feelings" and stop "thinking" so much. This approach misses the point, for feeling and thought go hand in hand. It is only by getting the patient to associate to dreams, daydreams, fantasies, and slips that thoughts that are usually censored can be articulated; and when they are, the feelings associated with them generally well up of their own accord. Telling patients that they are not allowing themselves to feel their own feelings and that they are over-rationalizing everything is tantamount to suggestion (often leading to compliant attempts by the patient to appease the therapist with demonstrations of emotion) and to accusing the patient of resisting without interpreting the resistance (see Chapter 4).

7. See, for example, Seminar III, 57. The same notion is repeatedly expressed in his work throughout the 1950s.

8. As Freud says, "We call 'unconscious' any mental process the existence of which we are obliged to assume—because, for instance, we infer it in some way from its effects" (SE XXII, 70, translation modified).

9. See Breuer's account of the case in *Studies on Hysteria,* SE II, 21–47.

10. Indeed, one might say that the return of the repressed in the Other is what distinguishes neurosis from psychosis, for in psychosis the foreclosed material can be understood as returning in the real—the TV announcer believed to directly address the psychotic individual watching and no one else—or is articulated by the other with a lowercase "o."

11. Each of these glorious categories no doubt earned its "discoverer" academic fame and clinical fortune.

12. Another definition Freud provides is as follows: the obsessive takes *too much* pleasure in an early sexual experience (later feeling guilty about it), whereas the hysteric takes *too little*. See Lacan's remarks on that definition in Seminar XI, 67/ 69–70.

13. On Freud's broad definition of "sexuality" (far broader than that involving only heterosexual genital sex), see, for example, *Introductory Lectures on Psychoanalysis*, chs. 20 and 21.

14. The very terms "obsession-compulsion" and "obsessive-compulsive" tend to be misleading, suggesting as they do that all compulsive behavior falls into the diagnostic category of "obsession." It should be stressed, on the contrary, that *the drives are always compulsive*, regardless of whether they are conjugated in an obsessive or a hysterical mode.

15. See *Freud's Letters to Fliess*, trans. Jeffrey Masson (Cambridge, Mass.: Harvard University Press, 1988).

16. Phobia will be taken up briefly at the end of this chapter. It should be noted that Lacan does not *always* include phobia as a separate neurosis; see, for example, Jacques-Alain Miller's comments on this point in Miller, "An Introduction to Lacan's Clinical Perspectives," *Reading Seminars I and II*. Note, too, that Freud includes paraphrenia under neurosis, while Lacan includes it under psychosis (Seminar III, 282).

17. On the lost object and its genesis, see Fink, *The Lacanian Subject*, ch. 7. On "separation" and the kinds of figures provided below to illustrate the fundamental fantasy in hysteria and obsession, see Seminar XI, chs. 16–17, and Seminars XIV and XV. Figure 8.1 can be found in Seminar X (June 12, 1963). See also Jacques-Alain Miller's unpublished seminars (especially the classes given on March 9, 16, and 23, 1983, and on November 21 and 28, 1984), in which he formalizes Lacan's notions of alienation and separation; Bruce Fink, "Alienation and Separation: Logical Moments of Lacan's Dialectic of Desire," *Newsletter of the Freudian Field* 4 (1990), which is based in large part on Miller's work; and Fink, *The Lacanian Subject*, ch. 5. Separation is also discussed below, in Chapter 9.

18. Rather than talk about that time in chronological terms—that is, rather than say that there is no subject-object distinction until three months of age or one year—Freud and Lacan suggest that it is a logically necessary moment; for the infant is not, at the outset, constituted for itself as a thing or person that can be considered distinct from other things or persons.

19. As Lacan says in Seminar X, the plane of separation passes not between the child and its mother but between the child and the breast.

20. In 1973, Lacan drew an arrow from $\math$ to a in the table under the "formulas of sexuation" (Seminar XX, 73), confirming, in my view, the continued validity of the formula ($\mathbb{S} \lozenge a$) in obsession. Although these formulas were designed to conceptualize what Lacan calls "masculine structure" and "feminine structure," I believe that, within limits, we can associate masculine structure with obsession, and feminine structure with hysteria. In Seminar XX, he says the following about men: "By way of a partner, [a man] never deals with anything but object a . . . He is unable to attain his sexual partner, who is the Other, except [insofar as]

the partner is the cause of his desire. In this respect, . . . this is nothing other than fantasy" (75).

21. In Chapter 9, we will see certain affinities between this strategy and perversion.

22. In Chapter 9, I will explain separation, and the figures I have been using here to illustrate it, in somewhat more detail. Here I would like to provide something of a social-psychological (or psychologistic) explanation for the different approaches to overcoming separation found in obsessives (usually male) and hysterics (usually female).

Very schematically put, there is a tendency on the part of mothers, for example, to give somewhat more generously and selflessly to their male children right from birth. They give them the sense that *the boys are the ones lacking in something*—nourishment and warmth—that their mothers can provide. As a consequence, boys later attempt to overcome their separation from the mother—imposed during what Freud refers to as the castration complex—by fantasmatically completing themselves with an object related to the mother (the breast, a soft warm voice, a tender gaze, etc.). Since the boy has come to sense that he is the one who is lacking in something, he seeks in fantasy the object that can complete *him.*

With daughters, on the other hand, mothers are likely to provide nourishment and care far less willingly and for shorter periods of time (studies show that mothers breastfeed their male children 70 percent longer than their female children). A mother tends to give her daughter the impression that the mother is the one who is lacking in something, and that the daughter should give it to her: hence the daughter's later attempts to overcome separation from the mother by completing that Other with herself as object. She comes to sense that it is the mOther who is lacking and needs her as object to make good the mOther's loss.

If and when Oedipalization occurs, this strategy of completing the mother as Other is transferred to the male Other—usually to the father—but I would suggest that it arises first in relation to *the maternal Other*, not the father figure. (It is a widely attested clinical phenomenon for women to reproduce in their relations with their male partners their relations with their mothers, at least in part. We see this strategy at work in relation to both maternal and paternal figures, in the case of hysteria discussed in detail later in this chapter.)

Fathers obviously play a part here as well, insofar as they tend to view their sons as greater rivals for the mother's attention than their daughters, and are thus more vigilant in their efforts to separate sons from mothers than they are in their efforts to separate daughters from mothers. Indeed, they are often happy to let their daughters be a source of solace, consolation, and joy to the mother, sensing that the mother's relationship with her daughters makes up for certain inadequacies in the mother's relationship with her husband.

The differing approaches to overcoming separation that arise from this situation may or may not coincide with learned sex roles and societal notions about what women and men are and how they are supposed to behave. These approaches constitute fundamental relations to the Other that are often detected in the fact that a person repeatedly establishes certain kinds of relations with other people, regardless of his or her own notion of the kind of relations he or she would like to have: that is, it is the kind of relation one unwittingly establishes and reestablishes, despite goals inculcated at home, at school, and in the media regarding the importance of remaining autonomous, avoiding "codependency," and so on.

Obviously, certain fathers are more than happy to let their sons satisfy their mothers' unsatisfied wants, whereas others vigilantly keep mother and daughter apart; and certain mothers give their daughters the sense that the daughters are the ones who need something their mothers can provide, whereas others give their sons the sense that the sons must provide their mothers with the satisfactions they don't get from their husbands. But in providing a psychologistic explanation, I am confining my attention here to what we might call "statistical generalities" in contemporary Western societies.

Why do most fathers and mothers treat their male and female children so differently? Their own Oedipal rivalries and jealousies obviously play a significant role, as does the perceived greater importance of the male child due to the fact that he passes down the family name—this was especially true in earlier times, though it is still true to some extent today—and plays a certain role in economic production. All of this leads to the creation of contrasting attitudes toward male and female children that set future tendencies in motion, leading to the reproduction of "sexual difference" or (perhaps more accurately) of typical sex roles and different approaches to overcoming separation.

23. Lacan's formulation of the hysteric's discourse in Seminars XVII and XX could lead to a modification of this formula. See Fink, *The Lacanian Subject*, ch. 9; and below.

24. Just as the phoneme is the most elementary building block of speech, and the semanteme is the most elementary building block of meaning, the "matheme" is conceived of by Lacan as the most basic unit of psychical structure.

25. Lacan provides different versions of the mathemes of hysteria and obsession. In a 1960 text, he suggests that $(-\varphi)$, the "imaginary function of castration," is situated in neurosis under the barred subject:

$$\frac{\$ \diamond a}{(-\varphi)}$$

He suggests in the same text that $(-\varphi)$ can be situated under either term, and even seems to suggest that when it is situated under a, the fundamental fantasy is nonneurotic (he refers here to Alcibiades' desire for Socrates in Plato's *Symposium*). See *Ecrits*, 825–826 / 322–323.

In 1961 (Seminar VIII, 289 and 295), Lacan provides somewhat different formulas. Hysteria is written as follows:

$$\frac{a \diamond A}{(-\varphi)}$$

for the hysteric puts herself in the place of the object in relation to the Other. Obsession is written as follows:

$$\text{\AA} \diamond \varphi \, (a, a', a'', a''', \dots)$$

Here Lacan suggests that it is the "imaginary function of castration" that renders equivalent all objects $(a, a', a'', a''', \dots)$ of the obsessive's desire; castration here serves a function akin to that of mathematical functions, like $f(x)$, in which the different objects are subjected to the same function when put in the place of the variable, x. The obsessive subject is written $A̷$ here because he "is never where he seems to designate himself"; he says, for example, "I am a clerk, but that's only my day job—I'm really a screenwriter." Whatever the designation or definition provided, that is never really *it;* there is always something else.

Note also the different "Φ functions" Lacan provides for hysteria and obsession in another context: "The Φ function of the lost signifier, to which the subject sacrifices his phallus, the form Φ(a) of male desire, $A̷(φ)$ of woman's desire . . ." (*Ecrits,* 683). In Seminar VI (June 17, 1959), Lacan provides a still earlier formula for all of neurosis; he says that neurotics devote themselves to trying to satisfy all of the Other's demands at the expense of their own desire: $Ꞩ ◇ a$ is transformed into $Φ ◇ i(a)$, the latter designating the "barred phallus" in the presence of an object of desire—the object here being the image of the imaginary other or ego. This formulation was no doubt a forerunner of that found in *Ecrits,* $Ꞩ ◇ D$; there Lacan says that the neurotic confuses "the Other's lack with the Other's demand. The Other's demand takes on the function of the object in the neurotic's fantasy" (*Ecrits,* 823/321).

A great deal could, of course, be said about these early formulas; but I have decided not to present Lacan's notion of the "imaginary function of castration" in this book, as it seems to me that Lacan's later notion of the "phallic function," the symbolic function presented in Seminars XVIII through XXI as Φx, supersedes it in certain respects. See Fink, *The Lacanian Subject,* ch. 8. It should be noted, however, that in Lacan's later work, $-φ$ takes on the meaning of a loss (or minus) of jouissance that is "positivized" in object *a.* See, for example, *Scilicet* 1 (1968): 23.

26. The reader interested in Lacan's early mathemes should consult Lacan, "Subversion of the Subject and Dialectic of Desire"; and Seminar VIII, *Transference,* chs. XV–XVIII. See also the many varied commentaries by members of the Ecole de la Cause Freudienne in the extremely useful collective work *Hystérie et Obsession* (Paris: Navarin, 1986).

27. Descartes' formulation fits the obsessive quite well: "I am thinking, therefore I am." This perhaps unfamiliar translation can be found in the most recent English translation of Descartes' *Philosophical Writings,* by J. Cottingham (Cambridge: Cambridge University Press, 1986). The obsessive may substitute counting for thinking—counting, for example, his conquests, money, heartbeats, and so on.

28. As Lacan says, "The unconscious is the Other's discourse" (*Ecrits,* 312): it is not the message we meant to convey—it is some Other message, some foreign voice speaking within us. See Fink, *The Lacanian Subject,* ch. 1. The refusal to recognize the unconscious is another way in which the obsessive annuls the Other.

29. This connects up with Lacan's 1961 matheme for obsession: $A̷ ◇ φ$ (*a, a', a", a'''*, . . .).

30. As Lacan emphasizes in Seminar VI, "It is altogether clear, in our experience, that love and desire are two different things, and that we must call a spade a spade and admit that one can very much love one being and yet desire another" (June 17, 1959).

31. For an English translation, see Lacan, "On Freud's *'Trieb'* and the Psychoanalyst's Desire," trans. Bruce Fink, *Reading Seminars I and II,* 417.

32. See Soler, "Hysteria and Obsession."

33. As a representative of what Lacan calls the Other sex (the sex that is radically Other or different, unassimilable, for both men and women—that is, Woman; who, according to Lacan, does not exist), she is annulled or canceled out such that no encounter with the Other sex can occur. In Seminar VI, where he discusses male impotence, Lacan says that a man very often "fears the satisfaction of his desire . . . as it makes him depend henceforth on the person who is going to satisfy his desire, namely the Other" (December 17, 1958).

34. As Aristotle says, "The pleasures are a hindrance to thought, and the more so the more one delights in them, e.g., sexual pleasure; for no one could think of anything while absorbed in this" (*Nicomachean Ethics*, 1152b16–18). Obviously Aristotle had never met anyone quite like the obsessive in question!

35. In a recent issue of *Shape* magazine (vol. 14, no. 6, February 1995), a number of men were interviewed, virtually all of whom admitted to fantasizing about one woman while making love with another.

36. See Seminar XI, chs. XVI–XVII. Lacan borrows the term "aphanisis" from Ernest Jones, but does not use it in the same way that Jones does. Lacan suggests that there is a link between aphanisis and obsession, and between the nonfunctioning of aphanisis (of the "aphanisis function") and hysteria. Since the fundamental fantasy in hysteria does not emphasize the subject as conscious, thinking master of her own desire—that is, since the hysteric's wish is to be a desired object, not a thinking thing *(res cogitans)* or machine—aphanisis is not a concern, and symptoms often appear in the body, not in the mind. The obsessive is concerned about his tendency to fade; the hysteric is unconcerned with fading, but is concerned with her constitution as object. Language as Other is assimilated differently by the hysteric, and the "subject of the signifier" (that is, the subject implied by language, by the fact that we speak) is not threatened with fading.

It should also be noted that by pursuing an impossible desire, the obsessive, like the hysteric, seems—more than anything else—to want to go on desiring. Indeed, that seems to be the very nature of desire: to reproduce itself.

37. See Fink, *The Lacanian Subject*, ch. 8.

38. Lacan's commentary there has been examined by numerous prominent Lacanians in Paris. Jacques-Alain Miller devoted several sessions to it during his "DEA Seminar" held at the Ecole de la Cause Freudienne in 1988–1989. Readers of English can find illuminating discussions of it in Colette Soler, "History and Hysteria: The Witty Butcher's Wife," *Newsletter of the Freudian Field* 6 (1992); and in idem, "Hysteria and Obsession."

39. We might say that she relies upon the signifier of desire (the phallus) to sustain her position as desiring. As Lacan says, "It is by the intermediary of Mr. K. that Dora desires, though it is not him that she loves, but Mrs. K." (Seminar VIII, 425). In the table below the "formulas of sexuation" in Seminar XX (73), Lacan draws an arrow from Woman (in the French version, from *La*) to Φ, the phallus: a woman's desire has to *passer par*—"pass by," "go through," or "maneuver via"— the phallus, a male marker or symbol of sorts. The other arrow, from Woman to S($\emptyset$), concerns not desire but jouissance: the Other jouissance.

Hysterical triangles also form in homosexual couples, of course. The lesbian hysteric, for example, may well seek to detect a desire for another woman in her female partner (qua Other), and come to desire like her.

40. In many cases (though not in the case of the butcher's wife), if the hysteric is led to play the part of a man, it is precisely because the man in question—usually the father—is not playing "his part." When the father in a family refuses, for example, to separate the mother from her daughter, to enunciate and enforce boundaries—such as the daughter's right to have a certain space of her own, a diary and other personal affairs that her mother cannot go through—the daughter is often led to do so by establishing limits herself, in whatever way she can. In one case I supervised, the daughter, verbally abused by her mother for anything and everything while her father watched television in the next room, learned to "explode," as she put it, yelling in an extremely violent way to finally shut her mother up. This was not what the daughter wanted to do, for she felt that it was her father's job to protect her; but he refused to intervene. Here we see that the hysteric plays the part of a man *faute d'un vrai*—that is, because there is no real man in the picture, no man that will play the part assigned to him in a certain societal conception of what a father is supposed to do.

In the example cited, we also see a hint of the eroticization of the mother-daughter relationship (due, no doubt, to the fact that the mother would get herself "all worked up" in yelling at her daughter—in other words, that she was very vehement, passionate, and excited when she berated her) in the daughter's choice of the term "explode" to describe her way of reacting to her mother. And we see the "perverse" nature of the mother's behavior with her daughter, pushing the latter to the point at which she herself would enunciate a law, limit, or boundary beyond which the mother could not go, as if the mother were requiring her daughter to tell her when to stop (see Chapter 9 below on the importance of the enunciation of the law in perversion). The mother—most likely a hysteric herself—would, according to the unfortunate formulations put forward by certain psychoanalysts, probably be described as like a child in her search for boundaries. But if hysterics are to be considered "childlike," this is anything but a "developmental issue"; rather, the problem arises precisely because, during childhood, the law was so rarely enunciated in their households in a clear and definitive fashion. There is often a certain similarity between hysteria and perversion regarding the need for separation (see, in particular, the end of Chapter 9).

In other cases, the hysteric "makes the man" *(fait l'homme)*—that is, she makes the man in her life into a "real man" or true symbolic father figure by making him "do the right thing," getting him to act in a noble and just manner. He doesn't do so spontaneously, but she works very hard to ensure that he does so anyway.

41. As one patient expressed herself, "I delight in restriction." Lacan suggests that what is important is not that the anorexic does not eat, but that she eats *nothing*. "Nothing" itself is an object of sorts in hysteria, a cause of desire ("the nothing," as Lacan puts it). The anorexic gets off on eating *nothing*.

42. The translation I have provided here is truly an interpretation. The French reads as follows: "le désir ne s'y maintient que de l'insatisfaction qu'on y apporte en s'y dérobant comme objet." Sheridan's translation is, in any case, sheer nonsense.

43. This often arouses her own jealousy—proof that her desire is still alive. But who is she jealous of? The husband? The other woman? Both? The triangle of desire is often still more complicated, blossoming into a quadrilateral; see Lacan's comments on Dora's quadrilateral in Seminar III, 107.

44. Given the hysteric's revulsion toward sexuality, Lacan goes so far as to suggest that the butcher's wife would like to give her husband to her female friend so that he would act out his sexual urges with the other woman, not her. He writes more generally that "the hysteric . . . offers up the woman in whom she adores her own mystery [for instance, the 'inimitable' female friend who refuses herself salmon, just as the butcher's wife refuses herself caviar] to the man whose role she usurps without being able to enjoy it" (*Ecrits,* 452).

45. We see here that the obsessive also renders the partner's desire impossible. It is not simply his own desire that is impossible!

46. On Lacan's claim regarding the nonrelationship between the sexes, see Fink, *The Lacanian Subject,* ch. 8. The hysteric's motto here seems to be: "Be somewhere else now."

47. Jacques-Alain Miller suggests that (the demand for) love and desire may be directed to the same object more often among women than among men ("Donc," May 11, 1994). Perhaps desire and jouissance converge upon the same object more often among men.

48. See, for example, his comments in *Ecrits,* 604–607/243–245.

49. Lacan's exact formulation is more difficult to render in English: "Que l'Autre ne jouisse pas de moi!"—"Would that the Other never get off on me!" or "Let the Other never get off on me!" or "May the Other never get off on me!" or "Don't let the Other get off on me!" See Jacques-Alain Miller's commentary on this phrase in his 1985–1986 seminar "Extimité" (unpublished), February 5, 1986.

50. On this point see Colette Soler's remarks in "Hysteria and Obsession."

51. This quote comes from the extremely difficult article "Subversion of the Subject and Dialectic of Desire" (*Ecrits,* 826): "Castration makes of the [fundamental] fantasy a chain that is both supple and inextensible by which the fixation [*l'arrêt*] of object cathexis, which can hardly go beyond certain natural limits, takes on the transcendental function of ensuring the jouissance of the Other, who passes this chain on to me in the Law."

52. See Jacques-Alain Miller, "A Discussion of Lacan's 'Kant with Sade,'" in *Reading Seminars I and II: Lacan's Return to Freud,* 212–237; and Slavoj Žižek's many discussions of the obscene jouissance of the sadistic superego. In this sense, the jouissance from the relationship to the Other prohibited by the paternal prohibition is nevertheless obtained in a disguised manner.

53. This might be referred to as "suturing," to borrow a term that Lacan used in another context (Seminar XII, *Concepts cruciaux pour la psychanalyse*). This term was made famous by Jacques-Alain Miller in "Suture," *Cahiers pour l'Analyse* 1–2 (1966): 37–49. English translation: "Suture (Elements of the Logic of the Signifier)," *Screen* 18, no. 4 (1977–1978): 24–34. The openness to the Other is closed up or sewn up like a surgical incision, sutured back together.

54. And it will always be the analyst who is at fault, who is held responsible. The hysteric blames the Other, since it is the Other who grants her being, whereas the obsessive is far more inclined to blame himself.

55. See Fink, *The Lacanian Subject,* ch. 9. More generally, see Seminar XVII (where Lacan elaborates his "four discourses" at great length) and Seminar XX. Colette Soler discusses this transition from the hysteric's discourse to analytic discourse in Soler, "Hysteria and Obsession," *Reading Seminars I and II,* 276.

56. S_1 and S_2 have not been introduced at all in this book; readers should consult Seminar XI; and Fink, *The Lacanian Subject*, chs. 5, 6, 8, and 9. Briefly stated, S_1 is the master signifier, a signifier which, when isolated, subjugates the subject; when it is linked up with some other signifier, subjectivization occurs and meaning (written as *s*) results. S_2 is any other signifier, or all other signifiers; in the four discourses, it represents knowledge as a whole.

57. In the four discourses Lacan adumbrates, there is no obsessive discourse per se; the closest thing to the obsessive's discourse is, it seems to me, what Lacan terms the university or academic discourse. See Fink, *The Lacanian Subject*, ch. 9; and Seminars XVII and XX.

58. See Fink, *The Lacanian Subject*, ch. 8.

59. For a detailed discussion of limits in obsession, see Fink, *The Lacanian Subject*, 109–112.

60. The effect of having had such a sacrifice imposed upon him might have been quite salutary for Robert, had it occurred; but, as we have seen, it did not. The Rat Man, too, went into analysis due to an encounter with an authority figure (the "Cruel Captain") who delighted in corporal punishment and who seemed, to the Rat Man, interested in inflicting a sacrifice (payment of money for a pince-nez to the wrong person and/or ridicule) on him.

Just as the psychotic is likely to experience a psychotic break when an encounter with One-father occurs, the neurotic is likely to go into crisis when a direct encounter with the Other's desire or jouissance occurs.

61. Indeed, his last name was a very difficult one to live up to, being that of a great man known the world over.

62. As we saw in Chapter 3. See also Fink, *The Lacanian Subject*, chs. 1, 4, 5, and 7.

63. It was also occasionally articulated along the lines Lacan sketches out in Seminar VII—that is, as arising when he gave up on his desire; in other words, when he submitted to his internal criticism and symbolic ideals instead of doing what he "wanted." We might translate this, in light of Lacan's later formulations, as *giving up on his drives*. See, in this connection, Chapter 10 below.

64. Or, as Lacan once put it, the "turd of his fantasy." This turd is at the same time the subject himself: in the withholding of feces, it is the coming into being of the subject that is in question. There is perhaps some relation here as well to his dream image of a "figure cloaked in black and huddled over," an idealized woman he was stoning.

65. This division seems to grow quite directly out of the castration complex in boys, when it puts an end to the Oedipus complex by making mom off limits. The world of women becomes divided into two subsets: mom and all the rest. A boy's mother is rendered inaccessible by the father's prohibition or threat and, insofar as she is lost as the provider of the boy's most significant satisfactions, becomes idealized. Such an idealized mother figure, whose love is retrospectively viewed as having been perfect, cannot be imagined to have betrayed the boy's faith by actually having had sex with the boy's father; the boy must have been the product of an immaculate conception—hence the Madonna image. In less absolute cases, a boy's mother is characterized as having slept with the father only as many times as there are children in the family.

264

Should the boy later begin to seek out other women, they are generally criticized for some kind of imperfection—they are not smart enough, beautiful enough, and so on—and are sometimes even explicitly viewed as untrustworthy, unfaithful, not unconditional in their love (in other words, potential cheaters or whores who would put their own satisfaction before his). A woman who resembles the mother in some way, however, may be made into a maternal figure, gradually or very quickly acquiring all of the mother's characteristics in the boy's mind. If Freud is led to say that a woman often isn't happy until she has turned her husband into a child in order to mother him, the flipside of the coin is at least as common.

66. This should be understood in the fatalistic sense of the expression "Shit happens."

67. One might even be tempted to read in this the origin of Robert's obsessive stance—that is, his aversion to and guilt over jouissance. The mechanical nature of the phallic object suggests a need to deprive his own organ of jouissance, due, perhaps, to guilt stemming from his illicit watching of the scene. Had he been caught watching such a scene as a child? Moreover, unlike many obsessives, Robert claimed to be fascinated by women's orgasms. Did a sense of too much excitement derive from having watched such scenes, having procured enjoyment vicariously, and having been punished thereafter? Was every attempt to bring a woman to orgasm thereafter tainted by revolt against the father? Or was that only with "suitable"—that is, motherlike—women? None of these questions was answered in the course of Robert's brief analysis.

A fourth possible position adopted by Robert in the fantasy is that of the phallus as partial object, object *a*. This position is, as we shall see in the next chapter, reminiscent of a perverse position: the subject as the object that causes the Other's jouissance. Alternatively, Robert could, as phallic object, be understood as the *copula* between man and woman, the go-between, connection, hinge, or linchpin between father and mother, suggestive of a hysterical position. For the hysteric very often views him- or herself as at the center of a nexus of relationships and, more specifically, as that which makes possible a relationship between two other people. The hysteric in that sense is a facilitator, mediator, negotiator, or link between two otherwise unlinked people—mom and dad, for example.

Robert's four possible "subject positions" mentioned here should not be viewed as in any way mutually exclusive or exhaustive. Just as Freud tells us that the dreamer may be represented in virtually every character in his or her dream, the fantasizer may be represented in virtually every person and prop in his or her fantasy.

68. See Freud's paper "Remembering, Repeating, and Working-Through" (SE XII, 147–156). The scene may even have occurred as early as age four or five, given the uncertainty as to when Jeanne's father left the country. Note here that, as is often the case in hysteria, the event had been forgotten; in obsession, on the other hand, the event is generally remembered but not its affective impact. In the former, the representation of the event is itself repressed, whereas in the latter repression severs representation from affect.

69. I discuss this intervention at some length in the commentary following my presentation of the case material here.

70. In French, *la vue* means both "eyesight" and "sight" or "view"—that is, what

is seen. Thus, the problem with her vision was perhaps also related to what she had seen from the cold hallway in North Africa. Perhaps what she had seen was even, in some sense, fueling her artwork.

71. Obviously implying, in Freudian terms, that she had not resolved her Oedipus complex. In another vein, it seems likely that Jeanne's father was the sort of man who produces psychotic sons; luckily, he had five daughters.

72. The slip could also be understood to put her in their place, if we read *amoureuse,* a singular, instead of *amoureuses,* a plural; they are pronounced identically in French. In that sense, she would be the one who was in love. Alternatively, the slip could suggest a desire for female suitors, but no such desire was ever hinted at in Jeanne's associations to the dream.

73. "Masculine" and "feminine" are obviously approximate terms, with only conventional significations; see the detailed discussion of them in Fink, *The Lacanian Subject,* ch. 8.

74. Having Bertrand refuse her advances in the dream also constituted a kind of externalization of her own inhibitions, as we shall see. If he refused her, she wouldn't have to stop herself, as she usually did.

75. Jeanne also mentioned on one occasion that she could not stand it when "Bertrand a mal"—when he was hurting somewhere (had a stomach ache, for example)—because she would hurt there, too, by way of identification. It should be noted that *mal* ("hurt" or "evil") and *mâle* ("male") are generally pronounced identically in French.

76. It was a *choice* of words in that she could equally well have said "illegal," "illicit," "underhanded," "non-kosher" (*pas bien catholique*), and so on instead of "dishonest."

77. To receive money for sex makes sex acceptable, in a certain sense, since it becomes equated with "the universal signifier," as Lacan puts it, which almost everyone is obliged to honor. Virtually everyone understands the argument (even if they don't approve), "I do it for the money." It is extremely common to hear people say that they feel like prostitutes at their jobs, justifying all kinds of substandard work and not-so-kosher dealings because that is what they are paid to do. (Indeed, as one patient put it, "All work is prostitution.") In such a context, sex can be viewed as a necessary activity instead of something that is morally reprehensible. If, for a particular woman (like Jeanne), unpaid, "ordinary" sex is surrounded by a multitude of inhibitions and overwhelming feelings of guilt, anger, pain, betrayal, and so on, money could perhaps annihilate or neutralize many of those powerful affects. It is the great leveler or equalizer.

78. Lacan, as we have already seen, does suggest that the drives already include the parental Other to an important degree, and thus I do not want to suggest that there is an absolute opposition between the drives and the Other (as ideals). In the drives, the subject is constituted in relation to the Other's demands, and the latter, insofar as they are contradictory, may well already sow the seeds of reactions to satisfaction. See Chapter 10 for further discussion of this point.

79. Another dream seemed to attest to the fact that Jeanne was not disinterested in sex at every level: she had what seemed to be a sort of sexual encounter with her father in the form of "a whale with a long *trompe* [literally 'trunk,' but also a form of the verb *tromper,* 'to cheat on' or 'to betray'] and a microphone." It reminded her

266

of a music video she had just seen in which a girl with big red lips was holding a microphone and sticking it in her mouth. This could, perhaps, be viewed as an expression of the oral drive, which otherwise found expression only in Jeanne's relation to food, involving, it seemed, a few hints of anorexia.

Note that Freud, in his case of Dora, does not take Dora's "repudiation of sexuality" as an a priori, but rather as the result of early childhood experiences leading to considerable inhibition (SE VII, 87–88).

80. On interpretation as aiming at and hitting the real or cause, see Fink, *The Lacanian Subject*, ch. 3. Insofar as the scene in question fixated Jeanne, it served as an S_1, a master signifier. If the latter was, indeed, "dialectized" through my intervention (in the sense explained in *The Lacanian Subject*, ch. 6), then Jeanne as subject came into being as a breach or connection between, or linking up of, S_1 (as the real, that is, as yet unsymbolized, scene) and S_2 (the putting into words or interpretation of the real scene). In that respect, it was an instance of subjectification—that is, a coming into being of the subject where *it* (some foreign, impersonal force) had been. This is, after all, how Lacan interprets Freud's injunction, "Wo Es war, soll Ich werden." As I show in *The Lacanian Subject*, ch. 6, the flash of subjectivity between S_1 and S_2 likewise implies a loss, which it seems we can locate, in this case, in the loss of the jouissance (albeit a painful one) that had been provided by the symptom, for the latter no longer appeared thereafter.

81. Bertrand obviously reacted as if she had been carrying on a secret affair behind his back. Given his own apparent lack of satisfaction in the relationship, one might wonder why he was so opposed to her analysis. What was he getting out of their stymied relationship that he was so loath to give up?

82. We might be tempted to explain it on the basis of an overly close relationship with a parent, leading to excessive desire for that parent. When such a desire is taken in conjunction with a seduction incident (real or imagined), excessive pleasure results. But then why was it that the relationship with the parent was overly close?

83. See Fink, *The Lacanian Subject*, ch. 8.

84. Lacan also says that phobia is "the simplest form of neurosis" (Seminar VI, June 10, 1959). Freud comments on phobias: "It seems certain that they should only be regarded as syndromes which may form part of various neuroses and that we need not rank them as an independent pathological process" (SE X, 115).

85. As Lacan says, the phobic object—the horse in Hans' case—is Φ, "a phallus that takes on the value of all signifiers, that of the father if need be" (Seminar IV, 425). Elsewhere he qualifies "the phobic object as an all-purpose signifier for supplementing [or plugging up] the Other's lack [or the lack in/of the Other]" (*Ecrits*, 610/248).

86. In other words, the hysteric—unlike the pervert, as we shall see in the next chapter—is able to leave behind her role as the object that gives her mOther *satisfaction* (solace, sympathy, caresses, etc.), aspiring to be the cause of the Other's *desire*. If she seeks to complete the Other, it is at the level of desire, not jouissance. (Figure 8.3 involves desire, whereas the figure with which I represent perversion—the left-hand side of Figure 9.1)—involves jouissance.)

87. I provide a short account of little Hans' phobia and its relation to the paternal metaphor in Chapter 9, and will discuss phobia at greater length in the

sequel to the present book. It should simply be noted here that Hans' propping-up of the paternal metaphor is successful only as long as his horse phobia lasts. When it disappears, Hans does not, in my view (or in Lacan's in Seminar IV), become an ordinary neurotic: whereas alienation is instated, separation is not.

9. Perversion

1. See, for example, Robert J. Stoller, *Sex and Gender* (New York: Science House, 1968). Many of the individuals discussed by Stoller can be better understood as psychotics than as perverts. See the discussion of such individuals in Moustapha Safouan, "Contribution to the Psychoanalysis of Transsexualism," trans. Stuart Schneiderman, in Schneiderman, ed., *How Lacan's Ideas Are Used in Clinical Practice* (Northvale, N.J.: Aronson, 1993), 195–212. The earlier edition of the collection in which this article appears is better known to many readers: *Returning to Freud: Clinical Psychoanalysis in the School of Lacan* (New Haven: Yale University Press, 1980). See also Lacan's discussion in Seminar XVIII, January 20, 1971.

2. These "fine" diagnostic distinctions are included under the general category of the "paraphilias" in the *Diagnostic and Statistical Manual of Mental Disorders* [DSM-III-R], (Washington: American Psychiatric Association, 1987). The psychiatric authors of this all-too-widely used manual seem to adopt the more scientific sounding term "paraphilias" in order to avoid the seemingly less politically correct term "perversions." However, they go on to use the most crassly political and moralistic language in their detailed discussions of the paraphilias—for example, "The imagery in a Paraphilia . . . may be relatively harmless" (279); "*Normal* sexual activity includes sexual excitement from touching or fondling one's sexual partner" (283, emphasis added); and so on.

3. See *Écrits*, 610/248, where Lacan speaks of the "fundamental fetish of every perversion qua object glimpsed in the signifier's cut," implying thereby that the object as fetish is crucial in every perversion. The object as isolated by the signifier (as "cut out" of an undifferentiated ground, simultaneously creating both foreground and background) will be discussed later in this chapter.

4. See the fine discussion of *Verleugnung* in J. Laplanche and J.-B. Pontalis, *The Language of Psychoanalysis*, trans. D. Nicholson-Smith (New York: Norton, 1973), an indispensable book that provides encyclopedic analysis of Freud's most central and complex concepts. Note that, in translating *Verleugnung*, the French also sometimes use the term *démenti*—from *démentir*, meaning "to belie" or "to give the lie (to something)."

5. SE X, 11; see also SE XXIII, 276.

6. See Freud's reference to this term in SE XXI, 153.

7. See the discussions of this term in Bruce Fink, *The Lacanian Subject: Between Language and Jouissance* (Princeton: Princeton University Press, 1995). It should be understood in relation to Freud's related term, *Triebrepräsentanz*—the representative, at the level of thought, of a drive (for example, the thought "I want to sleep with my sister-in-law").

8. Or "representative of the drive" (*Triebrepräsentanz*)—that is, the drive's representative at the level of thought. Strachey translates *Triebrepräsentanz* as "instinctual representative."

9. Freud sometimes seems to suggest that it is castration itself that is repudiated—in other words, the *idea* that the mother's penis was cut off and that one's own penis could thus be cut off. In this case it would seem that one idea remains in consciousness—"Every human being has a penis"—while a diametrically opposed idea is put out of mind, and this is tantamount to Freud's own definition of repression.

10. As Lacan says, "By definition, the real is full" (Seminar IV, 218)—that is, nothing is lacking in the real. See also Seminar VI, April 29, 1959, where Lacan says, "The real as such is defined as always full." The same general idea is repeated again and again in Lacan's work. In Seminar X Lacan suggests that what he means by this is not so much that there are no holes or rips in the real, but rather that there is nothing *missing* in the real, nothing absent or lacking.

11. Indeed, as the hysteric teaches us, perception itself is not an "innocent" or scientifically objective process, giving us a "true view" of the "real external world." Each culture "perceives" differently, as a function of the distinctions its language engenders.

12. Consider how Lacan problematizes any attempt to draw clear lines between inside and outside in his use of surfaces such as the Klein bottle and the cross-cap in Seminar IX. See also Fink, *The Lacanian Subject*, end of ch. 8.

13. In other words, some repression has occurred. Note that if something is put "out of mind," it first had to be "in mind"—it first had to be a thought, had to be symbolized.

14. Theorists and practitioners who place little emphasis on the importance of language, law, and the symbolic are likely to think Lacan has systematized Freud in an infelicitous way, leaving out the importance of the mother. It should be clear to anyone who reads Freud carefully, however, that throughout his work the father is of capital importance. Lacan simply provides Freudians with the wherewithal to refute Freud's critics who stress the importance of the pre-Oedipal: with the advent of language and the law, the pre-Oedipal is rewritten or overwritten. "The pregenital stages . . . are organized in the retroactive effect of the Oedipus complex" (*Ecrits*, 554/197). The Oedipus complex has a retroactive effect on that which preceded it temporally, implying that it is a symbolic operation; for in the signifying process, the addition of a new signifier to a series (say, of the term "father's 'No!'" to the series "name-of-the-father," "father's name," and "name given by the father") transforms the meaning of what was said before. Since speech is the only tool at our disposal in psychoanalysis, what we deal with as analysts are the retroactively constituted meanings, not the pre-Oedipal relations that preceded them.

15. This is one instance in which Freud's terminology needs to be clarified by using Lacan's categories: the fetishist believes his mother has a penis—that is, a real, biological organ, not a phallus; for a phallus is a symbol—in other words, part and parcel of the symbolic order. Lacan sometimes loosely refers to the organ the child believes in as the "imaginary phallus," but this should generally be understood to imply the penis (the real organ) that the child imagines the mother has.

16. This expression is used in Shakespeare's *The Merchant of Venice*.

17. Freud says one thought persists in the id and the other in the ego (SE XXIII, 204), a formulation that leads to further problems in his own metapsychology.

18. Freud encourages us to understand this split in the ego in terms of knowledge. According to Freud, the perception of the female genitals is put out of mind because it implies that the father means business when he threatens to cut off the boy's penis (indeed, the boy believes that the father has already done it to the boy's mother); this newly realized possibility of losing the highly invested organ leads to considerable anxiety. The anxiety is dealt with not as in neurosis, where a symptom forms to bind or alleviate anxiety, but by the formation of a kind of split (*Spaltung*). The split is such that two bits of "knowledge" are maintained side by side in a kind of local suspension of the law of noncontradiction: "Women don't have penises" and "All humans have penises." There may be abstract, rote knowledge where the pervert simply repeats what those around him say ("Women don't have penises"), and yet simultaneously a recognition at some level that that is true, as the thought generates anxiety in the pervert. Alongside this, however, there is a kind of subjective necessity leading to a belief beyond all proofs, a disavowal of that intolerable knowledge ("It's small now, but it will grow"). The pervert knows full well that women do not have penises, but cannot help feeling that they do anyway ("Je le sais très bien, mais quand même").

Whereas neurosis consists in a defense against an incompatible idea involving sexuality—leading to a denial taking the classic form, "The person in my dream was *not* my mother," the idea coming to consciousness only thanks to the addition of the "not"—perversion involves a kind of split, according to Freud: the pervert says yes and no simultaneously.

19. Consider the importance in American culture—intuitively understood by every successful merchandiser—of getting something for nothing, of getting things for free. Consider too the eminent popularity of movies, books, and stories about bank robbers (e.g., *A Fish Named Wanda*), jewel thieves (e.g., *The Pink Panther*), and so on where the audience is led to identify with the criminals and enjoy their exploits leading to free millions.

20. At the very least, the obsessive's autoerotic behavior is transformed: if he continues to masturbate, it is in defiance of the paternal prohibition, and thus this prohibition becomes part and parcel of the masturbatory activity. The Other becomes included (not necessarily consciously, of course) in the fantasies that accompany it. One of my female analysands, for example, continued to masturbate while fantasizing about being watched by a powerful man.

This yielding of pleasure to the Other can also be understood in terms of sublimation, as Freud conceptualizes it.

21. According to Freud, a young boy's masturbatory behavior generally involves fantasies about the boy's mother, which implies that it is already alloerotic—in other words, that it involves another person. I would even go so far as to claim that, beyond an extremely tender age, *there is no such thing as autoeroticism.* Even an infant's masturbatory touching already includes its parents, insofar as they first stimulated certain zones, showed interest in them, paid attention to them, lavished care on them, and so on. The connection to other people—which is evident in the adult's fantasies that invariably accompany "autoerotic behavior"— is so fundamental that there seems to be no *eroticism,* as such, without it. All eroticism is alloeroticism.

22. For example, SE XVI, Lectures 21–22.

23. Consider, for example, the behavior of little Hans' mother: whereas she beats her daughter Hanna, she takes her son into her bed, into the bathroom with her, and so on.

24. This is how I think we can understand what Freud means when he talks about the pervert's great narcissistic attachment to his penis, and his "excessive" drives. For drives are not constitutional or biological in origin, but come into being as a function of the Other's demands (the anal drive, for example, comes into being due to the parents' demands that the child become toilet trained, that it learn to control its excretory functions). It is the mOther's interest in and demands related to the pervert's penis that are responsible for the intensity of the pervert's drives.

25. Though in cases of psychosis, this might well be the case.

26. Fetishism, which holds an important theoretical place among the perversions, involves the localization of a great deal of libido on a kind of substitute sexual organ (as we shall see in the case study discussed below), and this occurs to a much lesser extent in girls than in boys.

27. Similarly, Lacan defines Don Juan as a feminine dream, a dream of a man who is lacking nothing ("qui ne manque rien"; Seminar X, March 20, 1963). He also refers to Don Juan as a feminine myth (Seminar XX, 15). It should be noted that Lacan is not necessarily saying that there is absolutely no such thing as female masochism; rather, he means that men tend to see it in women because they want to see it in them, and that it is thus certainly far rarer than men would like to believe.

Lacan suggests that a man, via this fantasy that a woman is masochistic (implying, as we shall see further on, that she is trying to arouse anxiety in him), sustains his ability to get off on his own anxiety, which for him coincides with the object that serves as the very condition of his desire (the sine qua non of his desire). Desire merely covers over or dissimulates anxiety. "In the reign of man, there is always· the presence of some kind of imposture" (Seminar X, March 20, 1963), something I might be tempted to term a *masculine masquerade*.

28. "Let us, by definition, call 'heterosexual' those who, regardless of their sex, love women"; "L'Etourdit," *Scilicet* 4 (1973): 23.

29. See Jacques-Alain Miller, "On Perversion," in Bruce Fink, Richard Feldstein, and Maire Jaanus, eds., *Reading Seminars I and II: Lacan's Return to Freud* (Albany: SUNY Press, 1996). On page 319, Miller says of female perversion:

"You have to look for female perversion where it is invisible. Female narcissism may be taken as a perversion, as an extension of the concept. It is because Woman is Otherness as such or the Other that she spends so much time in front of the mirror—just to recognize herself, or perhaps to recognize herself as Other. Even if it is a myth, it is very important. You may find female perversion in narcissism, at the core of one's own image, or, as Freud proposed, in the child—the child used as an object of satisfaction.

"In the latter case, we have the mother and the imaginary object, the phallus. The mother here is responsible for the perversion of the male child, but at the same time uses the child as an instrument of jouissance. According to the preceding formula, you could call that perversion. Was the first perverse couple mother and child? Lacan, in the fifties, suggests that it is in the connection between the mother's own body and the child that you may find a concealed expression of female perversion.

"Insofar as female homosexuality eliminates the male organ, there is some difficulty placing it in the register of perversion proper."

It is not clear to me whether or not Lacan would have equated the "perverse" nature of the mother-child relationship with perverse structure, strictly speaking.

30. It should be kept in mind that such weak fathers are well documented in literature dating back at least to the time of ancient Rome, and that the argument that fathers have lost tremendous power since the last century seems a bit under-demonstrated.

31. Consider, in the following exchange (from SE X, 17), the way in which his mother tries to prevent him from having a desire for a woman other than herself by guilt-tripping him when he manifests such a desire:

HANS: "Oh, then I'll just go downstairs and sleep with Mariedl."
MOTHER: "You really want to go away from Mummy and sleep downstairs?"
HANS: "Oh, I'll come up again in the morning to have breakfast and do number one."
MOTHER: "Well, if you really want to go away from Daddy and Mummy, then take your coat and knickers and—good-bye!"

32. Indeed, as Freud tells us, the pleasure principle would have us achieve the lowest possible level of tension or excitation.

33. In this book, my comments on the two operations Lacan terms "alienation" and "separation" are fairly basic; for further discussion, see Fink, *The Lacanian Subject*, chs. 5 and 6. Note here that while the subject comes into being in language through alienation, he or she comes into being as a mere placeholder or lack (*manque-à-être*). It is separation that provides something more along the lines of being.

34. The father fails here to provide the "phallic signifier"—to "unscrew," for example, Hans' imaginary phallus (in one of the boy's dreams, the faucet in the bathtub, a symbol for his penis, is to be replaced by the plumber) and replace it with a symbolic one.

35. A subject position, like a symptom, is fundamentally a solution to a problem. Note here that the schema I have provided in Figure 9.1 of the pervert's solution bears a certain affinity to the hysteric's solution in Figure 8.3 (though in the former the subject side is altogether missing). There is, nevertheless, an important difference in register between the two: whereas the hysteric tries to be the object that causes the Other's *desire* (symbolic), the pervert becomes the object that causes the Other's *jouissance* (real)—that is, the object by means of which the Other obtains satisfaction. The hysteric, as we saw in Chapter 8, refuses to be the real, physical object by means of which the Other obtains satisfaction.

36. The analyst occupies the place of the analysand's question or lack of satisfaction: when there is no question—whether it involves one's reason for being or one's confusion over what gives one sexual satisfaction—or lack, the analyst cannot play his or her role. As Jacques-Alain Miller says, "You need a certain void or deficit in the place of sexual enjoyment for the subject supposed to know to arise" ("On Perversion," *Reading Seminars I and II*, 310).

37. Here, the first libidinal object (that is, the object that provides the child with jouissance) is the mother.

38. Lacan brings up the question of the lack of lack in a somewhat different context: it is most commonly believed that a child becomes anxious when its mother is absent, when she is not there with the child; Lacan suggests, on the other hand, that anxiety actually arises owing to a lack of lack, when the mOther is present all the time. "What provokes anxiety? Contrary to what people say, it is neither the rhythm nor the alternation of the mother's presence-absence. What proves this is that the child indulges in repeating presence-absence games: security of presence is found in the possibility of absence. What is most anxiety-producing for the child is when the relationship through which he comes to be—on the basis of lack which makes him desire—is most perturbed: when there is no possibility of lack, when his mother is constantly on his back" (Seminar X, December 5, 1962). What this suggests in the case of the pervert is that, given the overly close mother-child relationship, not only is the mother not perceived as lacking, seeming to desire nothing beyond her child (whom she "has"), but the child himself cannot sense a lack in his own life and thus cannot desire, strictly speaking—cannot come into being as a desiring subject. Desire, Lacan teaches us, is a cover but also a remedy for anxiety.

39. In perversion, there seems to be both a backward-looking and a forward-looking gesture: the former involves the attempt to give the Other satisfaction; the latter, as we shall see below, seeks to prop up or supplement the father's act of naming. In neurosis, too, there are both backward- and forward-looking gestures: the former involves the attempt to become what the Other desires—in obsession, to perfectly incarnate the signifier of the Other's desire (Φ), in hysteria, to perfectly incarnate the cause of the Other's desire (a)—while the latter involves the attempt to shake free of one's fixation on the Other's desire, this being the analysand's path.

40. Consider his comments about the advantages of fetishism: "We can now see what the fetish achieves and what it is that maintains it. It remains a token of triumph over the threat of castration and a protection against it. It also saves the fetishist from becoming a homosexual, by endowing women with the characteristic which makes them tolerable as sexual objects. In later life, the fetishist feels that he enjoys yet another advantage from his substitute for a genital. The meaning of the fetish is not known to other people, so the fetish is not withheld from him: it is easily accessible and he can readily obtain the sexual satisfaction attached to it. What other men have to woo and make exertions for can be had by the fetishist with no trouble at all" (SE XXI, 154).

41. Binding anxiety is, obviously, something that can also be understood in terms of satisfaction, for it lowers the level of tension, as required by the pleasure principle; similarly, the pervert's enactment of separation can be understood in terms of satisfaction, as we shall see.

42. If we take le désir de la mère (the mother's desire for the child, or the child's desire for the mother) as a given, the onus very often falls upon the father to bring about triangulation and separation.

43. A person's concrete actions often give us a far better sense of his or her fundamental fantasy than the fantasies of which he or she is aware, especially at the beginning of an analysis.

44. Originally published in Scilicet 1 (1968): 153–167; translated by Stuart Schneiderman as "Fetishization of a Phobic Object," in How Lacan's Ideas Are Used

in Clinical Practice, 247–260. Page references in the text are to the English edition. The case study, as written by Tostain, is less useful to most English readers than to French readers well versed in Lacanian theory, since it simply *alludes* to many complex notions without explaining them (this is true of much of the work done in French on Lacan). When the case study is taken in conjunction with the discussions in the present book, however, the reader should find it quite fascinating.

45. We could say, in some sense, that she needs him to be a sickly child in order to be able to define herself in any way whatsoever, and in this case as a perfect mother. Thus, she makes him need her.

46. As Tostain puts it, from *being the phallus* for his mother, Jean can now raise the question of *having the phallus*. "Having," after all, is a symbolic affair: *possession is something that is guaranteed by the law.* The problem for Jean is that the father, while managing, in his own bungling way, to take away the imaginary penis from his son, does not manage to give him a symbolic penis—in other words, a phallus—in return. Being the phallus can be understood as imaginary or real (it involves being an object for the mother), whereas having the phallus is a symbolic function. On having and being, see Lacan, "Intervention on Transference," in *Ecrits*.

47. It is not entirely clear what a male orgasm involves at six years of age, but many patients do describe early sexual experiences in such terms.

48. Through his phobia of one button alone, he spares himself from ever having to help his mother get dressed again (and thus of having the same sexual feelings for her and painful jouissance), and expresses his wish for her to die; for the phobia forms the day his mother says to him, "What would become of me without my little man?" His phobic symptom seems to say: "Let's find out what will happen to you when you don't have me any more!" or "Would that something terrible would happen to you without me!" As Lacan says, separation involves questions that can be formulated as follows: "Can she lose me?" "Can she afford to give me up?" "Would it kill her to do so?"

49. A kind of *suppléance au Nom-du-Père*.

50. We shall see this again below, in the discussion of masochism and sadism.

51. See my translation of "Science and Truth," from which this quote derives, in *Newsletter of the Freudian Field* 3 (1989): 25.

52. Those schemas can be found in "Kant with Sade" (*Ecrits*, 774 and 778), and with slightly more explanation in Seminar X (January 16, 1963). For a detailed discussion of them, see Fink, "On Perversion: Lacan's 'Kant with Sade' and Other Texts."

53. This aim is no doubt present in the masochist's conscious or preconscious fantasy.

54. In the Old Testament, it is the *voice* of God that commands. In Judaism, it is the shofar sounded on Yom Kippur that recalls/re-presents the voice of God. Lacan discusses this at length in Seminar X (May 22, 1963).

55. Kant, for example, attempts to eradicate desire from a moral law that leaves no room for human feelings, attachments, and desires in its pursuit of universality (applicable to all cases); but morality is never detached from its medium: the parental voice that expresses desire and/or anger (passion or jouissance) even as it expresses a moral principle.

56. A comment made recently by a Pittsburgh judge.

57. Lacan draws many a link between castration and the sexual act for men. See, in particular, his discussions in the second half of Seminar X—above all, the class given on June 19, 1963.

58. Lacan is referring here to his four-term schemas for sadism and masochism, found on pages 774 and 778 of *Ecrits*.

59. See, for example, SE XXII, 82; and SE XX, 126.

60. As I mentioned before, Lacan suggests that the object serves a fetishistic function in all of the perversions: "the fundamental fetish of every perversion qua object perceived/glimpsed [*aperçu*] in the cut of the signifier" (*Ecrits*, 610/248). The fetishistic object is isolated by the parents' enunciation of a prohibition: the parents' words isolate the object, cut it away from its context, constituting it as such. In the case of weaning, it is very often the mother herself who withdraws and prohibits the child's access to the breast.

61. Here we see the encounter of an object (associated with jouissance) with the signifier (Seminar X, March 13, 1963).

62. It may seem as if the sadist is attempting to cast all loss off onto the victim, and to assert that he himself is still a whole object, lacking in nothing, having renounced nothing. The sadist "casts onto the Other the pain of existence, without seeing that in this way he transforms himself into an 'eternal object.'" Subjective division is thrust upon the Other, the partner, who is tormented. The loss of an object is required of the Other so that the sadist can consider himself whole. But insofar as he identifies with his victim, the sadist continues to seek separation.

A fine clinical example that illustrates this is found in Ferenczi's *Complete Works* under the title "A Little Chanticleer" (see also Dominique Miller's commentary in "A Case of Childhood Perversion," *Reading Seminars I and II*, 294–300). Ferenczi discusses the case of a little boy named Arpad, who joyfully imposes loss of life on chickens (whether staged with a fake knife or really carried out by the kitchen help), but then swoons to the floor himself as if dead, by way of identification with his victim. He is thus simultaneously executioner (or lawgiver, having his orders carried out by household servants) and the being that is executed.

A certain number of men who wind up on the police forces of the world no doubt qualify as sadists, since they take pleasure in letting their victims know what they are about to lose (life or liberty), while simultaneously believing themselves to be not so very different from their criminal victims. Police officers, military commanders, and politicians are very often depicted as considering themselves "above the law," yet they generally very much identify with those they squash, even as they squash them (as if to say, "This is what I myself deserve").

63. The Other as legislator can be associated here with the enunciating subject (or subject of enunciation) and the victim with the subject of the statement (or subject of the enunciated). These terminological links should be helpful in following Lacan's discussion in "Kant with Sade," though not if the reader attempts to use the current English translation (*October* 51 [1989]), which is riddled with errors.

64. The neurotic finds it exceedingly difficult to separate from the Other's desire, while the pervert works very hard to bring the Other's desire (as law) into being.

65. It is precisely because the mOther's lack has not been named that it can be filled with the child as a real object—the child as that libidinized object which

completes the mOther, bringing her jouissance. Once her lack has been named, she cannot be completed in that manner. Neurosis, perversion, and psychosis should not be viewed solely as completeness problems, but the dialectic of the whole and the not-whole is quite central to Lacan's thought and affords us an important perspective on the different clinical/structural psychoanalytic categories.

66. See, in particular, *The Lacanian Subject*, chs. 5 and 6. The substitutions shown here are found on page 69.

67. The two examples Lacan provides of this beyond of neurosis are Alcibiades in Plato's *Symposium* and the soldier in Jean Paulhan's *Le guerrier appliqué* (Paris: Gallimard, 1930).

68. For example, the myth of the libido as the "lamella," in "Position of the Unconscious," in *Ecrits*. Translated by Bruce Fink, in Bruce Fink, Richard Feldstein, and Maire Jaanus, eds., *Reading Seminar XI: Lacan's Four Fundamental Concepts of Psychoanalysis* (Albany: SUNY Press, 1995), 273–276.

69. A recognition, however small, by psychoanalysts of the importance of language and of the paternal function will hopefully lay to rest the kind of approach to perversion taken by an object relations theorist like Sheldon Bach, who, regarding sado-masochists, proffers the following banality: "One might say that these patients have to some degree failed to adequately integrate the mother of nurturance and the mother of frustration, or the mother of pleasure and the mother of pain"; Bach, *The Language of Perversion and the Language of Love* (Northvale, N.J.: Aronson, 1994), 17.

70. And a name, being a rigid designator, can satisfy only demand, not desire, strictly speaking.

71. Recall here, too, that Hans' parents refuse to enlighten him regarding the female genitals, and he remains convinced that his mother has a penis. Had they been willing to discuss sex more openly with him, he might have sensed that his mother, not having a penis, would want to get one via a man (though he might equally well have concluded that she simply wanted his).

72. The answer is provided in the fundamental fantasy.

73. The therapist would likewise do well to explain sexual difference, with pictures if need be. And in a case such as this one, the therapist would be advised to tell the boy that, since his mother does not have a penis, she tries to get one from a man, and failing that from her son. The point is to indicate that there is something a man has that she wants: she desires something outside herself, for she is lacking in something, something that can be named. Nothing is more anxiety provoking than a lack of lack.

10. From Desire to Jouissance

1. See, in this regard, the fine periodization of Lacan's work in Jacques-Alain Miller's 1993–1994 seminar, "Donc" (unpublished), upon which much of my discussion in this chapter is based. A short extract from that seminar has been published as "Commentary on Lacan's Text," trans. Bruce Fink, in Bruce Fink, Richard Feldstein, and Maire Jaanus, *Reading Seminars I and II: Lacan's Return to Freud* (Albany: SUNY Press, 1996), 422–427.

2. See, in this context, Freud's remarks in a letter to Fliess: "I was able to trace

back, with certainty, a hysteria that developed in the context of a periodic mild depression . . . which occurred for the first time at 11 months, and [I could] hear again the words that were exchanged between two adults at that time! It is as though it comes from a phonograph"; see *Freud's Letters to Fliess* (Cambridge, Mass.: Harvard University Press, 1988), 226 (letter dated January 24, 1897). Freud was thus quite aware that words are recorded or etched in our memories long before we can understand them. (See also page 234, letter dated April 6, 1897, where Freud mentions "hysterical fantasies which regularly . . . go back to things that children overhear at an early age and understand only subsequently.") This is why Lacan tells us it is so important "to watch what we say" around children: "Words remain"—they are recorded (Seminar II, 232/198). See, in this connection, Bruce Fink, *The Lacanian Subject: Between Language and Jouissance* (Princeton: Princeton University Press, 1995), ch. 2.

3. As Miller says, desire concerns the body as dead, as mortified or overwritten by the signifier ("Donc"). In Lacan's words, "The body constitutes the Other's bed, due to the operation of the signifier" (*Scilicet* 1 [1968]: 58). In other words, the signifier turns the body into the Other's terrain, domain, or medium.

4. The consequence to be drawn here is that termination is not an "issue" in psychoanalysis: the analyst continues to ask the analysand to come back, come what may. The analysand, when his or her desire is sufficiently decided, terminates analysis all by him- or herself, without spending weeks or months talking about how he or she will miss the analyst or summarizing the work they have done together.

5. See my translation of "On Freud's 'Trieb' and the Psychoanalyst's Desire," in *Reading Seminars I and II*, 419.

6. Oddly enough, the drives are what the analysand often characterizes as most foreign, most Other, when he or she first comes to analysis: "That's not what I want, but I find myself enjoying it anyway."

In Freudian terms, the desiring subject can, in some sense, be thought of as the ego (partly conscious and partly unconscious) which defends against the kind of satisfaction the id strives for. The ego finds objectionable and threatening the id's pursuit of satisfaction, for the id pays no heed to social norms and ideals in its selection of objects and orifices, partners and practices.

7. In *Scilicet* 1 (1968): 14–30.

8. In Chapter 7, I mentioned that psychosis is characterized by little control over the drives. The usual internal inhibiting forces—that is, the symbolically structured agencies such as the ego and superego (or ego-ideal)—have not formed to any great extent, and cannot brake the drives' automatic expression. In neurosis, the opposite is the case: the subject cannot achieve satisfaction of the drives because of excessive inhibition, and obtains satisfaction only in dissatisfaction or in torturing him- or herself—that is, only the jouissance of the symptom. Indeed, part of the problem is that, unlike the pervert, the neurotic does not want to know what it is he or she actually gets off on, because it does not fit in with his or her self-image. Metaphorically speaking, desire does not wish to know where true satisfaction comes from and systematically misrecognizes it.

9. Miller uses the expression *lever le fantasme* like the better-known expression *lever le symptôme*, a lifting or removal of fantasy that is like the removal of the symptom. See his "Commentary on Lacan's Text," in *Reading Seminars I and II*, 426.

10. As Lacan says (inverting the order of demands here), the Other "demands that we allow ourselves to be fed [that is, that we stop fidgeting, open our mouths, and so on] in response to our demand to be fed" (Seminar VIII, 238).

11. As Lacan says, "There is no devouring fantasy that we cannot consider as resulting, at some moment in its own inversion, from . . . the fantasy of being devoured" (Seminar XII, January 20, 1965).

12. Miller characterizes object *a* in this context as satisfaction itself: the object as satisfaction is discerned or isolated by the drive. As he says, "The object that corresponds to the drive is *satisfaction as object*. That is what I would like to propose today, as a definition of Lacan's object *a*: object *a* is satisfaction as an object. Just as we distinguish between instinct and drive, we have to distinguish between the chosen object [the sexual partner, for example] and the libido object, the latter being *satisfaction* qua *object*" ("On Perversion," in *Reading Seminars I and II*, 313).

13. *Ecrits*, 835; in English, "Position of the Unconscious," trans. Bruce Fink, in Bruce Fink, Richard Feldstein, and Maire Jaanus, eds., *Reading Seminar XI: Lacan's Four Fundamental Concepts of Psychoanalysis* (Albany: SUNY Press, 1995), 265.

14. Lacan gives us only a few examples of people who act as one might after traversing one's fundamental fantasy and freeing the drives from their inhibitions. One such example is the main character of Jean Paulhan's novella *Le guerrier appliqué* (Paris: Gallimard, 1930).

15. Miller, "On Perversion," in *Reading Seminars I and II*, 314.

16. Viewed in terms of separation, we can suggest that the drive takes the objec. with it, separating from the Other as desire.

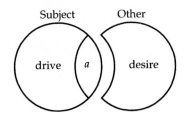

17. Not at his or her "good" (see, for example, Seminar VIII, 18).

18. Desire can also be associated with the pleasure principle, the drive with that which lies beyond the pleasure principle. In the words of Miller, the drive "is an activity that is carried out as a transgression [*infraction*] of the pleasure principle and that always ends in satisfaction—satisfaction of the drive—whereas the subject may suffer thereby, be unhappy about it, be besieged by it, and want to get rid of it" ("Donc," May 18, 1994). Desire, on the other hand, "is inscribed within the limits of the pleasure principle, in other words, desire remains the captive of the pleasure principle" ("Commentary on Lacan's Text," 423).

19. Castration is, after all, the imposition of a loss of satisfaction (for example, for a boy at the end of the Oedipal conflict, the loss of his mother or mother substitute as primary libidinal object). That loss is forever regretted by the neurotic, the subject being unable to focus on the remaining possibilities of satisfaction. Instead, he or she "loves" his or her castration, obstinately clinging to that loss, refusing to find satisfaction elsewhere.

20. Lacan's wager that psychoanalysis can take the analysand further than is often thought possible should, in my view, be taken up at many levels. I often hear therapists say, for example, that they felt that certain patients were not good candidates for therapy, and that their work with them thus took the form of social work or career/marriage counseling. How can we ever know in advance, until we have brought to bear our desire as analysts, whether or not someone can "do analysis"? Lacan's wager would, in my view, have us never presume that someone is incapable of undergoing analysis or can go no further in his or her analysis.

21. See *Ecrits*, 524/171.

22. As Freud tells us in his *Introductory Lectures on Psychoanalysis*, anxiety in a dream is often generated as a last-ditch attempt by the censorship to disguise the satisfaction the dreamer is obtaining from an activity or situation that the dreamer's "higher faculties" would deem unacceptable. When I asked a new analysand if she recalled any sexual fantasies, she said, "Not really," but went on to describe a repetitive dream in which she would feel the floor giving way before her and would anxiously try to reach firm ground. Her anxiety in this repetitive dream, mentioned in the context of sexuality, was in itself a kind of jouissance.

Let me simply recall here the intimate relation between anxiety and orgasm mentioned by both Freud and Lacan (see, for example, Seminar X, March 13, 1963). Freud often noted that certain anxiety attacks seem to take on an orgasmic quality, the person getting all worked up in a way that is reminiscent of a kind of sexual excitement. Anxiety attacks, "fits," and "panic attacks" thus provide satisfaction in a form that is often unrecognizable to the untrained eye.

23. Due to the blinders fantasy imposes upon us. As Lacan suggests, we all see the world through the lenses of our fantasies.

24. *Scilicet* 1 (1968).

25. This is one of the senses in which the Lacanian subject is "between language and jouissance": the subject can "have" *either* some sort of primordial pleasure *or* language, but not both (it is a "vel," that of the "forced choice" which the infant has to be "seduced," enticed, or encouraged into making in favor of language). As Lacan says, the subject "corresponds to the opposition reality principle/pleasure principle" (Seminar VII, 43)—in other words, the opposition between language and some sort of primordial, "easy" jouissance "before the letter." Fantasy is the attempt to bring the two elements of the choice—the subject of language and jouissance—together in such a way that they are "compossible" (to borrow a term from Alain Badiou's *Conditions* [Paris: Seuil, 1992]). Fantasy thus attempts to overcome the either/or, the choice made that was responsible for the advent of the subject and for a loss of satisfaction; it stages the attempt to reverse that loss.

The subject is also "between language and jouissance" in the sense that the subject is the link between a powerful affective experience and the thought (Freud's term here is "representation") that accompanies it. This link is often dissolved in obsession; for example, as an adult the Rat Man can see no relation between his anger and his father until Freud allows him to express his anger in the analytic setting and then interprets it as having something to do with his father. With this interpretation, Freud allows the Rat Man to come into being as the link between his affect (jouissance) and his thoughts (articulated in language) about his father. The powerful affective experience is, in Lacanian terminology, an S_1, whereas thought is an S_2. The subject is the flash between them that constitutes a link or connection.

26. This later approach on Lacan's part might be understood, in certain respects, as a return to a quasi-Freudian economic model—where satisfaction takes precedence—but a simultaneous synthesis of the economic and the dynamic models: in order for satisfaction to prevail, a new configuration of desire (as related to the ego and the unconscious) with respect to the drives (the id, and perhaps the superego insofar as the latter commands satisfaction of the drives) is required. The defenses against satisfaction might be considered to form one agency *(Instanz)*—the subject as desire—in a new topography, where the other agency is the subject as drive. These agencies do *not* allow of a one-to-one correspondence with Freud's.

Afterword

1. See Bruce Fink, *The Lacanian Subject: Between Language and Jouissance* (Princeton: Princeton University Press, 1995), end of ch. 8.

2. Precipitation is, of course, true of all understanding; see, in this connection, Lacan's comments in Seminar XX, 65.

3. "On Perversion," in Bruce Fink, Richard Feldstein, and Maire Jaanus, eds., *Reading Seminars I and II: Lacan's Return to Freud* (Albany: SUNY Press, 1996), 307.

4. Boileau's famous dictum "Ce qui se conçoit clairement s'énonce aisément," reads "straightforwardly" instead of "obscurely."

5. Style may, as Lacan himself repeats, be the man himself (*Ecrits*, 9), but is style identical to one's ideas? The relationship between the two is obviously dialectical. To express Lacan's ideas as I have here implies a loss of impact—of a certain unsettling, provoking effect on the reader—and a loss of the performative effects of his writing that are often so delightful. I can only hope that my writing "compensates" the reader for this loss in other ways.

RECOMMENDED READING

In this section, I first mention works of general interest that take up many aspects of psychoanalytic clinical practice, and then list short selections (usually just several pages or a lecture or two) of books or articles relevant to the preceding chapters. This should allow the reader to study or review only those pages in Freud's and Lacan's texts that are *directly related* to the discussion at hand, instead of requiring him or her to read through the whole of a theoretical treatise in search of one clinical notion. I have given precedence to works available in English, but, for those who read French, I have also listed works currently available only in French. I provide a very brief indication of the topics covered in each work cited when they are not immediately obvious from the title, and add the notation "difficult" if the uninitiated are likely to find the text challenging stylistically, conceptually, or both. Under each heading, works by Freud and Lacan are listed first, followed by those of other authors in order of importance.

General

Lacan, Seminar III, *The Psychoses* (New York: Norton, 1993). This seminar—which, for the clinician, is perhaps the most accessible and pertinent of Lacan's works that have thus far been published—has also been very competently translated into English by Russell Grigg. Of Lacan's numerous seminars, the only other ones currently available in English are Seminars I, II, VII, and XI; my translation of Seminar XX will be available shortly.
——— Seminar I, *Freud's Papers on Technique* (New York: Norton, 1988).
——— "Direction of the Treatment," *Ecrits*, 585–645/226–280; difficult.
Bruce Fink, *The Lacanian Subject: Between Language and Jouissance* (Princeton: Princeton University Press, 1995).
Bruce Fink, Richard Feldstein, and Maire Jaanus, eds., *Reading Seminars I and II: Lacan's Return to Freud* (Albany: SUNY Press, 1996). A collection of lectures given to students new to Lacanian psychoanalysis by the principal analysts of

the Ecole de la Cause Freudienne. The clinical papers included in this volume
are nowhere surpassed in English in terms of accessibility and clarity.

Bruce Fink, Richard Feldstein, and Maire Jaanus, eds., *Reading Seminar XI: Lacan's
Four Fundamental Concepts of Psychoanalysis* (Albany: SUNY Press, 1995). Second volume of lectures by the analysts of the Ecole de la Cause Freudienne
that present fundamental Lacanian concepts in a very clear and direct manner.

J. Laplanche and J.-B. Pontalis, *The Language of Psychoanalysis* (New York: Norton,
1973). The single best encyclopedic resource on Freudian concepts, written by
two of Lacan's prominent students.

1. Desire in Analysis

Freud, *Introductory Lectures on Psychoanalysis* (1917), SE XVI, Lecture 19; on resistance and repression.

———— "Analysis of a Case of Hysteria" [Dora] (1905), SE VII, 105; a counterexam-
ple of the analyst's desire.

Lacan, Seminar I, Chapters 1–4; on resistance, defense, and the ego.

———— "Introduction à l'édition allemande d'un premier volume des *Ecrits*," *Scilicet* 5 (1975): 11–17; difficult.

Colette Soler, "The Real Aims of the Analytic Act," *Lacanian Ink* 5 (1992): 53–60;
difficult. The journal *Lacanian Ink* is available in only a few bookstores, but can
be obtained by writing to *Lacanian Ink*, 133 Wooster Street, New York, NY,
10012.

2. Engaging the Patient in the Therapeutic Process

Freud, "Recommendations to Physicians Practising Psychoanalysis" (1912), SE XII,
111–120; on the analyst's stance.

———— "On Beginning the Treatment" (1913), SE XII, 123–144; on the analyst's
general approach.

———— "The Handling of Dream-Interpretation in Psychoanalysis" (1911), SE XII,
91–96.

———— "Remarks on the Theory and Practice of Dream-Interpretation" (1923), SE
XIX, 109–121.

———— "Some Additional Notes on Dream-Interpretation as a Whole" (1925), SE
XIX, 127–138.

———— *Introductory Lectures on Psychoanalysis*, SE XVI, 284–285; the ego is not
"master in its own home."

Lacan, Seminar III, Chapters 4, 7, 10, 12, and 13; on meaning and the symbolic, and
desire as a question.

———— *Ecrits*, 310–322/95–107; on time and the variable-length session.

———— Seminar VIII, *Transference*, translated by Bruce Fink (New York: Norton,
forthcoming), 435; the analyst as mirror.

———— Seminar X, "Angoisse," June 12, 1963; on the systemization of symptoms at
the outset of analysis.

———— "Geneva Lecture on the Symptom," *Analysis* 1 (1989): 10; on not putting the
patient on the couch too soon. The journal *Analysis* is available in very few

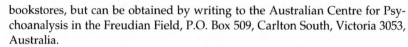
bookstores, but can be obtained by writing to the Australian Centre for Psychoanalysis in the Freudian Field, P.O. Box 509, Carlton South, Victoria 3053, Australia.

———— "The Freudian Thing, or the Meaning of the Return to Freud in Psychoanalysis," *Ecrits;* difficult.

———— "Subversion of the Subject and Dialectic of Desire," *Ecrits;* difficult.

———— Seminar V, "Unconscious Formations" (unpublished); on puns, slips, and parapraxes of all kinds.

Jacques-Alain Miller, "La sortie d'analyse," *La lettre mensuelle de l'ECF* 119 (1993): 31–38; on the emergence of an "autonomous" demand; difficult.

Michel Sylvestre, *Demain la psychanalyse* (Paris: Navarin, 1987), 66; the analyst as feigning not to have understood or heard correctly.

3. The Analytic Relationship

Freud, *Introductory Lectures on Psychoanalysis,* Lectures 27–28.

———— "The Dynamics of Transference" (1912).

———— "Remembering, Repeating and Working-Through" (1914), SE XII, 147–156.

———— "Observations on Transference-Love" (1915), SE XII, 159–171.

———— *Studies on Hysteria* (1895), SE III, Chapters 1–2.

———— Seminar III, Chapter 7.

———— Seminar VIII, Chapters 12–13.

———— "The Direction of the Treatment," *Ecrits;* difficult.

———— Seminar XI, *The Four Fundamental Concepts of Psychoanalysis,* Chapter 18; difficult.

———— "Intervention on Transference," *Ecrits;* in English in *Feminine Sexuality* (New York: Norton, 1982).

———— "Variations on the Standard Treatment," *Ecrits,* 332–336; not yet available in English.

4. Interpretation: Opening Up the Space of Desire

Freud, *New Introductory Lectures on Psychoanalysis,* SE XXII, Lecture 31.

Lacan, Seminar III, 184, 293–305.

———— Seminar VIII, translated by Bruce Fink (New York: Norton, forthcoming), Chapters 1–11 and 14–15.

———— Seminar XVIII, January 13, 1971 (unpublished).

———— *Ecrits* 106/13 and 588/228.

———— *Scilicet* 5 (1975): 16.

Bruce Fink, *The Lacanian Subject,* Chapters 3, 7, 8, 10.

5. The Dialectic of Desire

Freud, *The Origins of Psychoanalysis* (New York: Basic Books, 1954), 163–164, letter dated May 30, 1896.

———— "Project for a Scientific Psychology," SE I, 338–339 (on hallucination) and 353–356 (on deferred action).

—— *The Interpretation of Dreams*, SE IV, 146–151; the dream recounted by the "witty butcher's wife."

—— *Introductory Lectures on Psychoanalysis*, SE XVI, Lecture 21, "The Development of the Libido and the Sexual Organizations."

—— "Analysis Terminable and Interminable" (1937), SE XXIII, 252–253.

—— "Constructions in Analysis" (1937), SE XXIII, 257–269.

Lacan, "Direction of the Treatment," *Ecrits*, 621–636/258–271; difficult.

—— Seminar VIII, Chapters 15–18 and 25.

—— Seminar X, November 14, 1962 (unpublished).

—— Seminar XIV, "The Logic of Fantasy" (unpublished); difficult.

—— "On Freud's 'Trieb' and the Psychoanalyst's Desire," translated by Bruce Fink, in *Reading Seminars I and II*, 417–421.

—— Seminar VI, "Desire and Its Interpretation" (1958–1959). Seven sessions were edited and published by Jacques-Alain Miller in *Ornicar?* 24 (1981): 7–31; 25 (1982): 13–36; and 26–27 (1983): 7–44. The final three sessions, on Hamlet, were translated by James Hulbert as "Desire and the Interpretation of Desire in *Hamlet*," *Yale French Studies* 55–56 (1977): 11–52.

—— "Subversion of the Subject and Dialectic of Desire," *Ecrits*; difficult.

Colette Soler, "History and Hysteria: The Witty Butcher's Wife," *Newsletter of the Freudian Field* 6 (1992): 16–33. This newsletter, now defunct, is available by writing to the Department of English, Tate Hall, University of Missouri, Columbia, MO 65211.

—— "Hysteria and Obsession," *Reading Seminars I and II*, 248–282.

Comment finissent les analyses (Paris: Seuil, 1994), 163–210; a collective work.

Bruce Fink, *The Lacanian Subject*, Chapters 1, 5, 6, 7.

—— "Reading *Hamlet* with Lacan," in Richard Feldstein and Willy Apollon, eds., *Lacan, Politics, Aesthetics* (Albany: SUNY Press, 1995).

Elizabeth Roudinesco, *Jacques Lacan & Co.: A History of Psychoanalysis in France, 1925–1985*, translated by Jeffrey Mehlman (Chicago: University of Chicago Press, 1990). Discussions by different analysts of their analysis with Lacan.

6. A Lacanian Approach to Diagnosis

Freud, *Introductory Lectures on Psychoanalysis*, Lectures 23 and 28.

—— "Neurosis and Psychosis" (1923), SE XIX, 149–153.

—— "The Infantile Genital Organization" (1923), SE XIX, 141–145.

—— "The Loss of Reality in Neurosis and Psychosis" (1924), SE XIX, 183–187.

—— "Negation" (1924), SE XIX, 236–239.

—— "An Outline of Psychoanalysis," Chapter 8 (1938), SE XXIII, 195–204.

—— "Splitting of the Ego in the Process of Defence" (1938), SE XXIII, 275–278.

—— "Fetishism" (1927), SE XXI, 152–157.

Lacan, Seminar I, Chapters 4–5; recast by Lacan in *Ecrits*, 369–399.

Lacan, Seminar III, Chapters 1, 3, 20, and 25.

—— Seminar XXI, "Les non dupes errent," March 19, 1974 (unpublished); difficult.

Jacques-Alain Miller, "An Introduction to Lacan's Clinical Perspectives," in *Reading Seminars I and II*, 241–247.

Jean Hyppolite, "A Spoken Commentary on Freud's *'Verneinung'* ['Negation'],"
Ecrits, 879–887; in English in Seminar I, 289–297; difficult.
Bruce Fink, *The Lacanian Subject*, Chapters 5–6.

7. Psychosis

Freud, "Psychoanalytic Notes on an Autobiographical Account of a Case of Para-
noia [Schreber]," SE XII, 9–82.
Lacan, Seminar III.
——— "On a Question Preliminary to Any Possible Treatment of Psychosis,"
Ecrits, 531–583/179–225; difficult.
Jacques-Alain Miller, "An Introduction to Lacan's Clinical Perspectives," in *Read-
ing Seminars I and II*, 241–247.
Jean-Claude Schaetzel, "Bronzehelmet, or the Itinerary of the Psychotherapy of a
Psychotic," translated by Stuart Schneiderman, in Schneiderman, ed., *How
Lacan's Ideas Are Used in Clinical Practice* (Northvale, N.J.: Aronson, 1993),
184–194. The earlier edition of the collection in which this article appears is
better known to many readers: *Returning to Freud: Clinical Psychoanalysis in the
School of Lacan* (New Haven: Yale University Press, 1980).
Daniel Paul Schreber, *Memoirs of My Nervous Illness* (Cambridge, Mass.: Harvard
University Press, 1988).
Clinique différentielle des psychoses (Paris: Navarin, 1988). Includes commentaries by
many members of the Ecole de la Cause Freudienne; difficult.
Françoise Gorog, "Clinical Vignette: A Case of Transsexualism," in *Reading Semi-
nars I and II*, 283–286.

THE BUTTON TIE (ANCHORING OR QUILTING POINT)

Lacan, "Subversion of the Subject and Dialectic of Desire," *Ecrits*, 804–827/302–
325; difficult.
Slavoj Žižek, *The Sublime Object of Ideology* (London: Verso, 1989), Chapter 3.
Russell Grigg, "Metaphor and Metonymy," in *Newsletter of the Freudian Field* 3
(1989): 58–79.

THE EGO AS OBJECT

Freud, *The Ego and the Id* (1923), SE XIX, 19–39.
Lacan, Seminar II, 62–69/46–52.
——— "The Mirror Stage as Formative of the Function of the I," *Ecrits*, 93–100/1–7.
——— Seminar VIII, Chapters 23–24.
Bruce Fink, *The Lacanian Subject*, Chapters 1, 2, 4, and 5.

8. Neurosis

Freud, "Negation" (1924), SE XIX, 236–239.
——— *Introductory Lectures on Psychoanalysis*, Chapters 20–21.
——— "Constructions in Analysis" (1937), SE XXIII, 257–269.

Lacan, "On Freud's 'Trieb' and the Psychoanalyst's Desire," in *Reading Seminars I and II*.
—— "Direction of the Treatment," *Ecrits*, 604–607/243–245.
—— "Subversion of the Subject and Dialectic of Desire," *Ecrits*, 820–827/318–324.
Jacques-Alain Miller, "Donc," May 11, 1994; unpublished seminar given in French.
Bruce Fink, *The Lacanian Subject*, Chapters 1, 5, 7, 8.

HYSTERIA AND OBSESSION

Freud, *The Interpretation of Dreams* (1899), SE IV, 146–151; the dream recounted by the "witty butcher's wife."
—— "Notes upon a Case of Obsessional Neurosis [Rat Man]" (1909), SE X, 158–249.
—— *Introductory Lectures on Psychoanalysis*, SE XVI, 261–269.
—— *Freud's Letters to Fliess*, translated by Jeffrey Masson (Cambridge, Mass.: Harvard University Press, 1988), 141 (letter dated October 8, 1895), 144 (letter dated October 15, 1895), 145 (letter dated October 16, 1895), 154 (letter dated December 8, 1895), 164–169 (Draft K), 187–190 (letter dated May 30, 1896).
—— and Joseph Breuer, *Studies on Hysteria* (1895), SE II, 21–47.
Lacan, Seminar III, Chapters 12–13.
—— Seminar VIII, Chapters 15–18.
—— "Direction of the Treatment," *Ecrits*, 621–627; on the "witty butcher's wife"; difficult.
—— Seminar X, June 25, 1963; on desire in obsession.
—— Seminar XI, 67 / 69–70.
—— Seminar XVII, *L'envers de la psychanalyse*, Chapters 1–5; on the hysteric's discourse; difficult.
Jacques-Alain Miller, "H₂O," translated by Bruce Fink, in *Hystoria* (New York: Lacan Study Notes, 1988).
Hystérie et Obsession (Paris: Navarin, 1986). Includes commentaries by many members of the Ecole de la Cause Freudienne; difficult.
Colette Soler, "Hysteria and Obsession," *Reading Seminars I and II*, 248–282.
—— "History and Hysteria: The Witty Butcher's Wife," *Newsletter of the Freudian Field* 6 (1992): 16–33.
Bruce Fink, *The Lacanian Subject*, Chapters 7, 8, and 9.

PHOBIA

Lacan, "Direction of the Treatment," *Ecrits*, 610–611/248–249.
—— Seminar IV, *La relation d'objet* (Paris: Seuil, 1994), Chapters 12–24.

ALIENATION AND SEPARATION

Lacan, Seminar XI, Chapters 16 and 17; difficult.
—— Seminar XIV; difficult.
—— Seminar XV; difficult.

Jacques-Alain Miller, "Du symptôme au fantasme et retour" (unpublished seminar), classes given on March 9, 16, and 23, 1983; "1,2,3,4" (unpublished seminar), classes given on November 21 and 28, 1984. Miller's is *the* seminal work on alienation and separation.

Bruce Fink, *The Lacanian Subject*, Chapters 5–6.

———— "Alienation and Separation: Logical Moments of Lacan's Dialectic of Desire," in *Newsletter of the Freudian Field* 4 (1990): 78–119; this text is largely based on Miller's "Du symptôme au fantasme et retour" and "1,2,3,4" (unpublished). A number of substantive errors were introduced into this article by the editors of the newsletter. Please consult the author for clarification.

THE SUPEREGO

Jacques-Alain Miller, "A Discussion of Lacan's 'Kant with Sade,'" in *Reading Seminars I and II*, 212–237.

9. Perversion

Freud, *Introductory Lectures on Psychoanalysis*, Lectures 20–21.

———— "The Infantile Genital Organization," SE XIX, 141–145.

———— "Negation" (1925), SE XIX, 235–239.

———— "Fetishism" (1927), SE XXI, 152–157.

———— "An Outline of Psychoanalysis," Chapter 8.

———— "Splitting of the Ego in the Process of Defence" (1938), SE XXIII, 275–278.

Lacan, Seminar IV, *La relation d'objet*, Chapters 6–11.

———— Seminar X, "Angoisse" (1962–1963), December 5, 1962; January 16, 1963; February 27, 1963; March 13, 1963; March 20, 1963; March 26, 1963; May 22, 1963; June 19, 1963; and July 3, 1963.

———— "Kant with Sade," *Ecrits*; avoid the unusable translation in *October* 51 (1989); difficult.

———— "Position of the Unconscious," *Ecrits*; see translation by Bruce Fink in *Reading Seminar XI*.

Jacques-Alain Miller, "On Perversion," in *Reading Seminars I and II*, 306–320.

———— "A Discussion of Lacan's 'Kant with Sade,'" in *Reading Seminars I and II*, 212–237.

René Tostain, "Fetishization of a Phobic Object," translated by Stuart Schneiderman in *How Lacan's Ideas Are Used in Clinical Practice*, 247–260.

Moustapha Safouan, "Contribution to the Psychoanalysis of Transsexualism," translated by Stuart Schneiderman in *How Lacan's Ideas Are Used in Clinical Practice*, 195–212; clinical examples are used to illustrate the difference between perversion and psychosis.

Traits de perversion dans les structures cliniques (Paris: Navarin, 1990). Includes commentaries by many members of the Ecole de la Cause Freudienne; difficult.

10. From Desire to Jouissance

Lacan, "On Freud's 'Trieb' and the Psychoanalyst's Desire," *Ecrits;* 851–854; translated by Bruce Fink in *Reading Seminars I and II,* 417–421. Difficult.

———— Seminar X, March 13, 1963.

———— "Proposition du 9 octobre 1967 sur le psychanalyste de l'Ecole," *Scilicet* 1 (1968): 14–30; difficult.

Jacques-Alain Miller, "Donc" (1993–1994), unpublished seminar given in French. Several important pages have been excerpted and translated by Bruce Fink as "Commentary on Lacan's Text," in *Reading Seminars I and II,* 422–427.

Anne Dunand, "The End of Analysis," in *Reading Seminar XI,* 243–256.

Jean Paulhan, *Le guerrier appliqué* (Paris: Gallimard, 1930).

INDEX

Abraham, Karl, 52
affect, 212, 215, 278–279n25; repression and, 113–114
Alcibiades, 275n67
alienation, cause of desire and, 55; defined, 271n33; language and, 86–87, 271n33; neurosis and, 162; paternal function and, 91–94, 178–179, 248–249n39; perversion and, 174, 175–179, 187, 191–192, 193–195; and subject as drive, 209–210
alloeroticism, 269n21
analysand: demand of (*see* demand); desire of (*see* desire); engaging of (*see* technique; preliminary meetings); friendship attempts by, 11–12; seductiveness of, 230n15. *See also* subject
analyst: advice by, 22, 230n19; as cause of analysand's desire, 38–41, 52–53, 57–59, 210; desire of (*see* analyst's desire); exasperation of, 16–17; as imaginary other, 32–33; as judge, 35–38; as no master of knowledge, 31, 32, 216–217, 232–233n8, 245nn8,9; as person/individual, 31–33, 35, 134; separation from, 62–63, 70–71, 206; as symbolic Other, 31–33, 45–46, 104–106; techniques of (*see* technique)
analyst's desire: capacity for analysis and, 278n20; castration and, 70; defined, 6–7; jouissance crisis and, 9–10; and knowledge, resistance to, 7–8; late or canceled sessions and, 20–21, 227–228n17; as motor-force of therapy, 4–5, 206, 227–228n17; scansion and, 16; unpredictability and, 64–65. *See also*

countertransference
analytic discourse, 133
analytic relationship: beginning (*see* preliminary meetings); Freud on, 40; judgment by analyst and, 35–38; real face, 210; and subject supposed to know (*see* subject supposed to know); suggestion and, 28–30; symbolic vs. imaginary relations and, 33–35; terminating, 70–71, 206. *See also* sessions; treatment
"Anatomy is destiny," 162
anchoring point. *See* button tie
angst, 61
anorexia, 116, 117, 126
anxiety: affect and, 215; of castration, 33–34, 269n18; desire and, 176, 270n27; in dreams, 278n22; Freud on, 215; lack of lack as producing, 177–178, 275n73; neurotic vs. realistic, 60–61, 168–169; Other's desire as producing, 60–61; perversion and, 174, 187, 190–192, 272n38; of separation, 174, 272n38; symptoms as binding of, 179
aphanisis, 124
Aristotle, 44, 260n34
authority, 80–81. *See also* paternal function
autism, 91, 247n30
autoeroticism: as alloerotic, 226n15, 269n21; obsession and, 172; perversion and, 171, 172; sacrifice of (*see* castration)

Bach, Sheldon, 275n69
Badiou, Alain, 278n25
betrayal, 157, 215–216
Bettelheim, Bruno, 252n71